TO BE
DISPOSED
BY
AUTHORITY

THE AUDEN GENERATION

SAMUEL HYNES

The Auden Generation

*Literature and Politics in England
in the 1930s*

THE BODLEY HEAD

LONDON SYDNEY

TORONTO

For Mandy and Jo

Copyright © Samuel Hynes 1976
ISBN 0 370 10381 5
Printed in Great Britain for
The Bodley Head Ltd
9 Bow Street, London WC2E 7AL
by Unwin Brothers Ltd, Woking
Set in Monotype Baskerville
by Gloucester Typesetting Co. Ltd
First published 1976
Reprinted 1976

You cannot tell people what to do,
you can only tell them parables;
and that is what art really is, particular stories
of particular people and experience, from which
each according to his own immediate and peculiar needs
may draw his own conclusions.

AUDEN

Psychology and Art To-day (1935)

. . . if one conceives that the subject of writing is
the moral life of one's time, in the same way as
the subject of Greek Tragedy is moral, and *Everyman* is
a morality, and the subject of *Tao Te Ching* is the art
of ruling and being ruled; then to-day one is in
a very difficult situation. The precise difficulty is
to write about this moral life in a way that is significant:
to find the real moral subject.

SPENDER

Writers and Manifestos (1935)

CONTENTS

Preface, 9

PREFACE

This book is about the making of a literary generation—the young English writers of the 1930s. Several things should be said about the nature and the limits of the subject. First, I am concerned with one generation of writers, the men and women born in England between 1900 and the First World War, who came of age in the 'twenties and lived through their early maturity during the Depression. They are above all the generation *entre deux guerres*, and their relation to both wars is an important part of this book. I am interested in how the development of this generation of writers was affected by the circumstances of their times, how the war behind them and the war ahead entered into their work, and how the forms of imagination were altered by crises. I do not take the generation beyond the beginning of the Second World War; the decade of the 'forties has a different history. Nor do I consider, except tangentially, important works written during the 'thirties by older writers. Of course those other works are part of the circumstances of the time: one could not be a young poet in the 'thirties and be unaffected by *Ash Wednesday* and *The Winding Stair*, or be a young novelist and unaware of *Work in Progress*. But these are relevant to this study only insofar as they influenced younger writers.

I must also stress the point that I am dealing with a *literary* generation, and that this is a literary study. I assume that a close relation exists between literature and history, and I think that this relation is particularly close in times of crisis, when public and private lives, the world of action and the world of imagination, interpenetrate. I do not believe that literary history can be separated from social and political and economic history, and the reader will find that the context of literary events in this book is history in that larger sense. Nevertheless, the subject is literature, and specifically the growth of literary forms.

9

I have organized the book in a straightforward year-by-year chronology. I am aware that certain simplifications enter with such a method: it seems to assume that all imaginations work at the same rapid pace, and does not allow for a varying lag-factor between the stimulus and the work; and it seems also to assume that in all cases the stimulus is in immediate history. But the works I am concerned with here were not, in most cases, long in the making; all of the principal writers of the 'thirties generation were rapid and prolific writers. Most of them wrote for a living; some of them had propagandist motives that encouraged immediate publication. And the pace of the time itself, and the sense of time passing and an end approaching, gave a special quality to the 'thirties that made the relation between a work and its historical context unusually close. Not every work was topical in an obvious way (though there is a good deal of topical material in most 'thirties writing), but almost every work of importance is demonstrably related to its historical moment in mood and tone.

The 'moment', strictly speaking, is the time of composition, but that is not always easy to determine, and I have used instead the date of publication. In most cases the difference was not great; for example, Auden's 'Spain' was written between January 1937 (when he went to Spain) and April (when copy went to the printer), and was published in May, and Rex Warner's *The Professor* was written between the Austrian and Czechoslovakian crises (that is, between March and September 1938), and was published in November of that year. But there is also a theoretical justification for using publication dates. To the degree that literature *creates* as well as *records* consciousness, it begins to exist when it enters history—when publication makes it a public reality. *New Country* and Spender's *Poems* are both historical facts of 1933, with historical causes and historical consequences.

To write about the *literary* existence of a generation is to accept a necessary restriction of subject: you will be writing almost entirely about the middle-class members of the generation. English literature has been middle-class as long as there has been an English middle class, and the generation of the 'thirties was not different in this respect from its predecessors; most of the writers I deal with here came from professional families, and were educated at public schools and at Oxford or Cambridge. Virtually no writing of literary importance came out of the working class during the decade. The poor did find symbolic ways of expressing their needs and feelings—in Hunger Marches, in protests, in the East End resistance to Mosley's invasion—but these were not literary ways. This is scarcely surprising if one considers the conditions of working-class life during those years, the unemployment, the Dole, the diet of bread and margarine, and all the rest of it; it is simply one of the facts of the time. So when one generalizes about the generation, it must always be with the implicit qualification that there was a large majority whose lives did not find expression in language. This is of course true of any generation; what is different about the 'thirties is that, as political and social awareness grew among educated, middle-class young people, their sense of the need to speak to and for the poor and the workers grew too, and this becomes, for the critic-historian, another literary problem.

A further point to be made is simply a gloss on my phrase, 'the making of a generation'. I assume that a generation grows in definition by the interaction of consciousness and circumstance. One might say that a generation does not really exist until it has been made conscious of its identity, and that for such consciousness it must depend on the special awareness of its artists, and on their ability to create the forms appropriate to their own particular circumstances. Surely most of the members of any chronological group, even the most articulate ones, are neither spontaneously aware that they *are* a group, nor capable of defining their special existence. It took Gertrude Stein to explain to the post-war expatriates that they were a Lost Generation, and it took Hemingway to show them what she had meant. Evelyn Waugh's contemporaries didn't know that they were Bright Young People until Waugh told them they were; then they looked back to Oxford and the Hypocrites' Club and saw that they were significant. So it was with the 'thirties: the generation grew into consciousness as its artists devised the forms in which they could express contemporary history, and that new consciousness evolved and changed as events, and the expressions of events, occurred. There is not, then, a Thirties Generation that exists through the decade, with a fixed and definable set of characteristics; rather there is a consciousness that develops and changes as circumstances change.

It is only when a period has passed that it solidifies and becomes history, and we begin to think of it as a set pattern of events, forces, and consequences. At the time, history feels fluid and uncertain, the forces that time will eventually confirm don't yet know that they *are* the significant ones; in studying the past, we must try by an act of imagination to recover that sense of fluidity. In the Myth of the Thirties, for example, the Left plays a powerful role, but in the actual period the role of the Left was not clear, nor its principles and practices established. The Communist Party of Great Britain had been in existence for less than ten years when the decade began—like disillusionment, it was a post-war phenomenon. The *Daily Worker* began publication in 1930, and the *Left Review*, which was the nearest thing to an official organ that the intellectuals of the Left had, did not appear until 1934. The whole question of what a British Communist would be—how he would behave, what he would think about art and literature, and what kind he would himself produce if he were an artist—all these questions were unanswered, even unasked, in 1930. The 'thirties was not a time of political orthodoxy, but a time when orthodoxy was being worked out, and this includes orthodoxy in literature.

In a study of a literary generation, the process of 'growing into consciousness' will necessarily involve questions of the functions and forms of art. The decade of the 'thirties was a time of crises, and the most important writing of the period is best seen as a series of efforts to respond to crisis. Auden posed the problem very acutely in the mid-'thirties when he wrote, in a birthday poem to Isherwood:

> So in this hour of crisis and dismay,
> What better than your strict and adult pen
> Can warn us from the colours and the consolations,
> The showy arid works, reveal
> The squalid shadow of academy and garden,
> Make action urgent and its nature clear?
> Who give us nearer insight to resist
> The expanding fear, the savaging disaster?[1]

In these questions there is a new and different conception of the literary act, adapted to a sense of the critical nature of the time. The writer must be *strict* and *adult*, adjectives that impose moral commitment and discipline upon the act of writing. By his pen—in his role as a writer, and not simply as a citizen—he will make men aware of the need for action, and of what action means. His insight will give men strength to resist their enemies, without and within. This is more than simply a moral theory of literature, it asserts a direct relation between literature and action in the public world; writing becomes a mode of action.

There is no precise name for the kind of writing that Auden was approving in that poem. It is not simply didactic—the focus on action makes it more insistent, less abstract than that. Nor can it be described as propaganda—*strict* and *adult* ask for more than a party line. Auden was urging a kind of writing that would be affective, immediate, and concerned with ideas, moral not aesthetic in its central intention, and organized by that intention rather than by its correspondence to the observed world. The problem that he posed was not simply a formal one—finding an alternative way of writing a Georgian lyric or a realistic novel—but something more difficult: he was asking for alternative *worlds*, worlds of the imagination which would consist in new, significant forms, and through which literature could play a moral role in a time of crisis. This idea of a new kind of literature raises questions of fundamental importance—of the nature of language, of history, of the meaning of action, of heroism. These are not all strictly literary questions, but they are all questions that the writers of the 'thirties concerned themselves with; their works, the major writings of the generation, can all be understood as efforts to solve the crucial problem that Auden posed.

If we consider some major examples, we will see how difficult it is to give a generic name to them: what term will cover *Paid on Both Sides*, *A Gun for Sale*, *Vienna*, *The Wild Goose Chase*, *Goodbye to Berlin*, *The Road to Wigan Pier*, and *Autumn Journal*? All of these, in their different ways, might be taken as efforts to make action urgent and its nature clear. All deal, to some degree, with problems of politics and action. All are departures—in some cases quite extreme departures—from the formal traditions of pre-war writing;

all take their forms to some extent from their conceptual content, rather than from tradition or from observed reality; all embody a sense of crisis.

It is clear that the young writers of these books, and 'thirties writers generally, were very conscious of the special formal properties that their generation's best work had. In criticism and reviews they commonly used terms that identify this element of conceptual form: terms like *fable*, *myth*, and *allegory*. These terms have different literary ancestries, of course, but in the 'thirties they were used more or less as synonyms; it is one more evidence of the generation's separation from the past that they should use such traditional terms without reference to traditional examples: an allegory is an allegory *now*, not a work that resembles Bunyan's. I don't think terminology is an important issue here: any of these terms will do if one uses it consistently, and with an awareness that it covers a wide range of formal variations. What *is* important is to see the process by which these young writers groped toward forms for a new set of problems, and what factors affected their decisions.

I have adopted Auden's term—*parable-art*—because he provided contemporary definitions of what he meant by it. In his essay, 'Psychology and Art To-day' (1935), Auden wrote:

There must always be two kinds of art, escape-art, for man needs escape as he needs food and deep sleep, and parable-art, that art which shall teach man to unlearn hatred and learn love . . .[2]

And in the introduction to *The Poet's Tongue* (also 1935):

. . . poetry, the parabolic approach, is the only adequate medium for psychology. The propagandist, whether moral or political, complains that the writer should use his powers over words to persuade people to a particular course of action, instead of fiddling while Rome burns. But Poetry is not concerned with telling people what to do, but with extending our knowledge of good and evil, perhaps making the necessity for action more urgent and its nature more clear, but only leading us to the point where it is possible for us to make a rational and moral choice.[3]

The distinction between parable and propaganda seems to me a useful one, and so does the echo of Auden's poem to Isherwood. It all comes together: poetry is parable-art, parables teach (but love, not ideology), and that is what a strict and adult pen must do in a time of expanding fear and savaging disaster. Art remains Art, but it performs a social role.

The definition that emerges is something like this: a parable is functional—that is message-bearing, clarifying, instructive—but it is not didactic. Rather it is an *escape* from didacticism; like a myth, it renders the feeling of human issues, not an interpretation of them. It is non-realistic, because it takes its form from its content, and not from an idea of fidelity to the observed world. It is moral, not aesthetic, in its primary intention; it offers models of the problem of action. The working out of the meaning of parable, in theory and in a parabolic practice, is a process that continued through the 'thirties, and gave a kind of formal continuity to the diversity of 'thirties writing. And all that time history continued to offer new fears and new disasters, the public world pressed in more and more urgently upon the private world. Out of all that—the works, the crises, and their interactions—a generation discovered itself, and found its own expression. That is what this book is about.

My study of a decade has taken half a decade to research and write, and during that time I have been generously helped by the American Council of Learned Societies and by the National Endowment for the Humanities; I am glad to express my appreciation for their assistance here. Northwestern University was also liberal with funds and with released time from teaching and administrative duties, for which I am also grateful. I would also like to thank the following for their advice and assistance: the Librarian of Exeter College, Oxford; the staff of the University of Sussex Library; the staff of the Cambridge University Library; the directors of Mass-Observation Ltd; the staff of the Northwestern University Library; Quentin Bell, Barry Bloomfield, Mrs John Carleton, Sam Carmack, Arthur Crook, Mrs Valerie Eliot, William Empson, Brother George Every s.s.m., P. N. Furbank, Barbara Hardy, Laurence Lafore, Edward Mendelson, Sir Denis Proctor, Kathleen Raine, Leonard Skevington, Stephen Spender, T. Stanhope Sprigg, Rex Warner, Antonia White, Ian Willison, Charles Wintour, Alex Zwerdling.

A portion of Chapter X was first published in *Modern Irish Literature: Essays in Honor of William York Tindall* (New York: Iona College Press, 1972). The poem 'Awake! Young Men of England' by George Orwell is reprinted with the permission of Mrs Sonia Brownell Orwell and Secker & Warburg Ltd. The 'Preface' to *Oxford Poetry 1927*, by W. H. Auden and Cecil Day Lewis, is reprinted with the permission of the Estate of W. H. Auden, and of A. D. Peters & Co Ltd., agents for the Day Lewis estate. "I want the Theatre to Be . . ." is reprinted with the permission of the Estate of W. H. Auden.

I

1914-28

The Generation's Beginnings

I

A generation is, first of all, people of roughly the same age in
roughly the same place. But not all groups of contemporaries have
thought of themselves as separable from the stream of history.
What makes a generation aware of itself as a collective entity must
depend on two things: consciousness of unique shared experience,
and a sense that that experience distinguishes persons who have
shared it from those who have not, or who live through it in other
ways. English men and women born during the first decade of this
century are a generation in these terms: they shared two catastrophic historical experiences—the First World War and the
economic and political events of the 'thirties—and shared them in
particular ways because of the age at which they encountered
them. I am concerned in this book with the second of these experiences, and the ways in which living through the 'thirties affected
the literature that this generation produced; but I must begin
with the earlier period, because it was the peculiar shaping force of
the generation.

Every memoir about the time makes clear that the First World
War dominated the lives of those who were children then as much
as it did the lives of their elders.[1] Perhaps more so, for the young
had no real experience of the Edwardian world before the war;
for them, awareness of the world and awareness of the war came
at the same time. The War was a new kind of experience for everyone involved in it—vaster in scale, more prodigal of lives and of
materials, more mechanical and brutal than any previous war had
been. It was also new in that it was the first English war to make
much of the Home Front and of the role of civilians, including
children. At schools, boys learned to drill and to march and girls

learned to bandage, dormitories were cold and the food was dreary, and there were no sweets. It must have seemed to children, as the war went on, that a war was simply the sum of small discomforts and of large losses; for them it meant sacrifices without glory, arms without enemies and bandages without wounds, but it also meant the absence of fathers and brothers.

For the boys there was one great consolation: they were training for the brief and violent glory of the trenches. In their schools the lengthening Rolls of Honour, the memorial services, and the exercises of the Officers' Training Corps must have made school life seem only a stage in their preparation for battle, the beginning of a continuous process sustained by common values. For this was the last war in which the values of the public-school tradition—courage, self-sacrifice, honour, duty, playing the game, all that—seemed transferable to the battlefield. Older brothers had gone off in the spirit of Rupert Brooke, and younger brothers stayed behind and drilled, and wrote patriotic verses, like the poem that young Eric Blair (who became George Orwell) wrote in 1914, and saw published in the *Henley and South Oxfordshire Standard*:

Awake! Young Men of England

Oh! give me the strength of the lion,
  The wisdom of Reynard the Fox,
And then I'll hurl troops at the Germans,
  And give them the hardest of knocks.

Oh! think of the War Lord's mailed fist,
  That is striking at England today;
And think of the lives that our soldiers
  Are fearlessly throwing away.

Awake! oh you young men of England,
  For if, when your Country's in need,
You do not enlist by the thousand,
  You truly are cowards indeed.[2]

All the clichés are there—the evocation of England, the glorification of sacrifice, the image from medieval, romantic battle, the emotive language of courage and cowardice. It is a poem written not so much by a boy as by a tradition, and a tradition that was at its end.

And then the war was over. For the young generation the great opportunity had been missed, the marching and the drilling had been for nothing; the schoolboy soldiers had not performed their heroic deeds, the high suffering had not included them. The effects of the end of the war on the young were complex. At the schools there was an immediate schoolboy reaction against soldiering: at Eton (by Orwell's and Anthony Powell's accounts), at Lancing (by Evelyn Waugh's) the OTC became a joke, and boys vied with each other at being the most unmilitary. At Eton the boy-soldiers of one house turned out for an inspection all wearing horn-rimmed spectacles, and counted off 'one, two, three, four, five, six, seven, eight, nine, ten, knave, queen, king, ace'.[3]

With this unmilitary behaviour went a correlative reaction against the 'Old Men'—the generation of leaders who had declared war and had directed its continuance—and by extension against everything that might be associated with that generation of pre-war elders. Orwell later remembered this period of his life as a kind of revolution:

> Throughout almost the whole nation there was running a wave of revolutionary feeling which has since been reversed and forgotten, but which has left various deposits of sediment behind. Essentially, though of course one could not then see it in perspective, it was a revolt of youth against age, resulting directly from the war. . . . By 1918 everyone under forty was in a bad temper with his elders, and the mood of anti-militarism which followed naturally upon the fighting was extended into a general revolt against orthodoxy and authority. At that time there was, among the young, a curious cult of hatred of 'old men'. The dominance of 'old men' was held to be responsible for every evil known to humanity, and every accepted institution from Scott's novels to the House of Lords was derided because 'old men' were in favour of it. . . . And of course the revolutionary mood extended to those who had been too young to fight, even to public schoolboys. At that time we all thought of ourselves as

enlightened creatures of a new age, casting off the orthodoxy that had been forced upon us by those detested 'old men'.[4]

As this first post-war generation went up to the universities, they seem at first to have withdrawn from recent history, and to have tried to live as though there had been no war, as though 1914–18 had dropped out of time. If such a reaction was possible anywhere, it would be within the walls and within the traditions of Oxford and Cambridge. 'Despite everything,' Claud Cockburn recalled,

> despite even the casualty lists of the war years, it would have been just possible at Oxford to imagine that the First World War had not taken place—or at least that it had been merely a big, ugly, necessary episode . . .[5]

And his cousin, Evelyn Waugh, also at Oxford, wrote:

> After my time there were jazz, cocktail parties, a constant com-ing and going to London, new smart slang and the cult of the rich; soon to be succeeded by the cult of the proletariat. But for a single lustrum we lived and spoke very much as our predecessors had done ten years before.[6]

But of course one couldn't live in 1920 as though it were 1910, and Waugh goes on to acknowledge that obvious fact:

> Some of us were sharply conscious of those legendary figures who, almost to a man, were wiped out in the First World War. We were often reproachfully reminded, particularly by the college servants, of how impoverished and subdued we were in comparison with those great men.

That was the point—the next older generation, which this one should have followed to maturity, was simply missing; there was a break in time, with no human link between the post-war young and the Old Men whom they blamed for the war. This gap where there should have been older brothers for models, together with the post-war feeling about the pre-war generation, isolated the young in a way that was new; they were like the survivors of some primal disaster, cut off from the traditional supports of the past, and so dependent upon themselves for such meanings as their lives might acquire.

Toward the war itself the feelings of the young men of the next generation were deeply ambivalent, a mixture of revulsion at the brutality and waste of it, guilt at not having fought in it, and envy of those who had; and all of these feelings contributed to the generation's sense of its own particular identity. 'We young writers of the middle 'twenties,' Christopher Isherwood later wrote, 'were all suffering, more or less subconsciously, from a feeling of shame that we hadn't been old enough to take part in the European war,' and he confessed that 'like most of my generation, I was obsessed by a complex of terrors and longings connected with the idea "War" .' Orwell shared at least the longings: 'As the war fell back into the past, my particular generation, those who had been "just too young", became conscious of the vastness of the experience they had missed. You felt yourself a little less than a man, because you had missed it.'[7]

This sense of the opportunity lost, of the test that one had failed without even having taken it, is expressed in many memoirs of the time, and is, I think, an important factor in the collective consciousness of the whole generation of young men who came of age between the wars. Philip Toynbee, for example, was born twelve years after Isherwood, yet he gives a very similar account of his youthful feelings about war:

. . . it seems to me now that our picture of war was as falsely romantic, in its different way, as anything which had stirred the minds of Edwardian boys, brought up on Henty and the heroics of minor imperial campaigns. The desolate No-Man's-Land pictures of Paul Nash; Bernard Partridge cartoons of the Kaiser; songs from *Cavalcade* and the compassionate poems of Wilfred Owen had made a powerful, complex and stimulating impression on us, so that we felt less pity than envy of a generation which had experienced so much. Even in our Anti-War campaigns of the early thirties we were half in love with the horrors which we cried out against, and as a boy, I can remember murmuring the name *'Passchendaele'* in an ecstasy of excitement and regret.[8]

These ambivalent feelings, the terrors and longings, the excitement and regret, were fed, as Toynbee suggests, by the literature

of the war. Most of the best known novels and memoirs were not
published until the end of the 'twenties, but the war poets came
earlier—Sassoon and Graves before the war had ended, Wilfred
Owen's *Poems* in 1919—and out of their books, and Barbusse's *Le
Feu* and a few others, a new literary myth grew. I don't mean
anything very complex by the word *myth*; simply that young
people get their sense of history from books, and their *feelings* about
history from novels and poems. Before the war, ideas about war
had come to young people from Henty and Kipling and Sir Henry
Newbolt (certainly these must have been among Rupert Brooke's
sources). But these ideas had not survived the war, and so a new
myth appeared.

The first formulation of the myth is in the preface for a book of
war poems that Wilfred Owen wrote in the last months of the war
(he was killed on 4 November 1918). It is brief, and apparently
unfinished, but it is important in the history of twentieth-century
poetics, and of the 'thirties generation. Owen wrote:

> This book is not about heroes. English poetry is not yet fit to
> speak of them.
> Nor is it about deeds, or lands, nor anything about glory,
> honour, might, majesty, dominion, or power, except War.
> Above all I am not concerned with Poetry.
> My subject is War, and the pity of War.
> The Poetry is in the pity.
> Yet these elegies are to this generation in no sense consolatory.
> They may be to the next. All a poet can do today is warn.
> That is why the true Poets must be truthful.
> (If I thought the letter of this book would last, I might have
> used proper names; but if the spirit of it survives—survives
> Prussia—my ambition and those names will have achieved
> themselves fresher fields than Flanders . . .)

Here, sketchily put down, is a whole theory of war-poetry, based
on a number of related ideas: about heroism, about rhetoric, about
Owen's generation, and about the function of poetry in a time
of disaster. Owen defines the proper language of war-poetry, and
explains why it is proper: the rhetoric of the past, the words that
the Old Men used, has been thrown away, '*dulce et decorum est*' has

become a bitter irony, and nobody will ever be a corner of a foreign field that is forever England. The language that is left, the harsh, unromantic language of actuality, will not allow rhetorical gestures, but it will serve well enough the function that Owen proposes for poetry—it will warn men against war, by telling them the truth about it.

In the kind of poetry that Owen described, the traditional celebration of military heroism would obviously not be possible. Nevertheless, Owen's poems (and Sassoon's and Graves') *are* about heroes, and even about glory and honour, though the meanings of those terms have changed (that surely is the sense of Owen's final parenthetical sentence). The new Myth of the War was not simply a rejection of former attitudes; rather it was a revision of them. Anyone who reads the war poets will sense at once the note of praise that comes through the violence, anger, and grief; men may not perform Great Deeds any longer, but they can be tough, stoical, and humorous under stress, they can be loyal to each other, they can feel pity, and they can perform their meaningless destructive duties faithfully and with skill. It is a myth without the flags and the martial music, but not without values.

Perhaps the most important thing to say about the post-war world, as the young saw it, is that it was full of this Myth of the War. The poets who had served as soldiers, and had partly made the myth, were heroes to those who came after, and Wilfred Owen in particular became a sort of martyred saint, whose words, 'the poetry is in the pity', were repeated like a prayer or a line of scripture.[9] Part of the appeal that these men had was that they were poets who were also men of action. War's greatest appeal, at least for artists, intellectuals, and introspective men, is that it makes the nature and urgency of action clear. In the years between the wars, when young men wondered whether to act, and if so, how, they looked back with admiration to the examples of those earlier poets, who *had* acted.

They were also, obviously, literary influences, the principal source of the most characteristic qualities of between-the-wars poetry. They offered a new tone, a new idea of imagery, and a new rhetoric. The tone was ironic, could be bitter or angry, and could hate and condemn, but it avoided the upper register of emotions, the range of nobility and splendour and high tragedy. The imagery was the true naming of ugly things, nature violated and defaced, death without dignity, the wreckage of waste and war. (The tradition of romantic pastoralism died, one might say, on the Western front.) The new rhetoric was the language that Owen had commended, stripped of the high-flown abstractions that had faded on the recruiting posters, reduced to the plainness of fact. Michael Roberts was surely echoing Owen when he wrote, in his *Critique of Poetry* (1934), that

> 1914 showed the disaster which followed when hundreds of millions of people gave the old responses to the old stimuli. Soldiers, and later civilians, saw that 'Honour', 'Courage', 'Patriotism', as they understood them, led to cruelty, lying, and blood-lust on a scale so gigantic that the foundations of civilisation were threatened.[10]

This is a statement about the morality of rhetoric; the case against those traditional abstract terms is that they 'led to'—that is *caused* —wicked emotions, which led to suffering and death. Roberts is making an extreme claim for the power of language to affect action, a claim that makes language almost a mode of action. This idea had a powerful effect on the language that poets of the 'thirties used; but it had another and more fundamental effect on their conception of the role of poetry in society. For if the old stimuli could lead a nation to a cruel and stupid war, then new stimuli might keep it out of the next one. It is striking that in the 'thirties poets did believe, or at least hoped, that poetry might alter action in such a fundamental way. Decisions about style and subject necessarily followed from this belief; and the belief itself followed from Owen's Preface, and from the Myth of the War.

But the most profound influence of the Myth of the War on the post-war years was a more general and less easily definable change in social attitudes and values, the ironic and anti-rhetorical aspect of the myth applied to belief and behaviour. John Lehmann, recalling his life at Cambridge in the 'twenties, put the change very well: 'When I look back on it,' he wrote,

> it seems to me that the Cambridge I knew was haunted inescapably by the old war; it was always there in the background

conditioning the prevalent sensibility, with its preference for tragedy and bitter wit, its rejection of cosy pretences and its refusal to accept any criterion of behaviour except one: does your action cause suffering to another?[11]

Lehmann is describing here what we think of as the characteristic 'twenties sensibility—the sensibility of *Point Counterpoint* and *Gold Coast Customs*, of *The Green Hat* and *Decline and Fall* and *Private Lives*. It was a product, he says, of 'the old war', but it was not confined to writings explicitly concerned with the war; indeed it is not unreasonable to say that *all* the serious books of the post-war decade were war books, *Crome Yellow* and *Mrs. Dalloway* quite as much as *A Farewell to Arms* and *Goodbye to All That*, and that what they shared was the sensibility that is implied by Owen's preface.

In this sense the war book above all others in the 'twenties was *The Waste Land*, and no account of the forces that formed the 'thirties generation would be accurate that neglected that power-fully influential poem. Eliot had an acute sense of what he called 'the immense panorama of futility and anarchy that is contemporary history', and he put that sense of history into his poem. And in 1922 contemporary history meant vestiges of the war: hence the two veterans who meet in the first part, and Lil's husband, who has just been demobbed, in the second, and the shouting and crying in part five, which Eliot's note identifies with the Russian Revolution. But beyond that, the world of the poem, with its heaps of broken images and its shocked and passive and neurasthenic persons, is a paradigm of war's effects, and of a world emptied of order and meaning, like a battlefield after the battle. And the *manner* of the poem—its ironic tone, its imagery, its lack of heroes and heroism, its anti-rhetorical style—is also a consequence of the war, an application of war-poet principles to the post-war scene.

The importance of Eliot's poem to the first post-war generation is nicely recorded in an episode from Evelyn Waugh's novel of those years, *Brideshead Revisited*. The aesthetes of Oxford have gathered for a luncheon in college rooms, among them Anthony Blanche, who is modelled very closely on Brian Howard, the most aesthetical and decadent of Waugh's contemporaries. It is Blanche who performs the symbolic gesture:

> After luncheon he stood on the balcony with a megaphone which had appeared surprisingly among the bric-a-brac of Sebastian's room, and in languishing, sobbing tones recited passages from *The Waste Land* to the sweatered and muffled throng that was on its way to the river.
> '*I, Tiresias, have foresuffered all,*' he sobbed to them from the Venetian arches;
>   '*Enacted on this same d-divan or b-bed,*
>   *I who have sat by Thebes below the wall*
>   *And walked among the l-l-lowest of the dead . . .*'
> And then, stepping lightly into the room, 'How I have surprised them! All b-boatmen are Grace Darlings to me.'[12]

There is an alternative example in Peter Quennell's memoir, *The Sign of the Fish*, in which Harold Acton, a similarly aesthetic undergraduate of the same generation, recites the entire poem to the guests at a Conservative Party garden fête. 'His audience's manners were severely tested,' Quennell recalls,

> as this dirge for a godless civilization, delivered in Harold Acton's rich, resounding voice, swept irresistibly above their heads; and one or two old ladies, who were alarmed and horrified, but thought that the reciter had such a 'nice, kind face', rather than hurt the young man's feelings by getting up and leaving openly, were obliged to sink to their knees and creep away on all fours.[13]

The point that both anecdotes make is that for this generation Eliot's poem was a manifesto, a weapon to be used against the philistines and the Old Men (and their Ladies). It seemed to belong to the young, and one might find it, as Quennell says, on the table of every literary undergraduate, though it is well to remember the sweatered and muffled throng—not all undergraduates were literary, and not all of them felt the need of a *Waste Land*. But for young men like Howard and Acton and Waugh and Quennell, and for those who followed them at Oxford and Cambridge, *The Waste Land* was an important factor in the process by which the post-war generation became aware of itself and its situation. It was a part of their effort toward self-definition.

Two or three years later, the young Wystan Auden, then an undergraduate at Christ Church, demonstrated the increased authority of Eliot in a conversation with his tutor, Nevill Coghill. As Coghill remembered the dialogue, it went like this:

Auden: 'I have torn up all my poems.'

Coghill: 'Indeed! Why?'

Auden: 'Because they were no good. Based on Wordsworth. No good nowadays.'

Coghill: 'Oh . . .?'

Auden: 'You ought to read Eliot. I've been reading Eliot. I now see the way I want to write. I've written two new poems this week. Listen!'[14] The conversation convinced Coghill that he would have to take Eliot seriously; Auden's advice, he decided, was 'in the imperative'.

The difference between Auden's *Waste Land* and Brian Howard's *Waste Land* is striking. For Howard and Harold Acton, the poem was a defiant gesture, something to shock the bourgeoisie with; but for Auden, the poem was a model, and Eliot a master who had replaced Wordsworth. In only a few years, from 1924 to 1926 or '27, an influence that began on the decadent fringe of undergraduate life had moved to the centre, and was reaching to perceptive young dons like Coghill.

To Eliot's young admirers, *The Waste Land* was the essential vision of the post-war world, and the generation's *donnée*. It is worth noting that the generation involved here includes both the friends of Waugh at the beginning of the 'twenties, and the friends of Auden at the end. Critics have tended to divide them into two groups, to identify the first as the aesthetes, the Bright Young People of Waugh's early novels, and the second as the Political Activists of the 'thirties; but in the 'twenties, when the two groups overlapped at Oxford, they were one post-war generation, sharing a view of society as decadent and emptied of values. And Eliot's poem seemed an immediate and authoritative expression of what they saw.

From its first appearance, *The Waste Land* was read as a work of primarily social and moral import, a public poem on public themes. It is possible, now, fifty years later, to see it as the private nightmare of a young expatriate having a nervous breakdown in Zürich or, in Eliot's own terms, as 'the relief of a personal and wholly insignificant grouse against life . . . just a piece of rhythmical grumbling',[15] but in the 'twenties such readings were not current, because they were not useful to a generation living in the shadow cast by the late war. The poem was about the consequences of the war, and when influential young critics wrote about it, they dealt with it in essentially public terms, as a sentence passed by the poet on post-war society. And by writing as they did they helped to fix this reading as the orthodox one.

I. A. Richards, then a young don at Cambridge, was especially influential, for he seemed, to the young men he taught, to occupy roughly the same place in post-war criticism that Eliot did in post-war poetry. Christopher Isherwood, who as an undergraduate attended Richards' lectures on modern poetry in the mid-'twenties, remembered him as 'the prophet we had been waiting for'. 'To us,' Isherwood recalled, 'he was infinitely more than a brilliantly new literary critic: he was our guide, our evangelist, who revealed to us, in a succession of astounding lightning flashes, the entire expanse of the Modern World.'[16]

Richards was the first English critic to develop a theory of modern poetry in terms of which *The Waste Land* was an important poem. His *Science and Poetry* (1926) takes what one might call a Waste Land view of the modern situation. In a chapter entitled 'Poetry and Beliefs', Richards wrote:

A sense of desolation, of uncertainty, of futility, of the groundlessness of aspirations, of the vanity of endeavour, and a thirst for a life-giving water which seems suddenly to have failed, are the signs in consciousness of this necessary re-organization of our lives. [By 're-organization' Richards meant the acceptance of a scientific view of the world.]

To this sentence the following footnote was attached:

To those familiar with Mr. Eliot's *The Waste Land*, my indebtedness to it at this point will be evident. He seems to me by this poem, to have performed two considerable services for this generation. He has given a perfect emotive description of a state of mind which is probably inevitable for a while to all meditative people. Secondly, by effecting a complete severance between his poetry and *all* beliefs, and this without any weakening of the poetry, he has realised what might otherwise have remained largely a speculative possibility and has shown the way to the only solution of these difficulties. 'In the destructive element immerse. That is the way.'[17]

It is, I think, a crucial passage: it claims the poem as a philosophical support for a certain philosophical attitude—what Richards elsewhere in the book calls 'the neutralisation of nature'; and it links the poem with the post-war generation, as a perfect account of an inevitable state of mind. Henceforth, if one did not feel a sense of desolation, if one did not immerse in the destructive element, one was not a meditative person. For young people, this is surely the way beliefs, and feelings about beliefs, are often formed. And if this is so, then the creation of a received view of *The Waste Land*, and of the poem's connection with a post-war state of mind, was a significant part of the formation of the 'thirties generation.

The interpretation of the poem that Richards urged was not an eccentric one; it simply ignored the private meaning, what Eliot meant when he called it a personal grouse against life. He was encouraged to read it as he did by Eliot's own critical writings, by the famous defence of difficulty in 'The Metaphysical Poets', for example, and more specifically by Eliot's review of *Ulysses*, published in 1923. The essay is a justification of what Eliot calls 'the mythic method', and a transparent defence of the way *The Waste Land* is put together; the method, he says, 'is simply a way of controlling, of ordering, of giving a shape and a significance to the immense panorama of futility and anarchy which is contemporary history'.[18] Such a vision of history separates the post-war world from all the past, and from past ideas of order and value; it must have both confirmed and helped to form Richards' understanding of Eliot's poem, and, more importantly, it must have helped to form the post-war generation's sense of its isolation from the world before the war.

If, as I believe, the Myth of the War and the post-war vision of the Waste Land were shaping forces in the imaginations of the post-war generation, then one would expect to find evidences of those forces in their writings. One set of evidences is the annual volumes of *Oxford Poetry*, published through the 'twenties and early 'thirties. Most undergraduate poems are not written by poets, and are not burdened with much originality; they express such undergraduate feelings as are thought at the time to be poetic, and they do so in the poetic manners that are currently in vogue. By reading them, one can discover what subjects, and what models, were considered appropriate for poetry by the undergraduate generation.

The most surprising thing about Oxford poetry in the early 'twenties is that it showed no direct influence of Owen and Sassoon and Graves. One does find a few war poems in the annual volumes, but they are invariably laments for dead youths in the Rupert Brooke tradition, as though war-poetry had ended in 1914. The reason for this is clear: the genre of true war poems was simply not open to the 'just too young', and the example of Owen was not seen as applicable to experience outside the trenches. But Brooke, who had never actually got to where the fighting was, remained a possible model, and behind him all the heroic verse that he had drawn upon; conventional sentimentality is there for anyone, it is in the public domain.

But of course most of the poems in these volumes are not about war, but about love—frustrated, rejected, or unrequited love. I suppose this is always true of undergraduate poems, though perhaps the love-objects are not always so sexually ambiguous as they are in this lot. The modern poetic models in the early years of the decade are Edith Sitwell, Hardy, and perhaps De la Mare; the tone, at its most 'modern', is decadent, a bit recherché. Then in 1925 Cecil Day Lewis arrives, bringing the early Yeats. The Auden generation is beginning to stir.

Auden himself appeared first in the 1926 volume, which he edited with Charles Plumb. Editors of previous volumes had not made their presence much felt, except through the poems of their own that they published, but Auden and Plumb chose to open theirs with a vigorous preface, which contains this passage:

In this selection we have endeavoured to pacify, if not to content, both the progressive and the reactionary. And to the latter, who will doubtless be in the majority, we would suggest that poetry which does not at least attempt to face the circumstances of its time may supply charming holiday-reading, but vital interest, anything strictly *poetic*, it certainly will not. If it is a natural preference to inhabit a room with casements opening upon Fairyland, one at least of them should open upon the Waste Land. At the same time the progressive would be unreasonable to expect confidence until he has proved that his destination justifies his speed.[19]

This is cautiously put, but nevertheless it is a kind of manifesto, an indication of a new direction for a new generation. And it is significant that the editors identify the *poetic* with whatever faces 'the circumstances of its time', and that this correlates with the window opening upon the (capitalized) Waste Land. Geoffrey Gorer, reviewing the volume in the student magazine *Oxford Outlook*, regretted that 'the Eliot school predominates to such an extent';[20] four years after the first appearance of *The Waste Land* it could hardly have been otherwise.

The volume for the following year was edited by Auden and Day Lewis, and the preface is considerably more sophisticated. According to Day Lewis, the editors wrote alternate paragraphs; two, both by Auden if this statement is correct, are particularly interesting. First, after denying that 'the undergraduate mind' exists, Auden wrote:

On the other hand, the chaos of values which is the substance of our environment is not consistent with a standardization of thought, though, on the political analogy, it may have to be superseded by one. All genuine poetry is in a sense the formation of private spheres out of a public chaos: and therefore we would remind those who annually criticize us for lack of homogeneity, first, that on the whole it is environment which conditions values, not values which form environment; second, that we must hold partly responsible for our mental *sauve-qui-peut*, that acedia and unabashed glorification of the subjective so prominent in the world since the Reformation.[21]

Auden makes two assumptions here: first, he takes for granted that he and his contemporaries live in a 'chaos of values'—that is, his assumed moral world is the world of *The Waste Land*; and second, he assumes that in such a time poetry will be a private order created out of that public chaos. This is the first assertion of a theme that recurs throughout the 'thirties, and embodies one of the central literary problems of the period—the relation between public and private experience in literature at a time of public disorder, the 'Private faces/In public places' theme that Auden put in his epigraph to *The Orators*.

The second passage of interest comes at the end of the preface:

> Those who believe that there is anything valuable in our youth as such we have neither the patience to consider nor the power to condone: our youth should be a period of spiritual discipline, not a self-justifying dogma. As for the intelligent reader, we can only remind him, where he experiences distaste, that no universalized system—political, religious or metaphysical—has been bequeathed to us; where pleasure, that it is but an infinitesimal progression towards a new synthesis—one more of those efforts as yet so conspicuous in their paucity.[22]

The immediate ancestor of these remarks is certainly Eliot, filtered perhaps through the interpretation of I. A. Richards (*Science and Poetry* had appeared in the preceding year). They are important to an understanding of the later development of the generation, because they express the sense that two of its gifted members had of the moral and intellectual conditions of their world as they approached maturity. They saw themselves surrounded by the post-war ruins of all of men's traditional beliefs; the young would have to start again from the beginning, where they found themselves, in the Waste Land.

The preface is therefore more a statement of problems than of solutions. Some of the problems are put in terms of poets and poetry, but the central question of values is treated as the common inheritance of the generation. The implication is that this question makes the generation different, not simp'y in the way that every generation has always differed from the one that preceded it, but in a unique way. And there is the further implication that this shared issue gives the generation a kind of coherence that is a potential strength.

The role that the preface assigns to the artist is a strenuous one, and the terms used are active and energetic: words like *conflict, struggle, effort,* and *discipline.* It is on this point—the idea that in a time of public chaos art becomes a mode of action—that the preface most anticipates the critical debates of the 'thirties—and it is no doubt for this reason that it was later referred to as 'the *Oxford Poetry* Manifesto'.[23] One might say that the 'thirties really began here.

Eliot came to a similar conclusion about the date of the crucial post-war change when he wrote, in 1939:

Only from about the year 1926 did the features of the post-war world begin clearly to emerge—and not only in the sphere of politics. From about that date one began slowly to realize that the intellectual and artistic output of the previous seven years had been rather the last efforts of an old world, than the struggles of a new.[24]

It seems at first odd that Eliot should have placed *The Waste Land* and *Ulysses* among the old world's efforts, but there is justice in this view; he and Joyce were the ancestors rather than the agents of the post-war change, and one can certainly see now that *The Waste Land* especially was a work that drew very strongly on war feelings and pre-war feelings, and looked at the past with regret and at the present with dejection. It was, among other things, a poem about the end of European civilization, not about beginnings.

A change began in the mid-twenties, then, which one might describe, as Eliot did, as the first struggles of a new world, and which was related to the emerging self-consciousness of the rising generation. But it did not occur all at once, dramatically, like a Great Awakening, and it did not reach all members of the generation. Two brilliant Oxford undergraduates felt it, and put their account of it into the *Oxford Poetry* preface, but two undergraduates don't make a revolution; around them, most of their contemporaries seemed quite unaware of events in the world outside. In the summer of 1926, for example, when the General Strike occurred in England, students went out in groups from Oxford and Cambridge to work as strike-breakers, without any apparent understanding of what it was all about; even members of the Oxford Labour Club enlisted as blackleg engine-drivers, bus-conductors, and dock-labourers. Isherwood later remembered the strike-breaking as a 'tremendous upper-middle-class lark', and MacNeice recalled that university students 'regarded the strike as an occasion for a spree; a comic phenomenon due to the Lower Classes; a comet that came from nowhere and dissolved in rubble and presaged nothing to come'.[25]

If the English lower classes were remote from the undergraduate world, Europe was even more so. Isherwood, looking back at his life at Cambridge in 1925, recalled how he and Edward Upward had invented private fantasies to escape into from the world around them:

> It seems odd now [he wrote] to think of the two of us, so excited, so passionately self-absorbed, in that little fog-bound room . . . when one remembers that this was the winter of Hitler's Munich Putsch, of Mussolini's final campaign against the democrats, of the first English Labour Government, of Lenin's death. Hitler's name was, I suppose, then hardly known to a dozen people in all Cambridge. Mussolini was enjoying a certain popularity: rugger and rowing men, at this epoch, frequently named their terriers 'Musso'. The Labour Government and all its works were, for our selves, comprehended in the withering word 'politics' and therefore automatically dismissed as boring and vile.[26]

Both Isherwood and MacNeice were writing at the other end of the 'thirties, with the developed political and social consciousness that their generation had gained by then. But what they say seems true of their contemporaries at the universities: that at that point in their lives they had no political awareness, no sense of social realities, no sense of the moment in which they lived as a point in history. The change of consciousness had begun, and the brightest of the young were beginning to see their situation as different from the past, and requiring new solutions. But it was only a beginning, a window that had been opened on the Waste Land.

In 1926 there was scarcely a "thirties generation' at all, if by generation one means contemporaries who are aware of their collective identity. But the special conditions of their situation already existed. They had been involved in the world in new ways— through the war that they had missed, and through the General Strike that they had helped to defeat. They had touched the public world, ignorantly and reluctantly by all accounts, but touched it nonetheless, and from now on they would be drawn into closer and closer contacts with the jagged and abrasive realities, with economics, with foreign and domestic politics, and with war.

III

It is not surprising that the published undergraduate writings of the generation in the 'twenties contain no significant parables of their state of mind: not even the most gifted writers reach that level of consciousness so early. There was, however, one curious invention of those years that is worth noticing—the fantasy-world that Isherwood and his friend Upward created, and called Mortmere. The invention of Mortmere began in the mid-'twenties, when the two were undergraduates at Cambridge; they imagined a fantastic village, 'a sort of anarchist paradise', as Isherwood later described it, 'in which all accepted moral and social values were turned upside down and inside out, and every kind of extravagant behaviour was possible and usual. It was our private place of retreat from the rules and conventions of university life.'[27] They began to write stories about the inhabitants of the village, who gradually acquired names and characters: Ronald Gunball, Raynard Moxon, the Reverend Welken.

Such fantasies are common enough; most of us invent worlds of our own at some time in our lives, as alternatives to what reality offers us. Children play 'let's pretend', because they have no power to change the actual, and adults have their pornography and their fantasies of power. Utopias are alternative worlds made systematic to instruct us, and so are some political systems: Communism offers an alternative world, and so, in the 'thirties, did Fascism. What all these examples have in common is the creation of a complete *other* world, in which reality is so altered that the rules for living are altered. Such worlds liberate us, for a time, from the

35

restraints of the actual world that we inhabit. They also criticize the actual, at least by implication, by offering an alternative for comparison. These alternative worlds are, in my term, *parables*: highly structured, non-realistic, significant systems that constitute judgments of life as it exists.

Isherwood called the parable-world of Mortmere a 'private place of retreat', and it is not difficult to propose a psychological explanation of its authors' need for such a place: Isherwood, the son of a father killed at Ypres, full of guilt about the war, insecure and snobbish, homosexual, repressed; and Upward, the rebellious son of a Nonconformist family, unhappy at school and an outsider at the university. But Mortmere was more than an escapist day-dream; it was self-consciously written down, the names and places were fixed, the 'world' consistent, the style careful. It became a work of art.

Not much of the Mortmere saga has survived, or at least not much has been published; there are only the fragments quoted in Isherwood's *Lions and Shadows*, and Upward's last contribution, 'The Railway Accident'. But from these bits we can see that Isherwood was being disingenuous when he called Mortmere an 'anarchist paradise'. It is not anarchism that Mortmere expressed, but paranoia. Reality there is fantastic, unpredictable, and violent, and the characters are sinister and depraved: the vicar is guilty of moral offences with a choirboy, and Gunball manages a brothel for necrophiles. At least some of the stories seem to have been pornographic, and over the one surviving episode there hangs an atmosphere of sexual perversion.

In 'The Railway Accident' a character called Hearn travels by train to Mortmere, survives a mysterious train crash, joins in the vicar's annual Treasure Hunt, and watches a duel in which a man is wounded. The narrative is an odd, unstable mixture of school-boy horseplay and adult violence that anticipates later 'thirties parables like Auden's *Paid on Both Sides* and Rex Warner's *The Wild Goose Chase* (in Auden's case it was clearly a direct source). But it is more than that. The world that it describes is a disjunctive, irrational one, in which nothing is fixed or predictable, and there is no way of distinguishing fantasy from fact. Details that seem individually ordinary—a man fishing by a lake, an acquaintance seen from the train—become parts of a sinister but incomprehensible plot, while the customary order in events—timetables, the sequence of stations on the journey, the seasons—dissolves into anarchy.

'Perhaps *The Railway Accident* can best be described as a dream,' Isherwood wrote, 'or a nightmare, about the English.'[28] *Nightmare* seems the better word, for like an actual nightmare the story expresses fears beyond rational formulation: what would life be like if it were as it appears to be, a 'chaos of values', emptied of meaning, logic, or order? Like a nightmare it is an imagined action, but distorted, discontinuous, and uncontrolled by any ordering principle. It is also, as Isherwood adds, a nightmare about the *English*, and that is important; the village scene, with its vicar, its squire, and its vicarage garden, is all very English, but it is an English scene that belongs to the sentimental, dead past. If it is nevertheless still there, co-existing with modern, post-war England, then the English are mad, and paranoia is the true vision.

Mortmere may seem an odd place for two undergraduates to invent as a retreat from rules and conventions, but it is an understandable invention for its time. It is a kind of young man's Waste Land—grotesquely comical, ridiculously violent, undignified, frightening, perverse, free of all restraints, and entirely empty of meaning. Seen in these terms, it has a place at the beginning of this study, as an early parable of the generation. It contains none of the obsessive 'thirties subjects, the social issues, the politics, the fear of war, but it does express the anxiety of the valueless post-war world, which is the primary *donnée* of the time.

II

1929-30

I

When Michael Roberts set out to define his generation, he described it in relation to war: 'sergeants of our school O.T.C.s, admirers of our elder brothers, we grew up under the shadow of war.'[1] Stephen Spender wrote at about the same time:

> Who live under the shadow of a war,
> What can I do that matters?[2]

The metaphor is the same, but the shadows are different, cast by different wars; it is one of the peculiar burdens of the 'thirties generation that it moved into the shadow of the coming world war before the shadow of the past war had faded.

The shadow cast by the past, the Myth of the Great War, had been developing since the war years, and the first poems of Sassoon and Owen; it was filled out and given the particularity of history by the prose writings published at the end of the 'twenties. Most of the books of permanent value about the war appeared then: T. E. Lawrence's *Revolt in the Desert* in 1927, Cummings' *The Enormous Room* and Blunden's *Undertones of War* in 1928, Aldington's *Death of a Hero*, Remarque's *All Quiet on the Western Front*, Graves' *Goodbye to All That*, Renn's *War*, Hemingway's *A Farewell to Arms* and Sherriff's *Journey's End* in 1929, Sassoon's *Memoirs of an Infantry Officer* and Manning's *Her Privates We* in 1930.

'To the historian,' Desmond MacCarthy remarked in 1930, 'the year 1930 will be remembered chiefly as that in which men's emotions first began to turn against the war.'[3] MacCarthy was obviously wrong in thinking that the turn *began* in 1930; it began while the war was still being fought. But wide-spread, *consciously* anti-war attitudes did develop later, and it was surely the flood of war books at the end of the 'twenties that made those attitudes commonplace. Indeed some observers feared that the sheer mass

38

of writing would turn those anti-war feelings into mere clichés. 'There is an obvious danger,' John Brophy wrote in 1929, 'that the repudiation of war may become a mere habit of mind, an affectation not sprung from actual feeling and conviction.'[4] And Edmund Blunden remarked: 'Now the danger is, perhaps, that the horror and crime of war are being transformed into a glib axiom, a generalisation which may not work at the hearts of the new generation.'[5]

That was one danger. Another was that the horror and crime of war would be lost in nostalgia, that the unique experience of war would in time come to seem enviable. By 1930 the generation of the Great War had made its record and completed its Myth. Like every generation of war veterans, it had become a secret society, and that society was closed: there would be no new members. 'The experience of that generation,' Brophy wrote, 'is likely to be unique: for if another war should be jockeyed or forced upon the world, it will be a scientific, chemical affair; machines will be met with machines, not with the nerves and muscles of mere men. Later generations may see whole cities destroyed overnight, populations slain in their sleep; but they will not know winter in the Salient, or the summer shambles of the Somme, Gallipoli, and Mesopotamia.'[6] Those names had become incantations, like Mark Antony's recitation of his kingdoms or Othello's naming of his travels; they invoked a numinous, closed world, full of suffering and death, but made heroic by time and memory. This is what the young Philip Toynbee was responding to when he murmured the name 'Passchendaele' to himself 'in an ecstasy of excitement and regret'; that ambivalent feeling about war was a part of the generation's sensibility, and it was to a large extent created by the retrospective literature of war.

Reviews of these books often had an elegiac, obituary tone, as though the authors were not only long dead, but belonged to some mythologized past, like the casualty lists of the Trojan War. This was especially true if the reviewer was himself a veteran, as for example Herbert Read reviewing Sassoon's *Memoirs of an Infantry Officer:*

He is a sensitive member of a generation destroyed by the

greatest catastrophe in modern history; and because it was so destroyed, this generation cannot ever justify itself. A realist might object to this manner of speaking as fanciful; he would point out that although ten million men were killed, a fair number survived, and that surely some of them had a very jolly time. But in affairs of the spirit we do not count heads, and it was the spirit or vital faith of a generation that perished, not its bare existence.[7]

Read's assumption is that the war-generation no longer existed in the chain of human history, connecting their pre-war elders with the post-war young: the survivors of the war had withdrawn into their myth. Their abdication of a place in the present is yet another factor in the formation of the 'thirties generation's sense of isolation and separation from the past.

The quotation from John Brophy above suggests another important reason for the shift of feeling about the First World War that came at the end of the decade. 'If another war should be jockeyed or forced upon the world . . .': at the end of the 'twenties this possibility began to enter men's thoughts. 'It was probably about the Spring of '28,' another critic wrote in 1930, 'that the public first ceased to think of itself as "post-War",—and began to feel that it was living in the epoch "preceding the next Great War".'[8] It is striking how quickly this change spread, and how widely. One finds it not only in critical and political journalism of the time, but in the imaginative writings of the younger generation as well. In Evelyn Waugh's first novel, *Decline and Fall* (published in September 1928), the hero, Paul Pennyfeather, remarks that he expects another war, and Lord Circumference responds:

> 'D'you really and truly think so? That there's going to be another war, I mean?'
> 'Yes, I'm sure of it; aren't you?'
> 'Yes, of course. I'm sure of it too. And that awful bread, and people coming on to one's own land and telling one what one's to do with one's own butter and milk, and commandeering one's horses!'[9]

This is Waugh being satirical at the expense of country peers and schoolmasters, but the point is nevertheless clear: if this peer and this schoolmaster agree that a war is coming, it must be pretty obvious.

This expectation of a coming war became an insistent part of the consciousness of the 'thirties generation. It enters into—or perhaps one should say it intrudes upon—some of the best work of the decade's best writers, as a central image or an off-stage threat, as an obsessive metaphor, an image, or an allusion; in one form or another it seems always to be there, at the edge of the imagination, a fearful trespasser into private realms, a presence, a part of reality.[10] Even when actual warfare was not the subject, the language of war came readily to mind, as though war had become a natural metaphor for the relations among men. So Graham Greene, writing about politics and class in 1934, called his novel *It's a Battlefield*, and Auden, in *The Orators* (1932), imagined the struggle against bourgeois values as a farcical guerilla war. Indeed, social, political, and economic conflicts together seemed to amount to another war, a third shadow over the 'thirties that touched lives and imaginations as deeply as the shadows of those other wars, the one that was past and the one that was coming.

These wars were the forces that shaped the 'thirties generation. That seems clear now; but it was clear even in the early 'thirties to sensitive observers. Edmund Blunden made the point in 1931, in a review of the annual Oxford volume of undergraduate verse; after comparing the book to seventeenth-century miscellanies, he concluded that

Sedleys and Clevelands are . . . far from the modern spirit, or rather the mood of a generation which looks back to a world roaring with bursting bombs, looks immediately at a daily crisis in politics and the social fabric, and, if it has still strength to look ahead, half sees a world roaring with bigger and better bombs . . . I do not claim to discern how deeply the iron has entered into the soul of those who were in the nursery in 1914, but it seems obvious that they have grown up amid unnerving conditions, and such as destroy vision.[11]

What Blunden is noting here is a peculiar 'thirties state of mind, a sense of being bracketed by wars, like a lost battalion pinned

41

down by shell-fire that will eventually be on target. Gradually, as the decade went on, a new myth grew, the Myth of the *Next War*, an apocalyptic vision of approaching destruction and the end of civilization which became a part of consciousness, and so of literary imaginations of the 'thirties generation.

II

'Generations,' a book reviewer wrote in 1930, 'like wines of promise, can improve with age, and the post-war generation is beginning to settle.'[12] He was considering gastronomic writers in his review, but the same could be said of post-war novelists and poets: at the turn of the decade they were beginning to settle and to publish, and to become their own generation.

It seems appropriate that among the first to be noticeable were the two poets who had written their generation's manifesto in *Oxford Poetry 1927*. In the autumn of 1928 Auden and Day Lewis had left Oxford: Day Lewis was a schoolmaster in Scotland; Auden had gone to Berlin. Both were at work on long poems, their first attempts (and the first of their generation) at ambitious, large-scale treatment in verse of the problems that their manifesto had set down.

Day Lewis' appeared first: *Transitional Poem* was published by the Hogarth Press in October 1929. Formally it is not a continuous single poem, as the title suggests, but a sequence of thirty-four lyrics in various stanzas, divided into four parts. Day Lewis offered his own account of the poem's structure and meaning in a paragraph that introduces a string of footnotes at the end of the poem (the whole paraphernalia is very like that at the end of *The Waste Land*, and no doubt consciously so; Eliot provided the only model of what a serious modern poem should look like).

The central theme of this poem [he wrote] is the single mind. The poem is divided into four parts, which essentially represent four phases of personal experience in the pursuit of single-mindedness: it will be seen that a transition is intended from one part to the next such as implies a certain spiritual progress and a consequent shifting of aspect. As far as any definitions can be attached to these aspects, they may be termed (1) meta-

42

physical, (2) ethical, (3) psychological; while (4) is an attempt to relate the poetic impulse with the experience as a whole. Formally, the parts fall with fair accuracy into the divisions of a theorem in geometry, *i.e.* general enunciation, particular enunciation, proof, corollaries.[13]

This is very like Day Lewis' account, in his part of the *Oxford Poetry* preface, of the 'tripartite problem' of the modern poet; there he described 'the psychological conflict between self as subject and self as object', 'the ethical conflict' between Pure Art and the exigencies of existence, and 'the logical conflict, between the denotatory and the connotatory sense of words'. In both cases the problem is seen as a personal one: how does the individual poetic mind relate itself to the conditions of the world outside? It is the problem of public and private experience, which I have said (and will say again) is one of the central problems of the generation. Day Lewis' treatment of it is modern insofar as the contents of the mind that he reveals are modern—loss of faith, scientific ideas, images of the urban, industrial world—but there is nothing very new in the way these materials are used, and in the end *Transitional Poem* is a conventional young man's statement of the transition from adolescence to manhood, with the particular poetic themes customarily associated with that passage: love and lust, philosophic doubts, mind and imagination, pride and ambition, the power of poetry—all the subjects that young men write poems about. The four 'aspects' that Day Lewis enumerates are not, to my eye, at all distinct: the metaphysical and psychological sides of the problem interweave throughout the poem, and the ethical is scarcely apparent at all.

More fundamental to the structure than transitions are oppositions: mind/body, ideal/real, infinite/finite, love/fear, eternity/time. Day Lewis' use of these terms often echoes Yeats very closely, indeed the whole sequence is heavy with Yeatsian borrowings, and it is not surprising that Day Lewis used Yeats' word for such oppositions: he is dismayed, he says early in the poem, 'by the monstrous credibility/Of all antinomies'. But Yeats was content to live with his antinomies; Day Lewis was not, and one can see, from his restlessness here, that he would be an easy convert to an Hegelian system that would offer synthesis. *Transitional Poem* is not a political poem, and no political philosophy could possibly be inferred from it; but it expresses a need for certainty, for which 'single-mindedness' is Day Lewis' term, that would make dogmatic political belief attractive, and would later draw Day Lewis' unpolitical lyric gift in didactic directions.

When the poem first appeared, it was praised for its newness, and it came to be regarded as the beginning of a poetic revolution, an *Ur*-poem of the 'thirties. In the preface to the influential *New Signatures*, for example, Michael Roberts praised Day Lewis for breaking through 'the prevailing sterility', and quoted as evidence the following lines:

> Charabancs shout along the lane
> And summer gales bay in the wood
> No less superbly because I can't explain
> What I have understood . . .[14]

It is not immediately clear why this passage is different from the prevailing sterility, but no doubt it is those shouting charabancs, since Roberts (and many critics following him) took the use of 'imagery taken from contemporary life' to be a defining feature of the new poetry. Certainly Day Lewis did thrust images of modern civilization—gramophones, pitheads, loop-lines—rather randomly into his private lyric moods, and this suggests that he had at least recognized that one aspect of the new poetic situation was a changed relation between private and public experience. But the poem does not show that he had found a satisfactory formal way of dealing with it. If Roberts had continued his quotation for another stanza he would have had a far more typical example of Day Lewis' style:

> Let logic analyse the hive,
> Wisdom's content to have the honey:
> So I'll go bite the crust of things and thrive
> While hedgerows still are sunny.

This quatrain, with its familiar nature imagery and its hint of Shakespearian hey-nonny-nonny, is characteristic of the essential Day Lewis, and it is no doubt this sort of thing that the Marxist critic Philip Henderson had in mind when he said that Day Lewis had a 'natural, and after all quite Georgian, lyrical talent'.[15] And this is a fair enough judgment, if we take *Georgian* to be a descriptive, not a pejorative term. Certainly the most striking thing about *Transitional Poem* is how conventional it is, how well it attaches itself to the English tradition: the verse forms are regular, the allusions are classical, the natural details are Romantic. Romantic, too, is the constantly present 'I', the poetic sensibility focussed always upon its own condition. None of these qualities is deplorable in a poet, and none is really surprising in a twenty-four-year-old poet writing in 1928. What is surprising is that the poem was taken as a break-through into a new modernism.

It does, however, have one quality that points toward later and better works of the 'thirties: its thrust toward action. The first lyric begins energetically:

> Now I have come to reason
> And cast my schoolboy clout,
> Disorder I see is without,
> And the mind must sweat a poison
> Keener than Thessaly's brew;
> A pus that, discharged not thence,
> Gangrenes the vital sense
> And makes disorder true.
> It is certain we shall attain
> No life till we stamp on all
> Life the tetragonal
> Pure symmetry of brain.

Disorder without is what Auden had called 'the chaos of values which is the substance of our environment', and this opening passage is an early statement of the recurrent public–private theme, the self accepting the need to act in a changing public world. But the action here is put in very crude terms: 'pure symmetry of brain' versus disorder without suggests a too-easy confidence in the power of the mind to alter reality by thinking about it. Just how this is to be done the poem nowhere makes clear; it simply asserts, in a line that a note tells us is 'the refrain of a song sung by Miss Sophie Tucker', that 'there are going to be some changes made to-day'. One gets a general sense, throughout the poem, that a past is being discarded and replaced by a mature understanding of existence, but the particulars of this process are not specified.

Transitional Poem anticipates later poems in another, more explicit way: in it Day Lewis creates—though only briefly and in passing— a mythology of his own generation. This device may owe something to Yeats, who made his own mythology out of the people he knew, but it is a persistent feature of 'thirties writing, and I take it to be another aspect of the generation's separation from its own past. If there are no useable heroes behind you, then you will have to make heroes out of the people around you, and especially those who appear as agents of change. In this poem the mythic figures include 'the tow-haired poet', who is clearly Auden, and 'the hawk-faced man', who is Rex Warner, to whom the poem is dedicated. Here begins what Louis MacNeice called 'the myths of themselves';[16] here also begins the clubbishness, the view of the modern movement as private communications among friends, that is an irritating aspect of the whole generation.

Still, it is only a beginning: the title is right, the poem is transitional, between the Georgians and the poets of the 'thirties. Though it connects with what came after, it communicates very little sense of the generation's unique situation; Day Lewis did not yet feel that situation clearly or strongly enough to get it down. He felt disorder in the world, the chaos of values that Eliot and Richards had taught, and he tried to deal with it, but he gave to his theme no public dimension and no sense of urgency. The problem as he saw it then was primarily a private one, a crisis of belief that had no direct relation to the public world. So that world enters the poem not as a pressure, but as a set of details, gramophones and charabancs stuck in here and there, like raisins in a pudding; such details are not enough to locate the poem in contemporary time, to make it a piece of immediate history.

Most of all, the poem is not an alternative world. Day Lewis did not apparently feel the need to re-order reality entirely to conform to a new vision, and so his individual lyrics are like a series of commentaries or footnotes to the way things are—or, to be more precise, the way things *subjectively* are. The private life is the subject, and it remains private; it does not become, as later versions of private lives do, a parable.

Three months after *Transitional Poem* was published, Auden's *Paid on Both Sides* appeared in Eliot's *Criterion*. It is a nice bit of accidental symbolism that this, the first parable of the 'thirties generation, appeared in January 1930; more important, and not at all accidental, is that it did so under the sponsorship of the generation's principal influence and ancestor. For all through the 'thirties Eliot—classicist, royalist, and Anglo-Catholic though he proclaimed himself to be—managed to be both a model and a patron to the radical young.[17]

Paid on Both Sides is dedicated to Day Lewis, and one can see certain connections between Auden's first long work and that of his friend. There is, first of all, a common theme—the strenuous transition of a young man from immaturity to maturity; and second, a common moral context—the world-out-there that is taken for granted, a world as described in their *Oxford Poetry* manifesto, empty of values, yet the place in which one must live and act. Both are works of young men growing up in the 'twenties, and both are of their time.

But there the similarity ends. *Transitional Poem* is substantially traditional, familiar-sounding, and available to an ordinary reader of English verse; *Paid on Both Sides* is uncompromisingly 'modern': elliptical and knotted in its style, ambiguously located in time and space, unstable and untraditional in its mixture of tragedy, lyricism, and farce. Where Day Lewis is energetic and confident, beginning in arrogance and ending in peace, Auden is anxious, ambivalent, and sombre, and ends on a note of defeat. And where Day Lewis is relatively clear, Auden is sometimes impenetrably obscure. But if the play is more difficult than *Transitional Poem*, it is also more completely imagined, more fully realized in action and metaphor, more nearly an alternative world, a parable.

The word that Auden used to describe his play is not *parable* but *charade*, and it is worth pausing to consider the special kind of parable that this term suggests. A charade is a theatrical form distinguished by three features: it is *private*—for the entertainment of a small group of persons who know each other; it is a *game*; and it is *non-realistic*—in a charade, the actions carry meanings that are not

47

literally representational. *Charade*, then, identifies qualities that are noticeable and important aspects of this generation's writings —the private 'myth of themselves', the element of formal play and sometimes clownishness, and the common departure from the realistic rendering of experience. In these terms it is a generic name as applicable to major works of the 'thirties as *parable* is.

Paid on Both Sides has all of these characteristics, but it is not formally a charade at all. It is rather a mixture of traditional bits and pieces that together compose a puzzling and unstable play that belongs to no tradition. These elements, in their relation to each other and to the past, are like the fragments in *The Waste Land*: they make a form that denies the forms of the past. But unlike *The Waste Land*, Auden's play is built along a narrative line: it does tell a story, and the story carries significance, it is a disordered but comprehensible modern version of a tragic play, made out of bits and pieces of other literary traditions.

In the play a feud exists between two families, the Nowers and the Shaws, who live in the North of England at a time that is at once modern and primitive. John, the leader of the Nowers, is the son of a man killed from ambush by the Shaws; he is born, in the first scene, on the day of the ambush, and is dedicated by his mother to revenge his father's death. As a young man he continues the feud, though he has conflicting feelings about it: he helps a friend to escape from the fighting by emigrating, and he falls in love with Anne, the daugher of his enemy. In the middle of the play John kills Red Shaw, who had killed John's father, and orders a captured spy to be shot. Then, while the Shaws prepare to retaliate, he seeks to end the feud by marrying Anne. The wedding takes place, but the mother of the Shaws compels her son to murder the bridegroom, and the feud is resumed.

One can see, even in this bare summary, a parable of adolescence and maturity. For the young people in the play, the past is a curse: it is the feud, an inherited responsibility to continue a meaningless destructive pattern. The force of this responsibility is embodied in the two mothers; to be a mother's son is to be ruled by the past. The opposite of this condition is mature freedom, which is expressed in two ways, as love for a woman (John's marriage to Anne), which liberates a man from his mother's power, and as independent flight into the world (the man who emigrates) which liberates him from his past. In John's case the past is stronger than he is, his bid for maturity fails, and the killing goes on.

As a parable this seems straightforward enough, and not unlike some other modern expressions of the theme. But such a summary leaves out most of the elements that make *Paid on Both Sides* distinctive (and difficult). There is, to begin with, the 'world' of the play. Geographically it is the northern landscape of Auden's childhood, the limestone moors and hills of the Pennines that he has celebrated in many poems. The place-names are the harsh, Norse-sounding names common to that area, names that are closer to the language of the sagas than to an English countryside: Colefangs, Hammergill, Eickhamp, Nattrass, Garrigill. Some of them can be found on the most detailed maps of the region, and for all I know the others are the real names of obscure places, too; but none of them will be familiar to the average reader, and their location will remain uncertain. The date of the action is also ambiguous, for this world contains no cities and no familiar places, has no government and no laws, no trains or newspapers or policemen, yet there are mills and foundries there, schoolboys play rugby, and men kill each other with guns. It is a world that is at once primitive and modern, as our world can't be; but it is not ours, it is an alternative world.

Another problem of the world-of-the-play is the way the dialogue shifts back and forth between the saga-world of the blood-feud and what seems to be the small talk of an English public school, all about swimming matches and rugger teams. For example, three characters drinking together have the following conversation:

Walter: . . . How is the Rugger going?
Kurt: All right, thank you. We have not got a bad team this season.
W: Where do you play yourself?
K.: Wing 3Q.
W.: Did you ever see Warner? No, he'd be before your time. You remember him, don't you, Trudy?
T.: He was killed in the fight at Colefangs, wasn't he?

49

W.: You are muddling him up with Hunter. He was the best
threequarter I have ever seen. His sprinting was marvellous
to watch.

No single world of ordinary experience could contain both the
rugger team and the killing; they belong together only in Auden's
parable-world. Christopher Isherwood has explained how these
elements came together in Auden's mind:

> The saga-world is a schoolboy world, with its feuds, its practical
> jokes, its dark threats conveyed in puns and riddles and under-
> statements: 'I think this day will end unluckily for some; but
> chiefly for those who least expect harm.' I once remarked to
> Auden that the atmosphere of *Gisli the Outlaw* very much re-
> minded me of our schooldays. He was pleased with the idea:
> and, soon after this, he produced his first play: *Paid on Both Sides*,
> in which the two worlds are so inextricably confused that it is
> impossible to say whether the characters are really epic heroes
> or only members of the school O.T.C.[18]

This is no doubt a true account; certainly it sounds like the way a
bookish and rather immature young man might write a play,
drawing on the sagas he had read, and on boys' school literature,
for his material (he would find in *Stalky & Co*, for example, school
life treated very much as guerilla warfare). Saga would have the
advantage of being a tragic mode. Perhaps another advantage is
that it is a mode that is not a part of the direct English literary
tradition, just as the charade is not. For Auden seems to have felt
the need for a form that would not be propped up by traditional
attitudes and expectations, and so could contain a new statement;
the unfamiliarity and strangeness of the world of *Paid on Both Sides*
is in part a function of its separation from traditional models, and
that is the point.

I would suggest yet another literary source: one finds in *Journey's
End* and *Goodbye to All That*, and in the work of many minor war
poets, the same interweaving of war and school, the same school-
boy heroes and school games transposed to the battlefield, the
same misplaced adolescence. In recollections of that war, the experience of school seems to have played an important role as a
source of values—the only model for right behaviour that most

young soldiers had. In the war, young men with the sensibilities and interests of schoolboys were faced with a real challenge which was yet like a school game: highly competitive, played by the rules, requiring skill, endurance, and energy, and earning glory and the approval of parent-figures. Auden's young men are in the same sort of situation, and even speak in the same way: their terse, understated speeches and choked-back feelings surely owe as much to current war literature as to the sagas.

I take *Paid on Both Sides*, then, to be an apprehensive parable of immaturity, marked, inevitably, by Auden's homosexuality, but in a tradition that is not overtly homosexual—the Public School, First World War tradition of the games-playing male society. The feud-world in the play is the past of parents and the Old Men—destructive and repressive, and secure in its own rules. The alternative to that world is the life that Auden and his generation saw around and ahead of them—a life that was free, but emptied of values, requiring action, and specifically sexual action, as the price of maturity: in short, adult life in the post-war world. The best-known statement of this theme in the play is the chorus beginning 'To throw away the key', a brief parable of action as a voluntary journey into the unknown—not a *narrative* of a journey, but a statement of what is involved. To act, the poem says, you must throw away the key, reject the past, and commit yourself to the uncertain future (imaged as the crossing of a mountain). If you conquer the temptations and dangers of the journey you will reach the New Life on the other side, but what that life will be the poem does not say (to the immature, the mature life has no specific qualities except newness). As a poem of its time, the chorus speaks of both the anxiety and the need for action that the generation felt. It expresses strongly the common feeling that the past—past institutions, past values, past rules of behaviour—was of no present use, but it offers no guidance into the future: no politics, no ideology of any kind. What it describes is the state of mind of young men like Auden at the beginning of the 'thirties.

Paid on Both Sides is a charade, to be played among friends, and Auden's friends are in it: 'Edward' and 'Stephen' are surely Edward Upward and Stephen Spender, 'Layard' is a psychologist whom Auden met in Berlin, and 'Warner', whose sprinting was marvellous to watch, is certainly Rex Warner, who was a famous rugby player. Their presence makes the play another 'myth of themselves', like *Transitional Poem*. But Auden's charade is more than a private game, and a good deal more than a charade. As Isherwood's testimony points out, there are other parabolic forms involved: the saga, and the boys' school story. And there are still others that Isherwood doesn't mention—the Mummer's Play, the dream vision, and the chorus of classical tragedy. What all these disparate literary kinds have in common with each other and with a charade is that all are conventionalized, non-realistic presentations of meaning in action. They lead the imagination away from private feelings and from literal reality, toward those stylizations that generalize experience and carry abstract meanings. Auden, groping for a new form, mixed these elements up a bit uncertainly, and created a mixed and uncertain play; nevertheless it is an important first attempt at what he called 'an altering speech for altering things', a parable of his generation in the post-war world.

Auden speaks most generally through the play's chorus, which utters some of his finest and most memorable verse. The chorus performs two functions: first, the traditional normative choric function, generalizing the action and commenting on it. So, at the birth of John Nower, it is the chorus that speaks of the life force and the death wish:

> Can speak of trouble, pressure on men
> Born all the time, brought forward into light
> For warm dark moan.
> Though heart fears all heart cries for, rebuffs
>   with mortal beat
> Skyfall, the legs sucked under, adder's bite.
> That prize held out of reach
> Guides the unwilling tread,
> The asking breath,
> Till on attended bed
> Or in untracked dishonour comes to each
> His natural death.[19]

'Heart fears all heart cries for'—the whole ambivalent feeling of the young for maturity is in that line: it is the essential statement of the play.

Elsewhere the chorus provides the means by which the play's statements about life may be extended from the saga-world into the present time. It is in chorus speeches that we find most of the modern references, the images of industrial decay and commercial failure that compose the entropic adult world, as for example in this passage:

> The Spring unsettles sleeping partnerships,
> Foundries improve their casting process, shops
> Open a further wing on credit till
> The winter. In summer boys grow tall
> With running races on the froth-wet sand,
> War is declared there, here a treaty is signed;
> Here a scrum breaks like a bomb, there troops
> Deploy like birds. But proudest into traps
> Have fallen. These gears which ran in oil for week
> By week, needing no look, now will not work;
> Those manors mortgaged twice to pay for love
> Go to another.[20]

This dense mingling of public and private, school and war, nature and machinery, which in the poetry of the 'thirties becomes a familiar landscape, 'Auden Country', makes all seem subject to one natural law of dissolution. It brings the present economic world of 1930 into the poem, but without making it topical; the alternative world of parable keeps its own separate time, and its relation to the immediate present is not descriptive, but analogical.

The theme of entropy, the old life running down, emerges again and again in chorus speeches, most movingly in the final speech of the play:

> Though he believe it, no man is strong.
> He thinks to be called the fortunate,
> To bring home a wife, to live long.
>
> But he is defeated; let the son
> Sell the farm lest the mountain fall;
> His mother and her mother won.

His fields are used up where the moles visit,
The contours worn flat; if there show
Passage for water he will miss it:

Give up his breath, his woman, his team;
No life to touch, though later there be
Big fruit, eagles above the stream.[21]

It is a sombre ending, in the tone of classical tragedy: call no man fortunate who is not dead. Maturity is a long dying, death is a defeat; the mothers win, the son loses—which means, I take it, that continuity of life survives, but at the cost of individual life. In terms of the central theme of action, it is a dark reminder of the power of the enemy, the past.

Paid on Both Sides is the first important parable of a political decade, but it is not itself a political work. Its world predates politics, and the only relationship in it that might be called political is that between leaders and followers, masters and servants— the relationship, that is, of school and trench authority. But that relationship will become an important question in the following years, and one that will preoccupy many writers: what is the good leader, the Truly Strong Man? What are his strengths and weaknesses? how does the leader recognize his destiny? how are leadership and freedom related? John Nower is the first of Auden's leaders, and it is worth noting that he begins with a failure; there will be others.

But essentially, as I have said, the play is a parable of growing up, which embodies but does not explain the feelings of a young man facing maturity and afraid of it. This is an historical subject insofar as the problem was an especially acute one for Auden's generation, entering adult life in a world that seemed to be running down, and entering it without the support of inherited values. And it is this historical aspect that makes the play important to the critic considering the characteristic modes and themes of the 'thirties, as it was important to the young men of Auden's time.

As evidence of the latter point, consider the testimony of William Empson. Empson wrote the first serious essay on *Paid on Both Sides* in the Cambridge magazine *Experiment* in 1931. It is an acute reading of the play; but it is also a contemporary docu-

54

ment, a secondary statement of Auden's themes by a contemporary. Empson recognized that the play was a straightforward, sensible, and properly motivated tragedy, 'though very compressed, and sometimes in obscure verse', but he took it to be about 'the problems involved in the attempt to change radically a working system'. Already, a year after its first appearance, the play was being read as a political parable.

'One reason the scheme is so impressive,' Empson concluded,

> Is that it puts psycho-analysis and surrealism and all that, all the irrationalist tendencies which are so essential a part of the machinery of present-day thought, into their proper place; they are made part of the normal and rational tragic form, and indeed what constitutes the tragic situation. One feels as if at the crisis of many, perhaps better, tragedies, it is just this machinery which has been covertly employed. Within its scale . . . there is the gamut of all the ways we have of thinking about the matter; it has the sort of completeness that makes a work seem to define the attitude of a generation.[22]

It is significant that a member of Auden's own generation should see the play, at the time, as defining the generation's attitude. As the decade began, the generation was beginning to define itself, and to think of itself as a distinct group formed by distinct experiences; and in this process works of the imagination played a crucial role. Empson's essay is an acknowledgement of Auden's great contribution to the imagination of his generation; his gift for assimilating modern movements and systems of belief and transforming them into parabolic forms, and for finding the necessary images of immediate reality, made him a leader of his generation from the first, and a greater influence on 'thirties writing than any of his predecessors.

Paid on Both Sides is a general, large-scale map of 'Auden Country', that parabolic landscape that so dominated poetic imaginations in the 'thirties. The poems that Auden was writing at the same time also belong to that country: if the Charade is the large-scale map, then poems like 'The Secret Agent' and 'From scars where kestrels hover' are charts of local details, which fill in and complete Auden's alternative world. In the autumn of

1930 Auden put thirty of these poems with *Paid on Both Sides* to make up his first book, *Poems*. These are not the most famous of Auden's poems, and he thought ill enough of seven of them to discard them from the second edition, but if you read them straight through, as though they were one poem of thirty parts, you get a powerful sense of a whole imagined world, as you do from the Charade.

The poems add particularly to the map of the country in two ways. First, they add details of the new economic Waste Land (derelict machinery, rusted rail-lines), and of symbolic geography (principally images of borders and frontiers). These are images not of political concepts, but of psychological ones: the derelict world is the present from which young men must start, the border is the edge of the unknown and the beginning of uncertainty, and the world beyond it is the one that the young man must enter, if he is to act. As the decade moved on, these images took on heavier symbolic meanings as democratic Europe went on falling apart, and real European borders entered the general consciousness, dividing peace from war and freedom from tyranny; but the root-sense of the images remained the same—reality has its frontiers, on *this* side a dead security, on the *other* side the fearful threat that is unknown, but cannot be ignored.

The other element that *Poems* added to Auden Country was a new cast of characters, who stand as examples of how men have faced crises, and may again. The book is full of heroes—airmen, climbers, travellers, miners—whose acts are celebrated, even in failure:

> some acts are chosen
> Taken from recent winters; two there were
> Cleaned out a damaged shaft by hand, clutching
> The winch the gale would tear them from; one died
> During a storm, the fells impassable,
> Not at his village, but in a wooden shape
> Through long abandoned levels nosed his way
> And in his final valley went to ground.[23]

Among Auden's heroes are actual historical persons—'Lawrence, Blake and Homer Lane' in Poem XXII, and later Wilfred Owen and Katherine Mansfield. These are the self-selected 'ancestors' from whom Auden (and other members of his generation) chose to claim descent. They are all, to use a term that was common at the time, 'healers', and therefore important to young persons conscious of their society's sickness; and they are outside the main traditions of 'establishment' thought, rebels and sometimes martyrs. It was as though young writers, living in the Waste Land, were sifting the rubble in search of bits that they could use, among so much that was broken and useless. And by claiming the right to choose their own ancestors, they were denying the ancestors that the past had provided, and, in a sense, creating their own history.

By the time one comes to the end of *Poems*, one has experienced a world that is new to English poetry, and appropriate for dealing with the new realities of 1930. There was no inherited language that would do; even Eliot's heaps of broken images were not adequate to carry the necessary weight of meaning, the mixture of anxiety and urgency that composed the private feelings of young men faced with public crises. And there were no heroes—the 'twenties was a decade without heroes, and without any concept of heroism. *Poems* introduced a new state of mind, for a new decade; its world had to be invented, you might say, in order that the 'thirties could be experienced imaginatively. The creation of Auden Country is the most original literary achievement of the decade.

III

In the same year, the first of the decade, another generation-defining work appeared: Evelyn Waugh's *Vile Bodies*. It is a novel set in actual London—the geography is correct, and the street names are real and in the right places. But it is a London novel only in the sense that *The Waste Land* is a London poem; the city itself is an Unreal City, a fantasy of modern life lived in the absence of values.

You know on the first page that you have entered an allegorical world, when Mrs Ape appears with her angels: Faith, Fortitude, Chastity, and so on through the sacred virtues to Divine Discontent. Other characters' names confirm this point: Lord Chasm,

57

Lady Throbbing, Mary Mouse, Walter Outrage, Miles Malpractice. And so does the action, which is possible—you *could* have a party in a captive balloon, or enter a drunk debutante in an automobile race—but improbable, and inclining always to make one point, the accidental and aimless nature of modern life. The comparison with Eliot is an apt one: the world of *Vile Bodies* is a Waste Land, only it is a Waste Land inhabited mainly by Bright Young People.

The Bright Young People are the post-war generation, inheritors of the post-war mood that Richards had described: 'A sense of desolation, of uncertainty, of futility, of the groundlessness of aspirations, of the vanity of endeavour . . .' In the absence of causes or vocations, they spend their time going to parties:

> . . . Masked parties, Savage parties, Victorian parties, Greek parties, Wild West parties, Russian parties, Circus parties, parties where one had to dress as somebody else, almost naked parties in St John's Wood, parties in flats and studios and houses and ships and hotels and night clubs, in windmills and swimming-baths, tea parties at school where one ate muffins and meringues and tinned crab, parties at Oxford where one drank brown sherry and smoked Turkish cigarettes, dull dances in London and comic dances in Scotland and disgusting dances in Paris—all that succession and repetition of massed Humanity . . . Those vile bodies . . . [24]

This passage—in the narrator's own voice—is at the centre of the novel; it is an image of endlessness as depressing as the processions in Dante's Hell, an endlessness that even the syntax mimes, on and on, phrase after phrase, until it dribbles off, still not a sentence, only a catalogue of meaningless events.

The word that the Bright Young People use again and again for this condition in their lives is *bogus*: people are bogus, love is bogus, sex is bogus, politics is bogus. Even the Bright Young People are bogus; Adam Symes, in his job as gossip reporter, invents a whole new social set for his column, and they immediately begin to have lives and to influence people. The term is glossed for the reader in the course of a conversation between the wise Jesuit, Father Rothschild, and two elders of society, Lord Metroland and the Prime Minister, Mr Outrage. Outrage has been complaining about the wantonness of the young, and Father Rothschild replies:

> Don't you think . . . that perhaps it is all in some way historical? I don't think people ever want to lose their faith either in religion or anything else. I know very few young people, but it seems to me that they are all possessed with an almost fatal hunger for permanence. I think all these divorces show that. People aren't content just to muddle along nowadays . . . And this word 'bogus' they all use . . . They don't make the best of a bad job nowadays. My private schoolmaster used to say, 'If a thing's worth doing at all, it's worth doing well.' My Church has taught that in different words for several centuries. But these young people have got hold of another end of the stick, and for all we know it may be the right one. They say, 'If a thing's not worth doing well, it's not worth doing at all.' It makes everything very difficult for them.[25]

Bogusness, then, is not a simple expression of cynicism. It is a generation's judgment of a world emptied of significance, and a sign of their 'almost fatal hunger for permanence'.

As in Eliot, the emptiness of modern existence is ironically under-scored by reference to the magnificent visions of the past. Toward the end of the novel, for example, two Bright Young People set off on their honeymoon by air. The husband, looking down at the earth as the plane takes off, is reminded of something he once learned out of a poetry book: ' " This sceptred isle, this earth of majesty, this something or other Eden"! D'you know what I mean?—"this happy breed of men . . .".'

> Nina looked down and saw inclined at an odd angle a horizon of straggling red suburb; arterial roads dotted with little cars; factories, some of them working, others empty and decaying; a disused canal; some distant hills sown with bungalows; wireless masts and overhead power cables . . .[26]

What she sees down there is Auden Country: the decaying factories, the disused canal, the pylons; but *we* see it against the noble vision of John of Gaunt, just as in *The Waste Land* we see contemporary London against the city of Queen Elizabeth and Shakespeare.

The bogus present in which *Vile Bodies* exists is located in time chiefly by reference to two events: the First World War and the Second World War. Waugh was the first English novelist to see his own time as a period *entre deux guerres*, and that peculiar location gives his novel a good deal of its tone of human helplessness and aimlessness. The past war enters the novel in many ways: in the parlour of Lottie Crump's hotel, where there are signed photographs of young men in tight white collars or in Guards' uniforms, and photographs cut from illustrated papers, 'many of them with brief obituary notices: "killed in action".' Lottie's hotel is Edwardian, and it preserves the atmosphere of the world before the war; but it also reminds us that the war killed that world, and a generation of young men in white collars. Other passages confirm the point. Adam Symes makes his way to Marylebone Station:

It was Armistice Day, and they were selling artificial poppies in the streets. As he reached the station it struck eleven and for two minutes all over the country everyone was quiet and serious. Then he went to Aylesbury, reading on the way Balcairn's account of Archie Schwert's party. [27]

Later, a procession of the Great enters Lady Anchorage's grand party:

a great concourse of pious and honourable people . . ., their women-folk well gowned in rich and durable stuffs, their men-folk ablaze with orders; people who had represented their country in foreign places and sent their sons to die for her in battle . . . [28]

This, you might say, is the Bright Young People's version of the Myth of the War: it destroyed a generation; it was engineered by Old Men ablaze with orders; and it is now remembered for two minutes on one day a year.

The war that is to come enters the novel first in that same conversation of Father Rothschild, Lord Metroland, and the Prime Minister that I have already quoted. 'What do you mean

by "historical"?' the Prime Minister asks. 'Well,' Father Rothschild replies,

> 'it's like this war that's coming . . .'
>
> 'What war?' said the Prime Minister sharply. 'No one has
> said anything to me about a war. I really think I should have
> been told. I'll be damned,' he said defiantly, 'if they shall have
> a war without consulting me. What's a Cabinet for if there's
> not more mutual confidence than that? What do they want
> a war for, anyway?'
>
> 'That's the whole point. No one talks about it, and no one
> wants it. No one talks about it *because* no one wants it. They're
> all afraid to breathe a word about it.'
>
> 'Well, hang it all, if no one wants it, who's going to make
> them have it?'
>
> 'Wars don't start nowadays because people want them. We
> long for peace, and fill our newspapers with conferences about
> disarmament and arbitration, but there is a radical instability
> in our whole world-order, and soon we shall all be walking
> into the jaws of destruction again, protesting our pacific inten-
> tions . . .'
>
> 'Anyhow,' said Lord Metroland, 'I don't see how all that
> explains why my stepson should drink like a fish and go about
> everywhere with a negress.'
>
> 'I think they're connected, you know,' said Father Roths-
> child. 'But it's all very difficult.'[29]

Father Rothschild is making a fundamental connection between
the identity of the post-war generation and the prospect of a
coming war. From about 1930, predictions of war, and anxieties
about war, begin to enter English writing, and more and more
frequently as the decade passes; and at about the same time the
younger generation begins to write about itself *as* a generation,
to examine its own defining characteristics, and the way this generation is separated from those who are older. The First World
War had separated its combatants from the Old Men; now the
younger generation had its own war, and so it began to take note
of another important term in its self-definition—the Bright Young
People were, proleptically, veterans of the Second World War.

The theory of the causes of war that Father Rothschild proposes is very different from the common retrospective view of the First World War that I have called the Myth of the War. There are no villains in Father Rothschild's version: it isn't the Old Men who start a war, but the 'radical instability in our whole world-order'. This vast abstraction seems so encompassing as to be irresistible; how would one oppose such a force? And a generation faced with such an opponent might well react, as the Bright Young People do, by simply withdrawing from history, into parties, into a passive submission to accidental events. And that is another kind of definition. It is one of the important things about *Vile Bodies* that it takes the task of defining and thus explaining the younger generation as a principal subject; and by so doing Waugh contributed to his generation's self-consciousness.

The next war actually comes in the last chapter of the novel, in a vision of future warfare made up, as one might expect, out of the literature and films of the past war that were current at the time. The chapter begins:

> On a splintered tree stump in the biggest battlefield in the history of the world, Adam sat down and read a letter from Nina ... The scene all round him was one of unrelieved desolation; a great expanse of mud in which every visible object was burnt or broken.[30]

This, in 1930, is a highly conventional description of the Western Front of 1914–18. Only the weapons that the characters carry are imaginative projections into the science-fiction future: Adam carries a bomb for the dissemination of leprosy, and his opponent is armed with a 'liquid fire projector'. But perhaps one should also say that the *tone* of the chapter is a projection. There is a kind of placid cynicism in those last pages, in which we are told that neither love nor money, and certainly not war, has any value, and that this muddy desolation, this waste land of war, is the world (the chapter is titled 'Happy Ending'). This tone points forward, not back; for in even the grimmest of the First World War books there is a saving sense of value, a belief that men might perform acts of moral worth, even in a war, or at the very least there is anger at the destructiveness of it all. But in Waugh's happy ending there is nothing but a bland, cheerful negation, an attitude with which to confront what is coming.

Vile Bodies is a parable of bogusness that ends in the greatest bogusness of all, the war that is inexorably approaching. It is also a definition and a defence of the generation. If this seems a too solemn way to describe such a brilliantly comic novel, one can only say that comedy is serious, and that *Vile Bodies*, for all its wit, is a profoundly serious moral document, the sort of book that Savonarola might have written if he had been funnier. Though it is full of satiric sketches, I would not call it a satire; it is rather, I think, a surreal or expressionist attempt to record reality at a time when it seemed more and more to be, by any rational observation, unreal.

Waugh's novel stands, in many important ways, as a precursor of later writing of the decade: in its prophecy of war, in its consciousness of the separateness of the younger generation, in its contemptuous hostility to the politics of the establishment, in its irony, in its bitter, farcical wit, and perhaps most importantly in the way Waugh has gone beyond probability and beyond realism to create a parabolic world, a comical Unreal City of sad, yearning Bright Young People. The novel shares to a considerable extent in the world of Auden's poems—shares imagery, and shares one kind of character, the weak, inactive ones. But it is a transitional novel, linked to the 'twenties mood, and lacking qualities that distinguish later 'thirties writing and are already evident in Auden: the presence of heroes, the possibility of positive action, and the imperative tone. Waugh helped to define the beginnings, the place from which one had to start, but he didn't move with the generation, and his course for the rest of the decade is along a separate route.

'By the end of the 'twenties,' Aldous Huxley wrote in 1937, 'a reaction had begun to set in—away from the easy-going philosophy of general meaninglessness towards the hard, ferocious theologies of nationalistic and revolutionary idolatry. Meaning was reintroduced into the world, but only in patches . . .'[31] Was he right? In a way he was, but like most turns of mind this one was more complicated than it seemed. The philosophy of general meaninglessness—by which I suppose he means the Waste Land vision—was never easy-going; there was from the beginning a note of nostalgic regret at the passing of nobility and belief, and certainly the literary expressions of it—*The Waste Land* itself, *Point Counter Point*, *Vile Bodies*—acknowledged the need for a reintroduction of meaning. But as the 'twenties became the 'thirties, it was only a need; the ferocious theologies were still to come.

III

1931-32

I

'From 1931 onwards,' Stephen Spender wrote, 'in common with many other people, I felt hounded by external events.'[1] The date is not an arbitrary one: 1931 was the watershed between the post-war years and the pre-war years, the point at which the mood of the 'thirties first became generally apparent.[2] In the national economy, 1931 was the year in which the Depression seemed to settle permanently over England; more than two and a half million men were out of work by the end of the year, the threat of bankruptcy had caused the fall of one government, its successor had abandoned the gold standard, and the value of the pound had dropped by twenty-five per cent. Outside England, there were violent beginnings of disorders that would continue through the 'thirties: a revolution in Spain, and in Asia the Japanese invasion of Manchuria, which the European Left saw—perhaps a bit melodramatically—as the beginning of the Second World War. In British politics, it was the year in which the second Labour government collapsed; in August, Ramsay MacDonald, in trouble over economic policy, disbanded his government and created a coalition to deal with the national emergency. A General Election was called in October, and MacDonald's National Government confirmed in office with 556 seats in the House of Commons, against only 56 for the opposition. It was Labour's worst political defeat, before or since, and to persons on the Left it seemed to mean the end of any possibility of a Socialist government, or even of a strong Parliamentary opposition; at a time of crisis, the people had chosen a government that would proceed cautiously in the old ways. Whatever hopes for Left action remained, they would not be carried out within existing political institutions.

'National mood' is a difficult thing to assess, and perhaps such a uniform response to events never really exists, but by 1931 many people in England certainly had begun to see the crisis in which they lived as more than a temporary economic reverse—to see it rather as the collapse of an inherited system of values, and the end of a secure life. For many of them, the return of the National Government must have been less a vote of confidence than a confession of an inability to imagine an alternative; the ship of state was dead in the water, so why not leave the old crew on board?

Perhaps we may take as an expression of that mood the fact that one of the most popular West End shows of that year was Noël Coward's *Cavalcade*, a musical about the decline and fall of the English spirit, from the Boer War to 1930. Coward's handling of the finale strikes me as especially appropriate to the mood of the time. First Fanny, the musical comedy star, sings her song, 'Twentieth Century Blues':

> In this strange illusion,
> Chaos and confusion,
> People seem to lose their way.
> What is there to strive for,
> Love or keep alive for? Say—
> Hey, hey, call it a day.
> Blues, nothing to win or to lose.
> It's getting me down.
> Blues, I've got those weary Twentieth
> Century Blues.[3]

Then, as the curtain falls, the entire company sings 'God Save the King'. Was this meant as an irony? I think not, for this odd combination of despair and tradition is a musical equivalent of just what had happened in the October election: at a time of extreme national crisis a business-as-usual government had been returned to office. Obviously this was what the public wanted, in the theatre as well as in Whitehall: *Cavalcade* ran for nearly a year, and the National Government lasted out the decade.

But for the young, particularly, the pressure of external events must have made 1931 and the years that followed different from the years before, and with a difference that is more than simply an increased political and historical awareness. Spender's word is *hounded*, and he is talking about the pressure of the public life upon the private, the sense of immediate history as an aggressor against the private man. External events, if they are dire enough—a war, or the collapse of a society—challenge the value of private acts, and put the personal life to the test. For a young man (Spender was twenty-two in 1931) such a crisis, coming at a time when he was trying to define himself and his place in the world, must have been profoundly disorienting and disturbing.

When the young man is a poet, and the private act that he values is the writing of a poem, then a crisis in society becomes a literary problem. Is the role of a poet a defensible one in such a time? And if it is, what sort of poem should he write? Is the traditionally private content of lyric poetry, for example, appropriate to a time of public distress? In a situation that seems to demand action, can any poem be a sufficient act? These are all questions that imaginative writers faced throughout the 'thirties, and answered in various ways; they are the subjects of the best of 'thirties literary criticism, too, and they enter, colour, and sometimes distort many of the decade's best and most characteristic poems.

Spender wrote two poems in 1931 that show how these questions entered and disturbed his life: 'What I expected' (published in February), and 'I think continually of those who were truly great' (published in November). The general subject of both poems is heroism—not brave deeds performed, but the young man's dream of valuable personal behaviour. This is a theme that is understandable, perhaps almost inevitable, for such a young man in a critical time; for a great crisis seems to demand great action, and to offer youth a chance to enter maturity in a gesture of public glory. But *what* gesture? How exactly is one to act heroically in a time that is a 'chaos of values'? This is what the two poems are really about—the *problem* of heroic action; and in this they belong to their time.

'What I expected' is the more personal of the two, and the more negative. It deals with the disparity between the young man's dream of an heroic adult self, and his discovery of unheroic adult reality; this is, of course, a traditional subject—the disillusionment of growing up.

> What I expected was
> Thunder, fighting,
> Long struggles with men
> And climbing.
> After continual straining
> I should grow strong;
> Then the rocks would shake
> And I should rest long. [4]

It is a dream of violent energy and action, and of personal value coming naturally and inevitably out of personal effort (the point of all those strenuous participles): *fighting*—the myth of the war made that an inevitable heroic mode of action; and *climbing*—an heroic commonplace of the 'thirties, a sort of war-substitute, fighting height instead of men. Neither verb has an object: fighting whom? climbing what? The poem does not tell us; it offers no causes, only the value of individual, effortful struggle. As yet the problem of the generation has no form, and can only be expressed as a desire for intransitive action.

That is the dream; but the reality is different:

> What I had not foreseen
> Was the gradual day
> Weakening the will
> Leaking the brightness away. . . .

Once again the participles carry the meaning; here they indicate the processes of change that are the opposite of action, and that express the operation of time upon idealism, weakening it, leaking it away.

So far this could be any young man's poem of sensitive adolescence approaching adulthood. But it is saved from mere self-regard by the images that follow, images of public, social suffering that make the poem deeply expressive of a general mood of the time.

> The wearing of Time,
> And the watching of cripples pass
> With limbs shaped like questions
> In their odd twist,

> The pulverous grief
> Melting the bones with pity,
> The sick falling from earth—
> These, I could not foresee.

Cripples, the grieving, the sick—they are figures from the public world, urgent and demanding pity; their presence in the poem corresponds to the presence in the world outside of urgent suffering—the poor, the underfed, the unemployed. That is to say, they stand for the pressure of public issues upon private feelings, and the pity that they claim turns the theme of the poem—the failure to achieve heroism—from a private theme to a public one. There is no answer to the question that is posed by the cripples' limbs, but the question has been asked and noted, and public life has been brought into the private, lyric world.

The second poem is one of Spender's best known, and needs no elaborate commentary. It is also a young man's poem, a vision of heroism in traditional, romantic images. The vision is a noble and affirmative one, and the poem is very moving, and very youthful. Still, one must note that the vision is *retrospective*: the verbs are in the past tense, the truly great are gone. As in the other poem, they were climbers and fighters, but now they exist only in the waving of grass and the streamers of white cloud, and in the mind of the young man who thinks continually of their greatness, because he does not share it. So here again, though less directly, the separation of the present from the heroic past, and of the Self from the Hero, is made.

If we ask what makes that separation, we may find the answer in the final stanza of 'What I expected':

> For I had expected always
> Some brightness to hold in trust,
> Some final innocence
> To save from dust;
> That, hanging solid,
> Would dangle through all
> Like the created poem
> Or the dazzling crystal.

What is lacking, in the public world that the poem opens itself to, is an absolute value in terms of which heroic action would be possible. In the language of the poem it is *brightness, innocence*, a *crystal*, but we might draw more explicit value-terms from the poetic past: England, King, God, Honour—concepts that once were 'solid', but are no longer. But however we define it, the thing absent from the poem is an absent *value*.

Neither of these poems could be called polemical or political or topical: neither urges a cause or proposes an action, or links its subject explicitly to immediate history. Language and imagery are entirely timeless, with none of the contemporary urban-industrial content that came to be the mark of the generation (and that I have lumped together as 'Auden Country'). If they are nevertheless poems of their time, it is because they record a generation's state of mind, as young people confronted a troubled world in which they would have to act, but which had not provided them with values in terms of which to determine right action, or with a clear direction. That state of mind has a date of sorts, and these poems belong to the early 'thirties, when external events began to hound the occupants of private lives.

In such a situation, which seems at once to demand and to deny action, a poem is one possible response: if you cannot act directly, at least you can perform a *symbolic* action. But a poem is only one way of responding, and I am struck, as I read in the histories and memoirs of the 'thirties, by how often other actions that men performed were symbolic, and *self-consciously* symbolic, acts. It must always have been difficult, to the ordinary man, to take significant direct action on public issues, but it becomes more difficult, almost unimaginable, when the issue is a vast and threatening abstraction—Poverty, or Fascism, or War. In these cases, the only possible action may seem to be a private act that has only symbolic public meaning: defiance, self-immolation, the wild last gesture.

The Times of 14 October 1931 recorded such a gesture, and since it became a small part of the 'thirties myth it is worth describing here. Lauro de Bosis, an Italian anti-fascist poet, set out from Marseilles in a light plane on 3 October to drop political leaflets on Rome. He apparently reached Rome, but he did not return;

presumably he either crashed (he was not an experienced pilot) or he was shot down. Before he left France, de Bosis wrote and left behind him a curious document, 'The Story of my Death', which was published in *The Times*. It is an odd piece of writing, partly a political statement and partly a myth of himself; de Bosis is the Flying Dutchman, Rome is his Cape Horn, his plane is Pegasus—the whole venture is removed from the actual political world and placed in a mythic world in which individual acts carry meaning. And the death that he anticipates is a symbolic one; he does not claim that he will accomplish anything at all by his gesture, yet 'my death, however undesired by me personally, who have still so many things to achieve, could but add to the success of my flight'.

De Bosis' quixotic flight was an action that confessed the dead-end of action: he achieved nothing by it except his death, and the creation of a myth of himself. He was, in his own eyes, the solitary hero facing antagonists too strong and too impersonal to be resisted, antagonists who could only be opposed by a sacrificial gesture. This myth expresses a deeply felt problem of the time—the problem of individual action—and it is not surprising that de Bosis should have been remembered for a time as a symbolic figure. When John Cornford died in 1936 in the battle for Madrid, a Cambridge obituarist wrote:

> I could not but think, when I heard of his death, of Lauro de Bosis—the young Italian who went to Rome in his lonely aeroplane at the beginning of the October term of 1931, delivered his testimony, and died. John Cornford went to Spain in a sober English way, with a quiet resolution; but he was of the same stuff.[5]

Much of what young men did in the 'thirties might be described in these terms, as 'delivering their testimony', and many of the things they wrote which seem to violate the canons of aesthetics are better understood as testimonies, to be judged in other terms. But a testimony is not an opposing act: it is at best a surrogate for action. The 'thirties would demand a more direct commitment than that.

For the writers of the 'thirties generation, 1931 was an interim year. By this time they were young adults, out of the universities and on their own, but none had yet become an established literary figure—at least not established enough to earn a living from literature. And so they had scattered to various jobs: Auden was teaching in Scotland and Day Lewis in Cheltenham, Empson was Professor of English in Tokyo and Isherwood was giving English lessons in Berlin; Graham Greene was writing novels in a Cotswold cottage, and Orwell was hop-picking in Kent; in London Michael Roberts was teaching maths in a Holborn school, and Christopher Caudwell was editing a flying magazine. None of them published an important book that year, or one that added much to the definition of their generation.

They were not in fact really a *literary* generation yet. They shared a sense of their situation—as it had been defined by Eliot and Richards and the *Oxford Poetry* manifesto—and they felt hounded by the disarray of immediate history. But they had not determined their relationship as writers to those problems: the literary connection of private and public, the feeling self and the pressing world of action, was not clear.

A good example of this uncertain state of mind is Day Lewis' second long work, *From Feathers to Iron*, published in September 1931. It is, like *Transitional Poem*, a series of more or less formal lyrics on a personal, young man's theme—the gestation and birth of his first son. The dominant mode is pastoral; the poet had in fact just moved to a country cottage, and the poem records his delight in country living: 'Let's leave this town', the second lyric begins, and in the third he has gone 'back to the countryside'. The growth of the unborn child and the mother's changing states are systematically related to cyclical images of nature and the seasons—from autumn through the snows and anxieties of winter, to spring, birds, daffodils, and the birth—and the poem ends in natural rejoicing: 'Come out in the sun, for a man is born today!'

By this account, the poem sounds traditional and private, a poem that could have been written by any young Georgian, or indeed in another century. But it is in several ways a topical poem, marked by its time and by the public world. It is, first of all, framed by the dominating presence of Auden: at the beginning an epigraph from an as yet unpublished Auden poem, and at the end an epilogue, 'Letter to W. H. Auden'. Then, in the text itself, there are scattered so many 'contemporary' images, often borrowed directly from Auden, that one could use the sequence to make an inventory of Auden Country: frontiers, passes, railheads, engines, turbines, and mine workings; and climbers, soldiers, airmen, and miners. Such images do not coalesce into a pattern—the image-line that carries the poem remains the natural, seasonal set—but appear only as decorations, like illuminated letters in a manuscript. For example, poem XV begins like this:

> I have come so far upon my journey.
> This is the frontier, this is where I change,
> And wait between two worlds to take refreshment.
>   I see the mating plover at play
> Blowing themselves about over the green wheat,
> And in a bank I catch
> The shy scent of the primrose that prevails
> Strangely upon the heart.[6]

The initial image is of a railway journey (an important mode of transportation in Auden Country), with a change at the frontier, and even a refreshment room; but Day Lewis turns immediately away from it, to the birds and the primroses and the natural image-world in which he is more at ease, and on which the theme of the poem depends.

Why, then, are these images in the poem? Partly because Day Lewis was imitating Auden. Partly because he wanted to be a poet of his generation, and that seemed to require contemporary materials. But also partly, I think, because he felt, though not yet very clearly or precisely, that the contemporary world of industry and action, of frontiers and dictators, was a hovering threat to his private world, and had to be acknowledged, that a poem would not be a version of immediate reality that did not include some such references. Reviewers (at least when they were the poet's contemporaries) agreed. Michael Roberts, for example, called *From Feathers to Iron* 'a landmark, in the sense in which

Leaves of Grass, *A Shropshire Lad*, *Des Imagistes*, and *The Waste Land* were landmarks'.

> Since the beginning of the century [he wrote] poets have been trying to find a philosophy of life which would make them feel that they were participants in the social order, not fugitives or rebels, and they have been trying, too, to use the new images and metaphors made possible by the development of applied science ... Mr Auden's *Poems* ... showed the first marked advance, and now, in *Feathers to Iron*, we have the full solution: these images are used, not for their own sake, not because the poet's theory makes him choose images from contemporary life, but because they are structural: the thought requires precisely that expression.[7]

This is not, I think, true of the poem; but it is true of an idea of contemporary poetry toward which Day Lewis seemed to aspire, the idea that by using the language of the contemporary world poets would make themselves participants in it, and would thus make their poems actions.

Roberts went on to quote the first two stanzas of the poem, from which he drew this uncertain conclusion:

> Whether this represents the emancipation or the enslavement of poetry as an independent art we cannot yet say: poetry is here turned to propaganda, but it is propaganda for a theory of life that may release the poet's energies for the writing of pure poetry as well as provide him with definite standards which will make satire possible again.

As far as I know, this is the first time that *propaganda*, a word that was to figure largely in 'thirties criticism, was applied to a writer of the Auden generation. Roberts is not clear as to what the content of the propaganda is, and he does not even suggest that it may be political, but he understands that it is new, and that it may be the occasion for a new poetry. He liked his formulation well enough to use it again a year later in his preface to *New Signatures*, where he applies it not to Day Lewis, but to Spender's 'The Funeral'. The point would seem to be that propaganda is a generational quality, and so transferable.

One other book of poems was published that year that had important though indirect consequences for the definition of the generation. John Lehmann, just down from Cambridge, had gone to work for Leonard and Virginia Woolf at the Hogarth Press, and one of the press's publications in 1931 was a book of his poems, *A Garden Revisited*. The poems are the sort that any clever undergraduate might write, and many did—poems on personal or conventionally pastoral subjects, set in traditional metres, poems made out of other poems. There is nothing in them to locate them in time, none of the contemporary images that Auden and Day Lewis were using, no topical references, and no politics. The book nevertheless caught Roberts' eye, and he wrote to Lehmann about it. The two met, and out of that meeting came the idea for an anthology of the young poets, to be called *New Signatures*, with Roberts as editor. The preparation of that volume is the most important event of 1931 for the 'thirties generation, the event that affected them most as a literary generation. It was the first attempt by members of the generation to define, and to demonstrate, what it was that they shared that gave them a collective identity.

The book that Roberts and Lehmann produced has become a part of the 'thirties mythology. Leonard Woolf, who published it, later wrote that *New Signatures* 'was and still is regarded as that generation's manifesto', and he quoted in support of this view a remark by two younger critics that the book 'created a mild sensation then, and has since been taken to mark the beginning, the formal opening of the poetic movement of the 1930s'.[8] The latter parts of these two statements are certainly true, and indeed such remarks tend to be self-confirming; so long as critics believe and repeat that *New Signatures* was a manifesto and a formal opening, it will go on being accepted as that. But in fact it was neither, quite. If it was nevertheless important, it was for other reasons.

In his memoir, *The Whispering Gallery*, Lehmann recalls how *New Signatures* was related to the political events of 1931:

By the time of the General Election in 1931 I was already sufficiently converted [to Socialism] to share to the full the consternation and gloom that settled on all our circle at the collapse

75

of the Labour Government . . . But even as I reached this point of intellectual conviction, I began to move away from it, further to the left. The discredit of Labour made even staunch supporters of the Party in Bloomsbury mutter that perhaps far more radical measures of Marxism were necessary to defeat reaction and stop the drift towards a new war.

It was under the first wave of this disillusionment that work on *New Signatures* began . . .[9]

The suggestion here is that *New Signatures* was to be one of the 'more radical measures', and it was in this mood that Lehmann wrote the blurb for the book that he sent on to his friend Julian Bell. 'These new poems and satires,' he wrote,

> . . . are a challenge to the pessimism and intellectual aloofness which has marked the best poetry of recent years. These young poets rebel only against those things which they believe can and must be changed in the postwar world, and their work in consequence has a vigour and width of appeal which has long seemed lacking from English poetry.[10]

Lehmann was asserting that a *post*-post-war change had taken place in English poetry: a new generation had appeared to challenge the authority of Eliot, and to write a radically different kind of poem. The intention of the book was to define this new generation, while at the same time exploiting interest in it—that would be the intention of any such anthology, I suppose. But what is new is the terms in which Lehmann sets out his own notion of the generation. These poets, he says, are rebels, who think the world can and must be changed; and the implication is that poetry can do it. This idea of poetry as an instrument of change is a commonplace of 'thirties criticism, and one that had radical consequences for poetic rhetoric. Lehmann's paragraph is the first statement, so far as I know, of this idea set down as a principle, and it is significant that it should appear in connection with the first anthology of 'thirties poets, and that it should have, as an indirect source, the Labour defeat of 1931 and the movement of the younger generation toward the more militant Left.

If Lehmann's intention was to commission a book that would

be a radical political gesture, Michael Roberts was the wrong man to edit it, though in other respects he was an obviously good choice. In 1931 Roberts was twenty-nine, slightly older than most of the generation, and was already the author of a book of poems (*These Our Matins*, 1930), and an unpublished critical study (*Critique of Poetry*, written in 1930, published 1934), as well as many reviews of contemporary poetry. But more than that, Roberts was a thinker and a scholar. He had been trained as a scientist (chemistry at King's College, London, and mathematics at Cambridge), and taught mathematics and physics in a London school, but he was also widely read in philosophy and literature; when pressed to define his special subject, he decided that it was 'the history of English thought'. He regarded the poetry of his contemporaries as the latest phase in that history, and he was more interested in understanding its historical meaning than he was in exploiting its political possibilities.

The preface that Roberts wrote for *New Signatures* is the first serious effort by a member of the 'thirties generation to explain where they were, poetically speaking, and how they had got there. It is, understandably, a rather uncertain essay; there was no generational ideology yet, no common ideas about poetry and action, not even an enemy. What did exist in 1932, when the book appeared, was a sense of a new and urgent situation that could not be dealt with, even poetically, in the old terms, and this Roberts managed to communicate. His preface is a series of short struggles with a number of problems related to this new situation: the problem of poetic truth in a scientific society; the problem of urban and industrial imagery in poetry; the question of the poet's role in society; the problem of poetic difficulty; and the problem of reaching a popular audience. Some of these issues were inherited: difficulty came from Eliot, and the issue raised by science from Richards. Others seem to belong especially to the 'thirties: the whole matter of urban imagery, for example, and the search for an audience. These issues are all related to the central problem—how to write a new poetry for a new time—but they are not necessarily connected with each other, and their very incoherence may be taken as a truth about the circumstances in which young poets found themselves. Taken together, as

Roberts presented them, these questions gave a kind of definition to a puzzling historical situation; but more than this, by offering them as definitive of the generation, Roberts helped to fix the terms in which poetry and poets would be thought about, talked about, and written about in the years that followed.

The most interesting passage in the preface is one in which Roberts offers a general statement of the common condition of his contributors; it is the nearest he comes to a definition of his generation:

> The writers in this book have learned to accept the fact that progress is illusory, and yet to believe that the game is worth playing; to believe that the alleviation of suffering is good even though it merely makes possible new sensitiveness and therefore new suffering; to believe that their own standards are no more absolute than those of other people, and yet to be prepared to defend and to suffer for their own standards; to think of the world, for scientific purposes, in terms which make it appear deterministic, and yet to know that a human action may be unpredictable from scientific laws, a new creation.
>
> These are not really logical problems at all; they are aspects of an emotional discord which can be resolved neither by reasoning nor by action, but only by a new harmonisation such as that which may be brought about by a work of art. The fact that each of the writers in this book has solved this problem in his own way without recourse to any external system of religious belief therefore opens up new poetic possibilities.[11]

As an account of the beliefs shared by the *New Signatures* poets this surely claims far too much unanimity; but then Roberts was not really writing about them individually. Rather, he was describing the mood of the historical moment in which they all lived, and as an expression of that mood it is accurate enough. The passage is essentially an announcement of the end of all the comforting pre-war concepts—progress, the improvement of the human condition, absolute standards, a comprehensible, benignly determined scientific universe—and a weary agreement to go on with the human game anyway. This state of mind is very close to the 'chaos of

78

values' mood of the 'twenties, and Roberts' preface is a reminder that the 'thirties generation began in the 'twenties, and inherited the rejections and denials of Eliot and his contemporaries. But there is also something new here—the determination to act, even among negations, and the hope for a new poetry of a new belief.

The poets in *New Signatures*, like the issues in the preface, were various and not clearly connected, except in terms of certain shared backgrounds. Most of them were recent university graduates, and were acquaintances either of the editor or of Lehmann: from Oxford, Auden, Day Lewis, and Spender, from Cambridge, Bell, Richard Eberhart, Empson, and Lehmann. To these Lehmann added two poets he had met in London—A. S. J. Tessimond and William Plomer. It was a small and circumscribed group— not so much a generation as a circle of friends. But the poems that they contributed to the anthology do not suggest a school or a movement: they are very dissimilar—some public, some private, some traditional, some modern, some difficult, some transparently clear. There is nothing surprising in this, it must be true of any modern anthology, but the point is worth making because of the subsequent reputation of the book as a manifesto of the generation. It wasn't, and couldn't be; it was too various.

This point of the book's variety is most evident in the way that Roberts deals in his preface with politics. He felt compelled to say something about the political convictions of his contributors—no doubt Lehmann encouraged this line—but he was neither very clear nor very easy about the subject. What he wrote was this:

It is natural that the recognition of the importance of others should sometimes lead to what appears to be the essence of the communist attitude: the recognition that oneself is no more important than a flower in a field; that it may be good to sacrifice one's own welfare that others may benefit; to plough in this year's crop so that next year's may benefit: the return is certain, what matter who receives it.

This impersonality comes not from extreme detachment but from solidarity with others. It is nearer to the Greek conception of good citizenship than to the stoical austerity of recent verse, and its expression in many of the poems, and particularly in Mr Spender's 'The Funeral' suggests new possibilities for English poetry.[12]

Then follows the 'propaganda' passage borrowed from the Day Lewis review, and quoted above.

What Roberts says here has very little to do with communism as a political ideology; it is not much more than comradeship, team-feeling, the good of the school, all those collective emotions that these young men had felt long before they had any political ideas (and that their elders had felt in the trenches). But no more precise statement would have covered the range of *New Signatures* poets. The fact that Roberts nevertheless felt compelled to write this passage suggests that the need to acknowledge politics preceded any explicit expression of political ideas in the poems. It also preceded any confident feeling that political poetry was a good idea; Roberts was worried about a relationship that went on worrying his contemporary critics, the relation between poetry and propaganda, and the aesthetic consequences of political commitment. He had been uncertain about that relationship the year before, in his remarks on *From Feathers to Iron*, but if you place the two passages side by side you will see that in the intervening year his concern had taken a more specific turn. The 1931 version talks only about a 'theory of life', but in 1932 Roberts gives that theory a political identity, and calls it 'the communist attitude'.

There is only one note, one mood in the poems in *New Signatures* that recurs often enough to suggest some sort of common feeling. That is the note of apprehensiveness and impending crisis—the feeling that something is going to happen, soon, to all of us, that so dominates the entire decade. You find it most strongly expressed in Auden's 'Ode (To my pupils)', a poem that is a parable of this emotion. In it the army's youngest drummer waits to fight in a doomed struggle against a sinister enemy, for an unclear cause. The poem gives one a sense that the enemy is real, and that fear is real, but that nothing else is, and in this it expresses very powerfully the emotional state of the time. A correlative of this mood is the more positive response, the poem that celebrates action, a journey or a rebellion, any escape from passivity and the past;

Spender's 'Oh young men oh young comrades' is such a poem, and so are the extracts from Day Lewis' *Magnetic Mountain.*

Poems that express this feeling of crisis are political poems in a broad sense—the sense, for example, in which Spender used the word *political* in arguments about politics and literature: 'I used the word "political",' he later wrote in *World Within World,* 'in a very wide sense, to cover a fatality which I felt to be overtaking our civilization and which influenced our modern writing more explicitly than was generally realized'.[13] In this sense, many of the poems of *New Signatures* are political. But they are poems of political feelings rather than of political ideas; they are not polemical or ideological, and are rarely in the imperative voice. They simply acknowledge a political reality, the shared sense of imminent disaster.

The most immediate and alarming form of that disaster was the coming war, and at least one reviewer was struck by the presence of the war-theme in the book. 'It is remarkable,' he wrote,

> that no fewer than four of these writers feel themselves to be living 'under the shadow of war'. Under the shadow of future, nationalist war. And the possibility of war fills them, not with a sense of their own futility, but with indignation. They are indignant that anything so idiotic and wasteful as war should menace the creative promise of their generation.[14]

Indeed it is remarkable that as early as 1932 a number of young poets should make the shadow of the next war their theme. But it is also remarkable that a reviewer should be so struck by the substance of half a dozen poems in a book of more than forty poems. *New Signatures* does show that by 1932 the war had become a possible subject for poetry; but the quoted review shows also that the war had become, for some thoughtful persons, a preoccupation that made the theme stand out wherever it appeared.

New Signatures expressed a mood of the time, and we may call it political in a broad sense, but it did not achieve what Lehmann had hoped for—it was neither an explicit political gesture nor a challenge to pessimism. If it is an important book in the literary history of the 'thirties, this is not because it changed the relation between poetry and politics, but because it was the first anthology of 'thirties poets, and the first book to assert that this group had an identity derived from their unique position in history. From this point on, critics and reviewers began to refer to 'the *New Signatures* poets', to assume the uniformity that they did not have, and to take them as constituting a movement and a generation. The formal similarities among the poems in the book are in fact slight, and the differences great, and one gets very little sense of doctrine or of direction. What one does get is the mood: the sense of crisis, the menace of the future, the need for action; and these are the elements of what they did share, the sensibility of the generation.

One further point should be made, that the *New Signatures* poets were neither entirely new to the poetical world, nor at odds with the literary establishment. All of them had been published before: Auden, Bell, Lehmann, Day Lewis, Plomer, and Roberts in their own books of verse, and the others in various journals. Lehmann, Day Lewis, and Plomer had all appeared in the Hogarth 'Living Poets' series (*New Signatures* was also in that series), and Hogarth had also published two volumes of Cambridge poets, which included work by Eberhart, Empson, and Lehmann. So one might say that most of the contributors to *New Signatures* were already Hogarth 'house poets'. Of the others, Auden had been taken up by Eliot and published both by the *Criterion* and by Faber & Faber, and Spender would soon also be a Faber author. The point of this recitation is simply that a good deal of recognition had already been given to these poets, and most of it had come from the Bloomsbury establishment. Nothing could have been more conventional, or less revolutionary, than the way in which these young reputations were launched.

In spite of this support, the reception of *New Signatures* was not, as the myth would have it, extravagantly successful. Roberts' preface, which he felt was unsatisfactory, was not generally taken as a manifesto for his generation, or at least not as an adequate one; J. B. Priestley thought it 'for the most part wrong', and Middleton Murry could not see that it had any connection with the poems that followed. As for the poets, George Barker thought that they weren't really 'poets of their time' at all, and F. R. Leavis, writing anonymously in the *Listener*, concluded that '*New Signatures* . . . brings us no nearer to a poetry that shall be at once modern and popular'.[15] Sales of the book were modest: a thousand copies in the first year, less than two hundred the second. The sales continued, and by the end of the decade 2,400 copies had been sold and the contributors were famous; but they had not been made famous by *New Signatures*, it was rather the other way round.

III

The appearance of *New Signatures* was one sign that in the early 'thirties the generation was becoming conscious of itself. There were many others. There was, for instance, the Promethean Society, an organization of young radicals that met to discuss politics, 'sexology', philosophy, religion, and art, and published its own journal, the *Twentieth Century*. One might argue that a generation exists when it has such organizations and such journals of its own, and certainly the Promethean Society represented some definitive currents in the generation. An editorial in the first issue of *Twentieth Century* explained the Society's intentions:

> We want to cut across the field of contemporary party politics, accepting here, rejecting there, but always after detailed and impartial research. This attitude—the scientific attitude, and, to us, the only possible method of approach for anyone who cares more for intellectual honesty than for party, creed, or shibboleth—we will try to adopt and maintain in every branch of our work . . . With one exception—that of peace propaganda. Here we feel that it is not the time for a long period of research into the causes of war. Such research has a place in our scheme; but of far more immediate urgency, if we are to prevent ourselves and twentieth century civilization from crashing into complete ruin, is active and intense propaganda until total disarmament is achieved.[16]

This is a fair expression of dominant young ideas in the pre-Hitler 'thirties: the eclectic politics, the faith in science, and the pacifism are all there, and give to the time a sense of disorganized good intentions that have not yet been exposed to reality.

One also gets from *Twentieth Century* an impression of the generation's self-consciousness and its desire for self-definition. In the September 1932 issue, for example, an article appears under the

83

headline 'What Does the Public Want?', with the sub-title: 'Lock up the Old Men! Youth prepares for a coup d'état.' 'The truth, of course,' the anonymous author writes,

> is that a tremendous gulf separates *us* from *you*—you who remember something (a myth to us) called 'Pre-war'. What is it, this 'Pre-war'? *We* haven't the faintest idea. We hear tales of it. We see pictures of it. But we really cannot imagine what sort of beast it was. We never *experienced* it. We came afterwards.
>
> To those of us who were born (say) in 1906, and to whom the outer world only became a reality in 1914 (when our governess compelled us to destroy such of our possessions as bore the mark: MADE IN GERMANY)—to us, a state of crisis is perfectly natural. We have never known any other state.[17]

This is a definition in terms which have already become conventional: the war as a separating gulf, and crisis as an ordinary post-war state of affairs. What is new is the aggressiveness of the attitude toward the older generation. The 'Old Men' phrase is of course an inheritance from the reaction to the leaders of the First World War, but here it is applied to anyone who can remember what 'Pre-war' was like. No doubt a generation, as it becomes distinct and self-conscious, will inevitably separate the *we* from the *you*; but the flatness of this rejection is a new note.

The *Twentieth Century* ran for two years, from March 1931 to May 1933. During that time it published some of the generation's leaders, including Auden ('Get there if you can' and 'A Communist to Others'), Spender ('The Landscape Near an Aerodrome') and Michael Roberts, as well as an odd mixture of elders —Havelock Ellis, Wyndham Lewis, and Trotsky. And it caused enough stir to be noticed by the *Daily Express* ('250 Young Rebels Challenge the Whole World. Down With Everything. Marriage, Morals, Parliament' the headline read[18]). But by 1933 the notion that civilization could be saved by scientific research and eclectic radicalism was dead, and the journal and its Society were dead, too.

As the generation, in the larger sense, became definite, so the literary generation—the Auden Gang, the *New Signatures* poets, whatever one called that group of writers who became identified

with the decade—also began to become established and noticeable, at least among their contemporaries. This process had been
going on since the days of Auden and Day Lewis' *Oxford Poetry*
manifesto, but it accelerated rapidly in the years that followed. By
1929 Auden's taste for urban landscape was being quoted (and
illustrated with a photograph of the Oxford gasworks) in the
Oxford Outlook; in 1931 an Oxford undergraduate journal published a musical setting of a Day Lewis lyric; and in 1932 the
annual *Oxford Poetry* volume was dedicated to Auden, Day Lewis,
and Spender. The writers themselves helped a good deal in identifying the narrowest circle of the group by dedicating their books
to each other: Auden dedicated *Paid on Both Sides* to Day Lewis,
Poems to Isherwood, and *The Orators* to Spender; Day Lewis dedicated *Transitional Poem* to Warner and *The Magnetic Mountain* to
Auden; Spender dedicated his *Poems* to Isherwood; Warner
dedicated his *Poems* to Day Lewis; Isherwood's *All the Conspirators*
is dedicated to Upward. So that without any guidance except the
books themselves you could tell quite precisely who was *in* the
inner circle, and who was not.

In the summer of 1932 Virginia Woolf added another kind of
definition in her *Letter to a Young Poet* (published by her own
Hogarth Press, as *New Signatures* had been). Mrs Woolf was a
highly conservative critic when she addressed herself to poetry; she
believed in Beauty with a capital B, in clarity, and in decorum
(there were some emotions, she thought, that were not 'domesticated'), and she looked in poetry for ordinary, recognizable reality,
for real human characters and the 'world outside'. She did not
find those qualities in the young poets, she said, and it seemed to
her odd 'that these modern poets should write as if they had neither
ears nor eyes, neither soles to their feet nor palms to their hands,
but only honest enterprising book-fed brains, uni-sexual bodies
. . .'[19] By 'these modern poets' she meant *New Signatures* poets: the
examples she chose to quote are from poems by Auden, Lehmann,
Day Lewis, and Spender. She is severe in her criticism of their
poems—Auden 'breaks his machine because he will clog it with
raw fact', Spender is 'unintelligible', and they are all guilty of a
too-easy despair; but the very things that she complains of become
terms in a definition, and support the already existing idea of what

the generation was. The general effect of the essay is to re-affirm, with the authority of Bloomsbury, the *New Signatures* definition of the Younger Generation, and its separation from the immediate past.

Mrs Woolf's conclusion was that the young poets had been 'exposed to the fierce light of publicity while they were still too young to stand the strain', and she advised them to publish nothing before they were thirty. But of course her advice was itself further publicity, and made it even less likely that these poets could detach themselves from the public roles to which they were already assigned, as spokesmen for the Younger Generation in a Time of Crisis.

Peter Quennell, an Oxford contemporary of Auden and Spender, replied immediately in *A Letter to Mrs. Virginia Woolf*, a defence of his fellow poets which is also a further definition. By now, *definition* begins to seem an inadequate term, for what is building up is a sort of mythical figure, the Thirties Poet, who is neither one person nor another, but a generalization put in terms that are meant to explain his actions by describing his situation. 'He is dull,' Quennell explains:

> he would rather be that than meretricious; tuneless; it is a new music he hopes to sound—obscure and harsh; he prefers to call it experimental; for language, the medium through which he operates, is nowadays in the midst of severe crisis—a crisis probably more disturbing than has occurred since the Elizabethan Age.

But he is not a Poet in the legendary sense; that meaning is now extinct:

> He reads *The Criterion* once a quarter; and no man who makes it a duty to read that journal but bears its mark inscribed across his brow. I do not imply that he is necessarily an Anglo-Catholic; for all I can tell he may be a Communist or a young Hitlerite. But I feel certain that the prodigious melodrama of modern Europe casts its shadows in some form on to his mind.

And finally, he is defined by the now conventional allusion to 'Pre-war':

Be indulgent if he seems to you somewhat solemn! Remember
that of the placid pre-war universe—how tranquil and how
olympian it must have been! Was the pound really worth
twenty shillings, and were there parties every night and hansom
cabs? Did noblemen not write for the Sunday Press?—he can
recall barely five or six summers; then the War to End Wars
and so good-bye . . .[20]

Much of this is by now familiar: experiment, the crisis of language,
the extreme politics, the loss of the pre-war past. But there is one
new element: the shadow of Europe is a new shadow, and the
name of Hitler enters literary discussion for the first time. The
pressure of the public world has been increased, and given a new
name.

IV

Auden's *The Orators: An English Study* was published in May 1932,
two months after *New Signatures*. No doubt the attention given to
the anthology had something to do with the way the new work
was received: it was taken seriously by many reviewers, and was
treated as an important, though difficult, expression of the post-
war generation's state of mind. John Hayward, reviewing the book
in the *Criterion*, began his essay by defining the generation, as
though until that was done the book could not be properly
understood:

> The generation, for whom the last war is a confused memory of
> darkened windows, margarine and fearful visions in the pages of
> the *Illustrated London News*; of fathers and elder brothers return-
> ing on leave with bits of shrapnel and pressed wild flowers; of
> drawing-rooms littered with cretonne bags and skeins of wool;
> that generation has grown up since the publication of *The Waste
> Lead*, ten years ago. It has not been an easy or a happy appren-
> ticeship.
> Mr. Wystan Auden belongs to that generation . . .[21]

The defining terms are the war and *The Waste Land*; and Hayward
was not the only critic to relate *The Orators* to those sources.
    Hayward took note of the dust-jacket's assertion that '*The Ora-
tors* is not a collection, but a single work with one theme and

purpose', and rather diffidently suggested that the theme might be one of three: 'The value of Leadership; Society; The importance of group organization over the individual'; or, he thought, it might be a mixture of these. The latter view seems the right one, though all three proposed themes are really subsumable under the heading of Leadership. Leadership is a political subject, and in 1932 it was one of particularly critical importance. For recent events in England and in Europe had revealed a failure of democratic government, while at the same time a new kind of leadership was emerging in Russia, Italy, and Germany. Even if one did not understand the political implications of Fascism, National Socialism, and Soviet Communism, it was clear that they all offered strong alternatives to traditional democratic ideas, and heroic, mythologized Leaders. For the young in particular, who could not remember a time when their own political system had worked, this was the problem: on the one hand the apparent collapse of a traditional system that had seemed morally right and essentially English; and on the other, alternative systems that were foreign and violent, but were evidently effective. This is the situation that *The Orators* responds to, and in this sense it is not only a political book, but a topical one.

But there is another side to the problem—the private, psychological side. Why do men need leaders? How do they find them? And how does public power affect private lives? Auden had been reading psychology—Freud, Groddeck, Homer Lane, D. H. Lawrence—and he had come to believe that leadership was an individual psychological necessity. In a book review of September 1932, he wrote: 'Before a man wants to understand, he wants to command or obey instinctively, to live with others in a relation of power...' [22] And the following month, reviewing a book by Bertrand Russell, he elaborated on the key phrase, *a relation of power*. 'The trouble is,' he wrote,

that Mr. Russell refused to admit that man's nature is dual, and that each part of him has its own conception of justice and morality. In his passionate nature man wants lordship, to live in a relation of power with others, to obey and to command, to strut and to swagger. He desires mystery and glory. In his cerebral nature he cares for none of these things. He wants to know and be gentle; he feels his other passionate nature is frightening and cruel.[23]

In these terms the crisis of the 'thirties, and the consequent re-definition of the 'relation of power' in Western society, was a psychological as well as a political crisis.

The Orators is best understood as a series of parabolic utterances on this subject, the 'relation of power'. There is no continuing plot-line in the book, and no fixed cast of characters, though there are recurrent types, treated individually and in relation to each other—the Leader, the Young Man, the Enemy—and a general movement towards commitment and action. But such unity as the book has derives principally from its single theme, and from patterns of recurrent images, and in this it resembles its principal literary ancestor, *The Waste Land*. Like *The Waste Land*, it creates its own atmosphere, its 'world': a sick England with a sick people, its industries closed and its workers idle; the middle classes fearful and defensive, afraid of change, afraid of life; and the young, feeling the need for action, for a journey beyond the border of the familiar into a new life, but uncertain and afraid, and wanting a leader.

The parables of *The Orators* are, to use one of Auden's favourite words, diagnostic: each deals with an aspect of the central theme, and together they compose a complex image of the political and psychological situation of young men in England in the early 'thirties. The structure of the book is loose, and the line of thought is sometimes obscured by parody, by digressions into parables-within-parables, and by private jokes, but the central theme, 'the relation of power', remains central, though it takes different parabolic forms. The best way to deal with the book here is simply to begin at the beginning, taking note of the theme as it develops through its formal variations.

First, then, the prologue, a short poem beginning 'By landscape reminded once of his mother's figure . . .' Already one sees that this is a Freudian landscape; in it a young man takes a journey—a typical Auden journey of escape from mother and home—and becomes a hero, a prophet, a Jove. But when he returns to his own country he is condemned by a giantess-mother who cries 'Deceiver!'. The poem is a portrait of the young man as hero that recalls the situation in *Paid on Both Sides*, and establishes the basic psychological problem for the young man who would act: the past, and his own dependence on it, will prohibit and condemn his action. It also sets up another motif to which Auden returns: the private weakness of the strong public man.

After this prologue, *The Orators* is divided into three books: Book I, 'The Initiates'; Book II, 'Journal of an Airman'; Book III, 'Six Odes'. Roughly, these three parts divide up in this way: Book I is concerned with the need for Leadership, and its consequences; Book II is about the test of Leadership, seen subjectively; Book III is a series of comments on the theme, the voice of the poet addressing his friends and pupils on a subject that concerns them all.

'Address for a Prize Day', the first section of Book I, is a parody (the first of many in the book) of a speech at a public school. The speaker is a Leader and an acute diagnostician of the nation's sickness, which he describes in terms of the failures of love in the *Purgatorio*. The questions that he asks the boys are the right questions for this generation: 'What were the dead like? What sort of people are we living with now? Why are we here? What are we going to do?' and 'What do you think about England, this country of ours where nobody is well?' The questions are right, and the diagnosis is right—the sick need love. But the treatment is wrong: 'All these have got to die without issue'—a Final Solution before Hitler. Those whom the Leader condemns are indeed ill, and England is ill, and the situation does, as he says, call for 'some pretty stiff changes'; but if action means the extermination of the ill, does one still favour action? I take it that this 'Address' is a parable of one problem of Leadership—the apparently necessary connection of Power with Violence.

The following two sections, 'Argument' and 'Statement', are about Followers, the young who seek a Leader, and about their antagonists, the Enemy. The action takes the familiar parabolic form of the journey to a frontier by a conspiratorial band, through hostile, primitive country (which resembles the world of *Paid on Both Sides*). The young men dream of 'Him', a superhuman leader who will demand complete submission to his will, but in return will bring them over the border to a new life. But the journey fails, the leader dies or is betrayed, and the final note is of defeat and inaction; devotion to such a leader is, it seems, another kind of defective love, you can't love your way to the border.

The 'Statement' that follows is a catalogue of the conditions of men, the doers and the neurotic failures, the saved and the damned, who make up the *Us* and the *Them* of Auden's world. But here they are inextricably mixed together, and that seems to be the point—that in a sick society it is difficult to separate sickness from health, or right love from defective love. The section ends with this paragraph:

> The man shall love the work; the woman shall receive him as the divine representative; the child shall be born as the sign of the trust; the friend shall laugh at the joke apparently obscure. The boy and the girl shall not play together; they shall wait for power; the old shall wait in the garden, happy for death. The leader shall be a fear; he shall protect from panic; the people shall reverence the carved stone under the oak-tree. The muscular shall lounge in bars; the puny shall keep diaries in classical Greek. The soldier shall say 'It is a fine day for hurting'; the doctor shall speak of death as of a favourite dog. The glutton shall love with his mouth; to the burglar love shall mean 'Destroy when read'; to the rich and the poor the sign for 'our money'; the sick shall say of love, 'It's only a phase'; the psychologist, 'That's easy'; the ******, 'Be fair'. The censor shall dream of knickers, a nasty beast. The murderer shall be wreathed with flowers; he shall die for the people.[24]

This is a series of statements of the infinite varieties of love, which begins like a benediction, with love and procreation, but continues to restraint, prohibition, pain, death, and murder. What does it describe? A society in which men love their destinies? One in which defective love is exploited? Certainly a society in which children are controlled and women are subordinated, in which violence is approved, and in which the leader is 'a fear'. In short, a fascist state described in terms of the perversions of love.

'Address', 'Argument', and 'Statement' are all public modes of address, and express public aspects of the Leadership theme. The two sections that follow are in private forms: a love letter and a journal. Auden turns here to the private questions: what are the inner obstacles to leadership? what does leadership cost the sensitive young man who is tested by it? These are subjects that he had dealt with in *Paid on Both Sides* and in many poems in his first book, and, given the collocation of a young poet and a political crisis, they are probably inevitable. At any rate, in the middle of *The Orators* Auden turned inward.

'Letter to a Wound' is a parodic love-letter, addressed by a sick man to his own sickness, a wound that seems to represent a psychological abnormality, perhaps sexual (and if so, homosexual). Here love is directed inward, toward what is sick in the self; it is an extreme of self-regard, a condition that would make public, self-abnegating action out of the question. Yet the tone of the letter is not such as to lead a reader to condemn the writer of it: it is witty and self-aware, and self-accepting. The letter-writer is something of an artist, and in psychological terms what he has done is the essential act of the artist—he has acknowledged and expressed his psychic wound, the private neurosis that is the source of art. He is therefore a hero, of a traditional romantic sort—the introspective, suffering artist, the sort of man who might have written the works of Baudelaire or Proust. His presence here is a reminder of what public crisis does to conventional literary postures, the problems that it raises for the writer in search of a hero. It is no longer possible, in a time of crisis, to make the writer himself heroic; his gift becomes a wound that disqualifies him from entering the world of action, though it will still compel admiration.

Book II, 'The Journal of an Airman', is the longest part of *The Orators*, and the only one that has a narrative line. The Airman is a pilot involved in a secret revolutionary plot; his journal is a record of his plans, reflections, fantasies and anxieties as the day set for the revolution approaches. Like the letter-writer, the Airman is a neurotic, introspective man (Auden later said that his principal source was Baudelaire's *Intimate Journal*, which Isherwood had translated in 1930); but he has been thrust by the time's necessities into an active role—or say that he is the private artist-hero who must act as a public hero. In this he is a paradigm of the situation that seemed to confront the young artists of Auden's generation, and his thoughts and his fate are significant expressions of the generation's sense of itself.

His thoughts are primarily about the Enemy: who they are, and what they are plotting. They are, essentially, the middle class, the sort of people who live in suburban villas and belong to golf clubs and make polite conversation at boring parties—cautious, fearful, life-denying people. But they are also the older generation, the mothers and the Old Men who make patriotic speeches about war. The Airman is a shrewd analyst of their characteristics, but he is paranoid about their behaviour—every middle-class gesture is threatening in his eyes. (He is also a fantastic, surrealistic inventor of the bourgeois world, in a mode that recalls Mortmere, and no doubt was influenced by the Isherwood–Upward stories.) He regards his own behaviour with equal anxiety: he is a neurotic, a kleptomaniac, a homosexual, and he is afraid that on the day of action he will fail the Test. When that day comes, he finds the resolution of his fears in humility and self-condemnation, and though he prepares calmly to make his attack, it is in a mood of self-immolation. The fight against the Enemy, Auden seems to conclude, cannot be fought in public: the Enemy is ourselves.

One can see how a middle-class artist, writing about an essentially middle-class artist-hero, might come to such a psychological conclusion, accepting his own infection with the sickness of his society, and that such a conclusion might be taken as a private victory, and a kind of heroism. But in terms of the immediate political crisis and the problem of leadership, it is a defeat. The Airman fails as a leader because he loses faith in the value of leading, and out of his failure he gains a victory that seems to have nothing to do with politics, and no public consequences. The answer—if it is an answer—to political problems is a change of heart, self-knowledge, not a revolution.

The six odes that end *The Orators* are separable from the rest of the book, and some were published individually elsewhere. Here Auden, the poet and schoolmaster, speaks in his own voice, and addresses friends and students (and so adds to the Myth of Themselves). The odes repeat themes already established: the ambivalent feelings about the Leader, the psychological sources of social sickness and the paralyzing effects of fear, the need for love, for action, and for a change of heart. The parabolic forms are mostly ones that Auden had used before: a dream-vision, school and school games, a war against a sinister enemy beyond the frontier. Like the other parables in the book, the odes are diagnostic, but they do not prescribe, and, though the tone varies, the prevailing note is dark: 'Read of your losses', 'Grown used at last/To having lost', 'Not, father, further do prolong/Our necessary defeat'. If action is required, loss also seems inevitable.

The Orators begins with a parabolic prologue, and it ends with a similar epilogue—another journey poem, ' "O where are you going?" said reader to rider.' The terms are by now familiar: the passive, frightened person who sees terror in action, and the active man who makes his journey into the unknown anyway, because he must. But where exactly is he going? Is his action political? And will he arrive? The poem doesn't tell us; it only offers the alterna-- tives—a fearful action, or a frightened, sick passiveness.

Auden came to think of *The Orators* as a 'fair notion fatally injured'.[25] If the idea was to write 'An English Study' that would set the social sickness of England in psychological parables, then perhaps the fatal injury was simply that the book is too clever, too various, too disparate in manner to sustain a continuous theme. Or perhaps it is too literary, in an avant-gardeish way: St John Perse, Eliot, and Baudelaire are not the best models for public poetry. But it is not a fatal injury that the book is politically ambiguous. Later in the 'thirties, when the political sides had been drawn in black-and-white terms, it was described by a Marxist critic as being 'more like the plans for a Fascist *coup* than a Communist revolution',[26] but when Auden wrote it it was neither. Looking back thirty years later, Auden wrote: 'My name on the title page seems a pseudonym for someone else, someone talented but near the border of sanity, who might well, in a year or two, become a Nazi.'[27] Or, one might add, a Communist; but in fact Auden did neither. The point about *The Orators*, though, is that it records that stage in Auden's and England's history when the course was uncertain and the leaders absent, and only the sickness and the need for health were clear.

The lack of leadership, and the evident need for it, explains the odd presence of D. H. Lawrence in *The Orators*, and his continuing status among the young writers of the 'thirties. Auden mentions him by name in the first ode, when he recalls 'the hour in the night when Lawrence died', and he is also mentioned in Poems XXII ('Get there if you can') among the 'healers in our English land'. His influence on Auden's work of this time was considerable. 'Over the whole work,' Auden later said of *The Orators*, 'looms the shadow of that dangerous figure, D. H. Lawrence the Ideologue, author of *Phantasia on the Unconscious* and those sinister novels *Kangaroo* and *The Plumed Serpent*.'[28] You might expect that Lawrence, with his ideas of the absolute Leader and the obedient followers, and his celebration of blood, violence, and unreason, would have been hated and rejected by leftish young people, but in fact he remained throughout the 'thirties an heroic figure, tragic but wise in his understanding of the English sickness, a rebel and a protester. At a time of indecision and disorder in society, Lawrence at least offered an ideology, a diagnosis of the disease, and a cure for it that was an alternative to sick democracy. His influence as a writer was not great in the 'thirties, but Lawrence the Ideologue was as influential as Eliot, and 'the hour when Lawrence died' (on 2 March 1930) has its place among the beginnings of the 'thirties generation.

The Orators expresses the political uncertainty of the early 'thirties, but it also implies, in its obscurity, its shifting tones and mixed modes, an uncertainty as to the role of the writer in such a time. Clearly that role would be very different from what it had traditionally been—Auden and Day Lewis had recognized that fact in their *Oxford Poetry* preface in 1927—but different in what direction? As the 'thirties sense of crisis increased, this question began to seem a crucial one, and much of the critical writing of the decade is concerned with finding answers. But not the same answers.

Consider, as example, two essays published in September 1932, one by Day Lewis and one by Auden. Day Lewis' essay, 'The Poet and Revolution', was written in reply to a remark by Middleton Murry, editor of the *Adelphi*. Murry, commenting on the appearance of *New Signatures*, had given the poets his rather patronising approval, but had added: 'I doubt whether anything can be poetically very important nowadays.'[29] Murry was then passing through his Marxist phase, and he regarded poetry as a rather trivial activity in a revolutionary time. Day Lewis replied angrily in defence of poetry; of course poetry was important, he wrote, the poet was a kind of transmitting station (he found such imagery irresistible), receiving the truth about reality and broadcasting it to the world:

> If the capitalist system is dead, his poetry will expose the fact; it will have a dead ring; it may be none the worse poetry for that. If there is new life about, you may be sure he will catch it: he has sharp ears. It is for you to prove the new life, for him to record it.
>
> This is the paradox of the revolutionary and the poet. Each destroys, transforms, makes, from the fundamental and integral necessity of his nature; yet the true revolutionary does not function for revolution's sake, nor the true artist for art's sake ... It is as meaningless for a revolutionary to call poetry unimportant in the hour of revolution, as it would be for a poet to call revolution unimportant in the hour of poetry. We have both heard voices; we are both positive.[30]

Of all the 'thirties poets, Day Lewis was the one who tried longest and hardest to reconcile political commitment with a sense of the integrity of art; he was an active member of the Communist Party longer than anyone in his circle except Upward, and yet he remained what he always was essentially, a lyric poet. In 1932 he was not yet a Party member, and his little essay is far from orthodox; but it is nevertheless the first attempt by a 'thirties writer to put Poet and Revolution together, and to try to relate the terms to each other. And it asks the crucial question: 'What is the attitude of the poet to the political system under which he lives?' That question would be asked again and again in the years that followed, and answered in many ways, most of them as muddled as Day Lewis' first attempt was.

In the same month Auden contributed an essay, 'Writing, or The Pattern Between People', to *An Outline for Boys & Girls and Their Parents*, a sort of left-wing child's guide to knowledge, edited by Naomi Mitchison. Auden's essay makes an interesting contrast to Day Lewis's; its context is political, and it makes certain points

—mainly about the communal origins of art and language—that are compatible with Marxist theory, but in substance it is not really political at all. It offers no answer to Day Lewis's hard question about the poet's attitude to the political system under which he lives, and it does not deal with politics as a motive for writing: men write, Auden says, because they are lonely, and because they are mortal. His conclusion is a gloomy vision of the writer in the modern world that has social implications, but says nothing about political ideas; in the modern world, he writes,

> writing gets shut up in a circle of clever people writing about themselves for themselves, or ekes out an underworld existence, cheap and nasty. Talent does not die out, but it can't make itself understood. Since the underlying reason for writing is to bridge the gulf between one person and another, as the sense of loneliness increases, more and more books are written by more and more people, most of them with little or no talent. Forests are cut down, rivers of ink absorbed, but the lust to write is still unsatisfied. What is going to happen? If it were only a question of writing it wouldn't matter; but it is an index of our health. It's not only books, but our lives, that are going to pot.[31]

This vision of England—the centrifugal community, the lonely people, the sick society, and the writer, writing out of his loneliness but unable to find an audience—is a new version of the Waste Land, and another account of life in Auden Country. It has no clear political implications; like *The Orators*, it could lead to either right-wing or left-wing action. What it expresses is a sense of the time that, though not political, is a condition of politics, the ground-base of the more explicit political ideas that followed.

IV

1933

I

When Spender's *Poems* was published in January 1933, his publishers, Faber & Faber, announced the book as an event in an already important literary movement: 'If Auden is the satirist of this poetical renaissance,' the dust-jacket copy read, 'Spender is its lyric poet. In his work the experimentalism of the last two decades is beginning to find its reward ... Technically, these poems appear to make a definite step forward in English poetry.'[1] The confidence of this assessment (which was probably written by Eliot) suggests that Spender had arrived at his first published volume with an established reputation and a defined role in the dramatis personae of his generation; and clearly this was the case. That it was so was partly due to the previous year's publicity, and especially to *New Signatures*; but I think it had another cause, more general and less easily definable. New poets become a renascence when a public wants and needs a renascence, and Spender and his friends were celebrated almost before they were published because they seemed to offer new reponses to new problems. Their swift popularity is a sign of the general increase in social and political anxiety, and of the sense that established ways of responding to that anxiety no longer worked.

One evidence that this was the case may be found in the reviews of Spender's book. Critics did not follow Faber's lead, and write about experimentalism and technique; rather they took note of the social and political content of the poems, and praised Spender's ability to be lyrical about such subjects. Herbert Read, writing in the *Adelphi*, was typical:

Mr. Spender is conscious of his social heritage of chaos and despair ... perhaps the book's most notable quality is its social consciousness. and the perfect fusion of this often too intractable

98

material with the poetic idiom. Another Shelley speaks in these lines . . .[2]

In fact only the later poems in the book really fit Read's description; the earlier ones are introspective, often love poems. But social disorders were the time's problems, and they attracted the attention of reviewers; even *The Times Literary Supplement* reviewer, though he was troubled by Spender's 'unpoetic leaning' towards politics, praised him for the way 'he extends love and pity towards the hungry, the unemployed, and the oppressed'.[3]

By early 1933, the hunger and the oppression, and the chaos and despair, were worsening, both in England and abroad. In England unemployment had reached its highest point in mid-1932, and remained there. Hunger marchers demonstrated in London that autumn and fought with mounted police in Hyde Park. In November, Sir Oswald Mosley announced the formation of the British Union of Fascists, and his followers began to appear in the streets in their black shirts. Meanwhile, across the Channel there were riots in Poland and an anarchist uprising in Barcelona; and in January 1933, Hitler became Chancellor of Germany, the Reichstag burned, and the persecution of Jews and leftists began.

It is not surprising that in the context of such events the imaginations of young people were becoming increasingly engaged with the issues of the public world. One can see this process taking place most clearly by examining the undergraduate publications of Oxford and Cambridge. The *Oxford Outlook*, which had been Oxford's principal journal of arts and letters since the war, suddenly changed its nature with the issue of May 1932. Richard Goodman, a student-poet who was also a Marxist, became editor, and in his first issue featured Middleton Murry on 'Communism and the Universities' (in which Murry exhorted students to become communists), a short story about German workers, and his own poem, 'The Manifesto', full of red flags and marching masses. The journal then ceased publication, to appear a year later as the *New Oxford Outlook*, with a strong left-wing political leaning; 'the present editors believe,' an editorial explained, 'that there is now coming into existence some attitude—some outlook, in fact—less transient than the post-war poses.'[4] In the first issue this new

99

outlook was expressed in an editorial on the economic situation, an essay on 'How Nazis Think', and a poem entitled 'Diary of a Revolutionary', and in the second by a piece on 'Fascism and Communism in Oxford'. The change from the 'post-war poses' is clear, and so is the students' self-conscious self-approval that they have made it.

At Cambridge a new journal, *Cambridge Left*, began in the summer of 1933. There, too, the change in student consciousness is a subject for comment. In the first issue this 'Note on Poetry and Politics' appeared:

> The motives for writing, of those who are writing for this paper, have changed, along with their motives for doing anything. It is not so much an intellectual choice, as the forcible intrusion of social issues.
>
> Those who are left in their politics have to face certain problems as writers of prose or verse. Most of the present contributors are aware of the problems, but to formulate them successfully would be to have solved them. So it is most profitable to try and solve them by trial and error. That is what is attempted in this paper.[5]

The 'forcible intrusion of social issues' is very like Spender's phrase about being hounded by external events: both are accounts of that harsh invasion of the private life by public crises that is so definitive a part of the experience of the 'thirties generation.

Many of the issues that invaded young people's minds came from their immediate environment: poverty, unemployment, and the dole were there to be seen in any town, even in Oxford and Cambridge. Fascism and Communism were also visible: by 1933 Oxford had both a Fascist Club (opened officially by Mosley on May Day), and the October Club, for the study of Communism. But the issue that agitated them most was not visible, but was only an abstract possibility—the threat of another war. Student opposition to another war hit the British public with a sudden shock in February 1933, when the Oxford Union passed its famous motion that 'This House will in no circumstances fight for its King and Country'; but in fact the anti-war movement had been around for some time before it reached the Union. The first book on the subject published between the wars, to my knowledge, was a shilling communist pamphlet titled *Heading for War*, which appeared in 1929, and opposition to a capitalist war was a part of communist propaganda from then on, though it intensified in the early 'thirties. The May 1932 issue of the Marxist *Labour Monthly* contained six articles with *War* in the title, all concerned with the war that was coming, and in the same month *Outpost*, a Cambridge undergraduate journal, published an essay on 'The Danger of World War', and followed it in the next issue with a warning that 'the danger of another war is more obvious, and perhaps greater, than it was in 1914'.[6]

The Oxford Union was not even the first student group to pass an anti-war motion; on Armistice Day, 1932, the Debating Society of University College, London, resolved 'That in the event of a declaration of war, this house would not support the Government,' which differed from the Oxford motion only in not mentioning the King and not issuing from the Home of Lost Causes. And on the same day in Bristol the University Socialist Society placed a wreath on the university war memorial with the inscription: 'To the Dead of all nations, victims of a war they did not make—from those who are pledged to fight all such crimes of Imperialism.' (The Vice-Chancellor immediately removed it.)

The objects of these resolutions and demonstrations were not very specific. On Armistice Day, 1932, there was only one fascist state in Europe, and although Hitler was in power by the time of the Oxford Union motion, his government had not yet met, and the Reichstag had not been burned. So the enemy could only be defined in abstract and emotive terms: as capitalism, imperialism, armaments manufacturers, governments, and, the most emotive term of all, war itself. What these gestures expressed was not a party position or even a political ideology (the communists, for example, were against war, but they were also against pacifism), but simply anxiety, and fear of the vast and anonymous forces that seemed to have taken control of human destinies.

I assume that what students at Oxford and Cambridge and London and Bristol were feeling was also felt by a schoolmaster at Helensburgh and another at Cheltenham, by a classics don in Birmingham, a young novelist in the Cotswolds, a bookseller in

Hampstead, a maths teacher in London: that the generation extended to include anyone who was not a veteran of the last war, but might be a veteran of the next one. I assume that this generation shared the compassionate feelings that Spender's poems of the time expressed so well—feelings for the poor and the oppressed; and that above all other common bonds they shared a fearful revulsion at the thought of that possible war ahead. Political awareness for many young people must have begun here, with the recognition that what Father Rothschild had said was right, that wars don't start nowadays because people want them, but because the world-order has failed.

II

New Country, Michael Roberts' second anthology of writings by his contemporaries, was published in March 1933, a year after *New Signatures*. The second book carried the subtitle 'Prose and Poetry by the authors of *New Signatures*', and it has sometimes been treated by critics as simply a continuation of the first, but in fact the two books are very different, and their differences suggest some of the changes that had taken place in the generation and in the world during that year, including the change of consciousness that I have been describing in the universities.

First, there are the two titles: *Signatures*, the written mark of the individual, has become *Country*, the world out there, the moral landscape—another sign of the demand that the public life made on the attention of private imaginations. Then, the size and scope: *New Signatures* is a small book in paper boards, almost a pamphlet, some eighty pages of poems with a preface; *New Country* is large, cloth-bound, more than 250 pages long, and includes fiction and essays as well as poems. The expansion is a sign of the success of *New Signatures*, and of the improved public status of the contributors; but it also argues a revised notion of what is the appropriate form of expression for a serious young writer. Day Lewis is represented by four poems, but also by an essay, 'Letter to a Young Revolutionary', and Spender by poems and an essay on 'Poetry and Revolution'. These two essays by poets, with Revolution in their titles, are important: simply by being there among the stories and poems they assert that it is right and necessary that poets should think about political action, that the relation between the private and the public lives of artists seemed a close and inevitable one in 1933.

Day Lewis's 'Letter' is scarcely concerned with literature at all; his young revolutionary is not a poet, but simply a middle-class university student who is thinking of joining the Communist Party. Day Lewis offers him avuncular advice, such as an older man-of-the-world might give to a young man setting out for the Colonies or entering the Civil Service. Much of it is sensible advice, urging faith and patience, but it is quite clearly not based on experience, and some of it has that quality of boys' adventure story melodrama that one also finds in Auden:

> When it comes to the point will you, Jonathan Smith, be able to let off a revolver at Thomas Brown, bloated capitalist, cad, liar, bully, beast and public nuisance though you believe him to be? You can't go challenging him to a duel, remember; it's you or him, and the devil take the hindmost; back-street, hole-and-corner stuff; a rat's death for a loser.[7]

This is not a programme, it's not even advice: it is simply the intellectual's day-dream of action, in the language of public-school boys.

The most interesting passage in the 'Letter' comes at the end of a list of activities that Day Lewis is recommending for a left-wing student's long vacation. He urges him first to spend his time 'investigating the temper of the people' and 'the methods of capitalism', and then goes on to:

> 3. Promoting the will to obey. Not the capacity to be bullied; there is too much bullying already, far too much officious inter-ference, especially in the middle classes. But the will to obey. 'All men say they want a leader. Then let them in their souls submit to some greater soul than theirs,' Lilly says in *Aaron's Rod*. Not the obedience of man to his machine, his instrument, but the submission of a man to his natural leader. Create—recreate, I should say—that will in yourself and the people, and half your task is done. That is to say, if there is in you and your friends the new life which alone is justified in demanding spiritual

submission. Which brings us back to the beginning again. Be still in your own soul, as Lawrence would say: do you feel new life springing there?[8]

This use of Lawrence as a guide to young communists is odd, but not really surprising; after all, Auden did much the same thing, though more obscurely, in *The Orators*. And the point to be made is the same: Day Lewis might call the revolution that he looked for communist, but there is no ideology in his essay. What he was expressing was simply the desire for leadership in a leaderless time, and one feels, as with Auden, that he might as easily have become a fascist as a communist.[9]

The poems by Day Lewis that are included in *New Country* confirm that conclusion; what else are we to make of lines like these:

> We can tell you a secret, offer a tonic; only
> Submit to the visiting angel, the strange new healer.[10]

We may see Lawrence in this 'new healer', as we do in Auden's Leader, but the point is not one of literary influence; the question is, why were intelligent young writers in the early 'thirties influenced by this authoritarian and mystical element in Lawrence's writing, which to a later generation is likely to seem both unattractive and foolish? Obviously, it was because the question of leadership was an open one at the time, with the alternatives to democracy still untested, and only the failure of democratic leadership as an evident truth.

Day Lewis' 'Letter' is important as a symptom of a state of mind; its significance, one might say, lies in its confusion. Spender's 'Poetry and Revolution' is a different matter: it is important because it is thoughtful, lucid, and honest (the qualities that his best poems also have). The problem that Spender deals with is one that every artist in the 'thirties had to face: what is the right relation between art and action? It is a question that inevitably arose as soon as the generation began to take on definition: Roberts acknowledged it in his preface to *New Signatures*, and it is the issue that Murry and Day Lewis quarrelled over in their exchange in the *Adelphi*. But Spender was the first of the young writers to address the question at length, and with critical and moral intelligence.

Spender's essay is an act of self-defence against an invisible but easily imagined antagonist—a hard-line communist, with a set of accusations and demands that are new to literary discourse. This new opponent argues that the bourgeois artist is an idealist and an individualist, and that what he writes is necessarily bourgeois propaganda, whereas it is the duty of the revolutionary artist to produce revolutionary propaganda and proletarian art. Spender opens his defence with a defiant sentence: 'Of human activities, writing poetry is one of the least revolutionary,' and goes on to argue the case for a traditional view of the artist, even in a revolutionary time. There is, he says, an inevitable relation between an artist and his culture: a bourgeois cannot choose to join the proletariat *as an artist*, because his imagination and his creative sources are formed, and will remain bourgeois; and in any case there is no proletarian tradition for him to attach himself to. But what he writes need not be propaganda for his own class; if he is truly an artist, his work will perform art's historic role of revealing to men the reality of the present and the past. So art will serve the revolution by telling revolutionaries the truth.

Spender argued that artists should not let themselves be 'led astray into practical politics'. He based his argument on the conviction—which he held throughout the 'thirties—that there is a deeper sense of *political*, beyond party politics, which is simply the truth about historic public issues, and which it is the artist's responsibility to reveal. This is a romantic notion of the artist, as a man with a superior morality and a higher responsibility (that 'other Shelley' that Read heard is speaking here), but it is a strong defence against the demand for submersion of self in party.

One other point in Spender's essay must be noted. Arguing for the necessity of poetry, he wrote:

> Poetry is a function of language, it records the changing uses of words and fixes their meaning, it preserves certain words in their pure and historic meaning, it saves the language from degenerating into looseness.[11]

Discussion of the nature of language went on all during the 'thirties, especially among Marxist critics. The question, in Marxian terms, was whether language is to be understood as a part of the structure of reality, or whether it is a part of the changing superstructure that societies build upon reality. If the former, then it has an autonomous existence, but if the latter, it can be regarded as instrumental and relative. One can see that this is essentially an argument between language-as-art and language-as-propaganda, and that Spender, in urging the function of poetry as a preserver of pure meanings, was being conservative and counterrevolutionary, in spite of his expressed political sympathies.

The fact that these essays by Day Lewis and Spender were included among the stories and poems of *New Country* suggests two points, which the other contributions confirm: first, that these young writers had become more aware of the political ambiance of their time, and second, that they were by no means agreed on what the consequences should be for their work. One finds the words *communist* and *communism*, and the name of Lenin, scattered over the pages of *New Country* (there is none of this in *New Signatures*), but not the similarities of method and ideology that one might expect to accompany those terms. For some of these writers, this was no doubt because the exact nature and extent of their commitment was not clear; for others, it must have been simply that they didn't quite know how one went about writing revolutionary propaganda. They were, as Spender had said, bourgeois in their experience and in their literary culture; they had been raised on Eliot and Joyce, and they admired Forster and Virginia Woolf and Yeats. And where were the revolutionary models among those ancestors?

If you read through the stories in the volume, you find a range of techniques, from T. O. Beachcroft's working-class realism, through Isherwood's Forsterian story of sensibility, and Robert's satirical fantasy, to Upward's slightly Joycean interior monologue. The range of political content is also wide: Isherwood's story, on the one hand, is without apparent political meaning, while Upward's 'Sunday' was much quoted and admired as a statement about political commitment. The hero of the story is a neurotic, insecure young man who hangs about town on his day off, receiving, as Spender put it, 'the authentic, guaranteed *Waste Land* reactions, "a sense of desolation, of uncertainty, futility"'.[12] At the end he decides that he will act:

He will go back to his lodgings for lunch. He will read the news-paper, but not for more than a quarter of an hour. He will look out of the window and see the black hats and rolled umbrellas, but he will no longer be paralysed by disgust or apprehension. He will go out into the street and walk down to the harbour. He will go to the small club behind the Geisha Café. He will ask whether there is a meeting to-night. At first he may be regarded with suspicion, even taken for a police spy. And quite naturally. He will have to prove himself, to prove that he isn't a mere neurotic, an untrustworthy freak. It will take time. But it is the only hope. He will at least have made a start.[13]

It is a sign of the political uncertainty of the time that this nervous last hope—set, one notes, in the future tense, as a possibility only—should be taken as an example of political decisiveness, or for that matter as political writing at all. But it is nevertheless the most political story in the volume.

The poems in *New Country* resemble each other more than the stories do, no doubt because the generation had thus far been led by its poets, and so had been more influenced by the style of its own stars—especially by Auden and Spender, who appear here, not only in their own work, but scattered through the poems of Richard Goodman, Charles Madge, and Day Lewis. But even the leaders seem uncertain as to the poetic stance they should adopt. Consider, for example, the four poems by Auden included in the book: 'A Communist to Others', 'A Happy New Year' (a longish, muddled dream satire of which only the second part was ever reprinted), 'Prologue' ('O love, the interest itself in thought-less Heaven'), and 'Poem' ('Me, March, you do with your move-ments master and rock'). These four poems show an extreme range of styles—between what Leavis called Auden's 'guerrilla vein' and his denser and more literary manner; of tones—between the hearty-jocular and the inward-sensitive; and of subjects—between public issues and private feelings. Only 'Prologue' comes anywhere near being a good poem, and together the four suggest that Auden was simply not sure of what he was supposed to be doing. 'A Communist to Others' can only be explained as a con-scious (and unfortunate) attempt at direct propaganda, but if that is the poet's role, then what about 'Poem', which begins by imitating Hopkins and ends by imitating Yeats, and which deals with a relationship that may be either revolutionary or homosexual, or possibly both? Perhaps the best description of the lot is a couple of lines from 'A Happy New Year': 'these blurring images/ Of the dingy, difficult life of our generation.' The dinginess and the difficulty are there, all right, and so is the sense of a troubled generation; but these aren't sufficient to make blurred poems good.

Yet for all the uncertainties, *New Country* does have a kind of unity that *New Signatures* didn't have. One can discover the terms of that unity by examining Roberts' preface. It is very different from the preface that he had written for the earlier volume; that one was tentative and fragmented, more a set of possible problems than an argument, but this one is confident and assertive, and full of defining statements about his own generation and its political situation. By now the definition of the generation itself is fixed in his mind—it is 'the men who were just too young to serve in the war'; and so is their principal problem—they 'found themselves in a world which possessed no traditions by which they would regulate their lives'.[14] These statements slide into the argument with the ease of accepted truisms that don't require defending, and I take it that Roberts is simply restating what has by now come to be taken for granted.

As for the political situation, Roberts' preface sets it up in terms of two subjects: the nature of revolution and the condition of England, subjects which recur through the poems and stories in the book, and indeed run centrally through the writing of the 'thirties. I can give Roberts' sense of these terms best simply by quoting his preface:

On Revolution:

I think, and the writers in this book obviously agree, that there is only one way of life for us: to renounce the (capitalist) system now and to live by fighting against it.

It is time that those who conserve something which is still valuable in England began to see that only a revolution can save their standards.

On England:

> Plainly, you [the bourgeoisie] love your country, even though we cannot always understand you. And you see clearly enough the symptoms of her illness. Cannot you see that they are all symptoms of the one disease?
>
> It is not that we are pessimists: we have indeed greater faith in England than you.
>
> It is for us to prepare the way for an English Lenin . . .[15]

Roberts assumes that there must be a revolution to cure the English sickness, but that it will conserve and not destroy essential English values; and he speaks of the revolution in terms, like *faith* and *prepare the way*, that have an oddly religious tone about them. In his use of these terms he was representative of his generation, or at least of those articulate members of it who had contributed to *New Country*. What they were all expressing in these terms were ideas so central to the consciousness of the time that they might be called two of the generation's myths: the Myth of Revolution and the Myth of England. *Myth* is perhaps a bit pretentious for what I mean, but I don't know of a better word; I am thinking of the way ideas gather about them certain images and feelings, and then tend to be treated in terms of those accumulations. In the 'thirties, young English writers imagined England and the revolution in certain recurrent images that carried emotional loadings, and those complexes of images and feelings became attached to the terms themselves, and so became, loosely speaking, myths.

Revolution and *revolutionary* began to appear in the work of young English writers occasionally in 1932, and more frequently in 1933. Roberts' two prefaces are fair examples: *revolutionary* appears once in the *New Signatures* preface, but there are ten *revolutionaries* and two *revolutions* in the preface to *New Country*. The action that these words name also occurs more frequently in the generation's writings from this time on, in images that at first seem surprising—not the much-praised modern images that Day Lewis and Auden made current, but traditional images, from the Bible (Noah's flood) and from romantic pastoralism (spring after winter). Here, as an example, is a bit of Rex Warner's 'Four Choruses from "The Dam"':

109

When on the flooded plain the wreck settles and we build again, having decently laid to rest the remains of the strong ghost, we will turn back this river to land which long time or ever has waited for the life of water and for our great leader . . .

And some lines from an untitled poem by John Lehmann:

> But here is promise too among the wreck,
> New thoughts expand eclipsing forms that waste,
> The green of a new world, as the young trees
> In woods grow under withered boughs . . .[16]

And here, to move outside the covers of *New Country*, are stanzas from a poem by Randall Swingler published in June 1933:

> . . . It is time the late bud broke,
> The leaves of love uncurled,
> To submerge the whimpering self
> Amid the living world,
>
> To ride the storm, go on
> And let the dead lament,
> Expand the trade-routes, settle
> New regions of content.
>
> And love's first freedom find
> In this its certain hour.
> Bursting the dams, to loosen
> The equal flood of power.[17]

There are two things to be said about these examples (which could be multiplied many times from the publications of the period). First, they are all concerned with natural or supernatural change—change, that is, accomplished without human agents. And second, they are all *literary*: that is, they show the influence of that bourgeois poetic tradition that Spender recognized as an unavoidable source. The Swingler poem makes a third point, which I have noted before: that by 1933, the 'thirties generation was its own influence (Swingler's principal debt is obviously to Day Lewis).

Faith that an extreme change will come without human agency

is not a political belief, but a religious one, and there is a good deal that one could call religious in the Myth of Revolution. In many writings of this date, messianic figures appear: Warner's 'great leader', Day Lewis' 'new healer', Auden's 'Him'. And there are notes of what, in religious writing, one would call Enthusiasm —emotional, personal testaments that belong to the religious tradition of confession and conversion. Such a testament is Charles Madge's 'Letter to the Intelligentsia', a poem included in *New Country*. It is the confession of an alienated ex-public-schoolboy:

> Sitting alone on summer mornings, wondering
> How long the isolation would go on,
> Remembering Winchester . . .

He is sick; but then, he thinks, 'all men are ill . . . No getting better.' But a cure does come, and when it does it is miraculous:

> But there waited for me in the summer morning,
> Auden, fiercely. I read, shuddered and knew
> And all the world's stationary things
> In silence moved to take up new positions . . .[18]

Madge became a communist, and his poem urges the intelligentsia to join 'the team'. But the change he describes is not really a political one: Auden enters the poem not as an ideologue but as a healer, a Prophet or an Evangelist who brings the Good News. And of course Madge *couldn't* have got an ideology from Auden; if what he read was *Poems* or *The Orators* he could have absorbed at most the emotional beginnings of the Myth of Revolution.

It must have embarrassed Auden to be cast as a prophet in the Myth, but so he was. He appears again in *New Country* in a poem by Day Lewis, where he is invoked as 'Wystan, lone flyer, birdman, my bully boy!' (that is, as his own Airman), and both Day Lewis and Roberts quote in their essays unidentified phrases from Auden's poems, as one might quote from Scripture: 'in country houses at the ends of drives' and 'What do you think about England, this country of ours where nobody is well?' Clearly by 1933 Auden was a larger-than-life figure in a movement that was political in general intention, but was religious in tone, and literary in its manifestations.

England also appears again and again in both the prose and verse in *New Country*, in ways that suggest that these writers were as nationalistic in their way as the Georgian poets were. Their England is a curious mixture of contradictory elements, pastoral and derelict, lovable and sick, and their attitude toward their country is equally mixed, part love and part social criticism. So Auden, invoking Love on behalf of England, echoes Shakespeare's John of Gaunt:

> Here too on our little reef display your power,
> This fortress perched on the edge of the Atlantic scarp,
> The mole between all Europe and the exile-crowded sea;
>
> And make us as Newton was who in his garden watching
> The apple falling towards England became aware
> Between himself and her of an eternal tie,

but goes on to describe the present where

> inertly wait
> In bar, in netted chicken-farm, in lighthouse,
> Standing on these impoverished constricting acres,
> The ladies and gentlemen apart, too much alone.

And Day Lewis, in a poem from *The Magnetic Mountain*, addresses

> You that love England, who have an ear for her music . . .
> Cyclists and hikers in company, day excursionists,
> Refugees from cursed towns and devastated areas . . .

And Madge:

> Yes, England, I was at school with you, I've known
> Your hills come open to me, call me crying
> With bird voice . . .[19]

There is a good deal here that is in the tradition of Georgian 'week-end pastoral': the towns are ugly, the country is beautiful, and the spiritual force of England is linked to the natural world. But there is another, new set of conventions, which derive from Auden Country: images of industrial ruin and social sickness, of urban bleakness and poverty, and of the ordinary objects and actions of everyday life, and melodramatic images of guerrilla warfare against that dying society.

Like the Myth of Revolution, the Myth of England is essentially literary. It affirms, in its conventional pastoral images, that Shakespeare's England still exists, and that it still sustains lyric poets; but it embraces also a contrary set of images which carry the sense of England's crises—the problems that must be solved through action before the lyric vision will be valid once more. It is a myth that is by no means peculiar to *New Country* writers; you can find it as well in another important book of 1933, George Orwell's *Down and Out in Paris and London*, wherever Orwell's wanderings take him into the English countryside.

These two myths have common elements that are significant for the course of 'thirties writing: they are both literary, and both preserve a connection with the traditional past, and neither is strictly speaking either political or revolutionary. They share the sense of a nation in trouble and needing extreme change, but a nation that will retain its essential traditional qualities, including its literary qualities. These are myths to comfort young writers in a time of disorder and discontinuity, and it is from these shared myths, and not from common political, or for that matter aesthetic, convictions, that the *New Country* writers derived such unity as they had. It is surprising, to any one who has read the book through, that reviewers should have found political uniformity there, but they did. Bonamy Dobree, reviewing the book in the *Listener*, concluded that 'they are on the whole communists, but communists with an intense love for England', and Leavis, in *Scrutiny*, observed that 'the Communism of the Group offers an interesting study'.[20] A more interesting study would be to try to discover what notion of communism these critics shared that could be applied to such heterogenous writers. The point is, it would seem, that in the early 'thirties almost no one outside the Party had a very clear idea of what communism was.

One of the reviewers of *New Country* was Geoffrey Grigson, who dealt with the book in a characteristically severe way in *New Verse*. It is an important review, because both Grigson and *New Verse* were important—a good deal more important and more influential in the literary 'thirties than *New Signatures* and *New Country* were. In the six years of its publishing life—from January 1933 to January 1939—it published more good poems by young poets, and more unfavourable reviews, than any other English journal. *New Verse* did not exactly speak *for* the generation—it was too individualistic for that—but it spoke *to* the generation, and so both recorded the changing consciousness of the decade and helped to change it by the judgments it made. Grigson was an editor of independent mind, great intelligence, and strict literary values, who insisted on the naked distinction between good art and bad art, and he brought a moral ferocity to his work that made for a good magazine and many enemies. In the first number of *New Verse* he set down his intentions in founding it:

> The object of *New Verse* needs expansion in no complex or tiring manifesto. Poets in this country and during this period of the victory of the masses, aristocratic and bourgeois as much as proletarian, which have captured the instruments of access to the public and use them to convey their own once timid and silent vulgarity, vulgarizing all the arts, are allowed no longer periodical means of communicating their poems. . . .
>
> *New Verse*, then, has a clear function. When respectable poems (as it believes) are being written and forced to remain in type-script, it can add itself as a publishing agent to those few publishers who bring out (with conscience money) a few books of verse. It favours only its time, belonging to no literary or politico-literary cabal, cherishing bombs only for masqueraders and for the everlasting 'critical' rearguard of nastiness, now represented so ably and variously by the *Best Poems of the Year*, the Book Society and all the gang of big shot reviewers . . . If the poem is only one organism in the creation of which those [human] experiences are collected, concentrated, transmitted, it is the chief organism; and one (incidentally) in such an ulcerous period as our own which can serve magnificently.[21]

Grigson's critical goals are certainly clear enough here: he meant to run an elitist, highbrow magazine that would draw up sides in the traditional way—artists against philistines, good art against bad, avant-garde against rearguard—and would avoid political commitment. But the fact that he chose to put his intentions in the form of such an aggressive manifesto suggests that he knew from the start how strong the political pressures would be, even on a magazine of verse. The state of society that he describes is not unlike the account that Auden or Day Lewis might have offered; it is diseased (his term is *ulcerous*, a characteristically extreme version of the common metaphor), and it is nasty in a uniquely modern way. Such a view ought to have political consequences, but Grigson chose to resist them, at least within the pages of his journal.

His resistance was not very successful. In the second number he had to repeat, a little desperately, that *New Verse* was not political:

> ... *New Verse* has no politics. 'New' does not mean a deterministic end or postulate an unplanked-ditch between present-future and the whole past. It means only fresh, contemporaneous, new written, and we shall work to find verse to which these epithets belong, to publish criticism which is of value and not only of propaganda value. Individualism is required. If there must be attitudes, a reasoned attitude of toryism is welcome no less than a communist attitude.[22]

But in fact the reasoned toryism never appeared, perhaps because, among the poets and critics of Grigson's generation, it did not exist. The will to be wide-ranging was there, but the wide range wasn't.

New Country provided Grigson an opportunity to demonstrate his critical principles, and he reviewed it in the second issue. His strategy was to judge the contents on *his* grounds, simply as art, and to treat the political content as a dangerous kind of pollution. In his judgment, only Auden, Spender, and Upward were artists, though he grudgingly allowed that 'Day Lewis cannot make himself entirely a bad artist and symptoms of good art show in the verse of Rex Warner and Charles Madge'. But always the operative term is *Art*. So, in criticizing Day Lewis, he observed that 'briefly the best propaganda is art; and Day Lewis is too able to wither himself as a poet by being politically active'. As one might expect, he admired Spender's 'Poetry and Revolution' for its truth-telling, and for its sense of the danger that revolutionary ideas raised for the artist. And he despised Roberts: 'He does not think. He feels without thought, and feeling without thought is passive. It is sentimentality. It is not action in politics; or action in literature, which is art.'[23] The tone is characteristic of Grigson and his journal—harsh, contemptuous, and unforgiving; but then he was not simply reviewing a muddled book, he was writing a polemic against the enemies of Art.

It was a worthy cause, but from the beginning it was a losing one. *New Verse* was political, left-wing, and propagandist from its beginning, because the writers whom Grigson admired and wanted to publish were political. So, in the first number, one finds Auden's 'I have a handsome profile', two poems from Day Lewis' *Magnetic Mountain*, and Naomi Mitchison's 'To Some Young Communists from an Old Socialist'. And the second number, which contains Grigson's attack on propaganda-writers, also includes Charles Madge's explicitly communist poem, 'Instructions', an aggressive example of just what Grigson was deploring on another page.

By the third number, in May 1933, Grigson seems to have capitulated. The front-page article in this issue, an essay by Charles Madge entitled 'Poetry and Politics', is a direct attack on Grigson, and on the Spender essay that Grigson had admired. Madge begins:

> In the last number of *New Verse*, Geoffrey Grigson successfully confused the issues raised by Stephen Spender in his essay on Poetry and Revolution. These are important issues for readers of *New Verse*, so I ask them to pay attention while I start all over again.[24]

Madge's position was flatly contradictory of Spender's, a point that he made clear by simply reversing some of Spender's key sentences: of human activities, writing poetry is the most revolutionary; the problem which the poem solves is not the poem's, but the poet's problem; there is no world but the world and that world is the poem's world. The argument that follows is rather confused, but the principal point is clear enough: it is wrong to withdraw from life into a world of the imagination. Bad poets separate themselves from ordinary experience, travel, and write poems about the things they have seen (clearly this refers to

Spender and Lehmann); good poets stay at home, have jobs, and write poems that are not separate from the rest of their lives (Madge's example is Auden, the schoolmaster-poet). Salvation lies in commitment, and the essay ends with the quotation that was becoming the standard text on the subject, the last paragraph of Upward's 'Sunday', about the Geisha Café.

It is possible to admire an editor who would publish such a direct refutation of his own views, and it seems at first glance that in doing so Grigson was simply demonstrating his own objective standards. But the real point is simply that in 1933 even an editor as acute, intelligent, and dedicated as Grigson could not choose to be politically neutral. He might invite tories to express their reasoned attitudes, but none would turn up; and he might go on anathematizing propaganda, but propaganda would still be written, and it would be propaganda for the Left, and he would print it anyway, because it was by the best poets of his generation, and not to print it would be to falsify the spirit of his time. To Grigson's credit he kept *New Verse* as various as he could; and he raised his voice, in that noisy decade, against bad art. Forty years on, his journal retains its life, its acerb flavour, and its intelligence. There is no better guide to the literary tone of the 'thirties.

III

In 'The Poet and Revolution', Day Lewis had said of the revolutionary poet: 'If the capitalist system is dead, his poetry will expose the fact . . . If there is new life about, you may be sure he will catch it.' When he wrote those words he was in the midst of writing *The Magnetic Mountain*, and it is clear that that sequence of poems was intended to do just what he said: it was to put the dead life and the new life together in one poem, and by doing so to demonstrate that poetry and revolution were compatible.

Day Lewis was at work on the sequence throughout 1932, and as individual poems were finished they were published in various places—three in *New Signatures*, two in the first number of *New Verse*, four in *New Country*—so that by the time it appeared entire, his poetry-reading contemporaries knew a good deal about it. They knew that the mountain symbolized a goal for their generation, a new life; they knew that Auden was an important figure in it; and they knew that it satirized sick members of society. And they recognized that once more Day Lewis was following the dictates of his natural lyric gift, and making a long work out of short lyrics, as he had done in *Transitional Poem* and *From Feathers to Iron*.

What they couldn't know was that this time Day Lewis was trying for something more ambitious—a parabolic whole made of individual lyric parts, comparable, perhaps, to *The Orators*. And the sequence, taken together, *is* a parable in form: that is, it has a non-realistic narrative line that carries a central moral meaning. A young man prepares to leave a sick country and to seek a new, healthy one. Before he leaves he makes one last excursion of the country he is leaving, rejecting and condemning its sick inhabitants; then he exhorts other young men to join him in his strenuous adventure, and the poem ends. There is the embracing parable of the symbolic journey, and within it shorter sequences that are essentially parable-trials, or perhaps *arraignments* is a more exact term, of 'Defendants' and 'Enemies'.

The Magnetic Mountain addresses Auden directly in two poems, and is dedicated to him; and well it might be, for one can see at once, even from the sketchy description I have just offered, how much it owes to Auden's work. The journey is a recurrent motif in Auden's early poems, a trial occurs in *Paid on Both Sides*, and the Enemy is from *The Orators*. The tone of voice that Day Lewis adopts is also frequently Auden's: the Prosecuting Attorney confronting a felonious villain, the Scoutmaster haranguing a slack troop, the Head of School chastising a bully—all these are familiar voices from the Auden canon. Many characters in Day Lewis' poem are also familiar: spies and airmen, wicked press lords, dependent sons, and lonely adventurers; and so are the places: abandoned rail-lines, mines, and derelict mills. Day Lewis had been under Auden's influence since their Oxford days, but this time, as one critic put it, he had completely surrendered.[25]

But why the surrender at this time? Because Day Lewis wrote this sequence during the period in which the political consciousness of his generation increased so dramatically—roughly from the date of the defeat of the Labour Party in November 1931, to the beginning of Hitler's Chancellorship, in January 1933. It was a time of great change, and Auden had invented a rhetoric of change. To Day Lewis, Auden must have seemed, as he did to most members of his generation, a man of certainty who had solved his problems, private and public, poetic and political, simply by giving thought to them. And the style was the man, so that its authority, which was immense, lay not simply in its originality, but also in its apparent decisiveness.

Still, to imitate Auden is not to *be* Auden, and *The Magnetic Mountain* suffers a good deal by comparison with *The Orators*. Auden's work is wilfully obscure and private, but it nevertheless succeeds in convincing a careful reader that it deals justly with its theme. In his treatment of Leadership Auden has allowed for private emotions and frailties—for guilt, fear, anxiety, and the need for love—as well as for public virtues, and his use of the first-person in 'Letter to a Wound' and 'Journal of an Airman' makes possible a note of self-doubt and self-involvement. You may feel in the end that *The Orators* is imperfect, but you will not feel that it has been rigged.

The Magnetic Mountain is another matter. In it the oppositions that Auden saw to be complex have been simplified and hardened. Day Lewis has set dead life against new life, and Us against Them, and these antitheses are polar and absolute; death and corruption belong entirely to one side, and life and virtue to the other, and the speaker of the poem knows which is the good side, and is on it. In Auden's own terms, *The Orators* is a parable art, but *The Magnetic Mountain* is a work that attempts parable, but succeeds only in being propaganda.

The shortcomings of Day Lewis' poem as a parable are most apparent in the two series of 'arraignments' that occur in parts Two and Three. The first group, four 'Defendants', speak for middle-class security: Mother and Home, School, Church, Wife, and Marriage; they belong to the dead life, and the speaker rejects them all, though he speaks to the women with some tenderness. The second group are 'Enemies': Lust, the Press, Scientific Religion, Poetic Day-Dreaming; these too are cast off, this time more savagely and satirically. Together the two groups compose one collective antagonist, a social status quo that has much in common with Auden's Enemy. But Day Lewis' treatment is a good deal less subtle and less satisfactory than Auden's; his speaker is a superior prig, and the victories he wins are too easy. What, for example, is one to say of a young man who puts sexuality aside in these terms:

> Not hate or love, but say
> Refreshment after rain,
> A lucid hour; though this
> Need not occur again . . .
>
> Hands off! The dykes are down.
> This is no time for play.
> Hammer is poised and sickle
> Sharpened. I cannot stay.[26]

The failure here is partly a failure of tact, and partly of tactics. Political passion should not coarsen our responses to life, or to our antagonists: if they are worth opposing, they are worth exact treatment. But Day Lewis had set out to make commitment easy, and his opponents go down before him like ducks in a shooting gallery.

Still, the Enemies and their dead life are fairly explicit—one knows what Day Lewis is against. It is a good deal less clear what he is for. The parabolic journey in his poem is ostensibly a quest for the magnetic mountain, but in fact it is more an escape *from* than a journey *to*. This is a quality common to most such journeys in the writings of the time (for example, Auden's 'To throw away the key' in *Paid on Both Sides*), and it reflects a quite understandable state of mind: in a time of social stagnation and decay, the desire for change manifests itself as an almost physical need to leave the ruins, even though the destination is unclear; rejection is at least a kind of action. And so the particulars of the place left behind may be quite specific, while the place ahead is bound to be vague; and much emphasis will be placed on the merit of strenuous effort in itself, apart from the goal.

But though this is understandable, it gives to the note of praise and celebration of the new life a rather hollow ring. And there is a lot of this in *The Magnetic Mountain*—celebration of the mountain itself as though it were a clear symbol of explicit values, though in fact one cannot determine from the text just what the mountain does symbolize. What Day Lewis says is this:

> Near that miraculous mountain
> Compass and clock must fail,
> For space stands on its head there
> And time chases its tail.
>
> There's iron for the asking
> Will keep all winds at bay,
> Girders to take the leaden
> Strain of a sagging sky.
>
> Oh there's a mine of metal,
> Enough to make me rich
> And build right over chaos
> A cantilever bridge.[27]

But what is to be concluded from that? That the mountain provides strength, and cancels customary guiding instruments, and that it conquers chaos. In terms of the earlier parts of the poem, it seems to offer an alternative security that will be more strenuous and more manly than Mother, the Church, and the Middle Class. But beyond that one can't say much.

Nor can one say much about the young men who will seek it. They will be heroes, of course, self-sacrificing and dedicated; and they will be comrades:

> We are going about together, we've mingled blood,
> Taken a tonic that's set us up for good . . . [28]

And two of them will be 'Wystan 'and 'Rex'. It was a propos of *The Magnetic Mountain* that MacNeice coined the phrase 'myths of themselves', and perhaps this is the place to put that phrase in its context. MacNeice was writing about the strong personal element in the writings of Auden, Spender, and Day Lewis. 'The personal element,' he wrote,

is a bridge between the topical and the heroic; these poets make myths of themselves and of each other (a practice which often leads to absurdity, e.g. Day-Lewis's mythopoeic hero worship of Auden in *The Magnetic Mountain*). This personal obsession can be collated with their joint communist outlook via the concept of comradeship . . . Comradeship is the communist substitute for bourgeois romance; in its extreme form (cp. also fascism and youth-cults in general) it leads to an idealisation of homosexuality.[29]

Day Lewis' band of brothers is not homosexual, but it is certainly romantic, and performs essentially the same function for the literary revolutionary that bourgeois romance does for the shopgirl; it is a day-dream of belonging, an escape from fear and loneliness in a hostile world. In this sense, *The Magnetic Mountain* is the opposite of parable-art, it is escape-art: it rejects the present society, and imagines a revolutionary brotherhood, but it doesn't imagine the revolution.

Formally, the poem is an uneasy mixture of modes—propaganda trying to be parable, parable becoming escape, lyric sliding into polemic, and polemic lapsing into lyric. The lyric-polemic problem is partly a consequence of the form of the poem: the series of short lyrics encouraged Day Lewis' most pronounced poetic gift, and worked against his political intentions. The roots of lyric verse are in private experience, and cannot easily be cut off; in trying to use the lyric tradition for public subjects Day Lewis was putting two sides of his consciousness in conflict, and the resulting poem oscillates uneasily between a Georgian simplicity and histrionics. In the end, one must conclude that it was a poem written by the time, and across the grain of the poet's natural gift. If it survives at all now, it does so only in a few lines here and there that owe nothing to Auden, and have nothing to do with history, and so can live on as themselves, lines like these:

> You that love England, who have an ear for her music,
> The slow movement of clouds in benediction,
> Clear arias of light thrilling over her uplands,
> Over the chords of summer sustained peacefully . . .[30]

But the polemical poem is dead.

One thing remains to be said of *The Magnetic Mountain*: that like *The Orators*, it is a poem about Leadership, and a rather sinister one. For this Leader is a saviour:

Where then the saviour, the stop of illness? . . .
Alone who soars, who feeds upon earth—
Him shall you heed and learn where joy is
The dance of action, the expert eye.[31]

And his authority, like that of his equivalent in *The Orators*, seems to be absolute and irrational, and more out of Lawrence than out of Marx:

As needle to north, as wheel in wheel turning,
Men shall know their masters and women their need,
Mating and submitting, not dividing and defying,
Force shall fertilise, mass shall breed.[32]

It is a versification of Day Lewis' advice in *New Country*, about 'Promoting the will to obey'.

In Day Lewis' romantic politics of Comradeship, the saviour seems a benign mythical figure, a sort of Chief Scout. But in the spring of 1933, when the poem was published, the mythical Leader was already real: Hitler was Chancellor of Germany. A political possibility beyond customary democratic assumptions had been made actual, and if it was threatening, it also promised to be heroic and mythic; indeed the Nazis were already busy mythologizing themselves with all the teutonic ceremonies they could invent. The time seemed ripe for the return of heroes, and this had implications for literature, as well as for politics.

IV

While Day Lewis was writing his dream of heroic comrades, Auden was at work on two parables of his own which deny that dream. The first of these, 'The Witnesses', is a ballad-like poem in Auden's popular manner which manages to be both jocular and ominous; it is one of the most successful of Auden's parables of this period.

The poem is a cautionary tale, with commentary, told by two 'witnesses', figures with power over human lives that is neither explained nor defined. The parable that they tell is the story of Prince Alpha, a young man with all possible human gifts, who sets out, as Auden's heroes so often do, on a questing journey into the wide world. His adventures are fairytale heroics: he wanders the world, rescues maidens, overthrows giants, and slaughters dragons. At last he comes to a desert, and there, between two black rocks, he sits and cries:

> 'I thought my strength could know no stemming
> But I was as foolish as a lemming;
>   for what
> Was I born, was it only to see
> I'm tired of life as life of me?
>   let me be forgot.
>
> Children have heard of my every action
> It gives me no sort of satisfaction
>   and why?
> Let me get this as clear as I possibly can
> No, I am not the truly strong man,
>   O let me die'.[33]

And there, between the rocks, he does die.

This story, the witnesses tell us, 'has of course a morale', and they proceed to explain what it is. Prince Alpha was treated as he was because he had offended them. But what are they, exactly? Well,

> You are the town, and we are the clock,
> We are the guardians of the gate in the rock,
>   the Two,
> On your left, and on your right
> In the day, and in the night
>   we are watching you.

They represent, then, the idea of limitation itself: they are essentially the same as those 'Lords of limit' who are invoked in 'A Happy New Year':

> O Lords of limit, training dark and light
> And setting a tabu 'twixt left and right:
> The influential quiet twins
> From whom all property begins . . .[34]

Prince Alpha, because he thought his perfections were infinite, was destroyed by the knowledge of limitation, and, the witnesses remind us, 'we are watching you'. The parable of the failed quest is a warning: those who ignore or exceed limits are overtaken by disaster. The poem ends on a series of vivid, nightmarish images of terror, and a mild warning to be careful, and to remember the Two.

'The Witnesses' is an excellent example of what I mean by a parable. It tells a story of evident non-literal meaning, and it contains its own 'morale', but it is not didactic; the poem is more nightmare than allegory, and though nightmares may be parables of the unconscious, they are not entirely explicable, an essential obscurity remains. This is the way the poem struck an intelligent contemporary. Michael Roberts, in a lecture on 'The Fantastic Element in English Literature', said of 'The Witnesses':

> The important thing about the poem is, it seems to me, that Auden has managed to write a fantasy and an allegory at the same time. It is a nightmare which has been given a meaning, and the meaning is impressive and convincing because the nightmare-effect convinces us that there is something still more profound lurking behind the meaning.[35]

Another contemporary who was impressed by 'The Witnesses' was Harold Nicolson. He was at a house party in August 1933, at which Auden read the longer allegorical poem of which 'The Witnesses' was then a part, and, as he wrote in his diary, it disturbed him:

> It is not so much a defence of communism as an attack upon all the ideas of comfort and complacency which will make communism difficult to achieve in this country . . . A man like Auden with his fierce repudiation of half-way houses and his gentle integrity makes one feel terribly discontented with one's own smug successfulness. I go to bed feeling terribly Edwardian and back-number, and yet, thank God, delighted that people like Wystan Auden should actually exist.[36]

Nicolson's account of the allegory of the longer poem is essentially correct, but one would have to adjust it to fit the section that became 'The Witnesses'. For though the whole may be read as a poem about the difficulties of achieving communism (or any ideal social condition), the shorter parable within it is more general; it is about the obstacles to any human achievement that exist in the nature of things. There will be no Heroic Communism, Auden is saying, and no trip to the Magnetic Mountain, because there are no Heroes. The parable goes *behind* politics, to a more basic idea, the idea of limit. This is a political idea only in the sense that if you accept it, political consequences follow. (It is worth noting that Auden's sources for the figures of the Witnesses are not political, but apocalyptic: the Book of Revelations, 11:8–10, and Lawrence's *Apocalypse*.[37])

The phrase that Prince Alpha uses to confess his failure is an important one: 'I am not,' he says, 'the truly strong man.' Readers of Auden's *Poems* might remember that the phrase also occurs there, in '1929' ('It was Easter as I walked in the public gardens'). Auden later used it to describe T. E. Lawrence, and Isherwood develops the idea in *Lions and Shadows*. The original source of the phrase was a case history in Eugen Bleuler's *Textbook of Psychiatry*; a man named Wagner, a paranoid mass-murderer with homosexual tendencies, had written in prison a remarkable statement of his 'philosophy', which Bleuler quotes at length. It includes this passage:

> ... I want to remark to the Nietzsche followers that the key to a comprehension of his writings is weakness. The feeling of impotence brings forth the strong words, *the bold sounds to battle are emitted by the trumpet called persecution insanity*. The signs of the truly strong are repose and good-will. The strong man, about whom we palaver in our literature, does not exist. Furthermore, there is no such things as the strong man in the rôle of a tamer of the populace. The strong individuals are those who without any fuss do their duty. These have neither the time nor the occasion to throw themselves into a pose and try to be something great.[38]

The paradox, that the apparently strong and heroic are really the weak, clearly had a particular appeal for both Auden and Isherwood. The context in which Isherwood quotes Wagner in

Lions and Shadows makes the nature of the appeal very clear. Isherwood has been describing his early efforts to write a novel to be called *The North-West Passage*, and he explains the title in this way:

> It symbolized, in my mind, the career of the neurotic hero, The Truly Weak Man—antithesis of 'the truly strong man' spoken of by the homicidal paranoiac whose statement is quoted by Bleuler . . .

He then quotes the passage I have given above, and continues:

> 'The truly strong man,' calm, balanced, aware of his strength, sits drinking quietly in the bar; it is not necessary for him to try to prove to himself that he is not afraid, by joining the Foreign Legion, seeking out the most dangerous wild animals in the remotest tropical jungles, leaving his comfortable home in a snowstorm to climb the impossible glacier. In other words, the Test exists only for the Truly Weak Man . . .[39]

Auden's Prince Alpha is the Truly Weak Man, the neurotic hero, testing himself and failing. So is the Airman, and John Nower; so are Spender's climbers, and the principal male characters in Isherwood's early novels, and many other examples of the time. The Truly Weak Man is a central 'thirties character, and the Test is his typical situation. And it is clear why this should be so, at a time when uncertain and untried young men were struggling with the problem of Leadership and the nature of right action. For history seemed to have confronted them with a unique challenge—to devise the means by which the Truly Weak Man, the introspective neurotic that most young intellectuals take themselves to be, could make himself strong and effective in the public world of crises.

'The Witnesses' is a parable of heroism and limitation, and a cautionary tale. A more elaborate example is *The Dance of Death*, the political parable in dramatic form that Auden published in November. The *Dance* is a play about a concept that is central to Marxist theory—the inevitable decline of the bourgeoisie. This theme is explicitly set out in the first speech, when an Announcer says:

We present to you this evening a picture of the decline of a class, of how its members dream of a new life, but secretly desire the old, for there is death inside them. We show you that death as a dancer.[40]

What follows, however, is not the didactic argument that one might expect after such a beginning, but a clever and sometimes very funny parody of a musical comedy, with mock chorus routines and romantic ballads, like a Noël Coward revue. Auden connects the theme with the parody by making the whole set of musical comedy conventions into a symbol of the aimless, fatuous class that he is dealing with; the routines that they perform are their 'dreams of a new life'. So we see them trying sun-bathing (like the German youth-cults), nationalism under a demagogue (fascism), 'the will of the blood' (the doctrines of D. H. Lawrence as well as of Hitler), and flight into metaphysics. In each of these routines, a dancer figures as a Leader, but always a false one. In the last scene he dies, while the chorus sings a ballad of economic history to the tune of 'Casey Jones'. Karl Marx enters, and the Chorus sings, to the tune of Mendelssohn's Wedding March,

> O Mr. Marx, you've gathered
> All the material facts
> You know the economic
> Reasons for our acts.

And Marx announces: 'The instruments of production have been too much for him. He is liquidated.'[41]

The Dancer, Auden says, represents the death-wish of the bourgeoisie (a formulation which combines two important parable-sources, Marx and Freud); his death is the death of the class, which they secretly desire. But he is not a character in the ordinary sense, and neither he nor anyone else in the play has any individual identity. In the world of this play, individualism does not matter, and individual leadership can solve nothing. The force that matters is the one that the chorus sings about—economic determinism and control of the instruments of production. There can be no Hero in such a world, and the fatuous conventions of musical comedy make it possible to write a play that doesn't need one. The Dancer does have one kind of identity, though; he is the ultimate Truly Weak Man, the expression of the neurosis of his class, and his death may be read as Auden's resolution of the ambiguities of the Leadership theme in *The Orators*. Hereafter, the agent of change will be history.

In spite of the clowning and the farce, *The Dance of Death* is a serious work—a parable of Marxist economics that makes *The Magnetic Mountain* seem sentimental and undergraduate. Auden's statement of his dramatic principles, published in the programme of a *Dance of Death* production, makes the parabolic intention very clear (see 'I Want the Theatre to Be . . .', Appendix A below). It marks an important point in Auden's development—the point at which he bade farewell to Lawrence's will of the blood and acknowledged the abstract forces of history. It is also an important demonstration of the state of mind of many members of his generation at the end of 1933, when contemporary history had forced them to turn their attentions to politics and away from their earlier, more literary interests. This was more than simply a new political awareness; it was a transformation of consciousness, by which one set of preoccupations had been replaced by another.

The best account of this transformation that I know is in a letter that Julian Bell wrote to the *New Statesman* in December 1933, part of which reads:

In the Cambridge that I first knew [Bell wrote], in 1929 and 1930, the central subject of ordinary intelligent conversations was poetry. As far as I can remember we hardly ever talked or thought about politics . . . Only the secondary problems, such as birth control, seemed to need the intervention of the intellectuals.

By the end of 1933, we have arrived at a situation in which almost the only subject of discussion is contemporary politics, and in which a very large majority of the more intelligent undergraduates are Communists, or almost Communists. As far as an interest in literature continues it has very largely changed its character, and become an ally of Communism under the influence of Mr. Auden's Oxford Group. Indeed, it might, with some plausibility, be argued that Communism in England is at present very largely a literary phenomenon—an attempt of a second 'post-war generation' to escape from the Waste Land.[42]

Bell here makes three points that seem to me of especial importance to the understanding of the generation at this moment: (1) the literary nature of political opinion; (2) the influence of Auden; and (3) the continuing force of the Waste Land vision of English society. By writing the letter, he made still another point: that at the end of 1933 his generation was self-conscious about its own unique existence, and was finding terms in which to define itself.

V

One other document of this year needs to be noticed. In the summer of 1933 Gollancz published *The Brown Book of the Hitler Terror*, an anonymous compilation of the crimes of National Socialism from its beginnings through its first months in power in the spring of 1933. The book was apparently put together by the German communist Willi Munstenberg, as a major anti-Nazi propaganda effort by European communist parties: it was translated into 23 languages, and more than 600,000 copies were distributed.[43] But its English appearance, at least, gave no indication of its sponsorship; it carried no author's name, only the statement that it had been 'prepared by the World Committee for the Victims of German Fascism', and an introduction by Lord Marley, Chairman of the Committee, vouching for the accuracy of the contents. It was the first book in English to record in such sober detail the actual behaviour of the Nazis, and it must have been highly influential in creating the general English attitude toward German fascism.

The book is divided into chapters on the principal Nazi crimes, in an ascending order of violence: the burning of the Reichstag, the destruction of workers' organizations, the campaign against culture, brutality and torture, the persecution of the Jews, the concentration camps, ending with an appendix that lists 250 murders by Nazis. Each chapter is made up of short sections, with captions rather like newspaper headlines, containing narratives of incidents, accounts of Nazi theories, and quotations from newspapers, letters, and other documents. The tone is factual, realistic, and impersonal—the tone of good journalism or of documentary. But the contents make it something more than reportage, make it rather a surreal parable of the death of liberalism and the rise of terror as a national state of mind. The principal figures in the book—Hitler, Göring, van der Lubbe—are grotesques, and the incidents in which they figure seem distorted and visionary. But so do the other, more obscure incidents that the book records— the beatings of workers, the murders of Jews, the book-burnings. The whole account is like a nightmare, but one in which Europe, the dreamer, was awake, and knew the dream to be true.

If *The Brown Book* was a true history of existence in what had been a civilized European country, then it compelled any ordinary reader to alter and extend his sense of reality, of what was possible to men in the twentieth century. If it was true—and no one questioned the essential accuracy of the reporting—then reality meant something other, and worse, than men had thought, and human beings were capable of greater evil than liberalism had allowed for. *The Brown Book* did not create this change—the Nazis did that —but it helped to force a recognition of the change upon western consciousness.

The effect of the book upon literary imaginations is difficult to establish objectively,[44] but it must have been great, and it must have worked in something like the following way: as actual, verified human behaviour (in Germany first, but later in Russia and in Spain) became more and more violent, more brutal, and more extreme, the realistic impulse in literature turned away from imaginative forms, toward literal, documentary forms. This is partly because the imagination simply could not exceed what reality offered in terror, pity, and suffering; but it is also because in these circumstances the real might have a propaganda effect, and thus be a mode of opposing action, in a way that the imaginative could not be. Put this way, the process may seem perhaps more schematic and conscious than it was, but some such process clearly did take place, and the effects on imaginative writing are there to be observed. It is certainly true that from 1933 on, documentary writing assumed an increasingly important role among the literary genres of the 'thirties, and that literary realism virtually disappeared, overwhelmed, one might say, by reality itself.

V

1934

When John Lehmann published his second book, in 1934, he
called it *The Noise of History*. The title comes from one of his prose
poems, 'Morning', in which a woman sits in the garden of a
country house:

> The voices of her children, that come to her from the upper
> rooms of the house, bring her anxiety into sharper focus. She
> sees obscurely a future that will deny the values which her life,
> her well-filled house and quiet garden are teaching them. She
> hears the angry noise of history grow louder, like the noise of
> a landslide on an island coast.[1]

This is an example of a 'thirties theme that I have noted before—
the way in which, in a critical time, the public life invades the
private, and disorders and questions it. But the theme here has a
new urgency: the angry noise of history is more frightening and
more inexorable than 'public faces in private places'. What Lehmann's book records is the thrust of contemporary events into
literary consciousness, the present felt as forces in motion, as
history.

This is not the same as that sensitivity to a 'national mood' that
appears in the earlier years of the decade. *History* implies an
irreversible movement, causation flowing and spreading from public events to consequences, the shape that time assumes as it
passes. In 1933 and 1934, public events seemed to have such
shaping power that every human act, however private, must be
moulded by them. Thus Spender, writing a year's-end summar-
izing article on 'Politics and Literature in 1933', began it this way:

> At the beginning of this year something happened in Germany
> which has added to the political self-consciousness of almost

every contemporary writer in Europe. The Hitler party came into power in February, and in March the books of writers who have had the greatest influence on European literature since the War, were banned and even formally burnt in public squares.[2]

The rise of Hitler is taken as an event in the life of literature—perhaps the most important of 1933, more important than any book or poem. That is one significant point. The other is that Spender is here talking of a *European* event in relation to *European* writers. From here on, the movements in which English writers are caught up are international movements, and it becomes impossible to think of their writing in terms of English traditions: one touch of fascism makes the whole world kin.

The most imaginatively powerful events of 1933—the events that seemed to become instantly part of a new demonology—were the succession of Hitler to the German Chancellorship, and the burning of the Reichstag. The year that followed added more events to the same myth: in January the execution (by decapitation with an axe) of Van der Lubbe, the man convicted of setting the Reichstag on fire; in February the Socialist uprising in Vienna, and its suppression; in June the 'Night of the Long Knives', when Hitler purged his own followers by assassination; in July the murder of Dollfuss, Chancellor of Austria; in October the assassination of King Alexander of Yugoslavia.

In England one event seemed part of the same sinister mythology, and therefore deeply disturbing: in June Mosley's British Union of Fascists rallied in Olympia, a public meeting-hall in West London, and hecklers at the meeting were suppressed with a violence that shocked spectators. Mosley had promised 'something new in the political life of this country', and had provided it: 'I witnessed,' said the pacifist clergyman Dick Sheppard, '. . . scenes of great brutality such as I had never thought to see in England.'[3] That sense of violation, of un-English violence invading England, is also part of the story; henceforth no private world would be secure against the pressure of events.

That pressure is the subject of one of Auden's finest poems of this period, 'Summer Night' (first published in March 1934). The night referred to was an actual one, in the summer of 1933, and later, in the *Collected Poems*, Auden added the date to the title—not, I take it, to fix where he was and what he was doing, but to locate the private feelings of the poem in history. In that year, the poem begins, in England, a private and privileged life was still possible: one could lie on a moonlit lawn with one's friends and feel secure, and free to endure the 'tyrannies of love'. This private world of amorous love and 'kindness to ten persons' Auden renders in a static, timeless allegorical mode, as a Peaceable Kingdom:

> ... these evenings when
> Fear gave his watch no look;
> The lion griefs loped from the shade
> And on our knees their muzzles laid,
> And Death put down his book.[4]

It is a world without time, and hence without fear, or grief, or death. But it is sustained by a willed ignorance; the gentlefolk inside the garden

> do not care to know
> Where Poland draws her Eastern bow,
> What violence is done;
> Nor ask what doubtful act allows
> Our freedom in this English house,
> Our picnics in the sun.

There is an historical reason for Poland here; in June 1933 there were riots in Galicia, and no doubt they were reported in the papers that the members of the house-party read. But the point is really not so much the precise event as the fact that another world—a public world, subject to time and to historical forces—exists outside, and demands its place in private consciousness. Thus the moon that shines down on lovers in an English garden also climbs the *European* sky, and shines indifferently on churches and on power stations (that is, on fixtures of the past and present), on art galleries, and on

> The gathering multitudes outside
> Whose glances hunger worsens ...

The appeal of those multitudes is not to compassion—the house-party cannot protect itself by writing a cheque—but to history; the old, protected, private world will die, has already lost the will to live, and another world will replace it. That historical process Auden images in a little parable of a second Flood (an image, you may recall, that was also used by poets in *New Country*). The difference between this parable and the allegory earlier in the poem, of the private Peaceable Kingdom, is significant. The image of the private world was fixed and static, like a painting; this final parable is violently active, cinematic—a great force bursting 'the dykes of our content' and drowning the protected life, and, after the flood waters have subsided, a new life growing. The poem ends with a prayer (rather like the end of 'Sir, no man's enemy') that love, the prime value of that drowned private life, may survive to soften the world after the deluge.

One could call this a poem of historical determinism, and hence a Marxist poem: it is about the sickness and death of the bourgeoisie, and the revolutionary new world that is coming. It places the traditionally private feelings of lyric poetry in the public world of history, where politics and economics are real forces, and hunger is more urgent than love. But that fact, too, carries private feelings, and it is characteristic of Auden's poetic honesty that he acknowledges regret, praises the private virtues that will die in this historical change, and accepts his own historical place in the drowning world. It is a poem that is scrupulous in its pronouns, and does not pretend that *we* means the good, who will inherit the world, and *they* the past and the wicked others.

Auden's poem is a parable of the pressure of immediate events upon private lives. The details are not, strictly speaking, historical, but they are examples of what was actually happening at the time: violence, poverty, and hunger were parts of the time's consciousness. There is a similar effect, what one might call fictional history, in Graham Greene's *It's a Battlefield* (published in February 1934). Greene's first notion for the book, in a notebook entry of September 1932, was that it should be

a large inclusive picture of a city, the connecting link the conviction of a man for the murder of a policeman. Is it politic to hang him? And the detectives go out through the city listening . . .[5]

The novel that he wrote is roughly that, but one should add that the large inclusive picture he drew is of an *historical* city, located in real time and space—actual London, now, in an early 'thirties autumn. Greene managed this effect of historical reality by bringing together incidents that are imagined, but close to reality, and mixing them with names and places that are historical. The policeman is killed, for example, at a political rally in Hyde Park; there had been such a rally there in October 1932, the month after Greene made his first note, and fifteen people had been injured, including two policemen. The crimes that preoccupy the Assistant Police Commissioner in the novel are actual-sounding crimes: a trunk murder at Paddington station, a girl killed on Streatham Common. Newspaper headlines are quoted: 'Mr. MacDonald Flies to Lossiemouth', 'Disarmament Conference Adjourned'; MacDonald *was* Prime Minister, and had a house at Lossiemouth, the Disarmament Conference *was* in session. The streets that the characters move through are real London streets, meticulously named, and so exactly noted that you can follow each move on a London street-map without difficulty.

The effect of all this actuality is to impose upon the fictional action the restraints of particular historical existence: Greene's characters, like the figures in Auden's poem, are exposed to pressures that they do not understand and cannot control—the political, economic, and social stresses of a specific place and date: London, in 1933. Into their private lives the headlines enter like the noise of history: the Prime Minister leaves London, the Disarmament Conference adjourns. The Assistant Commissioner at his private policeman's task gets messages from the Home Secretary, who is under attack on the floor of the Commons ('it's a battlefield', his private secretary says). Greene is very good at this sort of thing: it is his version of the private/public theme, individuals in their private spheres echoing the crash and thunder of public conflicts. We will see him at it again in *A Gun for Sale*.

The private lives in the novel go on, the characters try to act out their feelings—their loves and hatreds and revenges—but they fail; in this world, private destinies are not determined by the desires of men's hearts, but by the incomprehensible pressures of historical reality. The headlines and the Home Secretary are there to remind the reader of this fact. A reader coming to the novel in 1934 must have felt very strongly that these characters occupied the same world that he did, and were moved by the same forces that he felt and found recorded in his evening newspaper.

The parabolic figure of this vision of man in history is set down in Greene's epigraph, a passage from Kinglake's description of the Battle of Inkerman, in *The Invasion of the Crimea*:

> In so far as the battlefield presented itself to the bare eyesight of men, it had no entirety, no length, no breadth, no depth, no size, no shape, and was made up of nothing except small numberless circlets commensurate with such ranges of vision as the mist might allow at each spot ... In such conditions, each separate gathering of English soldiery went on fighting its own little battle in happy and advantageous ignorance of the general state of the action; nay, even very often in ignorance of the fact that any great conflict was raging.[6]

This metaphor is picked up again and again throughout the novel: politics is a battlefield, London is a battlefield, the world is a battlefield. The Assistant Commissioner thinks of his policeman's task as a war:

> He was like a general left alone at headquarters to study the reports from every company; they littered his desk. But he was not sheltered in a château behind miles of torn country; the front line was only a hundred yards away where the trams screamed down the Embankment and the buses circled Trafalgar Square.
>
> It was hard, he thought, to get any clear idea of a war carried on in this piecemeal way throughout a city.[7]

And Conrad Drover, the deranged clerk who is trying to kill the Assistant Commissioner, thinks of his situation in the same terms:

> he might have been at the edge of a great army hidden by mist; and for a moment it was not a shoe, a fire, a lantern slide

which held his thoughts, but a faint memory of his secondary school, of a Latin lesson, of an army which waited on a hillside above a lake while an invisible enemy marched in the mist below.[8]

The image of war in the Kinglake passage has two components: the fighting, and the fog-bound isolation. Greene's novel-war is the same, individuals struggling alone, each ignorant of the great conflict in which they are engaged. But what is the war about, and who is fighting it? The Assistant Commissioner thinks:

> The war which he fought was a civil war; his enemies were not only the brutal and the depraved, but the very men he pitied, the men he wanted to help. . . . The buildings seemed to him then to lose a little of their dignity; the peace of Sunday in Pall Mall was like the peace which follows a massacre, a war of elimination; poverty here had been successfully contested, driven back on the one side towards Notting Hill, on the other towards Vauxhall.[9]

It is a war, then, of the law against those outside the law, of the rich against the poor, the haves against the have-nots. Not a holy war, not even a just war—the Assistant Commissioner thinks of himself as a mercenary—but simply a war that must be fought because it is already raging, two ignorant armies in a fog.

Most of the reviewers took note of the metaphor in the epigraph, and concluded that *It's a Battlefield* was revolutionary; *The Times Literary Supplement*'s man observed that 'from the general tone of the book it may be surmised that Mr. Greene's conflict is being waged for the overthrow of the existing order', and a critic in the Marxist journal, *Viewpoint*, wrote approvingly that 'Graham Greene . . . has some conception of the basis of the class struggle which he depicts against a wide and varied social background.'[10] But in fact the novel is not as clear in its politics as these remarks suggest. If we pursue the battlefield metaphor, the two armies involved are the army of the Law—Scotland Yard, prison wardens, the Home Office—and the Communist Party. The book is full of Communists, and a long scene is devoted to a Party meeting.

But neither army has right or justice or any other visible virtue on its side; both are full of internal conflicts, egotisms, suspicions, and deviousness. They are, like Kinglake's armies, separated, disorderly, and ignorant.

The nearest that Greene comes to pointing his political moral is in a long meditation by the Assistant Commissioner as he sits examining reports:

> ... he was upholding a system in which he had no interest because he was paid to uphold it: he was a mercenary, and a mercenary soldier could not encourage himself with the catchwords of patriotism: My country right or wrong; self-determination of peoples; justice. He fought because he was paid to fight, and only occasionally did the sight of some brutality lend conviction to the brain with which he fought. At other times the highest motive he could offer was that of doing his job; there were no abstract reasons to compel him to forbid this meeting, to break up that, to have this Socialist arrested for seditious speaking, to guard that Fascist's platform while he spoke in terms of bayonets and machine guns; it was the will of the organization he served. It was only when he was tired or depressed or felt his age that he dreamed of an organization which he could serve for higher reasons than pay, an organization which would enlist his fidelity because of its inherent justice, its fair distribution of reward, its reasonableness. Then he told himself with bitterness that he was too old to live so long. His thin face, yellowed by more fevers than he could count, lined by the years of faithful mercenary service, would grow for a moment envious at the thought of younger men who might live to serve something which they believed worthy of their service.[11]

This is surely an eternal human dream, the dream of a political instrument worthy of men's devotion. But in the 'thirties it was a particularly poignant one; for the causes were there, injustices and suffering and the threat of war were apparent to everyone. But where was the organization? And what political direction would it take? Greene's novel offers no answers: like *The Orators*, and some of Spender's poems, it is about, to use Greene's own phrase, 'the sense of violence and confusion',[12] a parable of the historical situation in the year of Hitler's first great triumph.

II

'Summer Night' and *It's a Battlefield* are works that acknowledge the force of immediate history but remain fictive. One gets from them the feeling of living in that historical time, but the historical particulars are imagined—they are typical rather than actual. Other young writers drew upon events of the time more directly, and wrote poems and novels that were historical in a more literal sense. History in 1933 and 1934 had taken on a new and terrible momentum: Hitler was in power, and it was clear not only that a war would come, but who the Enemy would be. To deal with this immediate history posed difficult problems, and especially for poets whose natural gifts were lyrical. I should like to consider two examples: Lehmann's *The Noise of History*, and Spender's *Vienna*.

Michael Roberts called these works 'occasional poetry', and admired their intentions. 'For many years,' he wrote, 'occasional poetry has been badly neglected . . . and Mr. Lehmann and Mr. Spender deserve commendation for their admittedly partisan accounts of the February insurrection in Vienna.'[13] And in a sense they *are* occasional: like the great modern poems in this genre—for example 'Easter 1916' and Auden's elegy on Yeats— they mythologize history. But Yeats and Auden are traditional in their materials; they deal with personal loss, the deaths of known individuals. Events in the early 'thirties set new problems: how do you write an elegy for a political movement? How do you grieve for strangers? And how do you assimilate politics into such a poem?

The Noise of History is divided into three parts: a series of short lyric poems, then a series of prose poems, and a final group of four short poems. In an 'Author's Note', Lehmann explained the chronology of this order:

The poems in this book were written during the latter part of 1931, and 1932, with the exception of the last, which belongs to the beginning of this year, 1934. The prose begins in 1933,

140

at the time of the Nazi conquest of power in Germany, and ends soon after the suppression of the February Insurrection in Austria. . . . The order is fairly exactly that of writing, and so follows the course of a gradually developing point of view.[14]

It is not uncommon for poets to date their poems when they gather them together, but it is unusual to locate them in time entirely in relation to political events. Lehmann is not saying that his poems are *about* political occasions; those occasions are important to the poems, but they function as factors in the 'gradually developing point of view' which is the real, central subject. In the poems, public and private interpenetrate and alternate, love gives way to terror, political violence intrudes upon personal relationships, and upon a poetic consciousness. The public events are actual and specific, and that is important; for this is not a book about *any* public crisis, but about *this* one, and its personal consequences.

The poems in the book are separable, and several were published separately—four in *New Signatures*, and six in *New Country*. Nevertheless they come together to compose a single work, not exactly a record—something more patterned and formal than that—a chart, perhaps, of Lehmann's private and public feelings, under the pressure of the time.

In this chart of feelings, one can follow several lines: the developing political point of view, beginning with an apolitical introspection, and moving through direct experience of political events to a firm feeling of commitment; the literal physical movement, from England to Vienna, to Berlin and back to Vienna; and the movement in time, through three crucial years. These are all interconnected, of course: time and place determine political opinions, but also emerging political convictions alter the angle of sight.

The first section of the book, the poems in verse, dates from the period between the Labour defeat of 1931 and the end of the Weimar Republic. The earliest of these poems are subjective and introspective, rather in the manner of the early Eliot: a separate, isolated observer observing himself being separate and isolated, as in these lines:

> This world behind the faces that you see,
> The moving lips and eyelids, eyes alight
> Like matches blown by wind, because you stand
> A little distance off and cannot change
> Your isolation for their many, bears
> The complete shape of art, the harmony
> And pattern of a film . . .[15]

There is a world in these poems, but it functions primarily as a correlative for subjective states: the subject is the self, and even an active theme like departure is treated privately, as escape from 'the habit and the self we have outgrown'.

Then, in the autumn of 1932, Lehmann left England for Vienna, and the poems move, too, begin to take note of foreign scenes and foreign faces, and most of all of foreign cities. Vienna appears as a complex symbol of human pride and human misery, aspirations and oppressions. Political feelings enter with a poem about the Karl Marx Hof, the Socialist workers' apartment block that was later to be shelled in the February Uprising. And, more powerfully than political ideals, terror enters—a political feeling, since the terror is political, but separated from ideas, reduced to the thing itself.

> Now terror advances, and the door flies open
> Sweeping aside barriers that scuffled with the wind,
> Now the dark assumes fingers, the unthinkable can happen,
> The wheels of the engine, terror on my flesh
> Advances in iron, on the rail, on the wound
> Flying open like a door, and the blood jetting warm,
> Shrapnel is no story, but irradiates with its flash
> The twist of the mutilated and the feeding worm,
> The cries of the tortured break in cells under my feet,—
> Comfort of busy streets, and flowers, and the flush
> Of morning over belfries are as paper in this hour
> Of the inrush of the wind, the naked claws of fate,—
> I am fixed beneath the shadow of terror like a hare.[16]

But amid these poems of terror, private feelings persist; friends meet, lovers touch, and 'in the dying city, and epoch, we are happy'. It is a principal strength of the book that this is so, that development is not away from private feelings into selfless dedication, but rather a private self becoming aware of the public situation.

The prose poems of the second section are all from the first year of Nazi power, from 1933 to early 1934. They repeat the noises of history that have sounded through the preceding poems: alarm bells ring, crowds roar, guns are fired, a knock sounds on the door. But there are also now specifically historical events: the Reichstag fire appears as an emblem of public terror, and the Austrian Uprising figures centrally. It would not be quite accurate to say that these are historical poems, or that the political events are the subjects: rather they are facts that have become symbols— symbols of the political hopes and fears that are now, in 1934, as much a part of reality as love, friendship, and death are. Here, for example, is a passage from 'Five to Twelve':

> In the uneasy silence, under the strata of snow, poverty, and despair that pressed on Central Europe, several faint noises could be distinguished.
>
> There was the sound, suddenly heard and then lost again, as if blown by the wind, of irregular troops advancing in mountain country, it might be to encircle this key-town or that.
>
> There was the echo of a vast crowd roaring, mixed with the crack of rifles and hiss of flames, from the streets of a capital far away in the north-west. And to thousands who stood by their machines in factories and generating-stations, it was like a sudden call to action.[17]

The event in the second paragraph is the Austrian Uprising; that in the third is the Reichstag fire (which Lehmann witnessed). But in both cases the events have been transformed by the pressure of political feelings into symbols, part of what I have called the instant mythology of the 'thirties.

In the prose poems, private feelings continue, and two poems are explicitly about love, but the introspection of the earlier poems in verse is gone, and the 'I' when he appears is in strongly-felt relations to other men. Lehmann nowhere says that love and politics are related; nevertheless the poems do seem to suggest that the ability to feel about other people can have both private and public consequences.

The final section of four short verse poems moves away from private feelings and political fears to visions of the future, when the fever of the old life is cured. The poems are weaker than those in the rest of the book, and seem dictated by political conviction rather than by true feeling—an affirmative coda for the cause, to encourage embattled men to resist. But that encouragement is the least persuasive element in the book: it is the confusion and fear that one feels most, the power of terror as an historical force, and the brave visions of a socialist future seem false, because they have no real roots in the historical present of the poem. What Lehmann had created ends with the prose poems: it is a parable of political terror, privately felt, an image of the emotional state of democratic Europe as fascism began to move. In this state the private feelings have a legitimate part, and offer an encouragement more genuine than political visions.

As poems, the parts of the book can be easily criticized, and were: the reviews of the book were on the whole unfavourable. Lehmann was still much under the influence of Auden in his verse, and of Bloomsbury belletrism in his prose, and he displeased political reviewers by his literariness, and literary reviewers by his politics. 'There is little good except the title,' Grigson remarked sourly, and even the *Daily Worker* gave only qualified approval: Lehmann was praised for becoming a participant in the battle against fascism, but, the reviewer added, 'As poetry, much of this book suffers from the uncertainty of its origin.'[18]

The failure of the book to win approval can be explained as a failure of style: certainly Lehmann had not escaped his literary origins, and these were not always adequate to the melodrama of immediate history. But the problem was also one of audience: in 1934, literary critics were not ready for the Reichstag fire, and the Communist Party was not ready for literature (though it was beginning to think about its function, as we shall see).

The February Uprising, which is one symbolic event in *The Noise of History*, is the whole occasion of *Vienna*. What happened, historically, is briefly and roughly this. In the early 'thirties in

Austria, political movements of the extreme right (nationalists, pro-fascists, monarchists) and the left (Social Democrats) had armed themselves against each other, and established what amounted to private armies. In early 1934 the government undertook to suppress the army of the Social Democrats. The Social Democrats resisted, first in the provinces and then in Vienna, where they were driven back into the working-class districts of the city and there were shelled into submission. It was a total defeat for the Austrian left, but out of it a heroic story of workers' resistance to fascistic force emerged, to be added to the 'thirties mythology of the class struggle.

Vienna is a poem not so much about the history of the uprising as about the mythology. It is not a narrative, though it includes narrative passages: it does not tell the whole story, it ignores chronology, and it does not explain. What Spender seems to have aimed at was the expression of his own personal sense of Vienna: the poem includes, but is not limited to, the public events of the uprising, and it deals with even those events in a private way.

Formally, *Vienna* is rather like *The Orators*: the same division into dissimilar parts, the same mixture of modes, local obscurities, jokes, sudden shifts of tone, the same overlapping of political and sexual problems. Like *The Orators* it is concerned with a sick society and the need for action, and for a 'healer'. But there is one essential difference: by the time that *Vienna* was written, violent political events had occurred, a failed revolution had become history, and hence susceptible to re-telling and mythologizing. *Vienna* has the quality that Ezra Pound said all epics have: it is a poem containing history.

There is another difference, too: Vienna includes an 'I' who is not an invented persona (like Auden's Airman) but an experiencing self. Spender had gone to Vienna shortly after the uprising, and he had witnessed the public consequences of failed heroic action. He was young, and he was politically in sympathy with the workers' action, and one gets from his account his spectator's excitement at the drama of events. But he was also a young man living a troubled and emotional private life, and elements of that life are also part of the poem. This gives it, along with its epic side, something of the character of a long lyric poem, in which all events are filtered through a private sensibility.

A confused city, apparently shortly after the violent suppression of the uprising, and a confused young man—a stranger to the city and its people, troubled in his own life, desiring love, uncertain of his sexual identity: these are the constituents of the poem. The young man observes, records, and feels the public themes—the authoritarian rulers, the brooding unemployed workers, the political antagonisms—but he also feels his private troubles, and weaves his introspection through the poem. Between the public themes and the private ones there is no necessary connection, except the identity of the poet-observer, but the implication is (as in *The Noise of History*) that history, *this* history of violence and betrayal, alters and inhibits love. The point is imperfectly made, and the poem remains in some ways fundamentally incoherent, but this assumption, which is so recurrent through the 'thirties, seems clear enough—that in a time of public catastrophe, private lives will be catastrophic, too.

I suggested, in discussing *The Orators*, that that work might best be considered as a series of distinct parables. *Vienna*, which resembles *The Orators* in so many ways, invites the same approach. Consider first, then, part one, 'Arrival at the City', the interior monologue of a young man in a Viennese *pension*. The society that he sees—or rather *feels*—around him is full of death: the living seem dead, a man is dying, outside bombs dismember senseless corpses. But it also contains positive forces: the workers are alive, the will to change conditions exists, there is the possibility of love. The relations among these elements is not clear, except that they all are recorded in one observer's mind; the whole section is phantasmagorical and obscure, a confused subjective vision, by an outsider, of a city in crisis.

The second part, 'Parade of the Executive', is primarily a speech, or a series of speeches, by the city's governors, describing their efforts to rule, their dependence on force and ceremony, their fear of the poor, and their anxious question: *What is wrong?* The section ends with the imagined arrival of a stranger, one of those vaguely messianic figures who turn up in many 'thirties works, who will answer the question:

> *What is wrong?*
>   Fear, fear in armies
> Breeds death.
>   Would he forgive us?
>   Would he
> Glance at a minister who smiles and smiles
> 'How now! A rat? Dead for a ducat.' Shoot![19]

That is, of course, Hamlet; but what is Hamlet doing here? Is he a persona of the troubled young observer, the man in the *pension*? Or is he another? A Leader? A Healer? It is not clear. But at any rate, the point of his answer is clear enough: Do not fear. . . . Shoot!

'The Death of Heroes', the third section of *Vienna*, is by far the most straightforward part of the book. It is a narrative of the uprising in the voice of a worker, and here political judgments are made: that the uprising failed because of the Social Democrats' 'fatal unconfidence', their failure to oppose force with force. And the harsh moral is drawn: only a ruthless Left can resist a ruthless Right. It is the death of moderation. It is also the beginning of hagiography, in the stories of the two worker-heroes, Weissel and Wallisch, two more examples of the 'thirties impulse to instant mythology.

The section that follows, and ends the poem, is by contrast the most difficult; it is also the most introspective, and the difficulty follows from that. The section is titled 'Analysis and Statement', and begins with five voices, labelled A to E, who speak of their weaknesses, their needs for love, and for a mode of action. They are apparently aspects of one person, the first-person speaking voice of the poem, an isolated, ineffectual, emotionally sterile young man who thinks of love for a woman as admirable and fertile, but cannot feel it, and who is drawn to the beauty of boys, but is troubled by those feelings. The problem is set entirely in psycho-sexual terms; sexual crisis seems to have been a crucial part of the Vienna experience.

But the solution that the poem offers is not set in sexual terms, but in vaguely revolutionary terms that seem to offer an alternative mode of action that will also be a cure for the 'desert' that the speaker feels in his breast. He imagines a stranger, another of those healing heroes who are central to the 'thirties myth, whose coming will drive out the sicknesses of the past, and all the introspective, self-regarding forms of love, the 'liars and buggers under the dark lid of centuries',[20] and will integrate the creative, revolutionary forces that are already gathering, into a new life.

> He greets the
> Historians of the future, the allies of no city,
> O man and woman minute beneath their larger day;
> Those burrowing beneath frontier, shot as spies because
> Sensitive to new contours; those building insect cells
> Beneath the monstrous shell of ruins; altering
> The conformation of masses, that at last conjoin
> Accomplished in justice to reject a husk.
> Their walls already rest upon their dead, on Wallisch
> Trapped in the mountains, on Weissel the engineer
> Who lied to save his followers 'I forced them after
> 'With my revolver'. On all the others. These are
> Our ancestors.[21]

Those are the last lines of the poem. They are visionary and positive, but without being very clear. Revolution apparently cures not only social sickness, but also private psychological sickness; the imagined stranger is at once a Leader and a Healer, and it is hard to say which the young man in the poem desires more.

Vienna is an unsuccessful poem, and one can see at once why it was likely to fail. Spender was attempting to mythologize immediate political events, to create an instant myth rather than allowing it to emerge; and at the same time he was trying to reproduce honestly his own feelings of the moment. So there is an uncertain mixture in the poem of politics and self, public and private, working in opposite directions, and obscuring each other. The problems of writing *personally* about public events in which one has played no part are very considerable (I can think of only one modern poet—Yeats—who has managed to do so successfully); there is an obvious temptation to make the self the subject and Spender did, so that, as one critic wrote of *Vienna*, 'we are led, on the whole, not only to pity for these Socialists, but also to a view of the poet himself in the act of being pitiful'.[22] Beyond those problems, there was another that has to do with dramatic form: the February Uprising was a disastrous defeat, of the kind only appropriate to tragedy. But tragedy and revolution are surely not compatible. In Marxist terms, historical reversals are not tragic but simply inevitable parts of the dialectical process, to be acknowledged and incorporated into a 'correct' understanding of historical change. So Spender settled for defeat, with a bit of revolutionary hope at the end.

Spender is an acute critic, of his own works as well as of those of others, and his comments on *Vienna*, and the feelings behind it, are helpful to an understanding both of the poem and of the time. Of this period in his writing life, Spender wrote:

> In poetry I was confronted with the dilemma of stating a public emotion which had become a private one, and which yet never became completely my own inner experience because, as I have explained, it invaded my personality rather than sprang out of it . . . To write about Fascism was then to write about the experience which had usurped the place of more personal ones. Yet I tried to relate the public passion to my private life.[23]

This seems to me a convincing and moving account of how political realities of the 'thirties made the relations between public and private modes of feeling the acute problem for writers that it obviously was. Spender saw *Vienna* as the extreme example of this problem in his own work:

> The most ambitious—and perhaps the least successful—attempt I made to solve the problem of making such a statement was in a longish poem called *Vienna*. . . . In part this expressed my indignation at the suppression of the Viennese Socialists by Dollfuss, Fey and Starhemberg: but in part also it was concerned with a love relationship. I meant to show that the two experiences were different, yet related. For both were intense, emotional and personal, although the one was public, the other private. The validity of the one was dependent on that of the other: for in a world where humanity was trampled on publicly, private affection was also undermined.[24]

Even the most well-disposed reader will have to take the love-theme on faith; it simply does not get expressed in the poem. But that is what Spender is saying in the passage quoted above, that the effect of public violence was to undermine private feelings, that political emotions may overpower and mask private ones. So that the very failure of his poem has a political meaning.

Spender titled the third section of *Vienna* 'The Death of Heroes', and Edwin Muir, reviewing the poem, described its subject as 'the most heroic episode of modern times'.[25] Paradoxically, the rise of European fascism had created a climate in which heroism was possible in life, and was therefore also possible in art. A hero, generally speaking, is a man who manifests public values in public actions, and after 1933 the values at issue, and the possible lines of action, were becoming clear. The fascists were consciously mythologizing their own party leaders and martyrs, and at the same time the Left was making heroes of imprisoned German communists, Viennese socialists, and Spanish revolutionaries.[26] But it was more than a matter of political propaganda, it was a change in the way men thought about action, and in the way they wrote about it.

Michael Roberts, who was always sensitive to new directions in current writing, took note of this change in an article titled 'The Return of the Hero':

Persistently [he wrote] in the work of these poets we meet figures such as Warner's engineer, 'Colonel Humphries', Auden's 'Gerhart Meyer from the sea, the truly strong man', Madge's Grant, all
> Those who were not afraid
> To dam the estuary or start the forest fire.

These figures represent something essential in humanity, magnified to heroic proportions. They represent the answer to doubt, uncertainty, and indecision, and the reintegration of divided personalities. The returning hero, the man who knows his own mind and is certain of his own desires is the antithesis of Eliot's Prufrock.[27]

Roberts' catalogue of names suggests an important point: that the return of heroism gives to the forces of history human faces.

Historical names also begin to appear in poetry: Van der Lubbe in poems by Auden and Spender, the fliers Parer and McIntosh in Day Lewis, the mountaineers in Roberts. *Vienna* is full of names: heroes like Weissel and Wallisch, and villains like Fey, Dollfuss, and Stahremberg. These names have taken on the meaning of their actions, and become mythic; the implication is that the individual acts of men matter, that men can behave in ways that are heroic or evil, and can alter events.

Roberts' use of Eliot for a comparison is also important: for he is taking note of a major change in literary tone that occurred when the sensitive, neurotic anti-hero of the 'twenties was succeeded by the man of action. The change is essentially a matter of generations, and it was perceptible at once to critics of the younger group. Dilys Powell, for example, writing in 1934, made the point in this way:

> When, however, we come to the new generation, to the work of Mr. Auden, Mr. Day Lewis, Mr. Spender, the nature of the conflict has changed. It has been externalized; it has become a battle, not within the poet, but between poet and environment. And the mood has suffered a violent reversal. The new verse has ceased to doubt and look back; it has begun to hope and look forward.[28]

Both Roberts and Miss Powell overstate their case a bit; Prufrock was not yet dead in 1934—he was alive, for example, in the introspective speaker of *Vienna*. But it is a part of the generation's growing sense of itself that it should see this break from the past, and from Eliot's example, in absolute and heroic terms.

III

In the writings of the Auden generation, history enters not only as events, but as a term. So Day Lewis, observing a communist, writes:

> Mark him. He is only what we are, mortal. Yet from the night Of history, where we lie dreaming still, he is wide awake . . .[29]

And Auden, revising the ending of his 'Prologue' at about this time, changes this line:

> And called out of tideless peace by a living sun

to this:

> And out of the Future into actual History.[30]

A small change, but a significant one, for it swings the poem away from an evolutionary version of human life to an historical one.

One might argue that the increasing presence of the word *history* is simply a consequence of the increasing pressure of historical events, the increasing volume of the off-stage noises. I would suggest that it is also a consequence of the increasing presence and authority of Marxist thought, and the dialectic of history, in the intellectual world of young writers. There is no way of knowing, now, how much of the literature of Marxism these writers actually read; but it is not necessary to read it to assimilate the terminology. It is only necessary to be around people who have read it, to listen to their conversation and read what they wrote. And by 1934 that must have been almost unavoidable, if one was young and a writer in England.

For 1934 was the year in which British communism formally addressed itself to the arts. In February the British Section of Writers' International was formed, and in October the British Section of Artists' International held its first exhibition. *Viewpoint*, 'a revolutionary review of the arts' published its first issue in April; it stood, an editorial announced, 'for militant communism and for individualism and metaphysics in the arts'.[31] In October it became the *Left Review*, the official organ of the British Writers' International, and the individualism and metaphysics were somewhat diminished. During 1934 the *Daily Worker* became a bit more literary, as though in response to a new market; novel-reviews began to appear on the weekly book page, and there was even a favourable notice of *The Noise of History* (it was the only book of poems reviewed there that year).

No doubt there was a connection between this activity and similar interest in literature in the Soviet Union, where the First Soviet Writers' Congress met in August. There Zhdanov had defined the party line on imaginative writing. 'Yes,' he said in his speech, 'Soviet literature is tendentious, for in an epoch of class struggle there is not and cannot be a literature which is not class literature, not tendentious, allegedly non-political.'[32] The effect of this official definition of the role of literature upon literary Marxists was evidently profound and immediate. 'All of us,' one of them wrote,

> writers in particular, feel that after the Congress literature will somehow become different, that it will rise to a new plane. And the literary historian of the future will, of course, treat the first Congress of Soviet Writers as an event marking the beginning of a new era in the history of Literature.[33]

The most obvious consequence of this movement in literary politics was simply that writers and their critics became more aware of the presence of political content, and seemed to accept the party view that all literature is political. 'Now in a time like the present,' a *New Verse* reviewer wrote in February 1934, 'saturated with politics, it is probable that much of the material of poetry will be political.'[34] And if that is the case, then the critic must look for political meanings (was *Vienna* Marxist? or was it fascist? or was it, as one critic suggested, Buchmanite?). One can see this becoming a habit of mind, so that even the non-political issues suggest political analogies—as when Spender, reviewing Roberts' *Critique of Poetry*, compares an argument about poetry and belief that he disagrees with to 'the attitude of mind which is considered desirable in a judge of the Aryan State'.[35]

That summer, when Geoffrey Grigson decided to survey the opinions of contemporary poets on the state of their craft, he made political commitment one of the questions: 'Do you take your stand with any political or politico-economic party or creed?'[36] Auden, Spender, and Day Lewis did not reply, but twelve other English poets did, and their responses are interestingly varied: four answered simply, 'No, I do not'; two said flatly that they were communists, and two others (Dylan Thomas and David Gascoyne) aligned themselves more vaguely with revolution; Edwin Muir supported Social Credit, and Wyndham Lewis wrote that he took his stand 'exactly midway between the Bolshevist and the Fascist'. Nobody admitted to conservatism, or to fascism, not even Roy Campbell, though he was by then far to

the right. Not every poet was enthusiastic about political commitment, but even the reluctant ones conceded the power or the
appeal of the Left. MacNeice, though he answered 'no' to the
question, added: 'In weaker moments I wish I could', and Norman
Cameron wrote: 'I believe that communism is necessary and good,
but I'm not eager for it.'[37]

Perhaps the most telling response to the survey, though, was
David Gascoyne's answer to a different question, 'Do you think
there can now be a use for narrative poetry?' 'What might be
useful now,' he wrote,

> would be a poem expressing the ever-rising feeling of crisis,
> anxiety and panic; a poem that would treat this feeling in a
> loose, universal and epic sort of way. I mean a poem narrating
> the contemporary Zeitgeist of Europe, or even of the World.[38]

It is a political response to a non-political question, not doctrinaire, but concerned with the feeling of crisis that was a part of
everybody's politics, and everybody's life—a feeling that, as Gascoyne recognized, united all of Europe, perhaps the entire world.
He is asking, essentially, for the kind of poem that Spender had
tried to write in *Vienna*, a poetry of immediate history that would
mythologize, and so make coherent, the enormous disorder of
the time. It is a gloomy sort of response, but it is also an optimistic
one, coming from a poet; for Gascoyne suggests that even in this
time of crisis a poem 'might be useful', though he doesn't explain
what its utility would be.

There is something of the same mood of Day Lewis' *Hope for
Poetry*, which was also published in that autumn of 1934. Day
Lewis set out in this, his first critical book, to explain his own
generation of poets to possible readers of poetry, and in so doing
to indicate the ways in which poetry 'might be useful', the sense
in which it still had a hope, even in a time of crisis. It is not a
particularly good, or a particularly original book, but it is the first
to be written on the Auden generation by a member of it, and
like many rather pedestrian books it is helpful for what it tells
us of the commonplaces of its time. In the course of explaining
his generation, Day Lewis repeats and fixes a number of the terms
by which the generation had come to define itself.

Day Lewis begins with a parable—appropriately, I would say, for a discussion of this parabolical generation:

> In English poetry there have been several occasions on which the younger son, fretting against parental authority, weary of routine work on the home farm, suspecting too that the soil needs a rest, has packed his bag and set out for a far country. Rumours of his doings come to our ears: they are generally unfavourable, and always distorted, for they have had to pass across seas. He is flirting with foreign whores, we hear, or with ghosts: he has wasted his fortune: he has forgotten how to speak English: he has shamed his father: he has gone mad in the desert: he died some years ago . . .[39]

This is the by-now-familiar poet's journey into the unknown: we have seen it already in *Paid on Both Sides*, *The Magnetic Mountain*, and, 'The Witnesses', and we will meet it again. It is a central parable for the decade, stressing as it does the necessity of breaking away from an exhausted past and from the family, and committing oneself to uncertainty in the name of action. A parable of revolution, one might say, though Day Lewis is careful to note that it has happened before, and so is in a sense a traditional act.

Once separated from his past, the young poet will be free to discover his real ancestors. This again is familiar territory, which we have visited before with both Auden and Spender, and Day Lewis is repeating a convention of his generation when he argues that ancestors are chosen, not given. One might take the argument further, and say that they are not really chosen, but rather are *created*; thus the ancestors that Day Lewis chooses—Hopkins, Owen, and Eliot—are redefined by him to suit his generation's needs: his Hopkins is a 'true revolutionary' who broke up the traditional forms of language and made them new; his Owen (also a 'true revolutionary') is primarily the great poet of pity; and his Eliot is chiefly important as the author of that great 'social document', *The Waste Land*. Together they provide a language, an attitude, and a vision of society: 'they are not merely the geographers but in a sense the creators' of the 'thirties poetical world.

Day Lewis takes certain aspects of that world for granted: that it was born amongst the ruins of the First World War; that it was cut off from its pre-war roots by the War; that it is a chaos of values; that it is a world 'inimical apparently both to poetry and to the social ideals which living poets affirm'. He recognizes that his contemporaries are inclined to speak in parables, that their poetry is 'a perpetual interplay of private and public meaning', that they have tried to absorb the data of science and technology into their work. And he praises, at the end of his essay, the emergent element of heroism:

> ... the mythopoeic faculty which we have claimed as one of poetry's greater powers, is evident in post-war verse. It is at work in the ancestor-worship we have already noticed, creating and drawing energy from the superhuman. We find it in the symbolic characters that raise their heads so often in these poems: Warner's engineer, 'Colonel Humphries'; Auden's 'Captain Ferguson' or his 'Gerhart Meyer from the sea, the truly strong man'. We do not suggest that these characters are immortal, but they are vivid and illuminating; they represent something essential in humanity magnified to heroic proportions; and they may be the forerunners of a new Achilles, a new Job, a new Othello.[40]

What I have said thus far about *A Hope for Poetry* makes it seem little more than a codification of ideas that were current when Day Lewis wrote it.[41] What it has to say about politics and poetry, however, is a good deal more interesting and less predictable. In 1934 Day Lewis was moving steadily closer to the Communist Party (he became a Party member the following year), and he gives a good deal of space to worrying about how one might be both a communist and a poet, and to defending propaganda as a poetic activity. Nevertheless, in the debate on Poetry and Propaganda of which the book is a part, Day Lewis comes in the end to be much nearer to the poetic individualism of Spender than to Madge's total commitment.

Of all his poetic generation, Day Lewis was the one who most wanted to believe in the communist faith. But he was an honest, intelligent man, and a self-consciously dedicated poet, and his doubts and criticisms creep in. So, when he looks to the left, he 'sees Communism, proclaiming ... "revolution for life's sake", the most whole-hearted attempt ever made to raise the individual to his highest power by a conditioning of his environment: yet here too he notices the bully and the spy, and wonders if any system can expel and survive that poison'.[42] And when he examines the revolutionary poetry of his contemporaries, he finds, as other critics had found, that it is often politically highly ambiguous:

> Its vague *cris-de-coeur* for a new world, its undirected and undisciplined attack upon the whole world-broad front of the status quo, are apt to produce work which makes the neutral reader wonder whether it is aimed to win him for the communist or the fascist state.[43]

(One should add that the best example of this ambiguity is Day Lewis's own *Magnetic Mountain*.)

To my mind the most valuable statement in Day Lewis's book is his formulation of the relationship that I have repeatedly referred to as the problem of public and private experience. 'In this poetry,' he writes, referring to the work of his contemporaries and himself,

> there is a perpetual interplay of private and public meaning: the inner circle of communication—the poet's conversation with his own arbitrarily isolated social group—is perpetually widening into and becoming identified with the outer circles of his environment; and conversely, the specifically modern data of his environment—the political situation, the psychological states, the scientific creations of twentieth-century man —are again and again used to reflect the inner activities of the poet. Such interchange of personal and (in the widest sense) political imagery, such interaction of personal and political feeling is to be found in poem after poem of the younger writers. It is my own experience that, when I have expressed some private experience in a poem, I have frequently discovered it to contain a 'political' significance of which I was quite unconscious while writing it. A year or two ago I wrote a sequence called 'From Feathers to Iron' which for me expressed simply my thoughts and feelings during the nine months before the birth of my first child: the critics, almost to a man, took it for

a political allegory; the simple, personal meaning evaded them.[44]

Day Lewis was the only critic of his time to see this interpenetration of public and private as a natural poetic process, and an understandable consequence of the post-war social situation. But, as his final point implies, it was also a problem; there is something wrong with the critical environment in which a poem about the gestation of a baby can be taken by *all* the critics as a political allegory. It is no solution of the problem simply to assume that all private references are public ones, though that was the common 'thirties response.

The hope for poetry that Day Lewis felt is not very explicitly defined in his book: when he got down to explanations, he reverted to what he really was as a poet, a sentimental Georgian who could talk about the nature of poetry in terms of 'the angel seen at the window, the air of glory'. As a contribution to Marxist literary theory the book is negligible, but it must have been reassuring to those traditional-minded readers who had feared that the young revolutionaries were bent on destroying English poetry. For what Day Lewis did was to place his own poetry, and Auden's and Spender's, at the end of a poetic line that runs back to the great figures of the past. In his criticism, as in his poetry, one can see a traditional sensibility, holding traditional ideas about poetry and poets, though he clothes them in the language of revolution.

One last word on the poetry of 1934—and a characteristically sour one—from Grigson. At the end of the year he wrote the annual article on 'The Year's Poetry' for the *Bookman*, and there he took note of the fact that John Lehmann had recently selected a group of poems by eight young English poets for the *New Republic*, and had there described his choices as 'well representative of the tendencies to be found in the English poetry of their generation'. The eight poets were Day Lewis, Auden, Lehmann, Julian Bell, MacNeice, Richard Goodman, Madge, and David Gascoyne—substantially a recapitulation of the *New Country* gang —and Grigson was not pleased with the selection. 'It is a pity, but true,' he wrote, that the poems included of Mr. Lehmann, Mr. Bell and Mr. Goodman ... and of Mr. Day Lewis are well representative of a new sentimentality of revolution-sickness made prominent in the last twelve months, more nauseating than the nature or love-sickness and pre- and post-War Georgians yearning to be able to converse with lambs.[45]

That is another way of putting what this chapter has been saying —that in 1934 the noise of history reached the ears of the young writers.

VI

1935

I

To say that 1935 was a critical year is in one sense merely to state
the self-evident: of course it was a year of crises, every year of the
'thirties was. In 1935 Germany re-occupied the Saar, and Italy
invaded Abyssinia, and the League of Nations failed to take adequate action to restrain aggression. But 1935 was also critical in
the literary sense; it was the year in which some of the best critical
writing by members of the 'thirties generation was published: *The
Destructive Element, Some Versions of Pastoral*, important essays by
Auden and—at a lower level of excellence—Day Lewis' *Revolution
in Writing*.

It is not surprising that a wave of criticism should have come
at this time. The young writers were in their late twenties and
early thirties, they had established themselves as poets and
novelists, and had been publicized by reviewers as *the* modern
movement—as the 'New Signatures Poets' or the 'Auden Gang'.
It was a natural point at which to pause and examine the theoretical bases of their work. One could cite many parallels of such a
critical pause among poets of the past: at about the same age
Wordsworth wrote the preface to the *Lyrical Ballads*, and Eliot
began the essays that became *The Sacred Wood*, and Yeats wrote
Ideas of Good and Evil.

But if this turn to criticism is a common thing in young poets,
the direction that the critical arguments took in 1935 is a function
of the time. The questions to which these critics addressed themselves were questions primarily about the social aspects of literature: what is its relation to immediate history? how does it reflect
the social background? what is its function in an unstable, perhaps a revolutionary society? These are questions that had been
asked before, in the years just past, and the critical writings of
1935 may be seen simply as further and more elaborate statements

in the debates on art and politics that had begun in the pages of journals like *Cambridge Left* and *Left Review*, and in *New Country*. Whether or not these antecedents are quoted or referred to, they are there, as part of the critical occasion, making a continuity of concern.

One can get a sense of the stage that the debate had reached in 1935 by considering quotations from three essays that appeared in journals at the year's beginning:

> It is already becoming more evident to serious writers that the prevailing 'consciousness' of the times is a political consciousness, and this is increasingly manifest in their work.
>
> (DAY LEWIS)
>
> We can no more forget the world of politics than the soldier-poets could forget the wounded and the dead.
>
> (MICHAEL ROBERTS)
>
> 'We can no longer permit life to be shaped by a personified ideal, we must serve with all our faculties some actual thing', Mr. Yeats has written in a recent preface. This seems to me to be true. The 'actual thing' is the true moral or widely political subject that must be realized by contemporary literature, if that literature is itself to be moral and serious.
>
> (STEPHEN SPENDER)[1]

At this time, midway through the 'thirties, young critics take it as given that political content is unavoidable for the serious writer; this is seen as a fact of history, a point that society has reached in the historical process—hence 'becoming', 'we can no longer', temporal phrases. Criticism is taken to be a function of the movement of history, and so, given the historical situation in 1935, it is correct and necessary that writers should be political.

But even if criticism is understood to be determined by history, even if the necessary subject is understood to be politics, the traditional literary considerations still remain: the artfulness of the work of art, the technicalities of technique, the private workings of the private imagination are still subjects that the critic— and especially the critic who is also an artist—will meditate upon. The important critical writings of this critical year try to deal with these questions in the context of public, political demands; they can best be understood as a series of defences constructed to protect literature and writers from the pressures of the time— pressures to be politically orthodox, to make art a class weapon, to abandon the traditional past, to simplify the complexities of art in the service of an urgent cause.

Both the sense of historical process and the critical defensive-ness can be seen very clearly in Spender's *The Destructive Element*, published in March 1935. Spender had set out to write a study of Henry James, an enterprise that seem on the face of it more Bloomsburyish than revolutionary; but his idea of the book changed, as he thought about it, 'into that of a book about modern writers and beliefs, or unbeliefs; which turned again into a pic-ture of writers grouped round the "destructive element", wonder-ing whether or not to immerse themselves'.[2] This three-stage change of mind corresponds to the three-part shape that the book finally took: first a section on James; then one on Yeats, Eliot, and Lawrence (in whom Spender saw the crisis of belief mani-fested); and finally a section on contemporary writers, for whom the fact of a world without beliefs is taken for granted as the base from which literary activity should begin. It seems reasonable to suppose that this form also corresponds to stages in Spender's own thinking about literature and belief, as his awareness of history grew during the early-'thirties years when he was writing the book. At any rate, the book he finally published is one in which the critical posture changes as the argument moves toward the present.

The 'destructive element' of the title is the phrase from Con-rad's *Lord Jim*, but that is not Spender's immediate source. As he explains in his introduction, he took the phrase, and the argu-ment of which it is a part, from Richards' *Science and Poetry*, and specifically from that influential footnote on *The Waste Land*. Richards had said of Eliot that

by effecting a complete severance between his poetry and *all* beliefs, and this without any weakening of the poetry, he has realised what might otherwise have remained largely a specu-lative possibility, and has shown the way to the only solution of these difficulties. 'In the destructive element immerse. That is the way.'

This comment, Spender says, 'really applied and applies to most of the serious literature of this century. We may take the pronouncement as a focal point from which diverge rays towards the past and the future.'[3] This may seem a considerable weight to put on a footnote, but indeed Richards' note did provide many of the literary intellectuals of Spender's generation with a conception of the modern writer's situation. It also provided Spender with a principle of selection for his book. 'All these writers seem to me faced by the destructive element,' he explained; 'that is, by the experience of an all-pervading Present, which is a world without belief.' And later in the book: 'I have chosen the writers in this book, because they are political-moral artists who are in the dilemma of Hamlet: they find their lives fixed in a world in which there are no external symbols for their inner sense of values. There is no power, and no glory.'[4]

Richards in his footnote, and in *Science and Poetry* more generally, had made two basic assumptions that were of value to writers of Spender's generation. First, he took for granted that the modern writer *must* accept a world without belief, because that was the philosophical point to which human history had come: that is to say, he dealt with the modern literary situation in long-range philosophical terms. This made it possible to think of the immediate situation not simply as a political crisis but as a stage in a process, to be accepted and responded to. Second, he proposed that the way out of this situation, for the writer, was a *formal* one—Eliot had found a form for unbelief, so others could, too. By making these assumptions, Richards extended the bounds of the problem, and provided younger writers with a link to the past: even in a world without belief, there was a tradition.[5]

Spender's sense of this tradition, and his place in it, is very clear: he begins with James, whom he sees as a great writer forced by his attitude toward a decadent civilization to create an inner world of art; then Yeats, Eliot, and Lawrence—'Three Individualists', Spender calls them—all moralists aware of the 'destructive element', but each seeking an individual solution to his problem.

163

Together these writers represent the art-tradition in modern English poetry and fiction; but they also represent the connection between that tradition and political reaction. Spender's achievement was to demonstrate their common element of social criticism, and to claim them, on the basis of that element, as the true ancêstors of his own generation. Once established, these ancestors could then be brought up, like troops held in reserve, to defend literary art from the demands of the propagandists.

The chapter in which Spender makes this defence most polemically, 'Writers and Manifestos', is an essay that had first appeared in the *Left Review*. As the title suggests, it belongs in a part of that running debate on art and politics that continued through most of the 'thirties, often with similar two-term titles: 'The Poet and Revolution', 'Politics and Literature', 'Revolutionaries and Poetry', 'Poetry and Revolution', 'Poetry and Propaganda'. Spender begins once more with Richards and the destructive element:

> The question is whether this despairing stage is now over, whether it is now possible for the artist to discover a system of values that are not purely subjective and individualistic, but objective and social . . .[6]

The answer is yes, he can find it in communism or socialism. But having said this, Spender immediately notes the serious problems involved for writers who adopt these values. The obvious problem is political: the ideological censorship in force in Soviet Russia and approved by writers in the *Left Review*. Another problem is more difficult to describe, but is partly moral and partly formal:

> if one conceives that the subject of writing is the moral life of one's time, in the same way as the subject of Greek tragedy is moral, and *Everyman* is a morality, and the subject of *Tao Te Ching* is the art of ruling and being ruled; then to-day one is in a very difficult situation. The precise difficulty is to write about this moral life in a way that is significant: to find the real moral subject.[7]

This is a difficulty for the artist because the 'real moral subject' may be political only in a very general sense—may be the lust for power, or the sense of guilt, or the pressure that the political, public world puts upon the personal life. This insistence on the moral subject is one of the principal motifs of Spender's book, and one of its strengths; but it is an argument for individualism —the *artist* decides what is moral—and one can see that it would offend the ideologues of the *Left Review*. The examples he cites, and his concern for the expression of non-realistic manifestations of the moral life, point to still another problem; Spender is defending the importance of literary form, the imaginative shapes that moral meaning may be given, and the right of the artist to follow his imagination, and to invent parables.

The word *parable* turns up several times in the book: for example, James' later novels are 'parables of modern Western civilization', and what Lawrence was really out to write were 'books that had the weight and translucency of parables or legends . . .'[8] Such sentences are part of Spender's argument against ideology: a work of art that is concerned with a serious moral-political subject will have moral weight, but if it is really a work of art it will be translucent—its meaning will shine out, but diffused by the strategies of the formal medium. Spender throughout his book defends the parabolic impulses of art—the difficult, the avant-garde, the experimental, the visionary—all of those strategies by which the writer protects his complex vision from simplification; and he rejects dogmatic communism because

> it seems likely . . . that the Communist explanation of our society is not adequate to produce considerable art: it is adequate only to use art to serve its own purposes.[9]

It is a difficult position to maintain, straddled between revolution and tradition, and exposed on both sides; but Spender managed to do it, and to write a skilful and moving defence of the necessity of art in a revolutionary time.[10]

At about the time that Spender was writing his book, and changing his mind about its direction, Auden, with his friend John Garrett, was preparing *The Poet's Tongue*, a poetry anthology for use in schools. It appeared in June 1935, with an introduction that is clearly the work of Auden. The anthology is, in its way, a political document. The editors chose poems from all literary levels—standard anthology pieces, skipping-rhymes, runes, riddles and word games, anonymous poems—with the intention of erasing the social distinction between highbrow and lowbrow, and presenting poetry as the whole variety of 'memorable words'. The poems were arranged (as Auden later arranged his *Collected Poetry*) alphabetically by first word, and without the author's name on the page—a method that stresses the community of poetry and eliminates the authority of individual status.

Left-wing critics took the political point at once. 'It is an anthology,' the *Left Review*'s critic wrote, 'that claims, not explicitly and so more weightily, that real English poetry has been shaped by the people in every generation.' In addition to its general political point, he found another significance in the anthology; it was, he said, a kind of manifesto of the Auden generation:

> It is as if the younger poets addressed us: 'Our writing is based on another tradition of literature than the one that has been usual lately with amateurs of the subject. We present our anthology as an indication of the tradition we mean. It will also help you to understand how we are writing, what we are writing about and the direction we are moving in.'[11]

Each of these remarks, taken separately, is more or less true: certainly *The Poet's Tongue* does contain more 'poetry of the people' than most anthologies do, and could be used to support the Marxist theory of the collective origins of poetry; and certainly some avant-garde poets—notably Auden—were drawing upon traditional popular forms like the riddle, the ballad, and the music-hall song that had not been a part of the art-tradition. But taken together the two remarks imply (and that was certainly the critic's intention) that there was a movement in modern poetry toward popular forms for explicitly political reasons, and this simply was not true.

One can see in Auden's introduction, for example, how he argues for a living and popular cultural tradition, but draws back defensively from the notion that this tradition should be used to advance any causes:

> The propagandist, whether moral or political, complains that

the writer should use his power over words to persuade people to a particular course of action, instead of fiddling while Rome burns. But Poetry is not concerned with telling people what to do, but with extending our knowledge of good and evil, perhaps making the necessity for action more urgent and its nature more clear, but only leading us to the point where it is possible for us to make a rational and moral choice . . . One must show those who come to poetry for a message, for calendar thoughts, that they have come to the wrong door, that poetry may illuminate but it will not dictate.[12]

Like Spender in *The Destructive Element*, Auden is concerned to assert the continuity of literature and the links between the modern writer and his past, and to assign to art a serious moral function; but he is also like Spender in defending the artist's right to use the tradition for his own artistic and moral ends.

In the introduction to *The Poet's Tongue* Auden remarks in passing on the relation between poetry and psychology: poetry is not, he says, a neurotic symptom as psychologists maintain; in fact, 'poetry, the parabolic approach, is the only adequate medium for psychology'.[13] He developed this extravagant claim further in 'Psychology and Art To-day', an essay that he contributed to Geoffrey Grigson's symposium, *The Arts To-day* (also 1935). Auden's essay is ostensibly intended to give a psychological account of the genesis of the artist and his place and function in society, drawing upon Freud but rejecting those Freudian concepts that diminish the value of art and the role of consciousness in creation. But in the end it is not so much an account of the art-psychology relationship as a defence of art against the reductions of any system.

Auden's strategy is to see psychology as an analogue for art, and with the same moral function:

The task of psychology, or art for that matter, is not to tell people how to behave, but by drawing their attention to what the impersonal unconsciousness is trying to tell them, and by increasing their knowledge of good and evil, to render them better able to choose, to become increasingly morally responsible for their destiny.[14]

The effect of this claim is to elevate art as a moral force; psychology cannot cure, it can only reveal, and art can do that better. Here Auden repeats the key passage from the *Poet's Tongue* introduction:

> You cannot tell people what to do, you can only tell them parables; and that is what art really is, particular stories of particular people and experiences, from which each according to his immediate and peculiar needs may draw his own conclusions.[15]

It is here that *parable*, in the sense that I have been using it in this book, enters Auden's critical language, though in this passage the meaning is not altogether clear—how, for example, does it differ from mimetic realism? And does it include, as it seems to, *all* stories? It seems, in this context, to be merely a name for indirection, and a way of asserting the moral function of literature.

'Psychology and Art To-day' is not primarily a political essay; nevertheless, politics enters the argument in two important ways. It enters first when Auden, at the end of the essay, compares Marxism and Freudianism as therapies for a sick society. The relation between these two modern systems was a problem that troubled many left intellectuals; Auden saw them as complementary, neither adequate to the whole task of curing the world:

> As long as civilisation remains as it is, the number of patients the psychologist can cure are very few, and as soon as socialism attains power, it must learn to direct its own interior energy and will need the psychologist.[16]

By arguing the mutual dependence of psychological and political 'treatment', Auden was in effect declaring his independence from either; both systems were useful analytical instruments, but neither was the Truth.

Auden's other political point comes in the last paragraph of the essay, when he returns to his idea of the moral function of art:

> There must always be two kinds of art, escape-art, for man needs escape as he needs food and deep sleep, and parable-art,

that art which shall teach man to unlearn hatred and learn love . . .[17]

Since this is a statement about changing the relations among men, it is political. Art, Auden is saying, can effect a revolution, but it will be an inner and moral one, the kind that he prayed for in the last line of 'Sir, no man's enemy': 'New styles of architecture, a change of heart.' (The whole passage, with its emphasis on love and its denial of the necessity of enemies and hatred, is directly opposed to the Marxist idea of inevitable class warfare; Auden remained what he always essentially was: an individualist, inclined more to Christianity than to any other system.) Like *parable*, this phrase 'a change of heart' turns up again and again in the writings of the 'thirties, as a name for the individualist's hope of a new world.

'Psychology and Art To-day' contains no literary criticism; what it does contain is a theory of art in terms both of individual human psychology (the artist as creative neurotic) and in terms of society (the work of art as moral instruction). There is no suggestion in the essay that collective political action is necessary, or that art should be in any way subordinate to political ends; on the contrary it is art that emerges as the principal agent in social change. Insofar as the essay is a partisan statement it is on the side of the one-man party of the artist, the individualistic maker of parables, against all ideologies. It is, as the *Criterion* reviewer of the book said, 'the best deliberate statement of his own aesthetic that [Auden] has made',[18] and for that reason it is an important document of the 'thirties.

Of the contributions made during 1935 to the continuing ideological debate on literature and politics, the most ingenious was William Empson's *Some Versions of Pastoral*. A contemporary reader familiar with earlier statements in the debate would have recognized as soon as he opened the book that he was reading an addition to that growing literature: the first chapter is entitled 'Proletarian Literature', and the first page is peppered with words like *propaganda, proletarian, workers, Russian, Marxist*. But as he turned the pages that reader would be puzzled by Empson's examples: Gray's 'Elegy', Marvell's 'The Garden', *The Beggars'*

Opera, Alice in Wonderland—what have these to do with the proletariat? The puzzlement was, I am sure, intentional on Empson's
part; individually the essays are brilliant examples of the analytical method that Empson had demonstrated in *Seven Types of
Ambiguity*, but packaged as they are, with this title and this beginning, they amount to an elaborate critical conceit, an intellectual's
joke at the expense of reductive communist critics.

The opening chapter, 'Proletarian Literature', is the most
theoretical, and ostensibly provides the foundations for the analyses
that follow. The immediate occasion for the essay was clearly the
publication of *Problems of Soviet Literature*, the report of the speeches
made by Zhdanov, Gorky, Bukharin, and Radek at the First
Soviet Writers' Congress in 1934. Empson quotes from Gorky's
speech, and attributes a remark made by Gorky to Radek, and
the whole line of his argument is a refutation of the critical position taken by the Russians. *Problems* was the first extensive statement of Soviet critical theory to reach English readers, and it
would seem appropriate that an English critic of the younger,
left-leaning generation, should examine the implications of the
theoretical position set out there. This is not to say that Empson
wrote a systematic critique of the book, but simply that he used it
as a starting point, a clear case of the problem at hand.

Empson begins his opening theoretical essay hesitantly, in the
role of the modest young Englishman, not really familiar with
these foreign concepts, but seeking definition:

> It is hard for an Englishman to talk definitely about proletarian
> art, because in England it has never been a genre with settled
> principles, and such as there is of it, that I have seen, is bad.
> But it is important to try and decide what the term ought to
> mean; my suspicion, as I shall try to make clear, is that it is
> liable to a false limitation.[19]

The goal, then, is simply to decide what proletarian art *ought* to
mean. What it usually does mean, Empson suggests, is simply 'the
propaganda of a factory-working class which feels its interests
opposed to the factory owners' '. Empson finds this sense uninter-
esting, and unlikely to produce good art, because it is based on a
bogus concept of literature, the communist aesthetic. He does not

define this aesthetic in much detail; he appears to take it for granted that his reader will know what the issues are—as though *everyone* had been reading *Problems of Soviet Literature*. The essential terms are clear, though: art should be by and for the workers, it should be propaganda in the class struggle, it should be, in Zhdanov's words, class literature, tendentious, and political.

Against this party-line definition of proletarian art, Empson sets these propositions:

> Good writing is not done unless there are serious forces at work; and it is not permanent unless it works for readers with opinions different from the author's.

> To produce pure proletarian art the artist must be at one with the worker; this is impossible, not for political reasons, but because the artist never is at one with any public.

> Politics and economics . . . do not provide an aesthetic theory.[20]

Separate art from opinion, separate the artist from his audience, separate aesthetics from politics and economics, and what you have is a theory of art opposed in all particulars to what Empson calls 'the communist aesthetic'.

How, then, *ought* one to define the term 'proletarian art?' Empson suggests that good proletarian art is usually 'Covert Pastoral'. *Pastoral* has a very broad meaning here, which Empson sustains throughout the book; it means simply 'putting the complex into the simple'. 'The essential trick of the old pastoral', Empson writes,

> which was felt to imply a beautiful relation between rich and poor, was to make simple people express strong feelings (felt as the most universal subject, something fundamentally true about everybody) in learned and fashionable language (so that you wrote about the best subject in the best way).[21]

But the core of this relation is simply 'a double attitude of the artist to the worker, of the complex man to the simple one ("I am in one way better, in another not so good")' and this Empson took to be a permanent truth about the aesthetic situation; for the artist is always the complex man, and his attitude toward

the simple will always be a divided one. If this is true, then proletarian art, being literature about the worker written by artists,
is only a particular type of the general case, and when it succeeds
it will succeed *as pastoral* (in Empson's terms). 'My own difficulty
about proletarian literature,' Empson admits,

> is that when it comes off I find that I am taking it as pastoral
> literature; I read into it, or find that the author has secretly
> put into it, these more subtle, more far-reaching, and I think
> more permanent, ideas.[22]

It is an ingenious argument, with several important consequences. First, it protects the artist from being 'proletarianized';
he remains the Artist—separate, intellectually superior, a conscious maker. Second, it preserves the idea of Art as artifact, the
sum of the artist's tricks. Third, it allows for submerged, 'secret'
levels of meaning below the conscious, polemical surface. And
fourth, it assumes that there is a relation between excellence and
complexity—that is, it makes the standard of judgment aesthetic,
not political.

Some Versions of Pastoral is, I have said, an elaborate joke; it
paradoxically defines an urban and realistic genre in terms of a
rural and artificial one, and by proposing that proletarian art is
simply one more version of Pastoral, it attaches the literature of
social realism to an old and often aristocratic tradition. But if it
is a joke, it is a serious one: by attaching proletarian art to the
pastoral tradition, Empson was taking it out of the hands of
Zhdanov and company, and restoring it to the artists. To communist critics he says, in effect: 'If you mean to formulate a sound
theory of proletarian literature you must account not only for
your novels about factory workers and five-year plans, but also
for the following related examples'; and he then offers the curious
series of literary works that constitute the rest of the book.

Empson was aware of the oddity of his examples. 'Probably
the cases I take are the surprising rather than the normal ones,'
he wrote in his first chapter, and in a letter to *The Times Literary
Supplement* he explained that 'the fact was simply that I had written
most of the essays before it struck me that they all bore on one
topic, and had interested me for that reason . . .'[23] This has an

unconvincing, after-the-fact sound, and one might better interpret it as something like this: 'I had written a number of essays on various subjects when I came upon *Problems of Soviet Literature*, and I thought that it might be fun to add proletarian literature to my studies, and invent a linking argument.' Still, the forging of that link, however arbitrary it might seem, had one important implication: by making it, Empson was asserting yet another traditional link between the political, revolutionary present and the literary past. As literary history, his versions of Pastoral make a very improbable sequence; but the very improbability of the line he drew has its point. His examples have virtually nothing in common except their complex forms, and so they demonstrate the eclectic range of English literature, and the variety of ways in which artists have put the complex into the simple. Like Spender and Auden, Empson was defending the variousness and complexity of serious literature against the simplifications of dogma, and relevance of the past against the apocalyptic visions of the mid-'thirties. It is not surprising that his book did not please left-wing reviewers, for it is literary-historical, individualistic, and eccentric, and consequently heretical. 'His scholarly attempt to meet the Marxists on their own ground,' wrote the *Left Review*'s critic, 'is invalid from the beginning . . . Certainly Mr. Empson is not yet a Marxist.'[24]

Revolution in Writing, published in the same month as *Some Versions of Pastoral*, is important in a different way. Day Lewis had made two crucial decisions that year—he had left his secure teaching position to become a free-lance writer, and he had taken 'the road these times should take'—he had joined the Communist Party. The argument of his pamphlet orbits around those decisions, and their consequences for him. One might expect that a statement written at such a point of commitment would be a brave manifesto, crammed with courage and convictions; but in fact it is full of hesitations, uncertainties, and qualifications. It is a catalogue of problems, and that is its value.

The pamphlet contains three separate essays, each dealing with a distinct aspect of the problem that Day Lewis faced, of being a revolutionary writer, and at the same time a professional writer, in a bourgeois society that appeared to be dying, but wouldn't expire. The question that the first essay, 'The Revolution in Literature', asks is essentially this: 'If a revolution is indeed coming, what will the future of literature be?' Day Lewis concludes that probably, 'whatever social system is coming, literature will be considered more and more as being ultimately . . . a guide to living. The temporary estrangement between literature and morality will be ended.' In his discussion of the moral role of literature he picks up Auden's term, *parable*; but he puts it to a use that suggests that he had misread his friend's argument. 'I am inclined to think,' he says,

> that it is poetry, oddly enough, which has the best chance of survival—poetry and the fairy tale, the two simplest forms of literature. Poetry, partly through metaphor but chiefly through rhythm, can penetrate into strata of man's mind that nothing else can touch. The fairy tale, the parable will survive, I believe, because it is a unique channel of education. [25]

This separation of poetry from the parabolic, didactic function of literature, he develops further:

> In the nearer future I think it likely that literature will divide into two main streams. On the one hand, morality writing—conveyed through fairy tales, allegory, satire, and perhaps a new kind of semi-religious drama based on the revelations of recent psychologists. On the other hand, a form of writing somewhat akin to music, depending on highly elaborated sounds, intense verbal subtlety and complex patterns of association. [26]

As prophecy, this is scarcely impressive; as an answer to the problem, it is no better. But as a record of a troubled mind, traditionally literary by nature, but convinced that a revolution in society and literature was taking place, it is of considerable interest. Looking for a future for literature, Day Lewis found it by assigning a different role to each side of his divided nature: morality writing for his political self, and 'a form of writing somewhat akin to music', and apparently without content, for his lyrical-poetical self.

The question in the second essay, 'Writers and Morals', is,

'How can I be a revolutionary writer in a bourgeois society (on which I am now dependent for the support of my family)?' The answer is, 'You can't', and the process by which Day Lewis reaches this answer is essentially a defence of his own vulnerable position, on the fence with all those who 'while fighting for the things-to-come, have to maintain a precarious existence on things-as-they-are'. He cannot solve his problem by simply making contact with the workers; that is difficult, and if he really *becomes* a worker he'll have no time for writing (here the argument approaches Empson's defence of the inevitable separateness of the artist). Nor can he solve it by expressing his Marxism directly in bourgeois literary forms. The middle classes will reject him, the masses won't understand him, and he'll have no market for his work. The day that Marx predicted will come,

> when the class war is about to be fought to a finish, disintegration of the ruling class and the old order of society becomes so active, so acute, that a small part of the ruling class breaks away to make common cause with the revolutionary class, the class which holds the future in its hands . . .[27]

But that day is not yet come, and in the meantime the revolutionary who is also a professional writer must go on straddling.

In the third essay, 'Revolutionaries and Poetry', Day Lewis poses the crucial questions in the first sentence: 'The questions are often asked—"What should be the attitude of Communists to poetry?" and "Is poetry of any value to the revolutionary?"' The answer, of course, is that poetry is valuable: as propaganda (he cites the effects of Sassoon's war poems), as a re-creation of language (Spender's argument in 'Poetry and Revolution'), as escape-art (Auden again). Good poems are valuable, even if written by a reactionary (*The Waste Land* is the example, as it often was on this point), because they give insight into the state of mind of a group of people. Like other writers in this critical-political dialogue, Day Lewis was not willing to assign to poetry a strictly instrumental role. But unlike the others, he was committed to a more or less orthodox line, and so he ended his pamphlet with another prophecy: 'The stage is set for the entrance of the proletarian poet.' And here he departs from Empson: there *can* be proletarian art, the obstacles are in society, not in the nature of the creative process. 'To speak to the workers and for the workers he does not need, as bourgeois poets do, to learn a new tongue: he has only to make poetry of what is his native language.'

Revolution in Writing is not a major critical work, as *The Destructive Element* and *Some Versions of Pastoral* are. But it is nevertheless important for the problems it poses and the questions it asks, important perhaps more as a symptom of the time than as an answer to any problem. One feels in it great honesty, a desire to confront issues, and a humility that accepts, and even anticipates criticism. As far as the theoretical content goes, the *TLS* reviewer was right when he wrote: 'It is all quite orthodox and singularly unimpressive' (though orthodoxy is not quite as easily defined, perhaps, as he suggests); but as an effort to examine the consequences of commitment it is worth a place in the literary history of the decade.

II

In *The Whispering Gallery*, John Lehmann writes of his feelings in 1935:

> Like so many of my contemporaries, I was haunted by the feeling that time was running out for a new world war. 'How to get out of this trap?' I noted in a journal at the time. 'How to find sanity and a clear thought again? How to defend oneself, to be active, not to crouch paralysed as the hawk descends? But there must be hundreds, thousands like myself in every town in Europe, wrestling with this nightmare.'[28]

There are two elements in this note that are characteristic of the time: the sense of nightmare, and the feeling of community with ordinary Europeans that the shared nightmare gave. A sense of community with Europe has not, traditionally, been an English feeling, but by 1935 many Englishmen felt it. For some, like Lehmann, it was a consequence of having been there, at the Reichstag fire and the Vienna Uprising; but most people must have taken it from the daily papers and the radio broadcasts. Some may have got it from imaginative literature, though the presence of Europe there is more a symptom of the growing awareness than a cause of it.

Of the 'thirties generation of writers, Christopher Isherwood was the one who had the earliest and most profound experience of Europe. He had gone to Berlin in 1929, and had remained there while it became the centre and source of the political nightmare. Auden and Lehmann and Spender all visited him there, and came away impressed by the austerity of the life that he had chosen: 'his renunciation of England, his poverty, his friendship, his independence, his work,' Spender wrote, 'all struck me as heroic.'[29] Why Berlin? Because for Isherwood and his friends Berlin meant liberation. 'One of my chief motives for wanting to visit Berlin,' Isherwood later wrote, 'was that an elderly relative had warned me against it, saying that it was the vilest place since Sodom.'[30] And certainly it seemed to have some customs in common with Sodom: in the last years of the Weimar Republic there were said to be 132 homosexual cafés in Berlin, all registered with the police. But Berlin offered more than sexual freedom: to be intimate with Germans was to cast off the emotions and rhetoric of the First World War, and so to reject childhood and become free and adult. And once the young English writers were there, they discovered that Berlin also offered a contemporary literature, and particularly drama, that was at once avant-garde and highly political, as England's was not.

Berlin first appeared in Isherwood's work in his second novel, *The Memorial* (published in 1932, but completed by the end of 1930, his second year in Germany). *The Memorial* is subtitled 'A Portrait of a Family', and most of it is just that—a novel of an English childhood and adolescence in an upper-middle-class family that is very like Isherwood's own, in the years during and after the First World War. It is a memorial to that life, an elaborate tombstone erected over a dead personal past. But in the latter part of the novel both the style and the centre of interest shift, from Eric, the adolescent Isherwood character, to Edward Blake, a shell-shocked veteran of the air war in France, who is the Truly Weak Man. Blake goes to Berlin in 1938, attempts suicide and fails, and is 'reborn' into an idle, promiscuous, homosexual life. The symbolism is excessively clear: Berlin is escape, the new and private life in which past, family, and English repressions are cast off, and a young man can be reborn into his own true nature.[31]

Mr. Norris Changes Trains is a more controlled, more ironic version of the same theme of liberation; another young Englishman goes to Berlin and finds a free life there. This character, William Bradshaw, is a figure of Isherwood himself (Isherwood was christened Christopher William Bradshaw-Isherwood, so William Bradshaw is the *inside* of his name). What Bradshaw does in Berlin is less melodramatic than what Blake does; in fact, he does nothing at all except observe the behaviour of others—he is the first of Isherwood's detached voyeurs, the Camera Eye. The world that he observes is Berlin during the critical years of 1930–3. It is, in a sense, a private world—Bradshaw knows no public figures, and has no public existence, being only a poor foreigner; but that private world is gradually invaded by the public world, the world of forces represented by the word *Europe*, what Lehmann had called the noise of history. The inevitability of this invasion is the central theme of the novel.

The private world is established first: Bradshaw and Mr Norris meet in a third-class compartment of the train that is taking William to Berlin for the first time. The public world intrudes briefly on the scene in the persons of passport control officers and customs officials, and there is an atmosphere of unexplained anxiety in the compartment, but nothing happens, except that a personal relationship is begun. It continues in private contexts—Frau Schroeder's flat, Mr Norris's flat, private dinners and parties at which Norris indulges his private taste for flagellation. In the early chapters there are occasional hints of the public realities of the time, as when someone shouts 'Red Front!' from a window, but nothing political occurs, and even when Mr Norris announces that he is a communist 'in all but name' it is passed off as a joke, and the conversation drifts back to his tastes in luxuries and perversions.

Gradually, however, the public, political world enters Bradshaw's life. At first the invasion is personal: he meets the Nazi Baron von Pregnitz and Otto, the communist pimp, and his girl, Anni, but he meets them as private persons—a homosexual, a pimp and a whore, and not as three figures in the turmoil of German politics. Then Hitler is mentioned, the winter of 1931–2 comes, and Bradshaw's narrative becomes public, a kind of history of a city in a state of civil war:

Hate exploded suddenly, without warning, out of nowhere; at street corners, in restaurants, cinemas, dance halls, swimming-baths; at midnight, after breakfast, in the middle of the after-noon. Knives were whipped out, blows were dealt with spiked rings, beer-mugs, chair-legs or leaded clubs; bullets slashed the advertisements on the poster-columns, rebounded from the iron roofs of latrines.[32]

From here on, the world of the novel opens up: election results are quoted, and scenes occur at public meetings and in the public streets, instead of in bedrooms, bars, and brothels, as in the earlier pages. As public violence increases, the private life recedes, and the private man is drawn out of his closed world, into the streets.

Most of these historical events are observed and recorded by Bradshaw coldly, as a newsreel film might report them. But there are two points at which his detachment fails, and they are crucial to the novel, since they are both *political* points, and reveal the nature of Bradshaw's political commitment. The first occurs dur-ing the description of the Communist Party meeting at which Norris makes a successful speech. The scene is reminiscent of the Party meeting in *It's a Battlefield*, and Isherwood may well have been influenced by Greene's novel; certainly he was aware of Greene's work. In a letter to Lehmann written while he was at work on *Mr. Norris*, Isherwood described his book as 'a sort of glorified shocker; not unlike the productions of my cousin Graham Greene'.[33] But whereas Greene's rendering of the meeting is satirical, Isherwood's manner is, as always, coldly objective, with one exception; when Bradshaw describes the audience he seems to become aware of his detachment, as though he were even detached from that, and could see it as a human flaw.

The hall was very full. The audience sat there in their soiled everyday clothes. Most of the men wore breeches with coarse woollen stockings, sweaters and peaked caps. Their eyes fol-lowed the speaker with hungry curiosity. I had never been to ι communist meeting before, and what struck me most was the fixed attention of the upturned rows of faces; faces of the Berlin working class, pale and prematurely lined, often haggard and ascetic, like the heads of scholars, with thin, fair hair brushed back from their broad foreheads. They had not come here to see each other or to be seen, or even to fulfil a social duty. They were attentive but not passive. They were not spectators. They participated, with a curious, restrained passion, in the speech made by the red-haired man. He spoke for them, he made their thoughts articulate. They were listening to their own collective voice. At intervals they applauded it, with sudden, spontaneous violence. Their passion, their strength of purpose elated me. I stood outside it. One day, perhaps, I should be with it, but never of it. At present I just sat there, a half-hearted renegade from my own class, my feelings muddled by anarchism talked at Cambridge, by slogans from the confirmation service, by the tunes played when my father's regiment marched to the railway station, seventeen years ago.[34]

The English young man sits outside, wrapped in his English past, in his class, his college, the war. It is a strong, because indirect account of the generation's relation to political action and to the working class. Bradshaw desires to belong to that class, but his motive is not a political one; he simply wants to belong to a human group that seems, when viewed from the outside, to be a living and energetic whole.

Bradshaw's other lapse from objectivity occurs when he learns that his friend Norris has used him, and betrayed their friendship. Ludwig Bayer, the communist leader who tells him of the betrayal, tries to reassure him. 'Mind,' he says, 'I have not said this against him as a man; the private life is not our concern.'[35] But it *is* Bradshaw's concern, and it is that life that has been violated, by the shabby public world.

It is Mr Norris, more than any other character, who represents the private life—Mr Norris with his wigs and his cosmetics, his whips and pornographic novels, and his odd capacity for affection. His life is private because it is free and furtive; for him, the public world is simply the antagonist, to be outsmarted and exploited, and not a locus of possible values or of moral issues. Insofar as the novel is the story of his game with the public world, it ends when that game ends. It is 1933: Hitler is in power, the communists are in hiding or in prison, Bayer has been murdered in the Spandau barracks, von Pregnitz has committed suicide. Mr Norris has fled to South America after being revealed as a double agent, and Bradshaw has returned to England. The public drama of Germany has been acted out to a tragic conclusion; in Berlin there is no private life left to be lived.

One can see now that in one sense *Mr. Norris Changes Trains* is a novel on a traditional private theme, the young man's education into life, like *The Great Gatsby* and Joyce's *Portrait of the Artist*. But reviewers in 1935 saw only the public side, and took the book almost as a documentary account of current history. 'It is chiefly as a picture of Berlin just before the Nazi regime that the book is valuable,' the *TLS* critic wrote, and William Plomer, reviewing it in the *Spectator*, agreed, though he went farther, and saw in the novel also a parable of the modern historical situation:

> It has value [he wrote] as a view of Berlin during the years pre-ceding Hitler's triumph, and accordingly as a study of social disintegration and upheaval, and it has a deeper meaning than that, for it may be taken as a comment on the state of civilisation in general during these last few years, and it may be that in the figure of Ludwig Bayer, a communist leader, we are tentatively to anticipate the possibility of a cleaner and better-behaved world.[36]

Isherwood has since protested against this view of the novel, on the grounds that he was a stranger to Berlin. But the camera is a stranger to its subject, too, and its record is no less valuable for that. It was inevitable that in 1935 *Mr. Norris* should have been read in this way, for serious books are read for what people need from them, and at this time what men needed—or thought that their fellow men needed—was the truth about Europe. Sensitive young men were a subject that could wait for better days.

In the same month of 1935 that *Mr. Norris* was published, another important work appeared to which Isherwood contributed the same European and political awareness that he gave to his novel. *The Dog Beneath the Skin, or Where is Francis?* was the third draft of a play that Auden had been working on for at least three years, with help from Isherwood on the first and third versions. All three texts survive, and it is possible to trace through them the generation's sense of what a revolutionary subject was, as it evolved during the early years of the decade.

The first version, *The Enemies of a Bishop, or Die When I Say When: A Morality in Four Acts*, was written in 1932. It concerned a white-slave ring, a group of escapees from a reformatory, and a lead-mine manager who seduces his assistant manager's wife with the help of the Devil. The theme of the play was the early-Auden faith in love and freedom. The Bishop, according to Isherwood, represented 'natural law', and was modelled on Homer Lane, the heterodox psychiatrist whom Auden admired at the time; his Enemies were essentially the same as The Enemy in *The Orators*—all those who distort and repress life, love, and freedom.[37]

Two years later Auden tried another version, and called it *The Chase*.[38] This play used some of the components of *The Enemies of a Bishop*, but shifted the focus from love and freedom to the class struggle. There is a strike at the centre of the play, and capitalists who oppose it. There is also a character—one of the escaped prisoners from the first version—who appears disguised as a dog, and a quest for a missing heir. Like the previous version, *The Chase* is set entirely in England, but its themes are very different, concerned with economic and social history, rather than with psychic sickness and health. The mood of the play is the anti-capitalist, pro-working class mood of the early 'thirties, the years of greatest unemployment, of the first Hunger Marches, and of the collapse of the Labour Party. It is a play about domestic political and social issues, as an educated liberal young poet might see them.

During 1934 Auden began to correspond with Isherwood about a third version of the play, and by the end of the year they had completed *The Dog Beneath the Skin*. The play, which was published in February 1935, shows many signs of its earlier existence: it is patched and layered like a too-often-mended garment, and it is partly for that reason that it reads (and plays) more like a revue made up of satirical turns than a continuous dramatic statement. It includes, for example, 'The Witnesses', which was originally a part of the allegorical poem that Auden wrote in 1932, and the Nineveh Hotel scene from *The Enemies of a Bishop*, and the Sermon from *The Chase*. There are passages of Lawrentian love, of psychological analysis, and of social concern for the poor and distressed, and at various points satirical comments on patriotic rhetoric, anti-German hysteria, and class attitudes. In fact, one can find on one page or another virtually all the ideas that engaged Auden's imagination, and the imaginations of his generation, during the first half of the 'thirties. What remains constant through all the versions of the play, and all the laminations of the final text, is the intention that Auden announced when he called his first version 'A Morality': the point changes, but the motive does not.

The principal difference between the final version of the play and preceding versions is that the *Dog* is about Europe. Most of the action takes place in imagined European capitals, and satiric scenes are devoted to European politics. The larger political world, the same 'noise of history' that invades private realms of feeling in *Mr. Norris Changes Trains*, enters the play, as it did not enter the earlier versions. For some of this change Isherwood is explicitly responsible. For example, the scene in which workers in Ostnia are executed by the king, while the queen comforts their widows, was suggested to Isherwood by the alleged behaviour of Frau Doll-fuss, the wife of the Austrian chancellor, during the Vienna Up-rising.[39] And it would seem reasonable that Isherwood, who had lived in Berlin through the early years of the 'thirties, would have pressed anti-fascist convictions upon his friend, who had spent those years as a schoolmaster in Scotland and England. But one must add that history itself was also pressing in, and that the shifts of scene and theme in the play corespond to a general shift in the focus of anxiety between 1932 and 1935.

The whole action of the *Dog* is developed from one of the two plots in *The Chase*—the search for a missing heir. This search leads Alan, the hero, through a repressive European monarchy and a lunatic fascist state and back to England, where he finds a native fascism establishing itself in his village. There Francis, the heir, reveals himself as the dog that had followed Alan on his journey, and the two go off together, after denouncing the leaders of the village establishment—the Vicar, the General, and the General's wife—to join 'the army of the other side.'

In a quest-plot like this one, one expects the object of the quest to carry the principal meaning. But what does Francis represent? Nothing very precise politically: he is against the Old Guard, that's clear enough, but it is less clear what the 'army' that he is joining at the end is all about. Spender, in an acute essay on the Auden–Isherwood collaborations, took note of this abrupt introduction of an unexplained force of virtue in the final scene:

> As this is the first we have heard of the army 'of the other side' throughout the play, this conclusion may seem rather surprising. But it is not really so, because the satire has been directed from 'the other side' throughout the play. The reason why the writers fail to represent that 'other side' whose point of view they implicitly accept is because whereas they know a great deal about the side of the bourgeoisie—from which they consider themselves disinherited—they know far less about the workers' side which they believe themselves to have joined. *The Dog Beneath the Skin* is a picture of a society defeated by an enemy whom the writers have not put into the picture because they do not know what he looks like although they thoroughly support him.[40]

This is very good, and points to a problem that dogged the middle-class, left-wing intellectuals throughout the 'thirties, and was much debated: how can one resign from one's own class and join another? or, another form of the problem: how can one write from the point of view of a classless society that doesn't yet exist?

Spender assumed that Auden and Isherwood were on the side of the workers, but reviewers of the play were less confident of what its political point really was. It was praised by the *Left Review* and by the *Daily Worker*, which took the play to be 'criticism, often pointed and effective, of a Europe distracted by Fascism and crisis'.[41] But it was also admired in the pages of *Action*, Mosley's fascist weekly. 'There can be no doubt,' E. D. Randall wrote there, 'that the text of the play is brilliant, and contains some magnificent verse. As a jocular superficial satire on the society of our day the whole production is clever and very funny.' But he added: 'Its propaganda message is pleasantly obscure.'[42] Apparently it was a play from which both Left and Right could derive pleasure and comfort, a point which was made by several critics of the middle. 'The "unity" for which the authors ask is presumably a corporate state of the Left,' *The Times* reviewer wrote. 'Why, on their own spiritual principle, it is more desirable than the corporate state of the Right which they satirize is not explained . . .'[43] And another reviewer remarked: 'The general trend of the play is revolutionary, but apart from one easily adapted scene the fascist helmet fits almost as well as the communist cap.'[44]

Politically *The Dog Beneath the Skin* is as ambiguous as *The Orators* and *The Magnetic Mountain*. Like those earlier works, it is more about stagnation, moral paralysis, and the need for action than it is about the exact direction that action should take. Francis cannot be interpreted as a symbol of any political doctrine; he is simply the man who can act, the Truly Strong Man. His antecedents in literature are not political leaders, but Auden's various questors, Spender's 'truly great', and Lewis' explorers—all those 'thirties heroes who were not afraid to enter the unknown.

But if the character is familiar, the scene is different. The opening chorus begins:

> The Summer holds: upon its glittering lake
> Lie Europe and the islands . . .[45]

And Europe-and-the-islands, taken as one place with one common set of problems, is constantly present in the play. The point is made most explicitly in the Chorus speeches, which urge the English audience to consider its European destiny:

Do not comfort yourself with the reflection: 'How very un-English'
If your follies are different, it is because you are richer;
Your clocks have completed fewer revolutions since the complacent years . . .
But already, like an air-bubble under a microscope-slide, the film of poverty is expanding
And soon it will reach your treasure and your gentlemanly behaviour.[46]

It is the existence of Europe, and not any political doctrine, that is the reality principle here. The point is one more version of the public-private theme: Europe exists, and thrusts its realities and crises upon insular England. There is one Enemy, and anyone who opposes that force belongs to the 'other army'. Action is no longer a matter of choice: it is an imperative.

That summer Auden returned to this theme of action in the birthday poem that he wrote to Isherwood. The poem is affectionately personal, recalling adolescence and summer holidays together; but it is also a poem about the present, and the pressures of public circumstance. In this 'hour of crisis and dismay', what can the artist do? Auden must have been thinking of *Mr. Norris Changes Trains* and *The Dog Beneath the Skin* when he praised the power of his friend's 'strict and adult pen' to warn and to reveal, to give 'insight to resist/The expanding fear, the savaging disaster', and to 'make action urgent and its nature clear'. But looking back on those works of 1935, one must conclude that Isherwood was a good deal clearer on the warnings and fears and disasters than he was on the nature of action.

Auden must have felt that, too, for the final stanza of the poem is a birthday wish that invokes above all a sense of relentless public forces at work among the private lives.

> This then my birthday wish for you, as now
> From the narrow window of my fourth floor room
> I smoke into the night, and watch reflections
> Stretch in the harbour. In the houses
> The little pianos are closed, and a clock strikes.
> And all sway forward on the dangerous flood
> Of history, that never sleeps or dies
> And, held one moment, burns the hand.[47]

Once more *history*, that favourite 'thirties word for unavoidable disaster, enters and thrusts the public world into a private occasion.

A birthday is a private rite in which public issues customarily have no place, and the presence of those issues here in a birthday poem is a sign of the disorder of the times. There are many similar examples, of which I will cite only two, both published in 1935: Auden's 'A Bride in the '30s' and MacNeice's 'Ode' (a poem on the birth of his son). Auden's poem is an epithalamium, but it contains 'the sixteen skies of Europe/And the Danube flood', as well as Hitler, Mussolini, Churchill, Roosevelt, and Van der Lubbe.

MacNeice's ode is similarly invaded by public elements—mob mania, newspapers, a bombing plane, Europe—which are all threats to a fulfilled private life for his infant son. What all these poems have in common is this sense of the violation of intimate private occasions, by politics, by war, by Europe, by the noises of history. They are poems that belong to their time.

III

I noted in the last chapter how heroes and myths of heroes returned to English writing in the 'thirties, as revolutionary politics seemed to make heroism once again possible. As that process continued, it became a subject for discussion as well as for representation: it was, after all, only a part of the propaganda war in which the Left and the Right were engaged. As Montagu Slater wrote in the *Left Review*:

> The Nazis pride themselves on giving the world a 'twentieth-century myth'. They succeeded but not as they thought. They gave us the story of the burning of a Parliament house, which is as if somebody had set fire to a symbol of the nineteenth century. They gave us the story of a man who was able to make world history his alibi. They unwittingly acquainted the world with a new quality of greatness which Dimitrov along with many others—Rakosi, Mooney, Conolly—have shown themselves possessed of.[48]

History provided the new greatness; and writers, it seemed, had only to draw upon that new source. So it is not surprising that, among the headings on the programme for the First International Congress of Writers for the Defence of Culture, in Paris in June 1935, was 'Formation of Heroes'.[49] One could once more be romantic about human behaviour; indeed, left writers had the support of Gorky for adopting 'that romanticism which is at the basis of myth and is highly beneficial in that it tends to provoke a revolutionary attitude to reality . . .'[50] It was all a part of the struggle.

Not many writers of Auden's generation had yet found it possible to create heroes. Auden's Airman, Isherwood's William

Bradshaw, the 'I' of Spender's *Vienna* are all uncertain, self-conscious young men who are aware of heroism as a human possibility, but unable to achieve it in their lives. And if you look further, to the early Waugh novels, to Greene's Entertainments, to *The Dog Beneath the Skin* or the poems of MacNeice, the evidence is the same: if a hero is a man who puts values into public action, then there are no early-'thirties heroes.

One writer of the group seems to offer exceptions. Day Lewis had already postulated, in *The Magnetic Mountain*, a possible heroism through revolutionary action, though in that poem it was only an *idea* of heroism that he celebrated. In 1934 he included in his 'symphonic poem', 'A Time to Dance', a narrative section based on recent history that seems, at least by intention, to be a brief heroic epic. The subject is a flight from England to Australia made by two Australian war veterans, Parer and McIntosh, in 1919–20. The flight, in a war-weary, condemned DH-9, took eight months, and it *is* heroic in its details of crazy, courageous struggles against odds, and disasters overcome. It is a good story, and Day Lewis tells it well enough; still, it is an odd tale for him to be telling just at the time when he was deciding to join the Communist Party, for it has no revolutionary content at all, no ideology, no politics. Parer and McIntosh are examples of the will to adventure and the gaiety of some men's courage, and nothing more.

Perhaps we can understand Day Lewis' motives if we examine another account of the Parer–McIntosh flight, written in the following year, in *Great Flights*, by C. St John Sprigg. Sprigg's book is a popular account, written for boys, of some adventurous long-distance flights; in a chapter titled '11,000 Miles' he describes the contest, initiated by the Australian Government in 1919, for a £10,000 prize for the first England-to-Australia flight made by Australians. Parer and McIntosh were among the six entrants; they finished second, but only because nobody else finished behind them. They reached Australia more than seven months behind the winners.

Sprigg's account is more factual than Day Lewis's, and concentrates on the flight of the winners. It is nevertheless a romantic story, in a book about the romance of flight (as Day Lewis' poem is a poem about that romance). The book begins:

There has been nothing like the great flights of the twentieth century since the historic days when Magellan and Columbus were exploring the unknown New World. In the same way the great long-distance pilots have been exploring the possibilities of the new world of the air . . .[51]

This is no doubt exactly the right way to begin a popular history of adventurous flying; but it is interesting, when one remembers that C. St John Sprigg is now better known as Christopher Caudwell, a member of the Communist Party, author of the best English book of Marxist literary criticism, who died with the International Brigade in Spain. Caudwell/Sprigg joined the Party at about the same time that Day Lewis did, late in 1935; at the time *Great Flights* was published he was at work on *Illusion and Reality* and deep in a study of Marxist literature. Yet his justification of the flights he describes has no element of politics in it.

'What good are these flights?' the practical man is inclined to ask . . . But it is unnecessary to answer the practical man; for the value of long-distance flying is not practical, any more than is that of exploring, sport, or mountaineering. All have values that are higher than the merely practical. The justification of long-distance flying is in its demonstration of human courage and skill battling against the dangers of a still unknown element.[52]

That last phrase must by now seem familiar: it suggests Day Lewis' Magnetic Mountain, Auden's frontiers, the mountains in Roberts' poems, the goals of Spender's 'truly great'. The First World War had destroyed the traditional British ideal of heroism in battle, but there was still the air, there were still mountains, and these offered metaphors for the challenge and danger of individual action, and the possibility of heroism.

I am assuming that the need for heroes is a human constant, though it is not always satisfied. I see no other explanation for the odd fact that the most heroic figure of the mid-'thirties, for the young men of the Left as well as for the rest of English society, was a man whose political views could not have appealed to the Auden

189

Generation at all—T. E. Lawrence. The desert campaign of 1916–18 in which he fought so courageously and inventively was the only campaign of the War in which individual courage could be a decisive factor; Lawrence emerged from it the last of the romantic military heroes, and fixed that image of himself permanently in the popular imagination with *The Seven Pillars of Wisdom*, which is surely the last of the romantic books of war.

In the years after the war Lawrence tried to evade his reputation, changed his name twice, joined the RAF as an enlisted man, and refused all public honours and appointments, but when he died, in May 1935, it was still as Lawrence of Arabia that he was mourned. Both King George V and the King of Iraq paid tribute to his gifts as a military leader, and *The Times* carried statements of grief and admiration from Winston Churchill, Field-Marshal Lord Allenby, General Sir Ian Hamilton, and Lloyd George. Even the Left agreed on his heroism: he was the only hero, wrote the Communist critic Ralph Fox, 'whom the English ruling classes have produced in our time, a hero who in his own lifetime gathered about him all the legendary atmosphere of the hero.'[53]

But though he was recognized as a hero, there was something new and disturbing about him. 'Part of the secret of this stimulating ascendancy,' Churchill said,

> lay of course in his disdain for most of the prizes, the pleasures and comforts of life. The world naturally looks with some awe upon a man who appears unconcernedly indifferent to home, money, comfort, rank, or even power and fame. The world feels not without a certain apprehension, that here is someone outside its jurisdiction; someone before whom its allurements may be spread in vain; someone strangely enfranchised, untamed, untrammelled by convention, moving independently of the ordinary currents of human action; a being readily capable of violent revolt or supreme sacrifice, a man, solitary, austere, to whom existence is no more than a duty, yet a duty to be faithfully discharged.[54]

Clearly Lawrence did not fit the traditional image of the hero. But perhaps he was the *new* hero, perhaps his life offered a new definition for the time. It is one of the characteristics of the 'thirties that

the urgencies and crises of the time seemed to demand new definitions: and just as there had to be new meanings for art and action,
for love and patriotism, new styles of architecture, new aesthetics,
so perhaps there had to be a new kind of hero.

To the young writers of the 'thirties, Lawrence seems to have
been that hero. He was an intellectual and a homosexual, a shy,
under-sized Oxford archaeologist who made himself into a man of
action as though by an act of will, and then withdrew again into
himself. Isherwood, in an acute essay, described Lawrence as a
divided man, an adolescent who had never matured, and a man
who 'suffered, in his own person, the neurotic ills of an entire
generation'.[55] And Auden saw him as a symbolic figure for the
time:

> To me [he wrote in 1934] Lawrence's life is an allegory of the
> transformation of the Truly Weak Man into the Truly Strong
> Man, an answer to the question 'How shall the self-conscious
> man be saved'? and the moral seems to be this: 'self-consciousness
> is an asset, in fact the only friend of our progress. We can't go
> back on it. But its demands on our little person and his appetites
> are so great that most of us, terrified, try to escape or make terms
> with it, which is fatal. As a pursuer it is deadly.' Only the con-
> tinuous annihilation of the self by the Identity, to use Blake's
> terminology, will bring us to the freedom we wish for, or in
> Lawrence's own phrase 'Happiness comes in absorption'.[56]

It is clear from this that Lawrence was the inspiration of the Air-
man in *The Orators*, as he was later to be of Michael Ransom in
The Ascent of F-6. He was the Neurotic Hero, the Truly Strong
Intellectual: Auden and Churchill agreed on that (Churchill's
oration on Lawrence is simply Auden's judgment translated into
Churchillese).

Lawrence was not a likely hero for the Left, any more than the
other Lawrence was. Nevertheless, the two Lawrences dominated
the imaginations of the 'thirties generation: two small, weak men
who had made themselves strong in the world; two neurotics who
had made their neuroses creative; two artists who had not been
content with art alone; two despisers of ordinary ambitions; two
outsiders who had refused to come into established society. For

young men of Auden's generation, these lives were parables of their own problem solved: 'How shall the self-conscious man be saved?' The answers in these cases had nothing to do with politics, but everything to do with action and with self-knowledge.

VII

1936

I

Looking back on the 'thirties, we can see in the history of the decade the shape of a tragic play—the initiating errors, the complicating actions, the climax, and the fall toward disaster and death. In that pattern, 1936 is the peripeteia, the point where the action turned: in that year Hitler reoccupied the Rhineland and the Versailles Treaty was finished, Abyssinia surrendered and the League of Nations had failed, the Rome–Berlin Axis was formed and the German–Japanese Pact was signed. And, most emotional and implicating of all the year's events, the Civil War in Spain began, and gave to the western world a parable-in-history of the struggle between the Left and the Right. And so, we think retrospectively, *that* was the year that was crucial, the moment when the tragic action might still have been altered.

But that is the completed view that history provides. Events only become peripeteias afterwards, when the tragedy has worked to its end, when order has been broken, and the kings are dead. To people living through the 'thirties, 1936 was not a turning point as it passed, but simply the latest and worst in a series of crisis-burdened years. Time was passing, the destructive forces in the world were growing stronger, war was certain to come soon, and its consequences would be catastrophic. 'Every active maker or sharer of an attitude,' a reviewer wrote that summer, 'is now obsessed with the quick arrival of the Doomsday of human culture. Things are all threatened, Mr. Auden and the Archbishop of Canterbury would agree . . .'[1] And this was not written in a political essay, but in a review of a book of poems; by 1936, Doomsday had become a commonplace.

The form that Doomsday would take was obviously a second World War. By 1936, war was a part of ordinary consciousness; it thrust itself into the major literary works of the year, as we shall see farther along, but it did so only because it was already obsessively present. The publication of books and pamphlets on the approaching war increased suddenly and enormously in 1935–6, books with titles like *The Roots of War*, *Challenge to Death*, *Poison Gas*, *Who's Who in Arms*, *Merchants of Death*, *The Coming World War*, *When Britain Goes to War*, *The Citizen Faces War*, *Next Year's War?*, *War Over England*. And as the threat became clearer and more vividly documented, the efforts to find a way to prevent it became more strenuous and more partisan. An example is the debate on pacifism that ran through 1936.

The English pacifist movement had been growing since the Oxford Union astonished the nation in 1933 by resolving not to fight for King and Country, and by 1936 two national pacifist movements were at the peak of their strength: Viscount Cecil had gathered some twelve million signatures to his Peace Ballot, which supported the League of Nations and rejected war as a solution to international problems, and Canon Dick Sheppard had enlisted 100,000 members in his Peace Pledge Union, pledged to renounce war and never to support or sanction another. The two movements were similar—they required only a written expression of conviction, a ballot or a postcard—and they expressed a similar point about the national mood, that very large numbers of ordinary Englishmen in 1936 were afraid that a war was coming; but neither was much more than a widespread expression of feeling, and neither developed a programme that was politically intelligent. Still, the movements were strong enough to affect the government's conduct of foreign affairs and, it was said, the policy decisions of German leaders, too.

Opposition to pacifism had also been growing. The Communist Party had been anti-pacifist all along, and so, at the other end of the political spectrum, had right-wing Tories like Winston Churchill. But by the middle of the decade they had been joined by young members of the left intelligentsia who a few years before might well have voted with the Oxford Union majority. A case in point is Julian Bell. In 1935 he edited and wrote an introduction for a book of recollections by conscientious objectors of the First World War, *We Did Not Fight*. The book is pacifist propaganda (it has a preface by Canon Sheppard), and Bell's introduction is firmly anti-war, but the position he takes is an oddly belligerent and un-pacifist one. He notes the enormous increase of popular opposition to war, and links it to the growth of radical movements in Europe since 1918, but he concludes:

> In such a situation the most active and ardent war resisters—at least among my own generation, those of military age—are more likely to take the line of revolutionary action than conscientious objection. This is not to say that more than a small minority of us are communists, or even socialists. But those of us who care about the human race and what happens to it have come to believe that only effective action counts ... I believe that the war-resistance movements of my generation will in the end succeed in putting down war—by force if necessary.[2]

At this point, Bell had rejected non-violence, and set one kind of violence against another as the likely solution. A year later he wrote a long essay, 'War and Peace: A Letter to E. M. Forster', in which he took the argument a long step further. By this time, late 1936, Bell saw that the immediate enemy, fascism, would have to be dealt with first, and that it could only be dealt with in war. 'At this moment,' he wrote, 'to be anti-war means to submit to fascism, to be anti-fascist means to be prepared for war.' Like most of his contemporaries, he took the war to be certain: 'The evil is inevitable. War will come, and the terror, hatred and enthusiasm of war, and the narrowness, the orthodoxy, the hatred of liberty and doubt.'[3] Bell had been persuaded, he said, by the Marxist analysis of the European situation. He continued to dislike communists, and to criticize the Soviet Union, but he could not refute their interpretation of history. This conversion of a Bloomsbury pacifist, a student of Lowes Dickinson and friend of Forster and Strachey, into a sort of upper-middle-class Marxist is dramatic because of Bell's connections, but the shift of conviction is typical of many members of his generation at this mid-point in the decade.

The pacifist issue was more formally debated in print in a controversy that began in April 1936, when Aldous Huxley, a supporter of Canon Sheppard, published a pacifist pamphlet, *What Are You Going to Do About it?*. Spender replied in an open letter to

Huxley that appeared in the August issue of the *Left Review*, and Day Lewis followed with his own pamphlet, *We're Not Going to Do Nothing*, in November (it was also published by the *Left Review*). As a debate, the argument is curiously disengaged, with Huxley arguing that war in the abstract was not necessary, and Spender and Day Lewis replying that in the present circumstances it was very probable, and urging support of a Popular Front.

The most significant aspect of the debate is not the details of the argument, however, but the fact that it took place between these antagonists, and in these terms. Here are two sides, polarized into hostile camps, one represented by a novelist, the other by two poets. All of them agree that war is a serious and immediate threat, and that the future of western culture is at stake, and they all agree that something must be done, and done by private individuals, acting together. They only disagree on the steps that should be taken. It is a paradigm of the situation of the time: the literary men, drawn from their work to debate in public the question of action against war, demonstrate the way in which war had become a part of the general consciousness, including literary consciousness.

The debate also demonstrates the way in which the situation encouraged the creation of polarities, the simplifying of issues into two-term oppositions. Julian Bell, in the course of an essay in which he attempts to define his generation, pauses to imagine the other side of the argument in these terms:

> while I have been writing these last pages, I have been acutely aware of 'the adversary'. He takes the form of an enthusiastic member of the Young Communist League and he bellows incessantly. That I am a social-democratic, social-fascist, weak-kneed traitor. That I am a bourgeois intellectual. That impartiality is a function of my rentier income, governing-class mentality, and desire to defeat and mislead the revolution; that all art is propaganda.
>
> I should not be surprised if this were true. Well, what of it?[4]

This is aggressively hostile, and it is caricature: Bell is accepting both a simplification of the adversary, and a simplified adversary version of himself. But he can do so only because such simplifications did exist, the terms he cited *were* bellowed, and bellowed in literary quarrels.

As the time became polarized, words like *communist* and *fascist* entered the language of literary criticism. John Lehmann was a prime example of the sort of adversary that Bell imagined; writing on 'Some Revolutionary Trends in English Poetry' he detected a 'semi-fascist flavour' in the school of Auden, Day Lewis, Warner and Upward, and 'potentially fascist thought' in *The Orators* and *The Magnetic Mountain*. Other critics considered that Auden passed muster because he had succeeded in 'resolving Communist faith to a personal poetic statement', and represented 'the attitude of the communist poets to the workers on the one hand, and, on the other, to the bourgeoisie . . .'[5] This sort of language, the language of political slogans and abuse, spread very widely into literary discussion, and into fiction and poetry as well. Even those sanctuaries that one might have expected to remain proof against that language were penetrated by it; Grigson's *New Verse*, for example, had announced itself opposed to 'politico-literary cabals' when it appeared in 1933, yet by 1936 it was publishing poems with lines like

> If you are with us you are red,

and

> Be Dead, or Red,

in poems that one might properly call 'polarized poetry'. (Not that such concessions gained Grigson any favour with the communists; he was still accused of persecuting Day Lewis for his political views, and of practising 'a sort of miniature literary Trotskyism'.[6])

The same adversary attitude toward the politics of writers is evident in John Lehmann's *New Writing*, a semi-annual miscellany that first appeared in the spring of 1936. It is the latest in the 'thirties series of 'New' publications: *New Signatures*, *New Country*, *New Verse*—newness was obviously a period value. But what *New* stood for changed. The newness of *New Signatures* was an uncertain experimentalism, with some politics here and there; *New Country* was more explicit and assertive politically, but still far from uniform in the fiction and poetry. *New Verse* began with an independent flourish, and though it was caught in the tide of the times, remained uncommitted, though leftish. But *New Writing* set out to be explicitly political and left. Since Lehmann had a hand in three of these four 'New' publications, one must conclude that the variable was the date: that what made *New Writing* what it was, more than anything else, was the movement of history.

The first issue of Lehmann's magazine appeared in the spring of 1936, and began with a 'Manifesto' that included this sentence:

> *New Writing* is first and foremost interested in literature, and though it does not intend to open its pages to writers of reactionary or Fascist sentiments, it is independent of any political party.

In fact, it was only independent of the Right, as reviewers remarked. The *Daily Worker* wrote of the second number:

> The truth is that it is a collection of imaginative writing, all, or nearly all, written from a single point of view—the point of view of a man who sees that the world is being more and more divided into two camps before his eyes, and knows that he must take his stand with the workers.

And the reviewer in the conservative *Criterion* made the same point, in his own terms:

> The fact that the editor finds it necessary to inform us of his comparative impartiality shows that he is aware of what may be said. That is, that *New Writing* is not concerned first with literature, but with left-wing propaganda.[7]

One could reach the same conclusion, simply by reading the notes identifying the contributors in any volume: a German exile, an anti-Fascist editor, a delegate to an anti-war congress, an author of books titled *Lenin* and *Communism*, a working-class writer.

The reviewers were right about *New Writing*; it was political and it was consistently left-wing. But Lehmann was not being disingenuous when he claimed that his magazine would be literary. He was as much a son of Bloomsbury as Julian Bell was, and his intentions were essentially those of his Hogarth Press employers—

to publish the best writers he could find. But he was caught in the press of political attitudes. 'I was inexplicably bewitched,' he later wrote of this period, 'by the idea that writers and artists had a large role to play in the struggle to prevent [war].'[8] And this is a bewitchment that was widespread, and very significant. If, in this time of crisis, art could be a mode of action, and could affect the public world of politics, then the artist's responsibilities were clear, and the line between art and polemics vanished. The logic of the position must have seemed irrefutable: how could you not use your art against war, if it would make a difference?

Among the young writers, Day Lewis was the most committed to polemics, as he was the most publicly committed to politics. Since the *New Country* days he had been the most active propagandist of his generation: he had been the first to write on 'Poets and Revolution', and he had defended his contemporaries in *A Hope for Poetry* and the more militant *Revolution in Writing*. By 1936 he, more than any other writer, was *the* communist poet and propagandist, and propaganda was taking up a good deal of his time; for example, in the autumn of the year he appeared in three consecutive issues of the *Left Review* with essays supporting the Popular Front, and not at all as a poet. It was inevitable, when Bell wrote his essay attacking bourgeois intellectuals who had turned communist, that he should entitle it 'The Proletariat and Poetry: An Open Letter to C. Day Lewis.' There was no more obvious example of the type.

Day Lewis' principal poetic work of 1936 was *Noah and the Waters*, a political parable in the form of a mediaeval morality play. The poet's intentions for the work are set out in two prefatory remarks in the published text. In an 'Author's Foreword', Day Lewis writes of the play:

> Its drama derives largely from the weight and imminence of the issue it represents and little from any conscious dramatic construction. This issue is the choice that must be made by Noah between clinging to his old life and trusting himself to the Flood.

What 'old life' and 'Flood' are to stand for is glossed by an epigraph, the passage from the *Communist Manifesto* that Day Lewis had also quoted in *Revolution and Writing*:

Finally, when the class war is about to be fought to a finish, disintegration of the ruling class and the old order of society becomes so active, so acute, that a small part of the ruling class breaks away to make common cause with the revolutionary class, the class which holds the future in its hands . . .[9]

This passage has always been a favourite of the intellectuals, and it was much quoted and discussed in the 'thirties. Left-inclined members of the educated middle class (like Day Lewis, whose father was a country vicar) could see themselves described and celebrated in it, as members of that heroic 'small part' that dares to break away and join the future. Day Lewis' morality play is a parable of that break: Noah is the bourgeois intellectual, and the Flood is the revolutionary class. The ruling class is represented by three burgesses, who antiphonally argue the case for the status quo. Noah is given two voices, since he is a divided man: one speaks his bourgeois fear of change and action; the other argues for commitment, gets the best lines, and wins the day.

Noah is a parable about an abstract political decision: the bourgeois intellectual's decision to join with the revolution. But it is also a personal poem about Day Lewis' personal dilemma, and his feelings about political commitment. The most convincing passage in the poem is the one in which the burgesses warn Noah of how the workers (that is, the Flood) will treat him, in terms that reveal the anxieties of a private, middle-class poet in a threatening political situation. 'We must warn you more crudely against these waters,' says one of the burgesses, and the others chime in (I will leave out the line assignments, since the burgesses are interchangeable):

> Don't imagine yourself indispensable to them
> I fear you are in for a cold reception
> Will damp your ardour or I'm much mistaken
> They are bound by their nature to let you down
> They will pour contempt on your delicate appetites
> The higher education is wasted upon them
> They will fling you overboard in mid-ocean . . .
> They distort the vision—through them you shall see
> Your death or survival a matter of indifference . . .[10]

Noah's response to this warning is a highly personal analysis of himself:

> I was always the man who saw both sides,
> The cork dancing where wave and backwash meet,
> From the inveterate clash of contraries gaining
> A spurious animation. Say, if you like,
> A top whom its self-passions lashed to sleep
> Pirouetting upon central indifference,
> The bored and perfect ballet-dancer engrossed
> By mere reiteration; but lately
> The one that cuts a figure on thin ice.
> —Who saw both sides and therefore could take neither:
> A needle midway between two fields of force,
> Swinging at last I point and prove the stronger
> Attraction.[11]

This speech seems directed not toward the political issue, or towards bourgeois intellectuals in the abstract, but toward Day Lewis himself, a young man aloof and unengaged by nature, capable of seeing contrarieties and making poems out of them, who commits himself at last against his nature, and involuntarily (as the compass metaphor implies). As in the case of *The Orators*, *Vienna*, and *The Noise of History*, the political parable becomes at a crucial point a personal confession.

In the end, Noah accepts the Flood. But then, we knew all along that he would—how could he not? For the Noah myth allows no choice, and contains no conflict: Noah is God's chosen survivor, and the flood is God's irresistible punishment. It is a parable of obedience, not of choice. And so the myth in Day Lewis' hands becomes not so much an expression of the issue that Day Lewis intended, as a confirmation and endorsement of the choice that he had already made.

The point is clearer, perhaps, if we look back at an earlier use of flood as a symbol of the coming revolution: Auden's 'Summer Night'. In that poem, the flood is a natural phenomenon that destroys but also enriches the earth, and the speaker accepts the likelihood of his own death as a regrettable but probable consequence of violent change; in political terms, he recognizes his own class connection and its implication and involves himself among the lost. But Day Lewis, by adding Noah, has made the natural image of destruction into something personal, the story of a man chosen by God for the small part of the ruling class that breaks away. His parable, in the end, is a form of self-congratulation.

Noah and the Waters has other faults as well. As Grigson shrewdly observed, it was politically unfortunate to represent the proletariat as 'an undifferentiated mass of H_2O, a substance which evaporates quickly, takes any shape and has only the force of gravity',[12] and one might add that the figure leaves the reader puzzled as to what happens to the working class when the waters recede. But this is simply to say what virtually every reviewer of the poem said in one way or another, that Day Lewis had not found an adequate parabolic form for the political meaning that he wanted to put into it. (Though perhaps one might argue that he *had* found the right parable for his deeper, unconscious intention, taking the Marxist idea of the class renegade who selflessly joins the other side, and embodying it in a myth of the personal survival of the only just man.)

The reviews were, without exception, unfavourable. The *New Statesman* thought that *Noah* was 'probably his worst book', Grigson in *New Verse* dismissed it as fake poetry and fake Auden, and even Michael Roberts, who had leaned toward generosity in his notice of *A Time to Dance*, could find little to praise. Not even the *Daily Worker* was impressed: its review was headlined 'way forward, but —"Noah" misses To-day's Real Problem'.[13] The review that Day Lewis took most notice of was Edwin Muir's, in the *Spectator*. Recalling the time in his autobiography, Day Lewis wrote:

> If my poetry had gained by the enlargement of my interests, it was now losing because of the many distractions this broader life had brought with it. I was first made sharply aware of this by a review Edwin Muir wrote on my *Noah and the Waters*: gently but firmly he pointed out how my poetry was deteriorating, becoming facile and careless.[14]

What Muir had actually said, in his review, was that Day Lewis had failed to give life to his parable: 'the allegory, instead of making the situation clearer, makes it more vague ... What Mr. Day

Lewis has actually done in this poem is to clothe in a poetic fiction a Marxian idea.' And he concluded:

> Mr. Day Lewis has been overpraised as a poet; but he has written some verse from which one can deduce at least that he is a man of talent. This last poem shows nothing but a devastating facility.[15]

The facility that Muir deplored must be related to Day Lewis' political convictions: he had made his parable too easy and too one-sided, because he was too committed to one side. Bell, from his Bloomsbury artist-and-socialist position, put it well when he wrote in his 'Open letter to C. Day Lewis':

> Almost always in your poetry comes the deadening voice of the bellicose civilian, 'We are right and you are wrong'. In your *Noah and the Waters*, for example, you put up against your salvationary flood only figures of fun and the defeatist second voice. Consequently your Noah never makes a real choice, and we never see our dilemma in his.[16]

The dilemma that *Noah and the Waters* really expresses is not Noah's, but Day Lewis's: not the problem of political choice, but the problem of how to make poetry a form of political action, and yet preserve the integrity of the poetic act. The poem is an example of a poem consciously used to impose political pressure (Day Lewis admits as much in the Author's Foreword when he says that the drama derives from the weight and imminence of the issue, not from the construction). But it is also an example of the way that pressure turns back upon the poet himself, and of the poetic consequences.

The poem is a failure and, it seems now, a violation of Day Lewis' natural gifts. What he could do, and did in places even in this bad poem, was to write about the English countryside with deep and convincing feeling. Roberts, who could find nothing else to praise in the poem, could say quite honestly and justly that 'in the choruses Mr. Day Lewis shows his intense feeling for the people and the hills and woods of England'.[17] But in the circumstances of 1936 that was not enough, and instead of good pastoral he wrote bad parable.

There is evidence that Day Lewis recognized himself that he had given up too much for his cause. In a new postscript to *A Hope for Poetry*, published in September 1936, he took note of

> a reaction from the recent preoccupation of poets with social justice, their possibly over-mechanized vocabulary, and often slapdash technique: a return to the ideals of poetic integrity and artistic individualism: a setting-out-again in the direction of 'pure' poetry.

And he praised the *Poems* of Louis MacNeice as the best book of verse to appear in the past two years. 'Apart from its poetic merit,' he wrote, 'it should be a salutary corrective to the sometimes facile optimism and mass-hypnotized rhetoric of the revolutionary poems.' He went on to criticize pure poetry and private art, but his final position was a revealing compromise:

> The function of those who uphold the ideal of pure poetry is, by their insistence on form and integrity, to correct the tendency of the rest of us to mistake gush for vigour and substitute rhetoric for imagination. Between the two ideals of poets of to-day, social justice and artistic integrity, a foundation should be laid for a poetic future not unworthy of the traditions we have inherited and the society some of us hope for and are fighting for.[18]

Day Lewis' Postscript suggests strongly that for him, in mid-1936, the tide of militant Marxism in literature was beginning to ebb. One might argue that this is a sign of the corrective value of harsh criticism, and that Day Lewis was simply responding to the reviews of *Noah*. But there are other evidences, too, that this was a year in which some enthusiasts drew back from their earlier convictions.

A good example is Michael Roberts. In February 1936 he published a new anthology, the *Faber Book of Modern Verse*, with a long introduction by the editor. Since Roberts had edited *New Signatures* and *New Country*, and had created in those volumes the image of the new generation of communist writers, readers must have turned to his new collection expecting to find there the revolutionary view brought up to date. But if they did, they were disappointed. For in the thirty-five pages of introduction Roberts never mentions politics or revolution at all, or only glancingly, to dismiss the whole business, as in this passage:

> Primarily poetry is an exploration of the possibilities of language. It does not aim directly at consolation or moral exhortation, nor at the expression of exquisite moments, but at an extension of significance; and it might be argued that a too self-conscious concern with 'contemporary' problems deflects the poet's effort from his true objective.[19]

The heroes of the movement scarcely appear in the introduction: Auden only for his definition of poetic parable, from *The Poet's Tongue*, and Spender to provide an example of a compressed metaphor.

All the concerns of the earlier introductory essays—the defence of industrial imagery, the arguments about propaganda and political attitudes and social purposes—are missing, too. Instead, Roberts writes about language, difficulty, tradition, poetic form. One might argue, on the basis of this change, that he had simply fallen under the influence of his new publisher, Eliot, and I think there is something in that; but Roberts' change of heart had other causes, too. He was not, I think, a political man by nature, only a temporary one by circumstance, and in the middle 'thirties he reverted to his inherent private self. The change came when it did because by 1936 reversion was possible; the tide of political literature was ebbing.

It may seem odd that this should be true of a year in which such crucial political events occurred: one might expect that the immediate history of 1936 would have fixed young writers in their most militant political postures. And indeed that is what did happen *in politics*. But in the relationship between politics and art the situation was different. The relationship had never been either clearly or uniformly understood by the young writers of the 'thirties generation: and if in the mid-'thirties the two terms began to slide apart, it was because they had never really been joined. By 1936 the *New Signatures* poets had come to be widely regarded as a group or a school, but in fact they were no such thing. They did not resemble each other in their work (except Day Lewis, who resembled all the rest at one time or another), and they did not have a common theory of literature. The best critical books of the generation—*The Destructive Element* and *Some Versions of Pastoral*—were heterodox, unsystematic, and individualist. Auden, the best critic of the lot, remained evasive, balancing Marx against Freud, speaking respectfully of Christianity, and never committing himself to any fixed position. Roberts' two prefaces had claimed for his poets and prose writers a revolutionary orthodoxy that was largely in his own mind (and perhaps in Lehmann's), but he had not made the orthodoxy very clear, and he had not succeeded in imposing it on the others or, it would seem, on himself.

What these young writers had in common was something a good deal less militant—the modern tradition, as articulated by Eliot and Richards. Their tradition was elitist, difficult, and individualist. When the Marxist critic D. Mirsky wrote of Spender in 1936 that he was 'gripped by an obsession—the obsession of the "independence" of the artist, of the necessity for him to fight shy of all party allegiances for fear of forfeiting his inner freedom,'[20] he must have thought that he was exposing a profound critical fault; and so he was in his own terms, which were those of *Problems of Soviet Literature* and the First Soviet Writers' Congress. But it might also be said that all he was really doing was accurately describing the idea of the artist that then prevailed among young English poets. Of course Spender argued that position; but so did Auden, so did Empson, so did MacNeice, so even did Day Lewis—it was a central part of their literary heritage. The swing in the early 'thirties toward political commitment and away from 'individualism' had been a deviation from the main thrust of the modern movement, and by 1936 the results of that swing were apparent: political commitment had produced no art of any importance, and no aesthetic that seemed adequate to a generation raised on Eliot's essays and the books of Richards; everything of importance in those years had been heterodox and individualist. So, in the mid-'thirties, a return to the main stream of modernism had begun. It would have been greater than it was, no doubt, had it not been for one event of that summer: in July, General Franco crossed the Straits of Gibraltar with his Moorish troops, and the Spanish Civil War began, and so for the rest of the decade commitment once more seemed a moral act of such obvious and compelling rectitude that the 'independence' of the artist was again suspended in the anxieties of history.

In the autumn of 1936 Spender reviewed three books for the *Left Review*: Auden and Isherwood's *Ascent of F6*, Auden's *Look, Stranger!*, and the second issue of *New Writing*. The review is not the political piece that one might expect, given the journal and the date; what concerns Spender primarily are the problems of the artist in the modern world—his isolation, his obscurity, and his difficulties in reaching an audience. These are problems that go back to the 'twenties, to Eliot and Joyce, and are part of the modern tradition; but they had a special urgency for writers in the 'thirties, for they all relate to the essential aesthetic question of the decade: how can an artist respond to the immediate crises of this time, and yet remain true to his art? This is the question that all those polemical essays are about—'The Poet and Revolution', 'Poetry and Politics', 'Politics and Literature', all those earnest efforts to make apparent opposites meet in a theory of literary action.

Spender's essay is different from the others, though, in that it does not go directly to the political aspects of the problems, but rather deals with them as problems of literary strategy, to be solved by finding *literary* ways of responding to urgent issues. 'Perhaps the best feature of the Auden–Isherwood dramatic style in *The Ascent of F6*,' he wrote,

> is the rhythmic contrast which the writers maintain between two entirely different methods of presentation: firstly, realistic scenes of political reportage; secondly, fables. There are two approaches to the contemporary political scene: the one is direct, or partially satiric, external presentation; the other is fantasy or allegory.[21]

He found, and praised, the same two approaches in the contributions to *New Writing*: 'the best stories in the volume are either very realistic fragments of actual life . . . or else they are allegories'.

What Spender was identifying in his essay were two alternative (and it might seem antithetical) ways of responding to Auden's challenge to the artist to 'make action urgent and its nature clear':

either the writer could record external actuality as strictly and objectively as possible, or he could compose a symbolic version of it. Spender's terms for these alternatives are *reportage* and *fable*, but one might propose others that would do as well: *realism* and *fantasy*, *presentation* and *allegory*, or the terms that I prefer, *document* and *parable*. Whatever the terms, the distinction is clear: on the one hand, the authority of sheer fact (or the illusion of fact), and on the other the authority of the imagination. Each kind implies its own aesthetic, its own ontology, and its own morality; for what is at stake is the true representation of the immediate world, with its crises and poverty, and its looming war. But though the approaches differ radically, the end is the same; it is the goal that Marx set for Marxists, not to describe the world, but to change it.

Both approaches appear throughout the 'thirties, and examples of both have already been discussed: of document, *The Brown Book of the Hitler Terror* and *Fascists at Olympia* and, in fiction, *It's a Battlefield* and *Mr. Norris Changes Trains*; of parable, numerous examples beginning with Mortmere and *Paid on Both Sides*. But 1936 is special for two reasons: new and more insistent examples of both began to appear, as though new formulations of the alternatives were necessary to meet the new anxieties of the time; and the terms began to be dealt with as opposite and alternative routes to the one goal.

We might consider two events of May 1936 as embodiments of these points: in that month the Left Book Club was founded, and the first issue of *Contemporary Poetry and Prose* appeared. Both the book club and the journal were literary experiments, both were left-wing and in their very different ways political, and both were aimed at changing the world by changing the contents of men's minds. But one was the extreme example of the documentary point of view at work, while the other was the principal English organ of Surrealism, which might be described as the extreme form of parable. The two were polar expressions of a common impulse toward political action through writing, and both belong equally to their moment in history.

The Left Book Club was founded by the Socialist publisher Victor Gollancz as an experiment in political education. His plan was to issue to his members each month selected political books on current subjects, at prices that could be kept low because the market would be predictable. The scheme was modelled on the successful commercial book clubs then in existence, but Gollancz's intention was more high-minded. 'What the Left Book Club is attempting to do,' he wrote in the first issue of *Left Book Club News*, 'is to provide the indispensable basis of *knowledge* without which a really effective United Front of all men and women of good faith cannot be built.'[22] The Popular Front had just won an election victory in France, and had the support of the Communist Party, and the initial motive of the Club was to support that policy in England by educating a Left membership. The first book chosen was *France Today and the People's Front*, by Maurice Thorez, General Secretary of the French Communist Party.

In later Club literature references to the Popular (or United or People's) Front were omitted. 'The aim of the Club,' a leaflet circulated at the end of 1937 stated,

> is a simple one; it is to help in the terribly urgent struggle *for* World Peace & a better social & economic order & *against* Fascism, by giving (to all who are determined to play their part in this struggle) such *knowledge* as will immensely increase their efficiency.

Knowledge, for the LBC, meant *facts*; of the 150 books distributed by the Club, only four could be called works of the imagination in the ordinary literary sense: three novels (Malraux's *Days of Contempt* and Hillel Bernstein's *Choose a Bright Morning* in 1936 and Cedric Belfrage's *Promised Land* in 1938), and one play (Clifford Odets' *Waiting for Lefty* in 1937). Of the other titles offered only one, or perhaps two survive: Orwell's *Road to Wigan Pier* certainly, and perhaps Koestler's *Spanish Testament*. To say this is not to judge either the Club or its books—permanence is not necessarily a part of the value of topical writing—but simply to note that the Club *was* topical, that it belonged to its time, died with its time, and left virtually nothing behind.

In its best years, though, in the last three years of the 'thirties, the Club flourished and grew far beyond anyone's expectations. From its first month its membership grew steadily, by from three to five thousand new members a month, until in the autumn of

1937 it reached more than fifty thousand members, a level which it maintained until the end of the decade. The Club circulated in all something approaching a million books—serious, often difficult books, books with statistical tables and no illustrations, in the plain orange and yellow covers that became a part of Left decor. Certainly it did affect the political education of many English people.

But though it began as an educational enterprise, it soon became something very different; the emphasis quickly shifted from *book* to *club*, and it became a society, a movement, almost a religion. Local groups for discussion were organized around the country and were listed in the Club's monthly paper. There were tours and summer schools, and a theatre club. The *Left Book Club News* became simply *Left News*, no longer a house organ but the voice of a movement. A club badge was devised, and rallies were organized, like that at the Albert Hall in February 1937, where Harry Pollitt, Secretary of the Communist Party of Great Britain, spoke in support of the Spanish Loyalists and the Popular Front.

At the end of December 1936, John Strachey, one of the Club's three Selection Committee members, summarized in the *Daily Worker* the principal Left achievements of the year that had just passed. His chief example was the Left Book Club:

As one of the selectors of the monthly choices of the Club [he wrote] I feel a certain diffidence in writing about the merits of particular books. But I feel no diffidence whatever in writing about the importance of the Club.

For the Club has become something quite different in scope and scale from anything which any of us ever imagined.

The truth is that the Left Book Club has become a movement. I have just heard that the membership has passed the 32,000 mark and that the 300th local group has been formed . . .

This growth has been achieved in seven short months. It means that there was, and is, a hunger for Socialist literature such as has never existed before in this country.

It means that we have only begun to realise our opportunities. It means that, if only we approach people in the right way, we can now win people to an acceptance and comprehension of Scientific Socialism, literally by the tens of thousands.[23]

The tone—something between a revivalist and a super-salesman —is odd but right for the occasion, for the LBC had something of both in its character.

For its members the LBC was clearly a haven, a collective something for the depressed and scattered Left to belong to (as the Peace Pledge Union was a haven, too, and also had its local groups in which to cling together). Many letters to the *Left News* make clear that joining the LBC was a kind of conversion, and that it was a commitment not to books and reading, but to involvement in Club activities. From the organizers' point of view, the Club became not so much an educational instrument as a political one—a means of manipulating Left opinion. It was not a Communist front organization (though there are those who still believe that this was the case[24]); Gollancz was certainly not a Communist, nor was Harold Laski, another of his book selectors, though John Strachey was, in all but Party card. Nevertheless, the Club's policies did not deviate significantly from Party lines; it supported the Popular Front, it defended Stalin in the purge trials, and it refused to publish 'Trotskyite attacks on the Soviet Union'.[25]

It is impossible to assess precisely the effect of such a movement. Certainly it organized the Left in a way that no political party could, and a *different* Left—the town and village groups, like the one in Gloucestershire that gathered round Day Lewis, the designated local group leader. It did a good deal to publicize the Loyalist cause in Spain and to collect funds for arms, and it must have contributed to the change in Left thought in the later 'thirties from pacifism to militancy. Above all it gave members of various Left persuasions the feeling that they belonged to one great cause—'the United Front', as Gollancz put it, 'of all men and women of good faith'.

The Left Book Club was built on documents, and on the proposition that facts were knowledge, but it was never simply a transmitter of facts. From the beginning it was a propaganda organization, designed to manipulate opinion by exploiting the information it provided; and so facts became partisan, a part of the struggle. This distorting process is probably inherent in the documentary position: particular realities, when organized, become an argument or an emotion, facts accumulate feelings, and it is the feelings, not the facts, that move us. One can see this principle demonstrated and argued in another important documentary movement, the GPO Film Unit. The Film Unit was established as an information-branch of the Post Office in 1933, with John Grierson, the most distinguished of British documentary film makers, as its head. Grierson, then in his mid-thirties, was already dedicated to documentary, which he defined as 'the creative treatment of actuality', and to the use of such treatment as a mode of persuasion. 'I look on cinema as a pulpit,' he said, 'and use it as a propagandist.'[26] Looking back from the end of the decade on his work with the GPO group, Grierson wrote:

> We were, I confess, sociologists, a little worried about the way the world was going . . . We were interested in *all* instruments which would crystallize sentiments in a muddled world and create a will toward civic participation.[27]

Gollancz might have said the same thing, in the same words, about his work with the Left Book Club.

But unlike the selectors of the LBC, Grierson was working within an art form, and this inevitably created a conflict of values, as it had for political poets. One can see this conflict very clearly in *Documentary Film*, a book published by Paul Rotha, a member of the GPO unit, in 1936. Rotha, a militantly left-wing member of the group, was explicit about his aims as a film-maker:

> Briefly, I look upon cinema as a powerful, if not the most powerful instrument for social influence to-day; and I regard the documentary method as the first real attempt to use cinema for purposes more important than entertainment.[28]

What those more important purposes were is quite clear—documentary was to serve as an instrument for spreading political, sociological, and economic knowledge, and as a counter-force to the bourgeois propaganda media—the national newspapers, commercial entertainment-films, and public education.

Grierson wrote an introduction to Rotha's book, and in it he both agreed with, and drew back from, Rotha's views. In agreement he wrote:

> Mr. Rotha is right ... when he associates the word 'propaganda' so persistently with the growth of documentary. The secret of its growth has certainly been in the public instruction it pretended.

(Though *pretended* is a loaded word.) But although he accepted the propaganda function, he qualified it with an artist's judgment:

> The controversialist's call is to action and to immediate action. The artist's call is to consideration. ... If, in propaganda, he shrinks to the writing of revolutionary war songs and the composition of political manifestos it is not that art and politics have been joined. All that has happened is that the artist has become a politician ... The great revolutionaries of our time in art were not Barbusse and Mayakowsky but Cézanne and Joyce.[29]

The problem that Grierson set for himself and his Film Unit—to 'make things known' and influence opinion without becoming a group of politicians—is the same problem that troubled all his generation of artists in the 'thirties: it is 'poetry and propaganda' all over again.

Of the films that Grierson produced during his four years with the GPO, the best known is probably *Night Mail*, a documentary of the night mail train run from London to Glasgow. It is known partly because Auden and Benjamin Britten worked on it: but it merits its reputation as a whole and successful work of art, a genuinely collaborative effort. The GPO's account of the film, as given in its official *Notes and Synopses*, makes it a flat and factual record: 'At 8:30 every evening, winter and summer, the Postal Special leaves Euston for Glasgow. It is a fast express, and carries no passengers. It is composed entirely of Post Office carriages, ...'[30] and so forth. This is from the spoken narrative of the film,

213

and describes its spatial and chronological structure, the journey of the train to Glasgow through the night. But *Night Mail* has another structure: it is a poem of contrasts—the dark and empty landscape through which the train rushes, and the bright, cheerful interiors of the carriages, where men work swiftly together, joking and talking as they work. That contrast makes it a film about loneliness and companionship, for which the letters that the train carries become symbols. One recalls the passage in Auden's early essay on writing: 'Since the underlying reason for writing is to bridge the gulf between one person and another . . .' That goes for writing letters, as well as poems, as Auden makes clear in the poem that ends the film:

> And none will hear the postman's knock
> Without a quickening of the heart,
> For who can bear to feel himself forgotten?

Night Mail is an excellent film, but is it propaganda? is it political? The answers, as with most rhetorical questions, depend on what you mean by your terms. The mateyness of the workers is a political point, though a rather complex one; the working class is a happy lot (happier than the rich?), but these workers are happy because they are doing their job (not striking, or on the dole). They are government employees, and the government is providing, through them, a service that bridges the gulf between one person and another. The GPO must have been satisfied that this was the film's principal message. But the essential loneliness that makes us long for letters cannot be touched by propaganda, and the film's fidelity to that condition makes it a work of art.

It is a work of art, and it is a parable—realistic in its texture, but double-levelled, symbolic, formal, and essentially moral. And so *Night Mail* demonstrates an important point: the way in which the documentary method, in an artist's hands (or in this case in several artist's hands), tends to escape the limits of the literal and to express other and more complex meanings. It's rather like what Empson said about proletarian literature: when it comes off, one reads into it, or finds that the artist has put into it, 'more subtle, more far-reaching, and I think more permanent ideas'.

Documentary appears as a literary term, and as a critical issue, in reviews of the first issues of *New Writing*. Several reviewers took the occasion to make distinctions between literature or art and documents: for example Stonier, in the *New Statesman*, remarked that Lehmann had been wise, 'failing the work of art, to rely on the document', and Chapman in the *Criterion* took it as obvious, 'from the amount of merely documentary work', that literature was not *New Writing*'s first concern. Stonier praised and Chapman condemned, but the implication is the same: the document is an inferior form, though perhaps forced upon the editor by some external pressure.[31]

This issue was argued most explicitly in John Brophy's review of the second number, in the *Daily Telegraph*:

> When 'documentation' becomes not a means but an end in itself [Brophy wrote], when fiction is written for the purpose not of entertaining (using that word in its fullest sense) but of recording recent events with more intimacy and freedom than journalism (and perhaps the law) will allow, it is time to call a halt . . .

After describing the contents of the volume, Brophy went on:

> In one way or another the book tells you a great deal, and vividly, about the lives of all kinds of people, most of them wage-earners, in different parts of the world, plasterers, sailors, Vienna Socialists, men smuggling arms into Spain, front-door canvassers in Paris, and so on. In brief, all these stories and sketches are 'documented'.
>
> But it seems to me that the contributors may be divided sharply into two classes. There are those who use the documentary facts as a spring-board, who leap from reality into imagination . . . Others, and they form the majority, appear to have gone the wrong way about their job—if that job really is the writing of fiction. In selecting, shaping and arranging incidents to make a story, they seem to have put the wrong question to themselves. Instead of asking, 'Is this necessary to the design I am making in my imagination?' they have asked, 'Is this true to life, does this stick to the facts?' Morally and socially, the second question may be of higher value than the

first, but once a story-teller allows it to dictate to his imagination, he may write excellently and interestingly, but he will write something other than fiction.[32]

For Brophy, as for the other reviewers, *art* and *document* are distinct and exclusive categories: one involves imagination and the other doesn't. But it is interesting that he does not make this distinction in order to argue the greater value of art; he allows that in terms of moral and social values documents may be more important. It is a concession that tradition made to the urgent mood of the time.

Lehmann had invited the art-document distinction by grouping certain of his 'documents' together under collective headings in his first two numbers. Such an organization was a way of demonstrating *New Writing*'s political commitment; for it was this kind of writing that would play the large role that Lehmann imagined for literature in the struggle ahead, if any writing would. He must have been pleased when reviewers took up the point, and he quoted most of Brophy's review in an advertisement for the second number that he ran in the *Left Review*: to Left readers, it would be a testimony to the seriousness of the volume that it was so documentary as to disturb the *Telegraph*'s critic.

The emergence of documents as a literary category is obviously related to socialist realism and the First Soviet Writers' Congress. But the causes are more complicated than that. There does seem to have been an audience in the mid-'thirties hungry for writing that gave the appearance of fact, and that hunger cannot be explained in political terms alone. The impulse was perhaps the same impulse that turns us all to the morning papers, knowing that they will contain no news that is not bad; it is the desire to know the worst, to believe in our own ability to face reality, however grim it may be. Some readers must have shared Gollancz' naive faith in the power of facts to save the world; no doubt others, like Yeats' hysterical women, felt that in disastrous times times art and imagination were frivolous, and facts were inherently serious. To all these possible readers, the recording of events was a moral act, and one that took priority over merely aesthetic issues.

III

Documentary was one obvious way of putting the verbal and visual materials of art at the service of urgent issues. Another, and far less likely, way was Surrealism, which came into prominence in England at about the same time, in late 1935 and 1936. The movement had existed in France by then for more than a decade, and advanced members of the 'thirties generation had known about it since their undergraduate days: there are references to Surrealist painting in both the *Oxford Outlook* and *Experiment* before 1930. Michael Roberts was aware of French surrealist poets in 1932, and a year later Hugh Gordon Porteus was finding 'a modified surréaliste technique' in Auden:[33] in 1933 one could see paintings by Miró and Ernst in a London gallery, and there was a Dali show in London in 1934. But the movement had engaged English imaginations so little that in 1936 David Gascoyne (then barely twenty years old) could be described as 'England's only wholehearted surrealist'.[34]

It was Gascoyne and another equally youthful surrealist, Roger Roughton, who gave the movement in England its first real momentum. Gascoyne published *A Short Survey of Surrealism*, the first English book on the subject, in December 1935 (Cyril Connolly, who knew all about French movements, headed his review disdainfully, 'It's Got Here at Last!');[35] and Roughton's *Contemporary Prose and Poetry*, which during its brief life was the leading English surrealist journal, first appeared six months later. The thrust that they gave did not last long; virtually everything that was notable in English surrealism had happened by the end of 1936: the best surrealist novel, Hugh Sykes Davies' *Petron*, appeared in the autumn of 1935, Gascoyne's book of surrealist poems, *Man's Life Is This Meat*, in May 1936, Roughton's 'Lady Windermere's Fan Dance' in October, and *Surrealism*, a collection of essays edited by Herbert Read, in November. And in the middle of this year, the International Surrealist Exhibition, England's first major surrealist show, opened in London.

In such a brief flowering, English Surrealism scarcely had time to become a movement, in the French sense; there were no real leaders (certainly no English Breton), no factions, and no doctrinal controversies, or at least none that have left traces. But for that short period there were plenty of surrealists around, plenty of surrealist paintings and poems, plenty of manifestos; it may not have been a movement, but it was a highly visible phenomenon while it lasted.

The moment of highest visibility was 11 June 1936, when the International Surrealist Exhibition opened at the New Burlington Galleries. The opening was a sort of Dadaist happening: one of the exhibitors, Sheila Legge, appeared as the 'Surrealist phantom', strolling through the crowds dressed in white samite, her head and face covered with roses, and carrying at first a pork chop and later, when the chop had gone bad in the heat, a model of a human leg; and Dali delivered a lecture while dressed in a diver's suit with the helmet closed (and nearly suffocated). William Walton, the composer, brought along a kippered herring, which he attached to an 'object' by Miró; Miró was said to be pleased by the addition.

These goings-on received wide publicity, and set the tone in which the show was generally received. One critic, Raymond Mortimer, compared the show to Roger Fry's First Post-Impressionist Show in 1910, as the expression of a *Zeitgeist*; but most reviewers adopted a tone of condescending amusement, with praise for established artists like Picasso, Chirico, and Klee, and a few dismissive words for the rest. Only the far Left and the far Right were really censorious. 'The general impression one gets,' said the *Daily Worker*, 'is that here is a group of young people who just haven't got the guts to tackle anything seriously and attempt to justify themselves by an elaborate rationalisation racket,' and *Action*, the fascist weekly, recommended cold baths and long runs in the country.[36]

One can understand why a Marxist, committed to socialist realism and the propaganda function of art, would have found the show frivolous and unsympathetic. His hostility would have been increased by the catalogue, for there he would have found Breton quoting Marx and Engels, and Herbert Read claiming a kinship between surrealist art and Marxism:

Do not judge this movement kindly [Read wrote]. It is not just another amusing stunt. It is defiant—the desperate act of men too profoundly convinced of the rottenness of our civilisation to want to save a shred of its respectablity.

The philosophers, said Marx, have only *interpreted* the world in different ways; the point, however, is to *change* it. The artists, too, have only interpreted the world; the point, however, is to transform it.[37]

Defiant? Desperate? The Marxists remembered the pork chop and the kipper, and were unconvinced.

And indeed the connection between Marxist doctrine and the surrealist Phantom does seem at best remote; still, it is of some historical importance to see how they happened to come together at the New Burlington Galleries. Because Surrealism reached England when it did, late in the history of the movement, and in the mid-'thirties, it contained disparate elements, mixed together, which had existed separately in France; it was as though the whole history of Surrealism had to be telescoped and got through in a single year. On the one hand there were signs of the Dadaist origins of the movement, in the jokes played at the expense of society and of art—the *objets trouvés* in the exhibition, the nonsense poems in the journals. On the other hand, there were many evidences that some surrealists took the movement in dead earnest, as the truly urgent art for the time. In 1935–6, just as Surrealism was surfacing in England, the French movement was urging its commitment to Marxism and revolution, and that political commitment crossed the Channel intact, and was taken up as a promise of a richer alternative to socialist realism. Surrealism would achieve that long sought-after goal of the intellectual Left, the reconciliation of Marx and Freud; the public world of political action would combine with the most private world of subconscious mental experience, and art would achieve two important and apparently incompatible conditions at once: it would be individual, and it would be revolutionary. The subconscious, probed deeply enough, would reveal itself as objective and collective, and the expression of it in art would destroy bourgeois restraints, and thus assist the revolution.

English critics had noted the problem of Surrealism and politics before, but only in relation to French examples (since there were no English ones). [38] But in 1936 the problem became English, and one finds a curious unilateral courtship going on, with surrealists plighting their troth to Marxism and the revolution, and Marxists angrily declining to be betrothed to such dubious suitors. Gascoyne began, in the introduction to his *Short Survey*: 'It should by now be clear to Marxists that the surrealist attitude is totally in accord with the Communist philosophy of dialectical materialism.' [39] And Herbert Read, in a lecture given during the Surrealist Exhibition, added more aggressively: 'The Surrealist is naturally a Marxian Socialist, and generally claims that he is a more consistent Communist than many who submit to all manner of compromise with the aesthetic culture and moral conventions of capitalism.' [40]

Communist responses were not encouraging. Reviewing Gascoyne's *Short Survey*, the *Left Review* observed:

> There is no doubt that surrealism is a revolt against the smug ineffectualness of bourgeois art. It is probably the most interesting, if somewhat mystical, art movement in Europe; it has many artists and writers of great talent and genius, including Picasso. But there seems to be no evidence for its claim of being proletarian, Marxist, or more revolutionary than the communist party. ... surrealist art, in spite of undoubted talent and genius, remains the complete expression of bourgeois decadence, appreciated and patronised chiefly by a very limited and sophisticated group of bourgeois intellectuals. [41]

In the *Daily Worker* a reviewer of Gascoyne's book categorically condemned the surrealists' political line as 'definitely opposed to that of Communism', and another, reviewing Read's collection of essays, concluded that 'the obscurantism of the surrealists is qualitatively identical with the obscurantism of the Fascists'. [42] There would be, it appeared, no marriage.

Yet the courtship went on. Surrealists continued to talk revolution and Marxist solidarity, as though they all agreed that an artistic movement needed some heavy political ballast to keep afloat in a time of crisis, and in their writings about the movement they went on trying to solve the problem of how to be a surrealist and a communist, an individualist and a collectivist at the same time. But so far as I can discover nobody who started from the opposite camp took any trouble to try to reconcile his beliefs with those of the surrealists: the Communist Party line was firmly and consistently dismissive, and all the yearning was in the other direction.

The case of Roger Roughton illustrates the problem. In 1936, Roughton was a gifted young man of nineteen who was already writing striking surrealist poems. He was also apparently a Party member—certainly he thought of himself as a thorough-going communist. When Roughton wrote in his political role, as he did when he reviewed Gascoyne's *Short Survey* in the *Daily Worker* in April, he took a hard, censorious party line, condemning the surrealists for attacking Stalin and the Soviet Union, and Gascoyne for trying to organize intellectuals outside the Party. Yet in the following month Roughton published the first issue of *Contemporary Poetry and Prose*, which is essentially a surrealist literary journal, and there among the contributors is Gascoyne, 'England's only wholehearted surrealist'. In this issue there are also surrealist-sounding poems and a surrealist story by Dylan Thomas; the second number, a 'Double Surrealist Number', is devoted mainly to translations of French surrealist poems. In neither is there anything that one could regard as political.

By the time the August–September issue of Roughton's journal was ready, two things had happened: the International Surrealist Exhibition had come and gone, and the Spanish Civil War had begun. These events come together in the first editorial that Roughton wrote, 'Surrealism and Communism'. The piece begins with what had become a conventional surrealist claim for revolutionary significance:

> Surrealist work, while not calling directly for revolutionary intervention, can be classed as revolutionary in so far as it can break down irrational bourgeois-taught prejudices, thus preparing the mental ground for positive revolutionary thought and action.

But from this point on the tone is that of the *other* Roughton, the Party member and *Daily Worker* reviewer:

Therefore it is all the more necessary that this revolutionary essence should not be adulterated by the contradictory attitude of individual surrealists.[43]

Roughton scolds Read for his ideological errors—calls him in fact a Trotskyist—and sets down the correct line: first, surrealists must work within the Party; and second, they must work for the United Front,

and not delude themselves . . . into imagining that there is any revolutionary part to be played *outside* the United Front—a theory which has been quashed once more by the example of the Spanish civil war . . .[44]

If they follow these simple instructions, Roughton concludes, 'there is no reason why there should be any quarrel between surrealism and communism'. And of course there could be none, since there would be no distinction between the terms. But these are instructions on how to be a good communist, and they answer none of the problems of the surrealist who wishes to be political while yet remaining an artist. The harmony that Roughton imagined between the two terms was to be achieved simply by submerging the art-term in the political-term.

In the journal itself, however, there was no such harmony. The issue in which Roughton published his editorial is called the 'Picasso Poems Number', and those poems are surrealist, but are not at all political. Nor is there any sign of politics or revolution in most of the other literary contributions. From this point on, Surrealism and politics co-exist in *Contemporary Poetry and Prose*, but without touching. The Surrealism is in the verse, and the politics hovers round the edges—for example on the back cover, which from the August–September number began to carry political slogans: 'Support the Spanish People Against Fascism', and 'Arms for the People of Spain', and in further editorials, like the one Roughton published in October, 'Fascism Murders Art', which asserts:

There is no longer a fence for intellectuals to sit on: they must choose between fascism and anti-fascism; and magazines of modern poetry can no longer pretend they are Something Apart.[45]

Perhaps the best expression of the problem that Roughton and his friends faced is a sheet that was tipped in to the November issue. It is headed 'Declaration on Spain', and is an appeal for the lifting of the embargo on arms shipments. As a political document it resembles many others of the time. The only thing that is unique about it is that it was issued by the 'Surrealist Group in England', and is signed by Sykes Davies, Gascoyne, Humphrey Jennings, Diana Brinton Lee, Rupert Lee, Henry Moore, Paul Nash, Roland Penrose, Valentine Penrose, Read, and Roughton —virtually the same group that had composed the 'English Committee' which sponsored the Surrealist Exhibition that summer, with Roughton added. It is a kind of surrealist United Front, Roughton appearing with Gascoyne and 'Trotskyist' Read, but the occasion has nothing to do with Surrealism, or with the journal in which the declaration appears.

In its first year *Contemporary Poetry and Prose* had published a good deal of surrealist writing, some of it very interesting. It had also done some political editorializing that was remote enough from the literary content so that Roughton felt obliged, in the last issue of 1936, to make a policy statement: 'It is necessary to point out,' he wrote,

that, although the editor is at the moment a member of the loosely-constituted English Surrealist group, *Contemporary Poetry and Prose* is in no way an official Surrealist magazine . . . Thus, the Surrealist group is not responsible for the political or other opinions expressed in the paper.[46]

And, one might add, the Communist Party is not responsible for the surrealist poems. The effect is of two activities being carried on simultaneously but independently: an avant-garde poetry journal is being edited, while round the back and in the editorials the urgent political issue of the time is argued. Roughton was performing both roles, but they were as separate as if he had been two people. He had not solved the problem of how to be at once a surrealist and a communist; he had only demonstrated that the problem existed.

Surrealism, I have suggested, is 'an extreme form of parable', a way of giving non-literal form to the contents of the unconscious. The actual forms, and their relations to the time, can best be seen by examining particular examples. First, then, a look at *Petron*, by Hugh Sykes Davies. Sykes Davies was the most sophisticated and most intellectual of English surrealist writers, and his book is to my mind the most satisfactory single work from the English movement. It is a prose narrative, but it is hard to define the genre more exactly than that; indeed Dent evidently regarded it as poetry, for it was published in a 'New Poetry' series. It might perhaps be described as surrealist-Gothic, or surrealist-picaresque, for it recounts the wanderings of a hero who has adventures that are often grotesquely horrible, though they are told in a relentlessly cheerful and accepting tone of voice. Petron's travels have no clear direction, and no end; he witnesses and suffers horror after horror—a murdered woman, an old man who divides his own fingers into tiny fingers with a pruning bill, a field of growing hands that open by day and close by night—but at the end he is still wandering, and the final sentence is 'Alas! he has still many years, many long years to live.'

The lonely journey that Petron makes may remind us of Auden's wandering heroes (in poems like 'Doom is dark' and 'To throw away the key'), and the journey into the unknown is certainly a parabolic form to which all these examples, and many others in the 'thirties, belong. But what exactly does Petron's journey mean? One might venture certain tentative propositions: that man is alone, that the world is irrationally violent and hostile, that the future is uncertain but is sure to be worse than the present, that time nevertheless moves on, and men survive to suffer further and more astonishing disasters. Put in those terms, Petron is a version of the nightmare of the 'thirties. Perhaps by realizing the nightmare of the time one might help to conquer it; a psychoanalyst would say so, and Sykes Davies was aware of psychoanalysis and its fundamental place in surrealist theory. 'Until we conquer these unconscious realms,' he wrote in the *Surrealist Bulletin*, 'we are always in danger. We wish to make this private world public—to put an end to loneliness.'[47] So *Petron* is another parable of private faces in public places, and another case of art understood as an action taken against loneliness.

Another interesting surrealist work of the same time is Roughton's poem 'Lady Windermere's Fan Dance', which appeared in the October 1936 issue of *Contemporary Poetry and Prose*. In the same issue Roughton ran his editorial, 'Fascism Murders Art', and one might expect that his poem would express the poetic consequences of that militant commitment; what it in fact says is this:

> Figures and trees in the street
> Are stretching and waving their arms,
> Reaching the time to repeat
> The errors; result of alarms
>
> Earlier heard in the night,
> Reports they once read on a wall.
> Finger still feeling the light
> Remember the hour of the fall
>
> When gently no one had saved
> With fingers in fingers of one,
> Hands from the barricades waved
> Or hands in the dark when they won.
>
> Sulphurous clouds from the bank
> Are killing the quick in the stream,
> Bodies from gunboats that sank
> Are menacing guns with a dream;
>
> Wavering over the sun
> Their arms are still greeting a king,
> Holding out hands for a gun,
> Impatient for shadows to spring.
>
> Arms of the fighters of tin
> And hands of the brave of a thought
> Signal the time to begin
> By quietly dividing by nought.[48]

Certainly the images and the tone are from the political world of the moment, and of the decade: barricades, gunboats, guns, and fighters are not literary, but literal, and so are the errors and alarms. Other elements are consistent with these images, though less explicit: 'The hour of the fall' and 'no one had saved' suggest all the losses and the failures of action that had passed in recent history: Berlin in 1933, Vienna in 1934, Abyssinia in 1935, and now Spain. Yet the poem is not either descriptive or narrative, and it is organized in an illogical way that surrealists would approve. Rhetorically, it moves like a bad dream, suggesting a logic that it does not have; the images stand in what seems a grammatical structure, but they make no statement, and express only the emotional effect of their own coexistence.

These examples suggest, and many others confirm the point, that Surrealism provided a means of expressing not political ideas, but the emotions *behind* 'thirties politics—the fears and anxieties, the sense of unknown and terrible dangers, and of possible violence and outrage beyond the projections of reason: in short, it provided a parabolic method for the social nightmares of the time. In this important respect English Surrealism might be said to be simply a new aspect of the post-war modern tradition, as represented by Joyce and Eliot—the tradition of history as nightmare. For it is Stephen Dedalus who said, 'History is a nightmare from which I am trying to awake', and Eliot who wrote of 'the immense panorama of futility and anarchy which is contemporary history', and there are surrealist nightmares in Joyce's 'Nighttown' episode and in the fifth part of *The Waste Land*, both with the elements of violence and madness that distinguish the later surrealists.

As some contemporary critics observed, this surrealist obsession with violence made the movement politically ambiguous, in spite of its repeated attachment to communism. Peter Quennell wrote in 1933 of 'that almost pathological worship of violence which seems to dominate so many modern French writers', and added that

In Surrealism, one seems to detect a similar need of violence—of revolution for its own sake, apart from its objects—translated with some ingenuity into literary and philosophical terms. The question arises whether it is not symptomatic of a larger movement, of which the spread has begun to be felt all over the world.[49]

The larger movement is fascism, in which violence against other men becomes a political act, and terror is a part of the ritual. The *Daily Worker* made a similar point, in a review of *Contemporary Poetry and Prose* in 1936:

> The attractions of surrealist poetry are that it embodies in the purest form the miraculous or magical element in art. But, on the other hand, the various forms of lust and cruelty which are to be found in the unconscious may be used as an occasion for mere sensationalism.
>
> And it is not much good inveighing against Fascist degeneracy if you are describing with relish orgies of torture and blood . . .[50]

By the end of 1936, the peak of the surrealist movement in England was past. One might argue that the Marxists had won, and by refusing to accept Surrealism as a political ally had destroyed its claim to be taken seriously. But I think that in fact what happened was simply that the movement was overtaken by history. Breton had said, and a reviewer quoted him approvingly in 1936, that 'the admirable thing about the fantastic is that it is no longer fantastic: there is only the real'.[51] One might alter that slightly, and say that as the 'thirties moved on toward the end, there was only the surreal; when violence becomes a commonplace, it doesn't need fantasy or the unconscious to express it. And so it might be said that Surrealism belongs to yet another modern literary tradition—the tradition of atrocities recorded, of which *The Brown Book of the Hitler Terror* is an early and vivid example. Auden, always so acute to the mood of the moment, must have felt this when he wrote, as the epigraph to *Look, Stranger!*, his 1936 collection, this poem:

> Since the external disorder, and extravagant lies,
> The baroque frontiers, the surrealist police;
> What can truth treasure, or heart bless,
> But a narrow strictness?

In a Europe in which even the agents of order were surreal and terrifying, Surrealism was unnecessary.

IV

Spender noted in his review of *New Writing* that it contained both *reportage* and *fable*, but separately, as two literary kinds. In the best writings of the 'thirties, the two kinds interweave, as Spender saw that they did in *The Ascent of F6*, and produce a dual-plane work with a strong realistic surface, which is yet a parable. This is true even in literary forms that would seem by their nature to be necessarily one kind or the other. Consider, for example, the travel book, traditionally a mode of reportage that depends for its principal interest on the exotic nature of its literal content. Writers of the 'thirties generation turned to travel writing in the last few years of the decade, and produced a number of striking books: *Waugh in Abyssinia* and Greene's *Journey Without Maps* in 1936, Auden and MacNeice's *Letters from Iceland* and Lehmann's *Prometheus and the Bolsheviks* in 1937, MacNeice's *I Crossed the Minch*, Orwell's *Homage to Catalonia* (a rather special kind of travel book, to be sure) in 1938, Auden and Isherwood's *Journey to a War*, Greene's *The Lawless Roads*, and Lehmann's *Down River* in 1939. What is most striking about them is that none is a travel book in quite the same sense that *Eothen* or Stanley's *Journal* is. The difference is in the degree to which the 'thirties writers turned their travels into interior journeys and parables of their times, making landscape and incident—the factual materials of *reportage*—do the work of symbol and myth—the materials of *fable*.

Why choose travel as the parabolic form? One might reply, quite practically, that by now the 'thirties writers were established enough to get publishers' advances for unwritten books, and that this was the age of feature-journalism, when writing about exotic places was a popular form of escape-art. By the mid-'thirties Waugh had already made a reputation as a writer of witty travel books, with *Labels* (1930), *Remote People* (1931), and *Ninety-two Days* (1934), and Peter Fleming had had a great and deserved success with *Brazilian Adventure* (1933). But the fact that travel writing was popular does not seem an adequate explanation of this burst of writing of so special a kind by writers who were primarily poets and novelists, and one must look further, into the peculiar circumstances of the generation.

One clear feature of the 'thirties is that as the decade passed, Englishmen became increasingly aware of the presence and importance of the world-out-there: as the Abroad became a threat, it became a reality. In the case of young writers this meant a shift of attention away from English subjects, toward foreign scenes and problems. This had happened quite early in the decade in some cases: Isherwood had gone to Berlin, Lehmann and Spender had gone to Vienna, Orwell had gone down and out in Paris, and all of them had written parables of the realities they had found. The travel books of the end of the decade simply extended the limits of out-there, as the perimeter of awareness and the community of disaster expanded—to Africa, to Mexico, to China, to the whole troubled world.

There is also the journey itself, the most insistent of 'thirties metaphors. As Auden first composed it, it was a journey over the frontier, out of the familiar and secure into the unknown and frightening, which had to be taken if one was to reach the new life. In the development of this metaphor, in poems like *Paid on Both Sides* and *The Magnetic Mountain*, details of landscape—the mountains, the pass, the rail-end—take on symbolic meanings of a kind that could easily be adapted to actual geography. So one might say that the travel books simply act out, in the real world, the basic trope of the generation.

And finally, there is the 'thirties concern with Heroism—the Truly Strong Man, and Auden's haunting question, 'What shall the self-conscious man do to be saved?' Travel offers the possible return of adventure, even of personal heroism, and the more so as it moves beyond the familiar civil landscapes, into the heart of darkness, or into war. It was too late for these poets and novelists to make themselves airmen or mountaineers, but they could all be travellers.

The first of this wave of travel books, Graham Greene's *Journey Without Maps*, seemed to announce at once, in its title, that it concerned a more than literal journey. And Greene stressed this difference in the two epigraphs that he chose for his book. The first, from Auden's epilogue to *The Orators*, is a condensed journey-parable:

> 'O do you imagine,' said fearer to farer,
> 'That dusk will delay your path to the pass,
> Your diligent looking discover the lacking
> Your footsteps feel from granite to grass?'

The second is a passage from Oliver Wendell Holmes, in which the life of an individual is compared to the pieces of a child's jig-saw puzzle map. 'If I could look back on the whole,' Holmes concludes, 'as we look at the child's map when it is put together, I feel that I should have my whole life intelligently laid out before me . . .' The two epigraphs gloss the two terms of the title: the *journey*, which will be fearful (and Audenish), and the *map*, which is not there because it is the map of meaning, and must be put together. It will be a parabolic journey, then, into the self and into the past, in search of meaning.

Greene explained the parabolic point more fully in the text, by comparing his journey to psychoanalysis:

> The method of psychoanalysis is to bring the patient back to the idea which he is repressing; a long journey backwards without maps, catching a clue here and a clue there, as I caught the names of villages from this man and that, until one has to face the general idea, the pain or the memory. This is what you have feared, Africa may be imagined as saying, you can't avoid it, there it is creeping round the wall, flying in at the door, rustling the grass, you can't turn your back, you can't forget it, so you may as well take a long look.[52]

This passage also suggests why Greene chose Africa; it promised, as no European nation could, an exploration of primitive life beyond Wordsworthian pastoralism, a kind of Jungian night-journey into the darkness of the self and of the racial memory: 'here in Liberia', Greene wrote, 'again and again one caught hints of what it was we had developed from.'[53] Like Lear on the heath, Greene went to Africa to discover the poor bare forked animal in humanity and in himself.

Greene's journey began at Freetown, in Sierra Leone. From there he and his companion and their African porters travelled inland, crossed into Liberia in the remote interior forests, and returned to the Liberian coast and civilization at Monrovia. It was a journey, Greene concluded, that exposed him to 'the worst boredom I had ever experienced, the worst fear and the worst exhaustion'.[54] It was an ill-planned, uncertain, and apparently quite arbitrary circuit, full of small hardships and discomfort, cursed by accidents and sickness, the whole thing curiously pointless-sounding. The life that Greene discovered in the African forest was strange without being dramatic, and fearful without being exciting; but it was what he wanted—it was the dark interior.

Journey Without Maps is essentially an interweaving of two strands: the narrative of this actual journey, with its particular observations, and the interior journey, composed of memories and reflections of the personal life. But there is also another element, which seems dictated by the spirit of the time: while Greene moves through the timeless, primitive world of interior West Africa, in the world outside the noise of history continues, and the reader is reminded of that other world, in which he himself must live—another heart of darkness that includes communists and Nazis, Hitler, political violence. So the book, in spite of its exotic material, is not escape-literature, as most travel writing is; it belongs rather in Auden's other and more serious category— it is parable-art.

Not all of Greene's reviewers were pleased with the parabolic aspect of the book; some complained that that wasn't what a travel book ought to be. But even those who wrote unfavourably about it got the point. For example, the *London Mercury*'s man wrote:

> Those who, like Mr. Greene, have looked at themselves through the eyes of Henry James, T. S. Eliot, and Kafka, look at the world chiefly as a stimulus for acute personal emotion. In the midst of the African forest we are made conscious not of Sir James Frazer's study of comparative religion, but of those famous notes to *The Waste Land*, of 'the seediness of civilization'.[55]

And he described the earlier part of the book as 'a nightmare of impression and sensation'. This is all very acute, for *Journey Without Maps* certainly is in the *Waste Land* tradition, and therefore also belongs with the other nightmares that I have been discussing. Perhaps one might say that Greene had gone to Africa to find the images of nightmare that surrealists found in their subconsciousness.

V

Another name for the nightmare is Doomsday—that feared and expected war that had brought so many documentary books in this year. Doomsday was also a subject for fiction, and it is striking how many novels of 1936 concerned a future war or a revolution, and its consequences: Storm Jameson's *In the Second Year*, Anthony Bertram's *The King Sees Red*, Barbara Wootton's *London's Burning*, Joseph O'Neill's *Day of Wrath*, Geoffrey Gorer's *Nobody Talks Politics*. Even H. G. Wells wrote one that year, *Things to Come*. These are all prophetic, admonitory, apocalyptic novels, but in texture they tend to be realistic, using actual settings, and describing a future that is not a distant science-fiction time, but a date just ahead (most of them put Doomsday at about 1940). And the war they imagine is not a futurist war, as in the early novels of Wells, nor an extrapolation of the First World War, as in *Vile Bodies*, but something very like the war that was actually fought in 1940, with air raids over London and civilians sheltering in the underground.

The coming war had entered into present-time, realistic fiction, too; by 1936, Doomsday was simply a part of reality. Orwell's Gordon Comstock, in *Keep the Aspidistra Flying*, thinks:

> Our civilisation is dying. It *must* be dying. But it isn't going to die in its bed. Presently the aeroplanes are coming. Zoom— whizz—crash! The whole western world going up in a roar of high explosives.[56]

And this passage is not offered as fancy or daydream; the enemy planes overhead are as much a part of Comstock's world as the advertising posters on the walls and the blowing leaves in the gutters. They are all part of one mood, which is the mood of the time.

The best single example of the way in which the real present incorporated the apocalyptic future, while remaining real, is Greene's 1936 novel, *A Gun for Sale*, a book that might be described as a war-novel before the event. It is one of Greene's 'entertainments', a thriller; but it is a thriller only in the sense that *Journey Without Maps* is a travel book: Greene has used the conventions of an escape-art to create parable-art.

Like most of Greene's novels of the 'thirties, it is a story of a manhunt, set in seedy, contemporary England. Raven, a hired killer, has murdered a minister of a foreign state, on instructions of an English armaments manufacturer, in order that a war should be forced on Europe. The murder is a purely commercial act: Raven is working for wages, and his employer, Sir Marcus, is stimulating trade, and neither is concerned for the consequences of his actions; and so our revulsion at the crime is a judgment of a world in which economics kills.

Greene has recalled that the plot line was suggested to him by two contemporary publications: a life of Sir Basil Zaharoff, the armaments king, and a report from a Royal Commission inquiring into the manufacture and sale of arms.[57] The novel therefore has the kind of base in immediate history that one finds in so much writing of the 'thirties—in *Vienna*, and *The Noise of History* and *Mr. Norris Changes Trains* and *A Time to Dance*, and later in *Autumn Journal* and the poems of *Journey to a War*. But it has another kind of topicality as well; for it is about the fear of war, and that is a feeling that all Englishmen shared in 1936.

The threat of war fills the novel: characters discuss it, newspaper headlines and hoardings report it, it is uttered in radio broadcasts and written on moving news-signs. But there is another war, too, a war that is less public and newsworthy, but is already going on—the war of the powerful against the weak, the rich against the poor, the 'big organized battalions' against the loners and the outsiders. We see this war most clearly in two principal characters: Raven, and Anne, the chorus girl he accidentally comes upon, who becomes for a time his ally. Raven is one of the wretched and rejected of the world, the son of a hanged criminal and a suicide, an asylum orphan, defaced by a hare-lip, unloved and incapable of love; 'there's always been a war for me', he says. Anne is a cheerful working-class girl, loyal to her class and against the big battalions.

The world through which these two figures move, the seedy and derelict reaches of an industrial city, is the battlefield of this war, and Greene describes it in battlefield images: a housing estate with its scarred fields and broken tree-stumps, the 'dark wounded ground' of the factory section, the industrial waste land through which Anne's train moves at the end of the novel, 'like a dying creature dragging itself painfully away through no-man's-land from the scene of a battle'.[58] It is a device that he had used before, in *It's a Battlefield*, and to make the same point: that a city is the scene of a continuous war for survival.

The core of meaning in the novel is in the relation between these two wars. The poor, like Raven, have always had their war; but now the same antagonists—the men who control money and power—threaten to extend that conflict onto another, more destructive plane, to bring all of Europe into war. This view of the coming World War as another economic assault upon ordinary people, as simply the class-struggle fought by armies, was a commonplace of Left rhetoric in the 'thirties, but Greene succeeded in turning it from rhetoric into parable.

A Gun for Sale is a parable in the rather special sense that the travel books and *Night Mail* are parables: that is, it is a symbolic, moral work with a strong realistic surface. Greene sustains a texture of actuality through his use of realistic-sounding particulars (the newspapers, the real London streets), and by his characteristic 'seedy' descriptive style. But in fact the world of the novel is fantastic, full of grotesques who function like the allegorical forms of monstrous vices: the spider-like Sir Marcus, Cholmondely the glutton, Acky the obscene defrocked priest. They fill the novel with the presence of evil, of which Sir Marcus' war would be the ultimate expression. Evil is already there, in these monstrous creatures; it needs only to be concentrated by 'the side that organizes', the big battalions of finance and industrialism, and war will come.

But though the world of the novel is peopled with monsters, there is only one scene that departs from surface realism, and that exception is an important one. An air-raid drill is called in the city, and all persons who go out into the streets are required to wear gas-masks. Medical students seize the occasion for a rag, and run about the streets tormenting passers-by. The masks they wear have erased their human identities and have turned them into 'masked monstrosities' that look like animals, and they behave accordingly, without any human sense of responsibility. The drill also frees Raven from his recognizable, deformed face; in a mask he is anonymous, and so can reach his enemy and kill him. The whole episode has a wild, surreal quality. It is the *only* surreal scene in the novel, and that suggests a point that has already been made: that war itself is surreal, and that the representation of it, or of surrogates for war such as air-raid drills, requires a more than realistic method to express its violence, its dehumanizing effects, and its fearfulness.

A Gun for Sale is perhaps most topical in the way it ends. Sir Marcus and Raven are dead, Anne has been reunited with her lover, and the war has been postponed. But only postponed; Anne thinks grimly, 'men were fighting beasts, they needed war'. The world peace is a precarious one, and as for the *other* war, it will go on as before, the strong against the weak. One is left with a sense of the fear of war, and of the helplessness of human efforts to avert it.

One review of Greene's novel is worth quoting at length as a contribution to this point by a distinguished novelist of his generation. Rosamund Lehmann wrote the following in the *New Statesman*:

Beneath his title *A Gun for Sale* Mr. Graham Greene has written An Entertainment. To my mind, it more closely resembles a long elaborate dream-experience: one of those dark disorganising circumstantial dreams which unwind in more or less logical sequence: dreams of immense conspiracies with oneself moving against an Enemy unseen, all-powerful, oneself in the predicament of being obliged to save the world. They are all there—the wicked faces, the shots, the solitary figures in the streets suddenly there and then not there, the sinister abnormality flickering without warning out of the bland normal surface, like a black snake out of an innocent crate of bananas. In a moment somebody will say something frightening, obscene . . . Mr. Greene has a remarkable capacity for building up and sustaining a Dark Tower atmosphere. Every detail is significant. Icy wind from the north, rain freezing in the gutters, fog, winter streets, tram-lines, shops decorated for Christmas, squalidly respectable residential areas, the sidings of a big station at night—all seems saturated with the menace of flight and pursuit.[59]

What is interesting about this review is that it is not really about Greene's novel, but is rather Miss Lehmann's own parable for the same mood, her own version of her generation's nightmare, 'the predicament of being obliged to save the world'. Like Greene's Anne, she saw this task as at once required and impossible; it was a dilemma that she shared with many of her contemporaries in 1936.

VI

One final example must be considered, a work that brings together many of the separate strands of this focal year—Auden and Isherwood's *The Ascent of F6*. Spender praised the play for the rhythmic contrast that it maintained between reportage and fable, 'two approaches to the contemporary political scene', and indeed it *is* both reportage and fable, but it is far more than a political play; it moves beyond the public issues of political action into private questions of the motives and the consequences of power.

As fable, *The Ascent of F6* is another version of a familiar Auden theme, the necessary journey over the border into the unknown. Its principal characters are familiar, too: the introspective young man who is forced toward a life of action, and the domineering mother who drives him. In this version the young man, Michael Ransom, is asked by the British government to climb F6, an unscaled peak on the border between two colonies, British Sudoland and Ostnian Sudoland. The natives believe that the first nation to reach the top of the mountain will rule both sides; the Ostnians are already preparing their climb, and British imperial interests are at stake. But in the end it is not the British officials, but Ransom's mother who persuades him to make the climb. He does, losing his party on the way, and at the top, in a hallucinatory scene, is united with his mother, and dies.

In choosing a mountaineer as their tragic hero, Auden and Isherwood were acknowledging a myth-making activity that was as prominent in the years between the wars as long-distance flying was, and for similar reasons. Those were the years of the great Everest expeditions—the British sent seven groups of climbers between 1920 and 1939—and of many other Himalayan and Alpine climbs, and these adventures were given the same sort of coverage in the press that the record-breaking flights were. *The*

Times reported British expeditions with great thoroughness, and even the *Daily Worker* gave most of a page to an account of a Russian climb.

For British intellectuals, mountain-climbing was more than a heroic myth; it was also a familiar activity, at first or second hand. Michael Roberts and his wife, Janet Adam Smith, were both serious climbers, and so were I. A. Richards and his wife (they were on the first expedition to climb the north ridge of the Dent Blanc in 1928). Auden, Greene, and Spender all had close relations who made reputations as climbers: Auden's brother and Spender's brother were together on one expedition with the great British mountaineer Eric Shipton. And so it is not surprising that the climber-hero appears in 'thirties literature from the beginning, in poems by Auden and Spender, and in verse and prose by Roberts. As early as 1930 Roberts, searching for a metaphor for Auden's poetic courage, compared him to Irvine and Mallory on Everest (a rather unfortunate comparison, since both climbers died on that expedition), and later, in his preface to *New Country*, he found in the companionship of climbing an image of his notion of communism.

While the climb in *F6* is a fable based on a 'thirties myth of heroism, it is also close to reportage. In the summer of 1936, while Auden and Isherwood were finishing their play, a British and American expedition was attempting Nanda Devi, a Himalayan peak on the border of India and Tibet, and its progess was being extensively reported. In some details, for example the choice of two men to make the final ascent, the action of the play is close to the actual Nanda Devi climb, and the whole treatment of the effort echoes press coverage of the expedition. But press coverage of such a gesture of public heroism is itself a kind of myth-making, and so even reportage becomes fable. This process is expressed in the play in the news broadcasts that report and interpret the climb to the British public, represented by Mr and Mrs A., exploiting the climbers in order to exploit the nation.

The problem in such a method of contrapuntal myths is that the work becomes too complex—not so much *dual*-levelled, as all parables are, as *multi*-levelled. E. M. Forster, reviewing the play in the *Listener*, found four ways of reading it, which amount to four levels of parable: the heroic, the politico-economic, the character-test, and the Freudian.[60] And he was right, they are all there in the play, as they are all there in a good many other works of this time; for these are the categories of problems that the generation faced and worried about.

On the heroic level, Ransom is a reticent and scholarly man of action, brilliantly able, but detached and self-examining. Everyone recognized at once, and Auden admitted, that the character was based on T. E. Lawrence. The description of him that is given in one of the play's news-broadcasts is a parody of the popular image of Lawrence:

> Eight stone six. Aged twenty-eight years.
> Short and blue-eyed.
> His first experiences the rectory elms and
>   the garden quarry.
> Kept a tame rook. Was privately educated,
> By a Hungarian tutor.
> Climbed the west buttress of Clogwyn Du'r Arddu
> While still in his teens. . . .
> Studied physiology in Vienna under Niedermeyer.
> Went to the Julian Alps,
> Conquered Triglav, mastered the Scarlet Crag.
> Disappeared into Asia Minor, appeared in the
>   Caucasus
> On two-headed Ushba, returned to England,
> In an old windmill near the mouth of the Nen
> Translated Confucius during a summer.
> Is unmarried. Hates dogs. Plays the viola da gamba.
> Is said to be an authority on Goya.
> Drinks and eats little but is fond of crystallized
>   apricots . . .[61].

'You,' his mother tells him, 'were to be the Truly Strong Man.' And he does become a public hero; but by doing so he reveals his inner flaw. As in the case of John Nower (in *Paid on Both Sides*) and the Airman (in *The Orators*), courage is the public face of private weakness, and leadership is a temptation to authoritarianism. This aspect of the play is one that the Group Theatre, which first produced the play in February 1937, stressed. An article on the play in the *Group Theatre Paper* for December 1936, described Ransom in this way:

> In Ransom, the leader of the expedition to F6, we have a complex study of the hero of action, a figure which has so often attracted the attention of the English theatre. But it is the hero of action in contemporary terms; who reminds us not of Tamburlaine or Agamemnon or Antony, but of T. E. Lawrence, or the dictators of the continent. The pleasant and easy task of lampooning and caricaturing the dictator is here abandoned in favour of an attempt to understand the springs of his conduct.[62]

This connection between Ransom's behaviour and the conduct of dictators is not one that the play makes explicitly; but apparently that was not necessary for politically conscious audiences in the mid-'thirties.

The politico-economic level of the play concerns the efforts of the British establishment to persuade Ransom to compete in the national interest against the Ostnian threat. Ransom is urged on by his brother (a Colonial Office official), by a newspaper peer, by a general, and by a titled lady—a gathering that collectively represents the centres of power in England and the Empire, and (what amounts to the same thing) upper-class self-interest. Like similar characters in *The Dog Beneath the Skin*, they are treated with broad, aggressive satire, and one is left in no doubt as to how the authors feel about the Establishment. But there is another point made here—that power corrupts, and that Ransom is corrupted by submitting to the will of the powerful. It is a point that leads to political quietism, an odd position for two writers of this activist generation to reach.

By character-test, Forster meant the understanding of the ascent as an interior journey of self-discovery. This theme is set up in the first scene, in which Ransom soliloquizes on the relation between Virtue and Power. It is closely related to the theme of heroism, for it turns on the question of whether the hero acts to acquire knowledge of himself, or to gain power and thus compensate for his own sense of his inadequacies. It is, one might say, the myth of the hero seen from the inside.

And finally, there is the Freudian level. The son is heroic to please his mother and win her love, and is destroyed by her. Both Auden and Isherwood had, in their separate earlier works, treated mother figures as Freudian carnivores (for example in Isherwood's *The Memorial*, and in *Paid on Both Sides* and the 'Prologue' to *The Orators*). Both knew a good deal about psychoanalysis, and the relation that they develop between Ransom and his mother has a classic case-study quality, though the frequency of the mother figure in their writings suggests that Mrs Ransom came from personal sources rather than from textbooks.

The interrelations among these various levels are not easily reconciled, and the authors had trouble ending the play satisfactorily. There were at least three different conclusions extant within a year of the play's first publication: the English published text, the Group Theatre's version, and the American text (which may have been the one used by the Arts Theatre in Cambridge in 1937). The problem is essentially a matter of that conflict of public and private themes that was so central to 'thirties writing. In one ending, the conclusion is political, a broadcast to Mr and Mrs A; another ends with Ransom and his mother, the private, psychological theme. These are not only different, they are contradictory; one stresses the political success at the expense of the private defeat, the other ignores the political and focusses on the defeat of the tragic hero. As one reviewer wrote, 'The fact that conclusions with very different implications are apparently thought interchangeable is alarming.'[63] But it is not altogether surprising; that uncertainty is a condition of the time and of the generation.

The Ascent of F6 poses the T. E. Lawrence question: 'What shall the self-conscious man do to be saved?' But it does not answer it, either on the personal or on the public level. Psychologically it says, as Auden had said all along, that heroes are Truly Weak Men. Politically, it demonstrates the ugliness of power, but its political alternatives are at best ambiguous. The Group Theatre identified the hero with European dictators, and Auden's friends accepted this, though with varying attitudes toward the fact. Spender, for example, took Ransom to be a fascist type, sympathetically dealt with, and was approving; but Day Lewis wrote:

The morality is much more questionable. As far as I have understood it, by erecting a colossal bogy out of Lord Acton's words, 'power corrupts ... all great men are bad', it asserts that the good man's responsibility must begin and end with his own soul. The implications of this are at best Oxford Group and at worst Fascist.[64]

Other Left critics found the play satisfactorily pro-worker and anti-capitalist.[65] Even allowing for the way in which words like *fascist* lost their shape in literary discussions of the 'thirties, one must conclude that politically the play was less than lucid, and less than resolved.

That may simply be a way of saying that *The Ascent of F6* is not a propaganda piece, but rather, like *Paid on Both Sides*, an eccentric tragedy of the between-the-wars generation; and like other tragedies, it is not fundamentally concerned with the sort of human problems that can be solved by taking thought or by taking action, by joining one group or by denouncing another, but with the problems that are beyond resolution, except by dying. You might call it The Self-Conscious Man's Tragedy, or The Tragedy of the Truly Weak Man, for the essential tragic point is that the self-conscious man strives to discover and judge his own motives, but that, like every tragic hero, he cannot know his motives until he has seen his actions.

This is more than a literary point: it is a statement of the problem that faced the generation, as the time for real action, actual fighting against an actual enemy, approached. The tragic resolution of the problem of action is death. The 'thirties had not, up to this date, been tragic in this sense, except in a remote way, in the working-class districts of Vienna, in the hidden camps of Germany. But at the turn of the year, as 1936 became 1937, the public dying had begun. The war in Spain had removed tragedy from the literary world.

VIII

1937

I

Some wars are literary events: they alter consciousness, and so compel literary imaginations to find new forms for describing the ways in which men kill men. These are the wars fought for the noblest causes and the highest-flown abstractions, in which men go into battle believing the rhetoric, and are changed by the violence of reality. The First World War was such a literary event, and in the 'thirties the civil war in Spain was another. It was not the first of the decade's wars—in 1936 the Japanese had been in China for five years, and the Italian campaign in Abyssinia had just ended—but it was the first to engage English imaginations. Unlike the others, this war was European and comprehensible: it was the first battle in the apocalyptic struggle of Left and Right that the 'thirties generation had been predicting for years. There is a sense of relief in the first writings about the Spanish war, a sense that at last what had been a rhetorical and prophetic conflict had become actual, that in the morality play of 'thirties politics Good was striking back at Evil.

At the beginning, the war in Spain seems to have acted upon young writers in the way that Auden had hoped serious writing would: it made 'action urgent and its nature clear'. The literary response was immediate and copious; indeed, one gets the impression that there was a great deal more writing done in England about the Spanish war while it was being fought than there was about the Second World War during its course. As was the case in 1914, the first of the war-writing was rhetorical and propagandist —Spain was not so much a place as the name of a cause, and the war being fought there was the Good War, a crusade in which the issues were unambiguous. (As Cyril Connolly put it, the Spanish war had its 'Rupert Brooke period'.[1]) But even then it was *literary* propaganda, poems and stories, many of them by established writers. The war began in July 1936, and by October the *Left Review* could run two stories and a poem about it. In November the Unity Theatre was performing 'Spain', a poem for voices by Randall Swingler, at rallies in support of the Loyalist cause, and in the same month Roy Campbell published a series of ten poems titled 'Toledo, 1936', celebrating the achievements of the Nationalists.[2] The flow of writing continued in the following spring: in March, the Left Theatre Revue included a one-act play about the International Brigade, and John Lehmann recalls how he scurried to get translations of war poems by Spanish poets for the spring issue of *New Writing*.[3]

As the war went on, this vision of it as a Left crusade changed for many English writers. The change was not a matter of switching loyalties or of withdrawing support—English intellectuals were overwhelmingly pro-Loyalist at the beginning, and remained so to the end[4]—but of coming to see the conflict, and war itself, more realistically. Partly this was an inevitable consequence of history: as attrition and defeats came, as the factions that composed the Loyalist side began to fight among themselves, as the Russians moved in to take command, the Good War came to seem soiled by sectarian bias and betrayal; anyone who read the daily papers could see that it was no longer an idealist's war.

Many young English writers had more than a newspaper-reader's knowledge of the real war. By the time it was a year old a considerable number of them had gone to Spain—to fight, or to work for the Loyalist cause in other ways, or simply to observe. They were encouraged to travel there by their own English political parties, and by the Loyalist government (which even organized an International Writers' Conference in Madrid and Valencia in the summer of 1937 to bring writers to the battlefronts); their journeys were publicized in advance ('Famous Poet to Drive Ambulance in Spain', a *Daily Worker* headline read when Auden departed in January 1937), and their observations were published in the English press. In these travels a new generation of writers was exposed to the realities of war, as the previous generation had been on the Western Front, but with some significant differences: this time it was a civil war fought between foreigners in a foreign country; and this time it was a war that was being fought for a cause in which the young believed. So though it seemed their own, it was not their own; and though it was ugly and destructive, it was worth fighting. The lessons of the First War's poets would clearly not serve for this one; one could only be Wilfred Owen with a difference. A new kind of war set a new literary problem—the task of finding literary forms for necessary violence.

The nature of the generation's new experience can be described best in terms of one of their dominant metaphors—the figure of the journey over the border that Auden had invented in his early poems. When these young travellers crossed over from France into Spain, they passed from the known world of peace to the unknown world of war, from the world of symbolic actions (the rhetoric, the resolutions, the protests and rallies) to the world of actual fighting and dying. Memoirs of English volunteers make much of the strangeness and emotional intensity of this passage: on one side of the border the familiar lives of ordinary men, on the other soldiers, passes, bullets, and uncertainty—all the fearful things that Auden had told them would be there, if they ventured far enough from security.

For the 'thirties generation, that frontier between peace and war must have had another, more particular meaning, because of the war that had hung over their childhoods: to enter the world of war was to take the Test that their fathers and brothers had passed in 1914–18. And for left intellectuals it was also a test of another kind, a test of commitment. The war in Spain was an enactment, in physical terms, of the revolutionary struggle that so much of their writing had been about: it was the 'action' of their propaganda. In essays in *New Country* and the *Left Review* young writers like Day Lewis and Upward and Spender had debated the problem of action: were literature and revolution incompatible? Should one give up writing to work for the cause? Was a poem an action? But always while the debating went on there had been, in the distance, the approaching day when the questions would be answered by the event, the day when the struggle would become physical and violent. And now, in Spain, it had begun, and the choice between art and action had become a real one, and not simply a point of literary argument.

For many young writers, the correct choice was obvious—no

merely literary act could equal the act of crossing the border. Most of the men who went first to fight were Communist Party members. John Cornford, the youngest and one of the most militant, reached the front less than a month after the war began. Others followed as their affairs permitted: Christopher Caudwell finished a draft of his *Studies in a Dying Culture*, wrote out careful instructions for publication in the event of his death, and left England in December; Ralph Fox, the Marxist critic, and John Sommerfield, the novelist, went at about the same time. So did Orwell, though not as a communist. The non-combatants, less totally committed to the Party or to the war, came along a bit later—Auden in January 1937, Spender in February, Bell in June. By then most of the volunteer soldiers were dead or wounded: Cornford was killed at the end of December (either on his twenty-first birthday or the day after); Fox died in January, Caudwell in February, Orwell was shot through the neck in January and returned to England. Bell, an ambulance driver, was killed by a shell in July. None of them had lasted more than a month or two in combat.[5]

It was from these young writers that the first real war-writing of their generation came back: Orwell and Sommerfield wrote from the fighting fronts, Auden reported from Valencia, Spender from Madrid.[6] These first pieces were essentially partisan reportage, but one can see in them how the writers were troubled and confused by the problem of dealing with a war that was both an ideological and an actual event, and that was at once theirs and not theirs. Often one finds an uneasy dissonance between the rhetoric of propaganda and the exact language of observation: in one paragraph the Great Cause appears in words appropriate to capitalized causes—words like *freedom, revolution, heroes*, and *courage* —and in the next the war enters with the bare shock of reality, the actual blood, the dying and the dead. As the war went on, and writers had more experience of it, this gap between the big words and the actualities widened, and became a subject in itself (the same thing happened in the best writing of the First World War, and perhaps it is an inevitable consequence of the experience of war). This was not necessarily a matter of disillusionment—some good writers died still believing in their cause, as they did also in the First War—but simply an awareness of the necessary disjunction between the words men fight for, and the ways men fight. But it creates problems of tone and of vocabulary for the war-writer, and especially for the writer who remains ideologically committed.

The first 'literary' writing from Spain came from two poets: Cornford, the combatant, and Spender, the observer. Cornford was at the front early in the war, and sent back two impressive poems: 'A Letter from Aragon' and 'Full Moon at Tierz: Before the Storming of Huesca'. He wrote as a communist, but he also wrote as a private man, young and frightened and shocked by the realities of war, and it is the interaction of these two sets of feelings, almost two languages, that makes these poems as memorable as they are. 'Letter from Aragon', the more particular and private of the poems, begins:

> This is a quiet sector of a quiet front.
>
> We buried Ruiz in a new pine coffin,
> But the shroud was too small and his washed feet
>   stuck out.
> The stink of his corpse came through the clean pine
>   boards.
> And some of the bearers wrapped handkerchiefs round
>   their faces.
> Death was not dignified.
> We hacked a ragged grave in the unfriendly earth
> And fired a ragged volley over the grave.
>
> You could tell from our listlessness, no one much
>   missed him.[7]

Cornford goes on to describe the shelling of a village, the screaming women and the children, and thinks 'how ugly fear is'. Up to the final stanza it is all particulars of death and suffering, an example of anti-heroic realism in the tradition of Owen and Sassoon. At this level of war, there is no politics; Ruiz and the screaming women could be on either side, death always smells, fear is always ugly. Only in the last lines Cornford introduces an Anarchist worker, who makes a speech:

'Tell the workers of England
This was a war not of our own making,
We did not seek it.
But if ever the Fascists again rule in Barcelona
It will be as a heap of ruins with us workers beneath it.'[8]

These last lines are lines that Owen couldn't have written, for they
assert, as Owen didn't and couldn't, that this war, for all its ugliness and fear, is a just and necessary one, in which the enemy *is* the
enemy, and heroism *is* possible: they bring into the poem the note
of history. And it is this element, above all, that distinguishes the
writing about the Spanish war, as a whole, from First World War
writing; for one of the most striking things about the best First
War poems is how empty of historical sense they are, how lacking
in causes and consequences, as though No Man's Land existed in
time as well as in space, separating these dreadful events from all
other human experience. But in the case of Spain the presence of
history was a necessary part of the reality for most writers: the war
was a cause, not a blood sacrifice. Still, as Cornford's poem demonstrates, the presence of history is a problem: the dissonance between
reality and rhetoric sounds ironic, and the brave words of the
Anarchist have a hollow ring, after Ruiz and the women.

'Full Moon at Tierz' is more ambitious and abstract, more
overtly communist, more ideological. It is not as successful a poem
as the more modest 'Letter from Aragon', but it is interesting for
what Cornford was attempting—to find a form adequate to the
moment as history. The problem is a difficult one, and especially
in a period when the traditional poetic ways of dealing with history
—the epic and the heroic drama—seemed to have died. In that
situation, how does a poet create the scale that historical significance demands, while at the same time preserving the immediacy
of the present moment? How can he record the dissonance between reality and ideology, and yet avoid the ironic note?
Cornford's solution was to set his historical moment—himself as a
soldier in the fields near Huesca, waiting for the battle to begin—
in a broad frame of Marxist history, made up both of actual
historical events and of images of the force of history itself. The
poem begins with a vast image of time, moving irresistibly forward,

like a glacier or a cataract, breaking down old orders, creating the present moment—the intersection of past and future where men stand free to act and so create *their* history. History is here an abstract, necessary force, but it is also a sequence of events: Cornford in the moonlit field stands at the end of a line that includes 'what the Seventh Congress said', Dimitrov's trial, the example of Maurice Thorez—the explicitly communist history that has led to the war against fascism.

But still, at the centre of this wide frame of history stands one young man, and at the centre of the poem he speaks for a moment in his private, young man's voice:

> Then let my private battle with my nerves,
> The fear of pain whose pain survives,
> The love that tears me by the roots,
> The loneliness that claws my guts,
> Fuse in the welded front our fight preserves.[9]

Then the poem opens out again, to the night and the moonlight that also falls on Germany and on England (in a passage that recalls Auden's 'Summer Night'), and concludes that all these places are one place, with one cause, and that the battle about to be fought will be fought for them all.

It is not, to my mind, an altogether successful poem, but it is an impressive one for a poet of twenty years to write in the midst of a war. Cornford had at least understood the poetic problem, and had made a first attempt to treat the Spanish war as a unique historical event, and to put the sense of history into the poem. By so doing he had turned his battle into a Marxist parable of history, in which the event draws meaning from the frame of historical necessity. That is not the same as writing propaganda, and certainly the poem is more than versified Marxism; the difference is the frightened boy in the centre, who reminds us, in his fear, how remote slogans are from acts.

Like Owen and Sassoon, Cornford wrote as a combatant, and that fact made his relation to the war somewhat simpler—there was at least a soldier-poet tradition. Spender, on the other hand, went to Spain as a propagandist—he was to broadcast from Valencia—and both the propagandist role and the non-combatant status must have created problems. And so, surely, did his poetic sensibility, which was naturally lyrical and emotional, and not inclined to deal in history and abstractions.

From the first, Spender reacted strongly against the distortions of reality that propaganda required. In April 1937, he wrote to the *New Statesman* from Madrid:

> People try to escape from a realisation of the violence to which abstract ideas and high ideals have led them by saying either that individuals do not matter or else that the dead are heroes. It may be true that at certain times the lives of individuals are unimportant in relation to the whole of future history—although the violent death of many individuals may modify the consciousness of a whole generation as much as a work of art or a philosophical treatise. But to say that those who happen to be killed are heroes is a wicked attempt to identify the dead with the abstract ideas which have brought them to the front, thus adding prestige to those ideas, which are used to lead the living on to similar 'heroic' deaths.[10]

This is a strong statement of that recognition that I spoke of, of the gap between the big words and the real things; it is also virtually a programme for Spender's war poems. Spender did not try, as Cornford had, to include both terms of this dissonance within his poems; rather, he separated individuals altogether from history and ideas. In his Spanish poems no distinctions are made between one side and the other, there is no enemy and no clear cause, there is not even, in most of them, an observing self. What remains is suffering individuals, and an overwhelming, unqualified compassion for them.

The poetry, then, is in the pity. Of all the English poets of the Spanish war, Spender was most clearly indebted to the example of Owen, and he was clearly conscious of his debt. In an essay published in the summer of 1937 (not long after his return from Spain), Spender called Owen the greatest English war-poet, and praised his anti-heroism and his truthfulness. What Owen opposed, Spender wrote, was 'the propagandist lie which makes the dead into heroes in order that others may imagine that death is really quite pleasant'.[11] This is very close to the language of Spender's report from Madrid; what it does is to claim Owen as an ancestor, a model of how to write war poetry that avoids propaganda and tells the essential truth, that 'for most of those who participate in it, a war is simply a short way to a beastly death'. Owen was not, for Spender, a technical influence (as he was for Cornford); his example was a moral one, a matter of truth-telling.

One can see Owen's influence in a poem like 'Ultima Ratio Regum', which was published shortly after Spender's anti-heroic report from Madrid, and which is clearly a product of the same experience. The title of the poem comes from the motto that was embossed on the cannons of Louis XIV: force is the final argument of kings. The poem dwells on the disparity between the powerful war-making world of money and arms, and the death of one boy.

> The guns spell money's ultimate reason
> In letters of lead on the spring hillside.
> But the boy lying dead under the olive trees
> Was too young and too silly
> To have been notable to their important eye.
> He was a better target for a kiss.[12]

Spender uses none of the brave abstractions that supported Cornford in his fears; the boy has no consciousness of causes, he is simply a natural thing, like the grass and the leaves, and like grass and leaves he dies. He dies for no principle, one cannot tell which side of the battle he was on, or even whether he was Spanish. He has no connection with the poet—he is neither a comrade nor an enemy—nor even with the battle in which he died: his death has no consequences.

To be truthful as a poet, Spender wrote of Owen, is to be truthful to your own experience. He, too, had experienced a war—that is, he had gone there, he had seen the dead—and his reaction was, like Owen's, one of undiscriminating pity for the victims of war. Like Owen, his pity extended even to the dishonoured dead (compare for example his 'The Coward' and 'The Deserter' with Owen's 'S.I.W.'). Like Owen, he wrote war-poems that do not contain history, or take sides, or deal in ideologies. But behind these similarities there is the deep difference: Owen had shared the experience of war, but Spender only observed it. This is not a point of morality or courage or any such personal judgment, but of poetry. There is something missing from Spender's war poems, some authority for the right to pity; without that authority, which perhaps a poet must earn by sharing in suffering, pity becomes a patronising, distant attitude. Spender's experience of war had been compassion for those who fought, and anger for those who made propaganda, but these feelings had been distanced by the fact that Spender was neither a soldier nor a Spaniard. His compassion is in the poems, but so is the distance. They are, even the best of them, the war poems of a tourist.[13]

Spender wrote many poems about the Spanish war, over several years; Auden wrote only one—'Spain'. He wrote it immediately after his return from his one visit to the war, and he seems to have got everything he had to say about the issue into it. Auden had departed for Spain in January with a certain amount of left fanfare; the *Daily Worker* announced on 12 January that:

> W. H. Auden, the most famous of the younger English poets, co-author of 'The Dog Beneath the Skin', recently produced in London, and a leading figure in the anti-Fascist movement in literature, has left for Spain.
> He will serve as an ambulance driver.[14]

But he didn't; he visited Barcelona and Valencia, and then quietly returned to England. He had little to say at the time about his experiences in Spain, but many years later he recalled one surprising reaction. 'On arriving in Barcelona,' he wrote,

> I found as I walked through the city that all the churches were closed and there was not a priest to be seen. To my astonishment, this discovery left me profoundly shocked and disturbed. The feeling was far too intense to be the result of a mere liberal dislike of intolerance, the notion that it is wrong to stop people from doing what they like, even if it is something silly like going to church. I could not escape acknowledging that, however I had consciously ignored and rejected the Church for sixteen years, the existence of churches and what went on in them had all the time been very important to me.[15]

This is reminiscence after nearly twenty years, and perhaps it is coloured by Auden's subsequent return to religion, but something certainly happened in Spain that diminished his commitment to the left line (which had never been very strong). The poem that he wrote after his return is the best of the English war-poems from Spain, but it is also the least partisan, the least passionate, the least concerned with actual war, and the least Spanish. The war in Spain is indeed not so much the subject of the poem as the occasion. What the subject is we may define by recalling Auden's remark about poetry in *The Poet's Tongue*:

> . . . Poetry is not concerned with telling people what to do, but with extending our knowledge of good and evil, perhaps making the necessity for action more urgent and its nature more clear, but only leading us to the point where it is possible for us to make a rational and moral choice.[16]

This is what Auden's poem does: it extends our knowledge of the crucial moral choice of the 'thirties—the choice between fascism and its opponent—by examining that choice as it was manifested in Spain in 1937. But it does not *make* the choice: its subject is moral decision, not political action.

Like 'Full Moon at Tierz', 'Spain' takes its form from a theory of history. Auden begins, as Cornford did, with a long perspective view of the process of historical change. He starts where European economic history starts, with 'the language of size/Spreading to China along the trade routes', and moves through the Middle Ages, the Renaissance, and the Counter-Reformation, to nineteenth-century science and engineering, seeing the European past as a record of consciousness altered by economic change.

At the fourth stanza the present begins to enter contrapuntally: 'Yesterday the Sabbath of witches; but to-day the struggle.' *Struggle* is a heavily ideological word, but in the poem it carries a meaning that is more general, and less specifically polemical, than simply *class-struggle*; it is rather the struggle or moral choice that goes on occurring *every* today, because in the present in which men live they must choose and act: the present is the point of intersection in time where Freedom becomes Necessity, and Choice becomes History. Though individuals (the poet, the scientist, the ordinary poor) and nations invoke the life-force to intervene and act for them, life only replies: 'O no, I am not the mover; Not to-day; not to you ... I am whatever you do ... I am your choice, your decision.' In 1937, that determining decision would be a decision about Spain, but the conception is one of general morality, not of particular politics.

In Auden's terms, every moment is a border-situation in time, a frontier between the known past and 'perhaps, the future'—*perhaps*, because the future depends on the decision made now, as the frontier is crossed. The future is therefore rendered in the poem in random images of peace, some solemn, some rather comical or ironic: the rediscovery of romantic love, the photographing of ravens, the bicycle races through the suburbs on summer evenings, 'all the fun/Under Liberty's masterful shadow'. They are random, because the future is composed of unselected options—it is perfectly free, because it is not yet history. There is no implication in the poem that the future will take any particular political form, or that it will be different in details from the present and the past; it will simply be people doing what they like.

But between past and future lies today, and today's choice, which waits in Spain to be made:

On that arid square, that fragment nipped off from hot
Africa, soldered so crudely to inventive Europe;
    On that tableland scored by rivers,
Our thoughts have bodies; the menacing shapes of our fever

Are precise and alive. For the fears which made us respond
To the medicine ad. and the brochure of winter cruises
    Have become invading battalions;
And our faces, the institute-face, the chain-store, the ruin

Are projecting their greed as the firing squad and the bomb.
Madrid is the heart. Our moments of tenderness blossom
    As the ambulance and the sandbag;
Our hours of friendship into a people's army.[17]

The striking thing about these lines is that they treat the Spanish war in psychological, not political terms, as an eruption of the sickness of modern society: in Spain, the enemy is *us*—our fears and greeds (as usual, Auden involves himself in the class he condemns); and the people's army is psychological, too, a sort of metaphor for loving feelings. It is more than a metaphor, though; in Spain 'our thoughts have bodies', what was mental has become physical, and therefore mortal.

The struggle, then, is a struggle between sickness and health, and Spain is a case. The treatment is immediate choice, commitment to some form of action:

To-day the deliberate increase in the chances of death,
The conscious acceptance of guilt in the necessary murder;
    To-day the expending of powers
On the flat ephemeral pamphlet and the boring meeting.

A chance of death, guilt, wasted time, boredom—these are random, unheroic, and not explicitly political (which side does one write the pamphlet for?). But they are actual commitments that a young poet might make or reject, occasions for moral choice.

At the end the poem returns to that abstract theme, to re-state it as directly and bluntly as the moral of a fable:

The stars are dead. The animals will not look.
We are left alone with our day, and the time is short, and
    History to the defeated
May say Alas but cannot help nor pardon.

Auden has since condemned this passage as 'wicked doctrine', on the grounds that it equates goodness with success. But in fact it does nothing of the kind; what it says is simply that History is Necessity, and that it is made by men's choices. Once it is made, help and pardon are irrelevant. It is a harsh morality, for a harsh time, but it is nevertheless a morality, and not a wicked one.

'Spain' is an extraordinary war-poem—diagnostic, abstract, detached, lacking all the particularities and feelings that defined the genre in the First World War and were continued by poets like Cornford and Spender. There are no battles in the poem, no dead boys or screaming women, no grisly details, and no personal voice testifying to war's hideousness. Not only is there no 'I' in it, there is no suggestion of direct observation at all; Auden's Spain is a shape on a map, or the earth seen from a great height, not a landscape. It is a pitiless poem; the poetry is in the pitilessness.

It is also an open and unresolved poem. This is partly inherent in the theme: moral choices must be made *now*, but the consequences are never clear. But it is also partly a function of the poem's date: in the spring of 1937, the future of the Spanish war, and the future of Europe that seemed to hang on it, were still uncertain. And it was partly an expression of Auden's own unideological position: he was certainly pro-Loyalist, and that shows in the poem, but he was unwilling to assign good and evil to causes in the simple way that other war-poets did, or to pretend that a good cause was necessarily a successful one. What he wrote instead was a poem expressing the difficulty and necessity of making moral choices in a disastrous time. In terms of my metaphor of the 'thirties as a tragic drama, Auden's 'Spain' is about the third act.

Immediate reactions to the poem depended on the ideological convictions of the reader. Richard Goodman, an admirer of Auden but a dedicated communist, wrote:

> 'Spain'—the best poem that Auden has yet written and, with Spender's 'Vienna', the only poem by an Englishman anywhere near being a real revolutionary poem—still deals with Auden's own personal reactions and personal interpretation of the Spanish struggle . . .[18]

and Edgell Rickword, another party member, protested that

> the setting-up of a pamphlet–poem antagonism, *i.e.*, social struggle *versus* inner struggle, is a reflection of the poet's continuing isolation, falsifying the perspective of social development and delaying the re-integration of the poet into the body of society.[19]

But other critics, less committed in their politics, gave it high praise; Clifford Dyment called it 'the best of the poems so far inspired by that unhappy country,[20] and *New Verse*'s anonymous reviewer thought it 'an organic, grave, sensible and moving statement, more reasonable and more free of bigotry than any other political poem written for some years'.[21] Such differing judgments in part reflect the political differences among the judges; but they also point to a quality of the poem that makes it important for its time. It is a poem that eludes partisan capture, or even generic definition; it is not about the simplifications of 1937, but about the moral difficulties.

II

Among the English writers who chose to fight in Spain and who died there, were two of the best of English Marxist critics, Christopher Caudwell and Ralph Fox. Their most important books, *Illusion and Reality* and *The Novel and the People*, both published in the first year of the war, take Marxist theory of literature farther than any previous English critic had taken it, and it is ironic that war and revolution should have come as a possible mode of action for intellectuals just as writers who seemed capable of solving the problems of Marxist criticism were beginning to appear. It was a case of theory overtaken by history, one might say; or perhaps more truly, theory overtaken by the primacy of action.

The Novel and the People was published in January 1937, probably a day or two before Fox died. It is an orthodox study of fiction in relation to society (Fox had been a communist far longer than most of the intellectual Marxists of his day, and was clearly better trained and more sophisticated in Marxist doctrine); it argues for socialist realism, and is anti-Freud, anti-Joyce, and anti-Proust. But it is not doctrinaire; Fox was an intelligent man, and a good writer, and he put his case well.

The most interesting section of the book is the tenth chapter, 'Man Alive', in which Fox discusses the trial of Dimitrov by the Nazis as an example of 'moral grandeur and courage', and 'an epic of our time'. Communists before Fox had seen Dimitrov as a mythic figure; Montagu Slater, in an essay written in 1935, commented on the way the Nazis had inadvertently made a hero of him, and Cornford used his name in that sense in 'Full Moon at Tierz', and there are many other references to his heroism in left literature of the time.[22] But Fox was the only one who saw Dimitrov's story as an unwritten novel, and examined it in detail as a parable for Marxists, created out of actual history. Fox was himself the author of two novels, and he describes this unwritten epic vividly and novelistically: the atmosphere—'Berlin on the eve of Hitler's coup, a kind of feverish madness in the streets and beerhalls'; the characters—Van der Lubbe, dull-witted, wandering, probably mad, the Nazis, the four men charged with the burning of the Reichstag; the humour—the black humour of Nazism; and the dramatic climax—the trial scene. As Fox tells it, in the present tense, it reads like the scenario of a strong political novel.

Still it stands a little oddly in the book, among other novels that had managed to get written. Fox was aware of the anomaly; 'This long digression,' he wrote,

> ... may perhaps be excused as an attempt to show that in our modern life there are extraordinary subjects crying out for imaginative treatment, subjects in which the fantastic is mingled with the heroic, brutality with the calm spirit of man, baseness with loyalty and the chuckling of the insane with the searing wit of the mind's courage. Out of it all emerges a personality the study of which can only enlarge our experience and knowledge of man, strengthen our belief in our own powers and deepen our perception of life.[23]

The point is well taken, and worth pausing over. What Fox is saying is that the historical events of the 'thirties restored action, violence, melodrama, heroism, tragedy, the conflict of good and evil—all those traditional literary elements that were despaired of in the literature of the 'twenties—to creative imaginations. Whatever else it was, the decade of the 'thirties was dramatic, and its drama involved moral issues of the greatest importance. The Epic of Dimitrov is one conceivable example, as Fox demonstrates; but the general point is a more important one, that at this moment in history an epic response to human events seemed once more possible.

Yet that epic was never written. Fox was the last critic to see it as possible, and perhaps Dimitrov was the last of the decade's possible heroes. Perhaps the heroic phase of the 'thirties—the period of Dimitrov's trial and the rising of the Viennese workers—had come to an end by 1937, when men were dying anonymously and in large numbers in Spain, for there can be no epic of modern war, and no real heroes, either.

Illusion and Reality is a less orthodox, less polemical, and far more original book than *The Novel and the People*, and it was immediately recognized as an important work. Auden, reviewing it in *New*

Verse, wrote: 'This is the most important book on poetry since the books of Dr Richards, and, in my opinion, provides a more satisfactory answer to the many problems which poetry raises.'[24] And the anonymous *Listener* critic agreed: 'As a contribution to aesthetics it deserves to make as deep an impression on current thought as did I. A. Richards' *Principles of Literary Criticism*'.[25] It is interesting that in both cases the comparison is to Richards. In 1937 the younger generation, then at the highest point of its political commitment, was ready to replace Richards, who had been such a powerful influence on their earlier ideas of poetry and society, and Caudwell's appearance was providential.[26] Politics would take the place of psychology, and capitalism of the 'chaos of values'. 'We have waited a long time for a Marxist book on the aesthetics of poetry,' Auden said. 'Now at last Mr Caudwell has given us such a book.'

A serious artist of left inclinations would be bound to admire Caudwell, for of all the English Marxists writing criticism at the time he gave to art the most significant role in society. For Caudwell, art's role was equivalent and complementary to that of science:

> As art tells us the significance and meaning of all we are in the language of feeling, so science tells us the significance of all we see in the language of cognition. One is temporal, full of change; the other spatial and seemingly static. One alone could not generate a phantastic projection of the whole Universe, but together, being contradictory, they are dialectic, and call into being the spatio-temporal historic Universe . . .[27]

Science, says Caudwell, is 'the consciousness of the necessity of outer reality', and art 'the consciousness of the necessity of the instincts'.[28] In this dialectic, literature is not subordinated to a cause, nor assigned a merely polemic role; rather, it *creates* the future by articulating ideas and hopes, which may then be realized in time. When Auden wrote that *Illusion and Reality* had long been needed, he was simply saying what was clearly true—that left poetry had long needed a theoretical defence against the Agitprop mentality, and now it had it.

He may also have had something more personal in mind. He

must have been reading *Illusion and Reality* while he was writing 'Spain', for Caudwell's book was published in March 1937, just as Auden returned from his visit to Spain, and his review of it appeared in May, the same month that 'Spain' was published. On the subject of history and individual action—the theme of Auden's poem—Caudwell had very similar things to say:

These changes [in society] do not happen 'automatically', for history is made by men's actions, although their actions by no means always have the effect they are intended to have. The results of history are the net product of actions willed by men, but the results of history are by no means willed by any men.[29]

And beyond such particulars Auden would have found a mind in many ways like his own: a synthesizing, diagnostic, polymathic mind, given to schematizing knowledge and history in elaborate diagrams, mixing psychology and politics in ways that pleased neither Freudians nor Marxists, essentially heterodox, essentially an artist's mind.

But how, one wonders, did Auden respond to his own appearance in *Illusion and Reality*? In the final chapter, 'The Future of Poetry', Caudwell discussed the relation of Auden, Spender, and Day Lewis to communism and the proletarian revolution. They were, he said, all bourgeois, at most in alliance with the proletariat, but not within the ranks.

Their attitude to existing society therefore can only be destructive—it is anarchist, nihilist, and *surréaliste*. They often glorify the revolution as a kind of giant explosion which will blow up everything they feel to be hampering them. But they have no constructive theory—I mean as artists: they may as economists accept the economic categories of socialism, but as artists they cannot see the new forms and contents of an art which will replace bourgeois art.

They know 'something is to come' after this giant firework display of the Revolution, but they do not feel with the clarity of an artist the specific beauty of this new concrete living, for they are by definition cut off from the organisation which is to realise it, and which therefore alone holds in its bosom the nascent outlines of the future. They must put 'something' there in the future, and they tend to put their own vague aspirations for bourgeois freedom and bourgeois equality.[30]

This is an acute analysis of much of the 'thirties writings of these poets—of early poems such as *The Magnetic Mountain*, 'Summer Night', and 'I think continually', but also of poems of the Spanish war. What Caudwell said about the future is exactly true of Auden's 'Spain'—Auden's sense of the future *is* set down in images of bourgeois freedom and bourgeois equality. And indeed Auden's posture was always that of a middle-class, educated man, sympathetic to the proletarian movement, but involved in the guilt of his own class. The same is true of Spender and Day Lewis at their best, and it is when they attempt to join imaginatively with the working class that they sink into bathos and empty polemical gestures. What Caudwell saw as a poetical failing is in fact a strength: the recognition—steady in Auden, intermittent in the others—that poetry comes out of the life one has lived, and that a bourgeois poet cannot make himself proletarian by an act of will.[31]

But then, neither could Caudwell. He could scold bourgeois artists like Auden for being Marxists in economics and bourgeois in their art, but the same was true of himself; his own poems are traditional in form and vague in political content, and his one serious novel is a psychological study without any political content at all. And the form in which he was most prolific—the detective novel—is the most middle-class of literary genres. Even *Illusion and Reality*, though it is a strenuous effort at orthodoxy, has never gained a secure reputation among other Marxist critics. Though his commitment to communism went farther than that of most of the 'thirties writers, his situation was essentially theirs: he was a gifted young man with an artist's sensibility, drawn to political action by circumstances, but remaining a divided man, an artist in spite of himself. As a Marxist critic he could write severe condemnations of his bourgeois contemporaries, and demand a new literature for a new time, but as an artist he could not imagine what that new literature would be. His final, visionary chapter is vague and rhetorical in the way that the end of *The Magnetic Mountain* is; he could no more prescribe the parable of revolution than Day Lewis could write it. Perhaps his decision to fight in Spain had something to do with this; perhaps he chose the only mode of action in which he could express with perfect clarity his vision of the future.

Auden did not respond to Caudwell's criticism, but Spender replied for both of them in his contribution to the *New Verse* 'Double Auden Number' in November 1937:

> From the point of view of the working-class movement [he wrote] the ultimate criticism of Auden and the poets associated with him is that we haven't deliberately and consciously trans- ferred ourselves to the working class. The subject of his poetry is the struggle, but the struggle seen, as it were, by someone who whilst living in one camp, sympathizes with the other; a struggle in fact which while existing externally is also taking place within the mind of the poet himself, who remains a bourgeois. This argument is put very forcibly by Christopher Caudwell in the last chapter of his book *Illusion and Reality*. Whilst accepting its validity as a critical attitude, may we not say that the position of the writer who sees the conflict as something which is at once subjective to himself and having its external reality in the world —the position outlined in Auden's *Spain*—is one of the most creative, realistic and valid positions for the artist in our time?[32]

This is a straightforward defence of less than total commitment and a flat refutation of Caudwell's own position, and it is interest- ing that here, at the peak of English Marxist criticism, a retreat from commitment is also apparent, as though it was first necessary to have the best possible Marxist aesthetic in order to be sure that it wouldn't do.

Spender's own retreat is the most public and best documented case. It occurred during 1937, just at the point at which he seemed to be most committed to communism. During the latter part of 1936 he had been at work on a book which would express, as he put it, 'a personal attitude towards communism'. The book was announced in October under the title *Approach to Communism*, but when it appeared, in January 1937, the title had been altered to *Forward from Liberalism*. That change, from arrival to departure, is significant. For what Spender had tried to do in his book was to attach communism to the English liberal tradition, making it simply the latest and most contemporary expression of those values of individual freedom and justice that had been held by the great liberal idealists, from John Stuart Mill to E. M. Forster: 'I am trying to do a portrait,' Spender wrote, 'of the mind of a person whose sympathies are idealist and liberal in the present moment of history.'[33] That phrase described many left-wing intellectuals of Spender's generation, but it certainly did not describe a communist.

Forward from Liberalism is, as Spender said, a personal book, and it is valuable for that reason: it is the best testament that exists of the state of mind of a young literary man of good will in the mid-'thirties—eager to be active in the service of humanity, but jealous in defence of the privileges of art, and experienced only in the life and thought of his own circle. 'This book,' Spender wrote midway through it, 'is an act of my will, it is an assertion on behalf of two things I very much care for, justice and poetry. If you like, I believe that the revolution must be an example of poetic justice.'[34] And what sort of revolution would that be?

Spender's book was published by Gollancz as a Left Book Club choice and got a mixed reception, even from the LBC selection committee itself. Harold Laski, who wrote the official LBC review, was totally admiring, and took Spender's experience and opinions to be essentially those of Club members:

> I believe [he wrote] that members of the Left Book Club will especially value his book because they will find in it the very effective definition of a road along which, perhaps less securely, they also have been travelling. It will perform for them the very great service of making them see what the choices are this generation has to make.[35]

But John Strachey, the most orthodox communist on the committee, attacked Spender bitterly for criticizing the conduct of the Moscow trials, and other communists joined in; the book was reviewed unfavourably in the *Daily Worker* ('It is clear that Spender has not come very far "Forward from Liberalism" '), in the *Left Review* ('the standard of self-criticism of Communism is precisely that historical perspective which this book signally lacks'), and with avuncular severity in the *Labour Monthly* by Harry Pollitt, General Secretary of the Party in Great Britain ('completely wrong in many important and fundamental aspects of Communist policy').[36]

Spender's response was to join the Party, and to recant his remarks on the trials in an article in the *Worker*, and then to leave for propaganda work in Spain. 'The Communist Party warmly welcomes Comrade Spender to its ranks', the *Worker* announced, 'as a leading representative of the growing army of all thinking people, writers, artists and intellectuals who are taking their stand with the working class in the issues of our epoch, and is confident that in life and work with our Party Comrade Spender will reach complete unity with the outlook of Communism.'[37] But obviously that was not to be the case; by the end of the year he was writing the defence of individualism against Caudwell's attack that I have already quoted; and when asked to contribute to the pamphlet, *Authors Take Sides on the Spanish War*, he replied:

> I support in Spain exactly such a movement in liberal and liberating nationalism as the English liberals supported in many countries still groaning under feudalism in the nineteenth century.[38]

So the *Worker* was right, Spender had not come very far Forward from Liberalism, or if he had, he had brought Liberalism with him. His belief in distinterestedness, justice, objectivity, and the aesthetic experience as an end in itself had not changed much from *New Country* to *Forward from Liberalism*; what had changed, that brought him briefly into the Communist Party, was history. And history took him out again.

It was at about this time, though the date is uncertain, that Day Lewis began to retreat quietly from his activist position in the Party. In his memoir he recalls a rally, which must have taken place at some time during 1937, or possibly 1938, at which he suddenly realized that this was no place for a poet, and from then on he faded from the political scene. He did not resign from the Party or make any dramatic gesture of recantation; he simply ceased to be there, politically speaking. There is little political content in his essays and reviews after 1936, and though in his poems he continued to praise political workers and Spanish heroes, one finds a note of disenchantment in some of his verse of these years, as for example in 'Regency Houses', first published in May 1937:

> We who in younger days
> Hoping too much, tried on
> The habit of perfection,
> Have learnt how it betrays
> Our shrinking flesh . . .[39]

It is not really a political poem, but in the poet's own life it has a political relevance.

It was this general withdrawal of the literary Left from commitment that moved Empson to write his satirical 'Just a Smack at Auden', which appeared in *Contemporary Poetry and Prose* in the autumn of 1937. Empson's specific object was the limp and passive political postures of young writers like those in Auden's circle, and his poem is a catalogue of their useless gestures, each cancelled by the passive refrain:

> Waiting for the end, boys, waiting for the end.
> What is there to be or do?
> What's become of me or you?
> Are we kind or are we true?
> Sitting two and two, boys, waiting for the end.[40]

But though the smack was aimed at Auden, it struck a far larger target, for there was a general withdrawal from action evident among English intellectuals, as they came to see no alternative to waiting for the end. A number of factors were operating: the growing success of fascist powers in Europe; a greater public knowledge of the ways communism functioned in action, through the Moscow trials and the methods of Russians in Spain; the increasing propaganda for a Popular Front, which made it possible to be anti-fascist while avoiding communism; a greater awareness of the insuperable difficulties of being at once a communist and an artist. And perhaps one should add the simple fact that time was passing: in 1937 Auden was thirty, Day Lewis was thirty-two, Roberts was thirty-five. The men who had been sentimental Marxists in their youth were in their thirties, were reviewing for the *Daily Telegraph* and writing books on commission, some of them were married, some had children and mortgages; life was no longer an abstraction out of D. H. Lawrence, but a series of ordinary days.

An example of the general diminishment of revolutionary fervour after 1936 is Michael Roberts. As the editor of *New Signatures* and *New Country*, Roberts had been the midwife to the young generation of poets, and his introductory essays to those volumes had first set the political terms which gave the generation such unity as it had. In 1937 he surveyed the five years that had passed since *New Signatures*, and put his observations into an essay for *Poetry* magazine. Much of the language of his essay is the old terminology: *propagandist, socialist, communist, economic conditions*. But the mood has changed profoundly; the militancy and the celebration of newness are gone, and in their place is a sober poetical ecumenicism, as in this passage:

> Auden, Spender, and Madge are sometimes called communist poets, and Eliot a Christian poet, but their importance depends on the fact that they see more and speak more clearly than the ordinary communist or ordinary Christian. They aim at clear and exact speech in the interests of understanding, and the gulf which separates them from the ordinary politician is greater than that which separates the poets themselves. Thus the mood of Charles Madge's poem on Vienna (which is one of the best sonnets of our time) is one with which, I imagine, Mr. Eliot would deeply sympathize; but it would be wholly foreign to some members of the communist party.

Of the current mood of English poetry, Roberts wrote:

> Anger and bitterness and fear may have their own poets, and no doubt they would be popular, but I see no sign of the emergence of such poets in England today. The prevailing mood of Spender and Auden, as of Eliot, is one of grief and sympathy rather than anger or denunciation. It is in this sense that their poetry is political: they have a clear idea of the kind of life which they wish to see in Europe, and they express the temper in which more and more Englishmen wish those changes to be

made. To many people it seems that a combination of gentleness and knowledge, with firm convictions of right and wrong and readiness to act, is the alternative to doctrinaire ruthlessness.[41]

After the stridency of *New Country*, the values of gentleness and knowledge come as a surprise; and so does the fact that Roberts no longer claimed to speak for a generation, but for Englishmen.

In the same year, 1937, Roberts published his most ambitious and most impressive critical book, *The Modern Mind*. The book, he explained, was a 'study of some changes in the use of the English language; in particular, it traces the influence of material science on common speech, and it shows in turn the effects of these changes on our attitude to religion, poetry and science itself.'[42] That description is accurate so far as it goes, but it does not indicate Roberts' polemical intent: the book is an argument for the reality of 'the world of religion and poetry', and for the necessity of religious belief. Roberts' thesis is that since the Renaissance the steadily increasing authority of science had established the scientific version of reality as the only reality, and scientific language as the only way of expressing truth. Roberts was himself a scientist: he had, it will be recalled, read maths at Cambridge, and had been for many years a science master in various schools, and he had collaborated on a book on *Newton and the Origin of Colours*; but he believed that the extension of scientific method had had reductive effects on the possibilities of language, and therefore on poetry and imagination. Religion, he thought, was a counter-force, which nourished poetry because it expanded reality; indeed in some passages he seems to make religion and poetry virtually synonymous.

The Modern Mind seems at first a surprising book to come from a leading member of the *New Signatures* group; no other writer of his generation had publicly turned from a belief in communism to a belief in religion (though Auden took the same route shortly after). Roberts' friend George Every, an Anglican monk, reviewing the book in the *Criterion*, took it to be the end of Roberts' role as an influential figure for his generation. 'Mr. Roberts is right,' he wrote:

to hold these things together we do need poetry. We need the larger reason in which conscience and imagination are included as component parts. And we need criticism, informed by critical standards, to help us to distinguish the genuine vision from the premature synthesis which may lurk under the guise of poetry as well as under the guise of philosophy. By his poetry and his critical acumen Mr. Roberts has come through. His vision is informed, but it is his own. He is no longer the leader of a band, but he has found his word.[43]

But in fact there no longer was a band: the *New Signatures* poets were rapidly disbanding, to become themselves. They had never really been a group or a movement, but by 1937 there was not even a factitious political unity to hold them together. Like Spender, Roberts had reverted to the liberalism that was his true position; the only difference was that Roberts was, in Bertrand Russell's phrase, a 'theological liberal'.[44]

Robert's book is most typical of its time in its concern for the nature of language, for the 'thirties preoccupation with the interaction of politics and literature had raised crucial questions of linguistic theory: is language a part of the structure of reality? does it develop out of thought, or out of action? is it collective or individual? should it be instrumental to political ends, or has it its own autonomous and intrinsic value? If one accepted the desirability of proletarian literature and socialist realism, then there were consequences for literary language; and if one defended 'poetic' language, one was also making a political statement. Even a writer like Roberts, who was not concerned in *The Modern Mind* with political issues, was being implicitly anti-Marxist when he defended the autonomous language of poetry and deplored the reductive language of science.

There was a curious burst of writing on the subject of language in 1937: one finds it in Fox's *The Novel and the People*, in West's *Crisis and Criticism*, in Upward's essay in *The Mind in Chains*, and most elaborately in Caudwell's *Illusion and Reality* (Caudwell, the most sophisticated of English communist critics, is interestingly close to Roberts on some basic points, and it is not surprising that later Marxists have regarded him as heretical in his linguistic theory). And with that burst, it came to an end, as the whole art versus propaganda, politics versus poetry debate did. No doubt this was partly due to the withdrawal of the literary Left from communism and action: waiting for the end did not require a theory. But partly it was a direct consequence of the Spanish war; for the two Marxist critics best qualified to continue the argument were Caudwell and Fox, and they were dead.

III

The end of left theorizing was also the end of proletarian literature as a political goal. The 'thirties had produced a few genuinely working-class writers who wrote well about their class—notably Walter Greenwood, James Hanley, and Ralph Bates—and left journals like John Lehmann's *New Writing* and the *Left Review* had sought out and published stories by coalminers and factory hands and men on the dole. But the notion that middle-class revolutionaries should write in this mode had never caught on, for obvious reasons; as MacNeice remarked to Auden, 'If one knows only bourgeois one must write about them.'

But the problem *behind* that talk remained: what should a socialist literature be in a time that demanded commitment? How, if not by socialist realism, should a serious writer render his sense of reality? In the mid-'thirties, various efforts had been made to transpose the descriptive function of realistic literature to actual events, and so make realism literally the real; I have discussed two of these efforts in the previous chapter—the growth of the documentary film movement, and the establishment of the Left Book Club. In 1937, two new developments of the new literary reality appeared.

In April 1937, a new monthly journal was announced, called *Fact*. In an editorial in the first issue, the editors identified themselves and their social role with the French Encyclopaedists; the encyclopaedists, they said, had spread *information*, in a form and in language that any one could understand, and by so doing they had related isolated errors to the system, and so produced action— the French Revolution. *Fact*'s editors aimed at the same programme and the same results: to spread information, and to achieve action. Clearly the enterprise belongs to the category of Documentary: it is one more effort to alter consciousness, and to effect action, by accumulating and transmitting facts. All of the contributing editors of *Fact* were socialists, and they obviously expected that the actions they caused would be socialist actions; but the journal was not proposed as an exercise in persuasion. Nor was it to be at all literary, in the customary sense, although three of the editors—Spender and the novelists Storm Jameson and Arthur Calder-Marshall—were literary people. Its aim was beyond literature, and beyond argument, in a realm of fact where language and reality meet.

The journal made a promising start, selling 10,000 copies of its first issue, a monograph on 'The New Economic Revolution' by Margaret Cole. But with the second issue it was in trouble. The principal item there was 'I Joined the Army', by 'Private XYZ', which *Fact* described as 'a very plain and unvarnished account of life in the Royal Tank Corps'. It appeared in June, the month of the Coronation, and perhaps partly for that reason printers refused to print and distributors refused to distribute a document that they considered seditious. The editor of the right-wing journal, *Truth*, wrote in an editorial that 'such propaganda comes perilously near sedition', and suspected 'a deeper design than merely to expose the evils of the Army . . .'[45] Clearly one man's facts were another man's conspiracy.

Fact survived these trials, and went on to publish, in its fourth issue, 'Writing and Revolt', a monograph consisting of four essays on the 'Theory' of revolutionary writing, and a number of examples. The theoretical essays are an interesting record of the state of left literary thought in 1937. Two simply continued the orthodoxy of earlier years: John Allen, writing on 'Theatre', argued for plays with political content, and praised the Unity Theatre Club's productions of *Where's That Bomb?* and *Cannibal Carnival*, two broadly satirical plays written by a London taxi-driver; Arthur Calder-Marshall, on 'Fiction', picked up Spender's terms, *fable* and *reportage*, and saw socialist possibilities in both. The third critic, Spender, writing on 'Poetry', took the occasion to execute a cautious retreat from the political front-lines: 'When I say that modern poetry is political,' he wrote,

I am not thinking of John Cornford giving up poetry in order to fight the fascists in Spain, but of the fact that the best poetry of our time, the outstanding poems of Thomas Hardy, the war poems of Wilfrid Owen, Eliot's *Waste Land*, much of Auden's poetry, is concerned with the individual faced by an unprecedented crisis in the history of civilization, and with far-reaching public calamities such as the Great War, the prospect of a greater war, and the crisis in the capitalist system . . . However much we admire the actions of a John Cornford or a Rupert Brooke, poetry is not the same as action and a poem is not the same as a political thesis. [46]

By defining *political* in terms of contemporary subjects and not in terms of convictions, and by including in the category poets who were not left-wing or even politically inclined in the ordinary sense, Spender divorced himself from propaganda and from party discipline. (He must have written the essay just after his first trip to Spain.)

The most important essay of the four, however, is that by Storm Jameson. Writing on 'Documents', she produced the first theory of documentary as a literary form. As such, her essay belongs to the mid-'thirties documentary movement, with the films of Grierson and the publications of the Left Book Club. But it differs in a fundamental way from the ideas of Gollancz and the LBC: though Miss Jameson wrote as a socialist, she also wrote as a novelist, and the goal she set was not simply the dissemination of information, but the creation of a great socialist literature.

Her argument is essentially this: in a time of revolutionary change a socialist literature must exist to record and interpret that change, but no such literature did exist in the 'thirties in England, because the actual lives of men and women, which should provide the materials of that literature, had not been sufficiently observed. The assumption is that imaginative literature depends on such observations, and that it is therefore the urgent and immediate task of socialist writers to observe and to record—that is, to write *documents*. Such works will be only instrumental to the final literary end, however; in the scale of literary art they will be inferior to what will come after, rather in the way that the dictatorship of the proletariat is an inferior stage en route to the classless society. But they are nevertheless necessary, if the great work, the socialist *War and Peace*, is to be written:

> The conditions for the growth of a socialist literature scarcely exist. We have to create them. We need documents, not, as the Naturalists needed them, to make their drab tuppenny-ha'penny dramas, but as charts, as timber for the fire some writer will light tomorrow morning.[47]

Throughout her essay, Miss Jameson is contemptuous of proletarian fiction: one does not become a socialist writer simply by imagining poverty, but by observing and recording the *facts* that compose the present moment, in this society; the ground of reality is always the real, visible world of men. The document is therefore superior to the proletarian novel, because to produce it a writer must go and look at reality—not emotionally ('there is no value in the emotions, the spiritual writhings, started in him by the sight, smell and touch of poverty'), but coldly, with a camera eye:

> Perhaps the nearest equivalent of what is wanted exists already in another form in the documentary film. As the photographer does, so must the writer keep himself out of the picture while working ceaselessly to present the *fact* from a striking (poignant, ironic, penetrating, significant) angle.[48]

If this cold documentary style is to be achieved, many customary literary elements must be discarded: atmospheric writing, the static analysis of feeling and thought, stream of consciousness, all commentary, all aesthetic, moral, and philosophic enquiry—in short, any technique that brings forward the sensibility of the author, as most modern literary techniques have done. The document that results from this austere and self-abnegating method will not be the new socialist literature, because it will not be imaginative, but it will build the foundation of fact on which some great socialist writer in the future may create that literature.

The programme of writing that Miss Jameson proposed was, in relation to traditional ideas of literature, *un*literary. But at the same time it was traditionally literary in the high value that it placed on writers and the written word. Unlike many of her fellow socialists, Miss Jameson did not consider that writing was inferior to direct revolutionary action, nor did she make the role of the writer a subordinate, propaganda-making one. The relation that she saw between writing and revolution was very general. 'Literature concerned with change and the changing world,' she wrote, 'is concerned with revolution, and with all the stages of revolutionary action'; but it is not necessarily concerned with the proletariat, or with the class-struggle, or even with effecting change. The writer understands the changes that occur around him; but the changes are caused by other than literary forces. Miss Jameson's essay is a testimony to a faith in the power of the written word to render reality, not to change it. Such rendering was, she said, 'a task of the greatest value, urgent and not easy . . . waiting to be done'.[49]

Casting about for examples of how that great task should be performed, she could find only one English example. 'George Orwell has begun on it,' she wrote, 'in the first half of *The Road to Wigan Pier*.' On the face of it, Orwell's book would seem to be a document, if any 'thirties book was. Orwell had been commissioned by the Left Book Club in the summer of 1936 to write a study of poverty in the industrial north of England. He travelled through the area during the autumn of that year, living with working-class families, going down a coal-mine, observing and recording, and wrote the book—apparently very rapidly—before he left for Spain in December. It was published as the Left Book Club Choice for March 1937.

Miss Jameson was careful to say that only the first half of *The Road to Wigan Pier* exemplified what she wanted. 'The first part,' she had earlier written in a review, '. . . is a social document as vivid, bitter, and telling as one could have asked. The second part is a document of another kind, much less interesting and less valuable, but more curious.'[50] One must make some such distinction in discussing the book, for it is two very different books in one cover: one is an account of a journey among the industrial poor, the other a personal testament of Orwell's own political convictions, and how they grew. The first book was the one that Gollancz and his club had commissioned, and they were pleased with it; but the second was unexpected and embarrassing—so much so that Gollancz felt obliged to write an apologetic fore-word to the Club's edition, explaining where the project had gone wrong. The first part he admired; it was, he said, a 'tribute to courage and patience' among the workers. But the second part was 'highly provocative', and he took pains to dissociate himself and his colleagues from some of Orwell's more objectionable remarks. It was clearly not the sort of thing that the LBC had had in mind.

In the first part Orwell does seem to have met most of Miss Jameson's requirements for the documentary writer: 'his job', she had written, 'is not to tell us what he felt, but to be coldly and industriously presenting, arranging, selecting, discarding from the mass of his material to get the significant detail, which leaves no more to be said, and implies everything'.[51] This part of the book is full of facts, presented and arranged in lists and tables and case histories, which make it look rather like a census report or the minutes of a committee on public welfare. The style is flat and descriptive, and the first-person narrator maintains a cool, obser-vant manner, never rushing forward, as Miss Jameson said he shouldn't, to tell his reader, ' " When I saw this, I felt, I suffered, I rejoiced. . . ." '[52]

Nevertheless, Orwell did get his feelings into the story—indeed they *are* the story. The journey that he took to Wigan was a per-sonal, symbolic one—a journey, not simply into the industrial north, but into poverty and into the working class. And because it became a personal book about feelings, much of it reads like fiction, and particularly like the Naturalistic novels that Miss Jameson and other left critics deplored.[53] Consider, for example, three highly emotive descriptive passages from Part One—two from the opening chapters, and one from the end. The book begins, not like a report, but like a first-person proletarian novel:

> The first sound in the mornings was the clumping of the mill-girls' clogs down the cobbled street. Earlier than that, I suppose, there were factory whistles which I was never awake to hear.[54]

That is a neutral enough bit of working-class scene-setting, but in the next sentence the tone changes:

There were generally four of us in the bedroom, and a beastly place it was, with that defiled impermanent look of rooms that are not serving their rightful purpose.

Beastly and *defiled* define the tone of the rest of the chapter, which describes life in a lodging-house in an unidentified northern industrial town. Everything that Orwell observes there is grotesque and disgusting—the filth, the stench, the loathsome food, the black-beetles, and worst of all the sickly, ageing, subhuman people who endure such an existence; the whole chapter expresses in a concentrated and relentless way the revulsion and disgust that were always Orwell's feelings about the lowest poor. There is much carefully rendered detail in the chapter, and a good deal of generalizing about the poor, but it is nevertheless not really a description of representative poor people so much as a complex, highly emotive image of poverty itself. Here, for example, is Orwell's account of his decision to leave the lodging-house:

> On the day when there was a full chamber-pot under the breakfast table I decided to leave. The place was beginning to depress me. It was not only the dirt, the smells and the vile food, but the feeling of stagnant meaningless decay, of having got down into some subterranean place where people go creeping round and round, just like blackbeetles, in an endless muddle of slovened jobs and mean grievances.[55]

The force of this passage is not in description (not even in the chamber-pot), but in the two metaphors, which are metaphors of personal feelings: the journey into poverty is a journey *underground,* and the poor that one finds there are not human beings, but disgusting insects. The passage is not so much about poverty as it is about middle-class feelings about poverty, how poverty degrades the poor, and how one draws back instinctively from degradation.

In the second chapter, Orwell makes another, very different journey underground, when he visits a coal-mine. The miners that he meets there are not 'the poor', but 'the workers', and they are treated as heroic figures of demonic strength and energy, who carry the industrial world and its parasites on their shoulders. 'In a way,' he writes, it is even humiliating to watch coal-miners working. It raises in you a momentary doubt about your own status as an 'intellectual' and a superior person generally. For it is brought home to you, at least while you are watching, that it is only because miners sweat their guts out that superior persons can remain superior. You and I and the editor of the *Times Lit. Supp.*, and the Nancy poets and the Archbishop of Canterbury and Comrade X, author of *Marxism for Infants*—all of us *really* owe the comparative decency of our lives to poor drudges underground, blackened to the eyes, with their throats full of coal dust, driving their shovels forward with arms and belly muscles of steel.[56]

Like the previous passage, this is not about the working class, but about middle-class *feelings* about the workers, feelings which sentimentally elevate working men to the level of heroes, just as Orwell's feelings about dirt and smells degraded the poor below the human level. But in both cases the essential image is the same—the subterranean journey. To experience the reality of lower-class life, you must go down, into the lower depths.[57]

The third example of Orwell's fictionalizing of his Wigan experience comes at the very end of Part One of the book, which is also the end of his account of his northern tour. He has turned, in these closing pages, to the home life of the working classes. 'In a working-class home,' he writes,

... you breathe a warm, decent, deeply human atmosphere which it is not so easy to find elsewhere. I should say that a manual worker, if he is in steady work and drawing good wages —an 'if' which gets bigger and bigger—has a better chance of being happy than an 'educated' man. His home life seems to fall more naturally into a sane and comely shape. I have often been struck by the peculiar easy completeness, the perfect symmetry as it were, of a working-class interior at its best. Especially on winter evenings after tea, when the fire glows in the open range and dances mirrored in the stall fender, when Father, in shirt-sleeves, sits in the rocking chair at one side of the fire reading the racing finals, and Mother sits on the other with her sewing, and the children are happy with a pennorth of mint humbugs, and the dog lolls roasting himself on the rag mat—it is a good place to be in, provided that you can be not only in it but sufficiently *of* it to be taken for granted.[58]

This is even less documentary, less objective than the two previous passages. It is not even based on immediate observation, but is, as Orwell confessed, his recollection of working-class interiors of his boyhood, a bit of middle-class nostalgia for an Edwardian past in which none of the problems existed that had sent him underground among the poor.

Two aspects of this vision are especially striking, when one considers that it occurs in a 'documentary' book written by a socialist. First, the political implications are essentially conservative—just keep the working classes working, and they will be happy, happier than *we* are; and second, the secure and cheerful life that they live is one from which middle-class intellectuals are excluded—*we* can never be *them*, and *they* can never be *us*. The fictional tradition operating here is no longer the proletarian novel: this passage is in the Dickensian tradition of the sentimental poor. It defines human happiness in terms of domestic security and family bonds, says nothing about class solidarity or political or social action, and makes poverty a happy, innocent state. It is a very odd paragraph indeed for a socialist to write.

Part One of *The Road to Wigan Pier* is a book that many middle-class literary intellectuals might have written, if they had made Orwell's journey. They would have felt, as he did, a sentimental admiration for 'the workers' and a fastidious disgust for the physical conditions of actual poverty, and they would have recorded their conflicting feelings in terms of novelistic conventions, as he did, because there *were* no conventions for literary documentaries. But the second part could probably only have been written by Orwell. Insofar as it is in any literary tradition, it belongs to the tradition of English confessional literature, with all those testimonies of sin and miraculous conversion that nonconformist religion has produced in such quantities; among the writers of his generation Orwell was probably the only one who regarded such penitent self-exposure as a literary virtue.

In Part Two, Orwell described the forces in his life that had

276

made him a socialist of the kind that he was—his birth into the 'lower-upper-middle class', his education at Eton, his service in Burma with the Police, his days spent among the down and out in Paris and London. Here Orwell examines the distortions of objectivity that will necessarily occur in his book, simply because *he* is the observer: he is class-conscious, he is snobbish, he feels guilt and shame about imperialism, he is drawn to and repelled by the lower classes. And his socialism is the product of these shaping emotions.

The socialism that emerges is not so much a political philosophy as a personal myth of the good society, of a state based on freedom, justice, and equality, but without any specified political principles. In this myth, the heroes are the working-class socialists —warm-hearted, unthinking, and weak on doctrine; and the villains are all the faddists of Orwell's own class, whose eccentricities found common cause with socialism—the 'Nancy poets', fruit-juice drinkers, nudists, sandal-wearers, Nature Cure quacks, pacifists, feminists, 'vegetarians with wilting beards', 'shockheaded Marxists chewing polysyllables, escaped Quakers, birth-control fanatics, and Labour Party backstairs-crawlers'. Most of the beliefs in this list are harmless enough and not necessarily incompatible with serious socialist convictions: what made them repulsive to Orwell is that they were all *ideas*, and ideas that members of the middle classes might adopt. In his vision, true socialism would be anti-faddist and anti-bourgeois; it would also be anti-Marxist, anti-fascist, anti-intellectual, and even anti-machinery and anti-progress. In short, in would be a movement of the sentimental, good-hearted English working class and of such others as could achieve that state—egalitarian ('we have nothing to lose but our aitches') and doctrineless, but full of simple virtue, with no more precise goals than liberty, justice, and a return to the dream of working-class life that Orwell had imagined at the end of the first part of his book.

The Road to Wigan Pier is ostensibly about poverty, but it is more profoundly a book about class. The primary subject is Orwell himself, as a representative of his own middle-class generation—repelled by poverty but sentimentally impressed by the workers, preaching universal socialism but despising middle-class converts, desiring a classless society but separated from the working class by his bourgeois background, his accent, and his ingrained prejudices. The frankest confessional passages in the book are those in which Orwell analyzed his own class attitudes, as for example when he explained 'the real reason why a European of bourgeois upbringing, even when he calls himself a Communist, cannot without a hard effort think of a working man as his equal'.

It is summed up in four frightful words which people nowadays are chary of uttering, but which were bandied about quite freely in my childhood. The words were: *The lower classes smell.*[59]

That confession drew a good deal of criticism from left critics, and Gollancz was especially distressed by it, but in fact it was in passages like this one, when Orwell was writing about himself and his prejudices, and demonstrating those prejudices in operation, that he wrote most brilliantly and imaginatively—more brilliantly than he did in any of his 'thirties novels. It was only when he turned to ideas, and to the political future, that his imagination failed him; like so many other writers of his generation, he could not imagine a socialist future or give it literary form. His book, like Spender's *Forward from Liberalism*, is a testament of departure but not of arrival; he was on the road to Wigan (that is, to that identification with the working class that he called socialism), but he hadn't got there.

Like *Forward from Liberalism*, *The Road to Wigan Pier* got the mixed reception that one might have expected: warm notices from liberals, but increasing hostility from reviewers as they were farther to the left. Laski, in the *Left News*, thought the first part 'admirable propaganda for our ideas', though he criticized Orwell's version of socialism, but Harry Pollitt, in the *Worker*, was entirely dismissive; Orwell, he wrote, was 'a disillusioned little middle-class boy', and his review was headlined: 'Mr. Orwell Will Have to Try Again.'[60]

Both of these books are documents of a sort, and belong in the documentary movement, away from the imagination and toward a literature of fact, which took place in the middle of the decade; but what they document is states of mind of young writers without political experience who nevertheless felt the immediate political situation as a crisis that had to be faced, and who were trying to find a literary form for the conviction. Both are, in their different ways, interesting but unsuccessful as documents—too subjective, too literary, too defensive of the rights of the individual imagination to achieve that cold, objective rendering of *facts* that was the documentary goal.

Another kind of effort to achieve that goal was the curious movement called Mass-Observation, which was organized early in 1937. M-O was essentially an attempt to avoid subjectivity and distortion in recording the realities of contemporary existence by applying anthropological methods of observation to ordinary English life. Its unique feature was that the observers would not be trained anthropologists, but untrained common people— thousands of them—who would record what they did and saw, and would forward their observations to a central office for organization, interpretation, and publication. M-O would be an 'anthropology of ourselves'; as the first M-O pamphlet put it:' Ideally, it is the observation by everyone of everyone, including themselves.'[61] Such a method would be a completely democratic science, in which everyone was at once the scientist and his subject; and the publications that resulted from it would be a democratic mass-art, the collective expression of the collective mind. The people, by observing and by reading the observations of others, would increase their social consciousness, and so be moved to social and political action. It was to be a movement in which artist and scientist would find a common ground, and would join with the masses to create documents that would transform society. But in fact it was from the start a mixture of such contradictory elements as would seem to guarantee its failure. It was at once literary and scientific, realist and surrealist, political and psychological, Marxist and Freudian, objective and salvationist. In its confusions of methods and goals it is a complex example of the confusions of young intellectuals of the time.

The whole thing began with a letter to the *New Statesman* published in December 1936. The writer, a Mr Geoffrey Pyke, had been thinking about the Abdication Crisis and the public's reaction to the King and Mrs Simpson:

Anthropologists and psychologists all over the world [he wrote] are studying the reactions of primitive tribes to sexual situations. There have been concentrated within the last ten days the reactions of the people of the British Empire to a sexual situation. Here in a relatively limited form is some of the material for the anthropological study of our own civilisation of which we stand in such desperate need.[62]

Mr Pyke leaves the story at this point, but two aspects of his letter are worth noting, because they continue through the history of Mass-Observation. First, the relation to a national crisis: M-O was ostensibly a science of the most ordinary life, but in fact it was initiated in the spirit of crisis, and continued to relate its social importance to the special nature of the period; and second, the sense of 'desperate need', which arises from the crisis mentality, and which gave to M-O a salvationist tone that is the opposite of what one expects in scientific work.

A few weeks later the *Statesman* printed a letter in reply to Pyke from Charles Madge, in which Madge described the creation of a group to undertake 'an anthropology of our own people', and called for volunteers.[63] Madge at this point described himself as 'poet and communist'; he had also been associated with the English surrealists, and there are signs of that association in his letter. What he was after, it seems, was a symbology of the mass-unconscious, what you might call the surreal content of ordinary minds. And the technique for revealing this content was to be a mixture of psychoanalysis and anthropology—psychoanalysis to deal with the hidden wishes, anthropology to turn the results into cultural generalizations. At this time, Madge was much interested in popular systems of symbolism—in newspaper astrology, in coincidences, in the mass-fantasies and exploitative symbolisms of the daily press, the phenomena that I have called the Instant Mythology of the 'thirties. He seems to have been particularly struck by two events of late 1936—the burning of the Crystal Palace, and the abdication of Edward VIII—and apparently it was the concurrence of those events that led him to organize his group. As he describes his method in the letter, the group sounds more like a surrealist seance than a scientific investigation, though the basic proposition of the movement has already been formulated, that 'only mass observations can create mass science'. What he needed now was someone to provide the science.

The *New Statesman* inadvertently provided one. On the same pages with Madge's letter there appeared a poem about cannibals, written by T. H. Harrisson, a young ornithologist turned anthropologist, just back from the Hebrides. It seems fitting, and expressive of Mass-Observation's unorthodox nature, that its two leaders should have met in this way, on a page of a left-wing journal, the poet pretending to be a scientist and the scientist posing as a poet.

In less than a month they were back in the *Statesman*'s pages, joined this time by Madge's friend and fellow-surrealist Humphrey Jennings,[64] with a letter announcing the creation of Mass-Observation, and inviting support. The letter described the scientific bases of the movement ('Mass-Observation develops out of anthropology, psychology, and the sciences which study man'), and its quantitative method (they hoped for 5,000 observers around the country), and offered a list of some possible subjects for study:

> Behaviour of people at war memorials.
> Shouts and gestures of motorists.
> The aspidistra cult.
> Anthropology of football pools.
> Bathroom behaviour.
> Beards, armpits, eyebrows.
> Anti-semitism.
> Distribution, diffusion and significance
>   of the dirty joke.
> Funerals and undertakers.
> Female taboos about eating.
> The private lives of midwives.[65]

This list is an odd one, mixing a serious subject for investigation like anti-semitism with others that have the intentionally ridiculous quality of the titles of some surrealist poems; it also has, here and there, what seems a rather superior and patronizing tone ('the aspidistra cult', for example, had been treated in that way by

George Orwell in *Keep the Aspidistra Flying*). Not surprisingly, established anthropologists and sociologists reacted to the new movement with stiff disapproval.[66]

Such a proposal, inviting the untrained to watch their neighbours and themselves and call it anthropology, was bound to succeed, and it did; in a few months a thousand offers of help had come in to M-O headquarters. For M-O created a use for dreary lives—at least they could be Mass-Observed—and stimulated observers to take an interest in things that they had taken for granted. They studied their own smoking habits, their behaviour in pubs, the ways they played the pools, and the jokes they laughed at in Blackpool, and they sent their reports to Madge in London. It was a movement made for bored and impoverished people in the midst of a depression; as M-O studies showed, it was most attractive to the lower-middle class, to single people, to residents of the provinces—to the lonely bored livers of unexciting lives—and it is clear that they sought and got emotional rewards from it.[67]

But it was also bound to fail. The goals of the poet and the scientist were never the same, and this became clear as soon as those goals were written down. In the first M-O publication, a pamphlet written by Madge and Harrisson in the spring of 1937, the authors' differences are so substantial as to require separate statements of the 'Basis for a Mass-Movement'. Harrisson's is vaguely salvationist, and sounds rather like H. G. Wells:

> Tom Harrisson believes that *Mass-Observation*, by laying open to doubt all existing philosophies of life as possibly incomplete, yet by refusing to neglect the significance of any of them, may make a new synthesis. This may lead to something less fierce, more understanding and permanent, than the present miserable conflicts of dogmatic faiths in race, politics, religion.

Whereas,

> In the other author's opinion, *Mass-Observation* is an instrument for collecting facts, not a means for producing a synthetic philosophy, a super-science or super-politics. The availability of the facts will liberate certain tendencies in science, art, and

politics, because it will add to the social consciousness of the time. *Mass-Observation* is not a party, a religion or a philosophy, but an elementary piece of human organisation and adaptation. It is one part of a general deflection of emphasis from individual to collective effort.[68]

So the scientist was the preacher in the movement, and the poet was the scientist (or perhaps simply the Marxist). The theory was that in M-O the artist and the scientist would meet on common ground, harmoniously, but clearly that would not happen. Harrisson withdrew to continue his study of one industrial town in Lancashire, and Madge stayed in London, accumulating reports from the several hundred observers and working at the organization and publication of material. There were quarrels and disaffections, memoranda and counter-memoranda, accusations and cross-accusations. The surprising thing is that, in spite of all the ill feelings, there were also publications, and publications that are of considerable interest in the intellectual history of the period, and particularly in the history of the documentary movement.

From the beginning, the founders of M-O had thought of it as a literary movement of a special kind. Harrisson wrote of the observers' reports that 'the result is in one sense anthropology, in another literature—and a far more accurate picture of life than any novelist can ever hope to give'.[69] Madge and Jennings, introducing a selection of M-O narratives, made much the same point:

The reports which are written for Mass-Observation come largely from people whose lives are spent in a world whose behaviour, language, and viewpoint are far removed from academic science and literature. Sociologists and realistic novelists—including proletarian novelists—find it difficult if not impossible to describe the texture of this world. After reading hundreds of Mass-Observation reports, we find that they tend to cover just those aspects of life which the others miss . . . It is not enough for such fiction to be *about* proletarians, if they in their turn become a romantic fiction, nor even for it to be *by* proletarians, if it is used by them as a means of escaping out of the proletariat.

Mass-Observation is among other things giving working-class and middle-class people a chance to speak for themselves, about themselves.[70]

This comparison with the proletarian novel, which Storm Jameson also made in 'Documents', is a fundamental point in documentary aesthetics: it is an attempt to take Socialist Realism back to a point beyond style and even subject matter, to its sources in proletarian consciousness. Since in M-O that consciousness is *mass*-consciousness, there is also an implied shift of the basis of artistic creation from the individual to the mass, and this provides both a theoretical foundation and a collective method for a new revolutionary art. The principle applied, at least in Madge's mind, to poetry as well as to prose; of the observers' reports Madge wrote in *New Verse*:

Poetically, the statements are also useful. They produce a poetry which is not, as at present, restricted to a handful of esoteric performers. The immediate effect of Mass-Observation is to de-value considerably the status of the 'poet'. It makes the term 'poet' apply, not to his performance, but to his profession, like 'footballer'.[71]

But though M-O was in theory a literary movement, the actual literary products of the first year's work were, with one exception, pretty minor—some extracted observers' reports in *Life and Letters*, and a collectively-written poem in *New Verse* (both accompanied by rather inflated assessments of their literary merit). The exception is *May the Twelfth*, a stout volume of more than 400 pages published in September 1937; it is the most substantial, and the most literary product of the entire movement. 12 May 1937 was George VI's Coronation Day, and the book is a mass-observation of that elaborate, symbolic event. Being focussed as it is, it has a unity which suggests that Madge was right, at least on literary grounds, in his initial attention to incidents like the Abdication; the shape of the ritual imposes a shape on the book. There is a chapter on the preparations, reported day by day, one on London throughout Coronation Day, another on the same day observed elsewhere in England and abroad, a chapter of individual reactions, and at the end a 'normal day survey' for March the 12th, showing how M-O would analyze more ordinary events. The whole is made up of the actual reports of observers, organized and occasionally analyzed by the editors.

Certainly *May the Twelfth* would seem to be a document in the sense that a documentary film is—it does render the actual, and in very visual terms. But it is also very literary, and no wonder, when one considers who put it together: the principal editors were Madge (poet) and Jennings (painter, poet, film-maker); they were assisted by T. O. Beachcroft (short-story writer), William Empson (poet), and Kathleen Raine (poet). Ruthven Todd (poet and novelist) compiled the index. It is not so surprising, then, that some passages, where the narrative shifts from one observer of the royal procession to another, sound rather Joycean, like the 'Wandering Rocks' chapter of *Ulysses*, or that fragments of recorded conversation recall Eliot's 'Coriolan'. But most often the book reads like a proletarian novel of urban life, put together by someone of avant-garde tendencies; only it is a novel without either a plot or any principal characters—that is, it is all documentation.

Or so it seems; but in fact the book is more carefully constructed than that suggests, and for clear polemical ends. In the first chapter, for instance, Coronation proceedings are carefully and ironically counterpointed with reports of the progress of the London bus strike; and throughout the book observers' reports are interwoven with popular journalism to produce a similar irony. Furthermore, editorial comments are scattered through the observers' reports, reading the events of the day as though they were images in a dream or in a symbolist poem: for example, this analysis of a report of seeing an illuminated London bus, decorated with a crown and portraits of the king and queen:

> The bus is an imitation Coronation coach—it appears and disappears—but the most important thing about it is that, as with the State Coach, its glamour is imaginary. The whole incident is a piece of make-believe such as children indulge in. The same *might* be said of the Coronation procession, if there were not such a weight of feeling attached to it that the make-believe side of the proceedings is almost wholly concealed.[72]

What the editors have made of the events of Coronation Day is an elaborate metaphor of politics and class. The final page says as much: 'Mass-Observation is more than journalism or film documentary, because it has the aim in view not only of presenting, but of classifying and analysing, the immediate human world.'[73] The motives are mixed, and the book is marred by the mixing. The materials are documentary, the presentation is literary, and the classifying and analysing are polemical; the book attempts to be at once scientific and political, to be comprehensive and yet readable, to record and to make judgments. In the end it fails, it becomes unreadable, but not because of the politics or the literariness; what kills it, finally, is the flat repetitiousness of the observers' reports—it is the *mass* in Mass-Observation that is numbing. The founders of M-O believed that the mass-consciousness could write a truer and better book than one man with his intuitions; *May the Twelfth* proves that they were wrong—writing will have to go on being an individual activity.

Madge made one other attempt to produce collective writing, and this one, being briefer, is more successful. To test his belief that there was a possible connection between M-O and poetry, he devised an experiment in which twelve Oxford undergraduates, all interested in the writing of literature, wrote one poem. First each noted 'predominant images' day by day (Madge was persuaded that days had such images—hence his fascination with the Crystal Palace fire); these were collected and compared, and the six which appeared most were selected. Next the group met and each member composed a single pentameter line for each of the chosen images. These were then arranged in order, and the best chosen by vote. The chosen images were then integrated into poems, the poems passed round, revised and voted on. The whole process took a month, and produced one eighteen-line poem.

The Poem
Believe the iron saints who stride the floods,
Lying in red and labouring for the dawn:
Steeples repeat their warnings; along the roads
Memorials stand, of children force has slain;

Expostulating with the winds they hear
Stone kings irresolute on a marble stair.

The tongues of torn boots flapping on the cobbles,
Their epitaphs, clack to the crawling hour.
The clock grows old inside the hollow tower;
It ticks and stops, and waits for me to tick,
And on the edges of the town redoubles
Thunder, announcing war's climacteric.

The hill has its death like us; the ravens gather;
Trees with their corpses lean towards the sky.
Christ's corn is mildewed and the wine gives out.
Smoke rises from the pipes whose smokers die.
And on our heads the crimes of our buried fathers
Burst in a hurricane and the rebels shout.

Madge said of this poem that it was 'much more a collective account of . . . Oxford than of any single person in the group.'

> It has the Oxford scene with its stone buildings, its situation in a valley, and its associations and history, with a moral. It has the sense of decay and imminent doom which characterises contemporary Oxford. It expresses a feeling of a responsibility together with a sense of that responsibility being neglected now and in the past. This reflection of the immediate scene is what is looked for in a collective poem.[74]

I'd put it rather differently, that it is a collective account, not of Oxford, but of the undergraduate state of mind at that point in history, and specifically of the *literary* undergraduates who performed the experiments. For literary undergraduates will tend to write in the manner and mood of their time. In 1937 this meant that they would be surrealists, sound like Dylan Thomas and Roger Roughton, and put *red* and *dawn* in the same line. The poem is interesting because it *is* collective—not an objective account of the Oxford scene, certainly, but an anthology of the image-content of undergraduate minds, and so a kind of document in the shape of a poem.

IV

A travel book is also, in a way, a document, arising from the documentary impulse to observe and record *facts*, and the burst of travel books by young writers in the mid-'thirties no doubt springs from the same impulse that produced *Fact* and Mass-Observation. But, as I remarked earlier, a record of travels may also be a parable; journeys in the 'thirties were often *symbolic* journeys, like those in the early poems of Auden, self-conscious crossings of the frontier between the known and the unknown, in search of some reality not visible at home.

In the summer of 1936 Auden and MacNeice travelled to Iceland, on commission to write a joint travel book for Faber & Faber. They seem to have done all the things that a travel-writer ought to do: they read the existing literature, they gathered useful information for other tourists, they took photographs, they studied the economy and made some convincing graphs. But the book that they wrote is a very eccentric travel book indeed; a substantial part is in verse (much of it in the form of a verse-epistle from Auden to Lord Byron), other chapters are letters to friends, one a parody letter from a fictitious deb. One might say, ungenerously, that it is a hasty and casual way of fulfilling a publisher's contract; or one might conclude that in the end what interested the two poets was the opportunity that a journey to Iceland provided for meditating on themselves, their generation, and immediate European history. The form, though odd, is not entirely new to Auden; he had tried before, in *The Orators*, to construct a parable out of heterogeneous parts. But this time he had a stronger framework in the actual physical journey to Iceland and back.

It is apparent from early in the book that Auden saw his journey as primarily a symbolic one. Chapter II, which is in the form of a letter to Isherwood, begins with Auden's parabolic poem, 'Journey to Iceland', a poem about the motives for journeying:

> And the traveller hopes: 'Let me be far from any
> Physician'; And the ports have names for the sea;
> The citiless, the corroding, the sorrow;
> And North means to all: 'Reject!'

The motive is escape—escape from the present moment in history:

For Europe is absent. This is an island and therefore
Unreal. And the steadfast affections of its dead may be bought
   By those whose dreams accuse them of being
    Spitefully alive, and the pale

From too much passion of kissing feel pure in its deserts.
Can they? For the world is, and the present, and the lie.[75]

To travel to an island—and especially to such a remote and
archaic-seeming one as Iceland—is to escape Europe. But such
an escape is no longer possible, or not for very long, as Auden
says in another passage:

I had the feeling . . . that for myself it was already too late.
We are all too deeply involved with Europe to be able, or even
to wish to escape.[76]

So the book, though it appears to record a temporary escape from
Europe and the present, is really about the generation's inescap-
able involvement in its time, and in contemporary European
disasters (while Auden and MacNeice were in Iceland, the Spanish
Civil War began, as though to underscore this point).

In the book, Iceland is treated throughout as a set of simplified,
archaic cases, from which modern morals for Europe may be
drawn. Of an Icelandic glacier, for example, Auden writes:

        the Markafljöt I see
Wasting these fields, is no glacial flood
But history, hostile, Time the destroyer
Everywhere washing our will, winding through Europe
An attack, a division, shifting its fords.[77]

And MacNeice makes his 'Eclogue from Iceland' a dialogue between two modern travellers and the ghost of a saga hero, through
which analogies are drawn between the saga world and the
present moment in Europe.

But much of the book is not about Iceland at all. The most
substantial poem, Auden's 'Letter to Lord Byron' is a highly personal literary-social-economic history of England, including
Auden's own career; and the book ends, not with the customary
traveller's farewell to his subject, but with 'Auden and MacNeice:

Their Last Will and Testament', a poem in which the poets distribute the things of their own familiar world among their friends
and enemies, as though they were writing not *their* will, but the
world's, drawn up in expectation of its imminent death. Many of
the details are private jokes, but the whole gesture of the poem
is serious, and the tone at beginning and end is sombre. The
authors begin, 'We . . .,

considering

The autumns, personal and public, which already creep
Through city-crowded Europe, and those in want
Who soon must look up at the winter sky and weep,

Do set down this, our will and testament:
Believing man responsible for what he does,
Sole author of his terror and his content.

And they end with a prayer:

And to the good who know how wide the gulf, how deep
Between Ideal and Real, who being good have felt
The final temptation to withdraw, sit down and weep,

We pray the power to take upon themselves the guilt
Of human action, though still as ready to confess
The imperfection of what can and must be built,
The wish and power to act, forgive, and bless.[78]

It is a very odd poem for the end of a travel book about Iceland,
since it has nothing whatever to do with Iceland, or even with
travel. But it is even odder at the end of a book concerned,
as this one is, with the feelings of two young men about Europe
in the mid-'thirties. For the poem has no political content, or
even any political implications; it deals with the sense of crisis
in terms of individual morality, and it expresses that morality in
religious terms. Action is as urgent as it was two years earlier,
when Auden wrote his birthday poem to Isherwood, but the
imperatives to *forgive* and *bless* are new. But perhaps the most
striking aspect of the passage is that it does not particularize the
crisis, or the source of evil, but offers only a general sense of the
human condition, as containing terror and guilt. What Auden

and MacNeice have done is to remove the growing sense of threat from the world of politics, and to place it in the world of morality. It is a significant change of heart.

Letters from Iceland is a failure that is full of brilliant successes—disorganized and unresolved, uncertain and fluctuating in tone, communicating nothing about Iceland so strongly as the authors' boredom with it, and yet containing some of Auden's finest verse, as well as good things by MacNeice. It has almost no shape at all, not even the shape of the journey itself; it begins en route, with a piece of the 'Letter to Lord Byron' that is placed there because Auden wrote it en route, and it ends with Auden and MacNeice back in London, without having travelled there. Weak endings, Frederic Prokosch said, were habitual in Auden: 'The future is always intruding, of course, and always unsolved (*v.* the bad endings to his plays, the badness of the Iceland book).'[79] And certainly it is true that Auden was unwilling, or unable, to write reassuring prophecies of the future—hence the vagueness of the future in his 'Spain'. The same point that I made about 'Spain' may be made here—that *Letters from Iceland*, coming out of the same mid-'thirties time, sees the same moral situation. Men live in history, and must act in it; the choice of actions is difficult, and the consequences are uncertain, but there is no way out of action, not even for poets. That is the whole point of the historical narrative that Auden addressed to Lord Byron: poets exist in history. And it is the point of the book.

I have written about the 'Last Will and Testament' as though it were the end of *Letters from Iceland*, but in fact there is one piece that follows it—'Epilogue for W. H. Auden', by MacNeice. This epilogue is a nostalgic reminiscence of the trip, written in the winter of 1936–7, when MacNeice was back in his Hampstead flat; but it is more than a reminiscence—it is also an expression of a mood of the time, filtered through MacNeice's melancholy, uncommitted, lonely nature. Auden had written, toward the end of 'Letter to Lord Byron':

> I'm home again, and goodness knows to what,
>   To read the papers and to earn my bread;
> I'm home to Europe where I may be shot . . .[80]

MacNeice, the gloomier man, wrote of doubt, loneliness and un-communicableness, and ended his poem with these lines:

> Our prerogatives as men
> Will be cancelled who knows when;
> Still I drink your health before
> The gun-butt raps upon the door.[81]

This is not simply poetical posturing or melodrama. In Europe men *were* being shot, and some of them were poets (Garcia Lorca was murdered in August 1936), and there *were* gun-butts rapping on doors. These passages render images of a possible reality that had not existed for earlier English writers; as the end of the decade approached, the alien and frightful violence of *The Brown Book of the Hitler Terror* was becoming domesticated in English imaginations.

One sees a similar change in the literary rendering of war. In the early 'thirties, war was a folly to be opposed through pacifist action:[82] the option of not fighting was still an open one, and most liberals chose it. Then in the middle years of the decade, as actual military action began in Abyssinia and then in Spain, war became a heroic resistance to fascism, in which the brave man would choose to join 'the army of the other side'. But it was still a *choice*, and the war that literary heroes like Auden and Isherwood's Alan went off to was still being fought somewhere else. But as the end of the 'thirties approached, war came to seem neither an elected action nor a foreign one, but a catastrophe that could happen right here, in England, and soon: it was the Apocalypse that would destroy culture. This was the line taken by the government in defence of its policies of appeasement; but even those on the Left who urged resistance and the Popular Front agreed that if war came it would mean the end of western civilization. The only thing that could be worse, they thought, was a fascist world.

That late-'thirties view of war was the one that my own gene-ration grew up with and went to war with, and it seems now an unavoidable, natural attitude. Yet the 'thirties was surely the first time in history when the belief was generally held that a war would have such dire and wholesale effects on all human values;

certainly nobody thought such thoughts before the First World War.

The new weaponry was obviously a factor—the combination of aerial bombardment and poison gas was a continuous nightmare of the 'thirties, which entered the literary imagination (for example, in Auden's 'James Honeyman', a poem of 1937 about a man who invents a poison gas, sells it to a foreign power, and is killed by it in an air-raid). But it also reached the scientific imagination, and a substantial literature on the technology of air-raids grew up in the mid- and late-'thirties, as the British government began to plan for air-raid defence.[83] In early 1937, factories in England were being opened to manufacture gas-masks, and local authorities were making plans for civilian protection; the first warning sirens were tested in March, and the first London depot for masks was established in the same month. The next month Nationalist bombers destroyed Guernica, and the point of the preparations became even clearer. In July, British troops fought a mock war on the south coast of England between Redland (the enemy) and Blueland, and the exercise included a practice bombing attack on a city, in which gas-masks were prominently used. The daily papers gave the war wide coverage, with photographs of gas-masked troops in bombed-out buildings.[84]

It wasn't only the weaponry that was different: so was the enemy. Germany had been a threatening, militaristic power before the First World War, but the English had not attached images of bestiality and murder to their opponents until after the invasion of Belgium. In the 'thirties the Nazis were attaching those images to themselves before the war began; no one had to invent atrocity stories in the Second World War—they had already happened. Neither the methods of war nor the men who fought it would be civilized this time, and it is not surprising that one finds visions of the next war as the Apocalypse in all kinds of writing of the time, from Aldous Huxley's *What Are We Going to Do About It?* to Virginia Woolf's *Three Guineas*.

This state of mind is expressed parabolically in MacNeice's play, *Out of the Picture*, which was published in June 1937, and was first performed in the following December. It is a useful example because MacNeice had always been the least political writer of his generation, and his play articulates a mood of the time unaffected by political ideas. The main plot-line concerns an indigent painter named Portright, whose only completed picture, 'Venus Rising', is seized by bailiffs for debts and auctioned off to a film star. Portright represents the artist and the individualist, and his painting, and Moll, the model for it, stand for art, love, and life. The film star and her psychoanalyst-adviser are the other side—society's parasitical life-deniers, the locus of money and power.

In these terms the play is simply another version (rather a conventional one) of the relationship of the artist to modern society. But it contains another theme that is of equal importance and of greater originality. The play begins with a news announcement of the failure of a peace conference, and as the action unfolds war is 'about to be declared', and then is declared; Paris is bombed, and the play ends in an air-raid on London. Portright, in a fit of rage, shoots the Minister of Peace who has precipitated the country into war, and is then poisoned by Moll to save him from prison or the army.

It is not a very good play—at best a clumsy offspring of *The Dog Beneath the Skin*, less clever, less poetic, and less dramatic than its parent. Nevertheless, it has two interesting aspects. The first is the way in which MacNeice treats war. War enters the play in two forms: as announcements on the radio, and as a Minister of Peace. The first gives to war a remote, invisible, but imminent power that is beyond human resistance; the second gives to government the same sort of power, for the same sort of destruction. There are no soldiers in the play, no armies, and no political issues; there is only war itself, approaching like a pestilence. When it comes, it comes first as news of destruction elsewhere:

RADIO ... and that is all that now remains of Paris. The destruction was completed under schedule time. The remaining population is calculated at not more than ...[85]

and in the final scene as an air-raid on stage. The destruction is not done by visible hands or for any expressed cause; it is simply destruction, which cannot be opposed or altered. What occurs is not so much the beginning of a war as the end of a civilization, as MacNeice says in a chorus-like speech near the play's end:

> It is going, going, among the flux of words,
> Three thousand years of a wordy civilisation,
> Tags and slogans, nursery rhymes and prayers
> Resolved at last to a drowning gasp for breath,
> Our world is going, going—going for a song . . .[86]

What is lost, as war comes, is commonplace reality, the pleasures of simply living. MacNeice had always been a celebrant of ordinary things; his self-proclaimed role of common man was a kind of substitute for political commitment, a way of being apolitical with a good heart. 'I am all against the rarefying effects of good taste,' he said in a BBC talk that he gave at the time his play was being performed:

> and have no sympathy with the idea that artists are people who should not soil their fingers with life. I don't agree that the style is the man. I always feel a vulgar curiosity to know what a man is talking about. In the case of pictures, I take a vulgar interest in their subject. In the case of music, I have a vulgar preference for something with a tune.[87]

This love of commonplace, particular life appears in the play in an elegiac naming of things that will be lost in the world of war. An off-stage Voice asks, 'When we are dead shall we remember?' And a Chorus answers:

> Shall we remember the jingles of the morning,
> The pipers, the pedlars and the brass farthings,
> The buds of music, the imagined darlings?
> No, we shall *not* remember.[88]

Moll, the model with the life-force, says, 'God be praised that things are as they are', but by the end of the play things aren't that way any longer. It is that sense of what is coming—the Apocalypse that will transform life or destroy it—that makes *Out of the Picture* so much a parable of its moment, a sad, bitter, passive goodbye to all that. 'A graceful elegy,' said the *Daily Worker*'s reviewer, 'on a decadent middle class.'[89] By 1937, the time for elegies had begun.

IX

1938

I

On 26 September 1938, *The Times* ran a leader on 'Poets and the Crisis'. The poets referred to were John Masefield, the Laureate, and W. H. Davies, in whose honour Masefield had just made a speech; the crisis was Germany's demand for the Czechoslovakian Sudetan lands (which was granted three days later at Munich). *The Times* took note of the 'poignant symbolism' of these two contemporaneous events, and spoke approvingly of the role of poets at such difficult points in history:

> At moments like this it is especially fitting that we should pay homage to poets—not for their own sakes (they are sufficiently blessed in 'their magic robes, their burning crown'), but for the sake of that clearer vision which their eyes, superimposed upon our own failing sight, can restore to us.[1]

Grigson, in *New Verse*, was derisive about the editorial—he called the writer a 'learned and sententious ape'[2]—and indeed it is a long way from the 'thirties generation's ideas of poetry, or for that matter of prose style. But in one respect *The Times* leader was not far from much of the writing of *New Verse* in this year of crisis; what they shared along with everyone else in England, young and old, right and left, establishment and rebel, was a deep political anxiety. The leader-writer came to a common point when he wrote, at the end of his piece:

> This is an evil time. We have need of our divinity. If the poets can help us to redeem it, let us salute them all, living and dead.

On this, at least, the editor of *The Times* and the editor of *New Verse* were agreed—it was an evil time.

This sense of crisis, of powerful and active evil at work in the world, dominated consciousnesses in this, the last full year of peace, and appeared everywhere in the written record of those days—in poems and novels and plays as well as in private letters and in *Times* leaders. *Crisis* here is not simply a term for a tense political situation—for the days when the Nazis entered Austria, or for those September negotiations that cost the Czechs their country; it names a state of mind in which men lived and wrote in those months when Europe slid downhill toward the Second World War.

Two issues of *New Verse* of that year provide two examples. Number 29 was published in March, the month in which Hitler moved against Austria. It contains two crisis-poems—neither, of course, *about* the immediate historical event, but both about the anxious expectation that such events would occur. Frederic Prokosch's 'Ode' is a longish poem built on a morning-to-evening progression which corresponds to his sense of current history, moving toward darkness and terror. It begins with a vision of European culture: the chaste basilicas and the spires, the lyrics and the madrigals, the poetry of Hölderlin and Racine. But that is the past; the present is fear and anxious questioning:

> O what is the lie, the chain, the terror?
> That furtive, sickening need that haunts our history?
> What was our sin? To imagine? And who are the
>   monsters?
> Dreams? We wait. And the world is shivering.

The darkness that settles over the poem as night approaches is clearly the darkness of present public evil. At midnight, the poet ends his poem on a dark meditation:

> Now one last time alone I shall walk the accustomed
> Path. The wind stirs the leaves, the wind not only
> Of night, but ours. The season's. The world's. And
> History's. Farewell. Nothing is certain . . .[3]

This apocalyptic sense of an end of everything—of the world and history and the private self—is a commonplace of the time, and Prokosch, a talented but somewhat derivative poet, was writing out of the general consciousness. Perhaps Grigson was right when he complained that Prokosch 'gets to his sorrow over Europe by a short cut';[4] still, sorrow over Europe was the subject that Prokosch chose in 1938, and it was a subject that Grigson was willing to publish in *New Verse*. Whatever the value of the poem as a poem, it is significant as a symptom of the time's mood.

A better but equally symptomatic poem from the same issue of *New Verse* is Bernard Spencer's 'Waiting'. The occasion of the poem is a private one: someone loved is undergoing a surgical operation in an upper room, while below in a waiting-room the speaker sits and thinks of the analogy between his private crisis and the world outside:

> Is it like that bad dream of knives, our counting the years
> Our listening to rumours until the guns begin and our
>   volted
> Delight in creating, our love, our famous words, and the
>   personal
> Order of our lives is devoured when our streets become
>   a furnace?
> I think so in times of despair, and the good in our random
>   culture
>   Woundable as a man is.
>
> Yet know that from our crisis leads no white stair to a
>   shut
> Door and the deftness of another's hands. What sickness
>   threatens
> Our freedom to lounge in the green world, to be happy
>   beneath the
> Clocks of its cities we largely know. If we live we have
>   the pride
> To be capable of action, to speak, out plainly. The wise
>   and passionate
>   Are on our side.[5]

This is more positive than Prokosch's poem was; here the nature of the sickness is known, and action is possible. Nevertheless, the poem is called 'Waiting', and its mood is passively apprehensive: reality is like a bad dream, the private world of love is threatened by public violence, and there is no surgeon who can cure the world's sickness. The mood is not so much one of hope as of the *will* to hope.

In the summer, 1938, issue of *New Verse* Grigson reviewed a number of recent books of poetry, and he took the occasion to remark on the point that I have been noting in Prokosch and Spencer—the relation between public and private events in the present time of crisis.

> After all [he wrote] ... it is quite easy to prove that we are in the first peculiar crisis of civilisation, and if poets say that rather often now in a good many different ways, is there a fact for us which is more important?[6]

Obviously for Grigson there was not; the crisis existed, and because it did, poets would write about it. It had always been the line of *New Verse* that poetry should be regarded as a serious response to present reality, and Grigson was only being consistent in allowing the crisis as a subject. But what is new in this passage is the point implied in *peculiar*: Grigson was not saying simply that another crisis had come along, but that the threat to civilization in the summer of 1938 was without precedent, the most important fact in the world. And because it was, it forced itself upon writers as a vast, insistent new problem, impossible to ignore, that would have to be dealt with in new ways.

Other writers at the same time were saying much the same thing. Orwell, for example, was feeling the same pressure of public crisis when he wrote to Spender about *Homage to Catalonia*. About half of the book, he reckoned, was 'controversial', but not because he enjoyed controversy:

> I hate writing that kind of stuff and am much more interested in my own experiences, but unfortunately in this bloody period we are living in one's only experiences *are* being mixed up in controversies, intrigues, etc. I sometimes feel as if I hadn't been properly alive since abt the beginning of 1937.[7]

And MacNeice, at best a reluctantly political man, felt the pressure of coming events strongly enough to end his *Modern Poetry* (which was published in the autumn of 1938) with this concluding sentence:

When the crisis comes, poetry may for the time be degraded or even silenced, but it will reappear, as one of the chief embodiments of human dignity, when people once more have time for play and criticism.[8]

Here the crisis is the ultimate one—the war itself—but the point is the same; private lives, private feelings, the private gestures of art are all vulnerable to the invasions of public catastrophe.

None of these writings that I have been quoting is addressed to a political subject: one is a review of poems, one a private letter about writing from one writer to another, the third a book about poetry. But because they are not political, they confirm what one might infer in any case, that in 1938 the sense of crisis, and of even greater crisis ahead, was never out of men's minds. And that constant consciousness of disaster must necessarily have had consequences for the forms that the imagination conceived.

One set of responses is evident in three political parables published in this year: Spender's *Trial of a Judge*, Auden and Isherwood's *On the Frontier*, and Warner's *The Professor*. Though formally very different, these three works share certain important elements drawn from a common view of the political situation. All deal with a European nation divided into extreme antithetical camps, fascist against communist. The fascists are rendered as brutal and irresistible—not men in a political movement, but a collective force of evil, stronger than good because it acknowledges no limits to human action. In each case the fascists seize power easily, and use it to destroy the humane, civil, *historical* elements in society; fascism is treated not as an historical event, but as the end of history—an apocalypse, a dark night the end of which is beyond imagining.

The *other* side, in all three works, is communism, and it is still the right side to be on, but communism is no longer seen as the inevitable power, with history on its side, that it was in writings of a few years earlier. And because it is weaker as a cause, its representative figures are not the active, positive heroes they once were: Spender's communists are a Chorus of Red Prisoners, who remain imprisoned; Auden and Isherwood bring their young student-hero reluctantly to the barricades, and kill him there;

Warner's Professor accepts the communist solution with reluctance, as a last chance, while he flees from the irresistible enemy. There are no Truly Strong Men in these books; the heroic phase of the 'thirties is over.

The characters who come closest to being heroes are nearer to tragedy than to epic action, and they are not communists, but liberals. Tragedy is the form men give to their sense of human loss, and it is striking, reading these books, how strong the sense of loss is that they record: in the division into two violent and diametrical camps, Far Left and Far Right, important mediating values have been cast out by both sides, tossed into the middle of the conflict, to be trampled down because they are irrelevant. These are the personal, human values inherited from the past: in public terms, they are the values of traditional humanistic liberalism; in private terms they are the values of love. In all of these books, the destruction of liberalism and love is the price of the struggle that is coming; but though that destruction seems necessary, it can nevertheless be grieved over, and each book is, in its way, an elegy for a lost liberal idea of European civilization. This is essentially a tragic theme, and the characters who express it best are Spender's Judge and Warner's Professor, both public men with public titles and reputations, who are defeated because they are liberals in a post-liberal time, but who are nevertheless sympathetic. They are not men of action—no line of action is possible for the liberal in this situation—but they are men of values, and of worth. It is a curious phenomenon of the late 'thirties that liberalism, which had been buried so deep by the Left in earlier years, should seem to rise from its grave like Banquo, and demand new sympathy.

One evidence that this was indeed so is the emergent role of E. M. Forster among the 'thirties writers of these years. Forster had always been an admired figure, but as the war approached he became much more evident as a hero, replacing those earlier cult-heroes, the two Lawrences. He seems, at first, a kind of parody of T. E. Lawrence: a shy, introverted, intellectual homosexual, inconceivable as a man of action. Yet in the crisis years he did act, in his way; he appeared, for example, at the Paris meeting of the International Association of Writers for the Defence of

Culture in 1935, and before that largely communist assembly he testified simply to his liberal beliefs.[9] He did so again in 1938, in an essay titled 'Credo', published in September in the *London Mercury*. The essay is a famous statement of Bloomsbury liberalism, affirming Forster's belief in personal relationships, democracy (but only two cheers for it), civilization, and 'an aristocracy of the sensitive, the considerate and the plucky'. If it now seems a bit self-indulgent and uninvolved, like a voice from the sidelines cautiously cheering, it is nevertheless a touchingly honest-sounding statement of Forster's personal faith; it must have taken some courage for a shy man to say in public, in 1938, 'I hate the idea of causes, and if I had to choose between betraying my country and betraying my friend, I hope I should have the guts to betray my country'.[10] Such testimony is a kind of action, of heroic action, even, and by making it as he did Forster became, ironically, a hero in spite of himself, and an example of liberal virtue. So, when Philip Toynbee reviewed *The Trial of a Judge* and *The Professor* together, it must have seemed natural to him to include with them Forster's *London Mercury* statement, and to make his review an essay on the condition of liberalism in the present time, with Forster as a living case of the problem that the Judge and the Professor exemplify:

> He is one of the very few members of the pre-war generation [Toynbee wrote of Forster] who have honestly confronted and recognised the limitations imposed on them by their period. He is a Liberal in every sense of the word and he has no illusions about the sad condition of Liberalism in the modern world. . . . Mr. Forster's beliefs are very few and very simple, but all of them are denied and repudiated by the modern *Zeitgeist*.[11]

To Toynbee there was clearly something heroic in the idea of confronting and recognizing limitations, and in uttering beliefs in the face of hostile, powerful opponents: in a time of crisis, the hero may be simply the man who testifies, and that man was Forster.

It is not surprising, then, that Forster appears as he does in the writings of younger men in the late 'thirties, that Connolly praised him in *Enemies of Promise*, that Isherwood admired and sought to emulate his tone in *Lions and Shadows*, that Auden and Isherwood's *Journey to a War* and Day Lewis' *Overtures to Death* are dedicated to him. The example of Day Lewis is particularly significant. *Overtures to Death* contains the last of his militantly political poems; by the time it was published, in October 1938, the poet had withdrawn from party action into the milder role of lyric poet and liberal. His obeisance to Forster must be taken as his public announcement of his change, a way of identifying himself with the hero of liberal values in liberalism's dark time.

Of the three parables that deal with the crisis of political values, Spender's *Trial of a Judge* was the first to appear, and perhaps for that reason it deals with the crisis most narrowly, as a problem internal to one country. It was published and first performed in March 1938, the month in which the Anschluss added Austria to the Third Reich, and six months before the Czechoslovakian crisis, but its historical source was events that took place much earlier, in 1932. At that time, before Hitler had come to power in Germany, Nazi thugs murdered a Polish Jew in Silesia and were acquitted of the crime when their party intervened in the trial. The date of the story is important, for it is a time when Germans might still have resisted fascism, and so the play is a cautionary tale for nations in which liberalism has not yet failed.

That is the principal theme of the play—the failure of liberalism and law under the pressure of fascism. At the play's opening, the Judge, a liberal, has sentenced five fascists to death for the murder of a Jewish radical, and in the course of the play he also condemns to death three communists who have wounded a policeman, though he thinks the law that governs such political acts unjust. Under pressure from his wife, a pro-fascist, and from his friend Hummeldorf, a politician, he reverses his sentence on the fascists, but lets the one on the communists stand. Later, when it is too late, he repents his decision; Hummeldorf removes him from his position, and in turn is removed from the government by the fascists, who execute them both. At the end the liberals are dead, the communists are in prison, and the fascists rule the country.

Spender called his play a tragedy. If it is one, it is a tragedy of liberalism; the principal line of action is the decline and fall of the Judge, who stands for the liberal faith in absolute justice and the rule of law, and who fails because his liberal values are weaker than the power of absolute, valueless evil. Certainly this is a shape that tragedy may take—the good man destroyed by his goodness, pulled down from his place by an antagonist that his values, however right and moral, are inadequate to deal with. The trouble with the play as a tragedy is that, though the Judge is the central figure, he represents no *power* in the play. His decision to free the fascist murderers is morally wrong, but it is politically insignificant; when he says in the last act that he should have acted differently, a communist prisoner replies that it wouldn't have made any difference: 'you are neither so wrong/Nor so responsible as you would like to be.' The conflict is between fascists and communists, and in this conflict the values of liberalism are irrelevant.

But even that is not much of a conflict, for the fascists seem from the beginning to be an irresistible force. This may be a fair historical judgment of what happened in Germany in 1933 (with Hummeldorf as Hindenburg), and certainly it is an accurate expression of the state of mind of young men like Spender in 1938. But it is not very dramatic. The conquest of liberalism is so easy and inevitable that the play seems to be entirely about consequences, one long Act Five. And communism, as a counter-force, scarcely exists; Spender gives the Chorus of Red Prisoners the last line, 'We shall be free. We shall find peace', but it is only a whispered line, and the reality of the final scene is not a communist's vision, but a liberal's nightmare, of a world mastered by fascism, from which history has been abolished.

If the Judge nevertheless remains the hero of the play, that is because he gets the best lines. But the fact that he does, while other, dimmer characters represent the active values of the play, suggests a basic problem, both in the play and in Spender's thinking. Goronwy Rees put the problem very clearly in a contemporary review, in which he wrote:

... Spender, to the spectator at least, has identified himself with the liberal Judge, and from this, I think, arises the sterility of his play ... For the Liberal middle class is not merely caught

304

on the horns of its dilemma, it is lacerated by them, and in its pain can make no objective judgment on its situation; if it could, the dilemma would not exist. All it can do is to lick and explore its wounds, and this is precisely what Spender does. His play is an exploration of the mental tortures of a class in decline ... Hamlet's doubts take five acts to resolve; they determine the tragedy. In *Trial of a Judge*, the doubts, fears, tortures, are subsequent to, and a commentary on, the tragic action.[12]

One other character in the play also has strong lines. The fascist leader speaks in the fifth act of his party's victory and the failure of liberalism in terms that are moving because they express the horror of fascism to the liberal imagination:

Those who opposed the walls of our advancing sea
Are crushed to pebbles. Their minds faded and failed,
O failed and faded like flowers before our enormous tide
Whose tall wordless movement does not resemble history
Taught in their libraries. For we are in no sense ideas:
We do not discuss and cannot be discussed.
Indivisibly we ARE, and by our greater strength of being
Defeat all words. Yet this Judge, in the last analysis believed
That an argument would govern the state which drew its form
From the same sources as the symmetry of music
Or the most sensitive arrangement of poetic words
Or the ultimate purification of a Day of Judgment ...
Yes, in his death, his body does not sleep
In a more rigid stupor than when he woke
To the overwhelming reality of our so-called barbarousness,
Which to him seemed a nightmare where his time fell asleep.[13]

What is nightmarish in this speech is the way the fascist removes his cause from the realm of politics and history and the ordered products of the human mind, and places it with irresistible natural forces—with the sea, the tides, and death itself. The enemy is no longer a political movement; politics has become fate.

Intermingled with this political theme is another, which is a continual private accompaniment to statements of public terror in these books: the theme of the destruction of love by the power of hatred. Petra the Jew is a lover as well as a radical, and he has been murdered by fascists; his brother assumes Petra's role of protector of Petra's fiancée (who is pregnant), and he too is killed. The Judge's barren and unhappy wife expresses her hatred of both Petra and the girl, and her joy in the growth of hate:

> In the larger hate which destroys the world
> The time is redeemed and I am content.
> Let the unconsidering compact bomb cut through
> Tenements and the horizontal thoughts
> Of civilisation. It was all false, false,
> Only my hatred and abrupt death were real.[14]

Fascism is the denial of love and life, and life-deniers are drawn to it. But personal feelings are also denied to those on the other side; in the conflict of Right and Left, it seems that there can be no place for private emotions: love, like liberalism and law, must wait for a time of peace.

By the force of its poetic language the play affirms the value of love, law, and justice; but its action demonstrates the power of barbarousness to destroy those values. The future that the Judge predicts is the only visible future:

> Of solemn words broken by rule, a future
> Of spiritual words burned up with libraries,
> And the triumph of injustice;
> Of tyrants who send their messages of terror
> Against the civilized and helpless.
> O let them witness
> That my fate is the angel of their fate,
> The angel of Europe,
> And the spirit of Europe destroyed with my defeat.[15]

For Spender, the spirit of Europe was clearly the spirit of liberalism, which had created European civilization, and the force that opposed and destroyed it was not a European political force, but the total denial of what Europe means. Against this power of barbarism there seemed only one possible barrier—the power of the proletariat, organized by the communists. But communism in the play is no longer a movement forward from liberalism; it is discontinuous with that creating spirit, an alternate violent force that would exact its costs in love and justice, as fascism did. It is also discontinuous with the workers as they actually are in the world of the play. As Rees put it,

> the working class appears, but it appears only under the form it takes in the mind of the Liberal, just, and humane Judge, that is, as an object of pity, compassion and sympathy, and as the subject of suffering, poverty, injustice.[16]

By the time he wrote the play, Spender was no longer thinking like a communist (if he ever had); but more important, he was not *imagining* like a communist, and though his choruses assert the triumph of the workers, his play is really an elegy for the death of liberalism and of Europe.

Spender called his play a tragedy; Auden and Isherwood subtitled their *On the Frontier* 'A Melodrama'. The intent of the subtitle was no doubt to acknowledge a broad-stroked technique, using stock-figures rather than developed characters and some rather stagey incidents. But in its political content the play is less simplified, and less propagandist, than Spender's is. The subject of *On the Frontier* is the way war starts, and the follies and suffering of ordinary people in war. The combatants are two invented European states, one fascist and one monarchist, and because the authors found neither system desirable they could withhold political partisanship, and attach their sympathies to the victims on both sides. The play is in fact against *both* states, because it is against nationalism as a cause of war. 'You see,' says Dr Thorvald (described in 'Notes on the Characters' as 'Middle-aged, pedantic, would have been a liberal under a democratic regime'),

> You see, I was brought up to think that a man's greatest privilege was to fight for his country; and it's hard to change one's ideas. Perhaps we were all wrong. War seems so beastly when it actually happens! Perhaps 'country' and 'frontier' are old-fashioned words that don't mean anything now. What are we really fighting for? I feel so muddled![17]

One is reminded of the *paysage moralisé* of Auden's earlier poems. In those poems, the frontier was always a place up ahead, beyond which was a New Country. But now, in 1938, he was *on* the frontier, and 'country' and 'frontier' were words that had no meaning. Those words had symbolized a courageous and adventurous quest into the unknown; but in the war that was coming there would be no adventure, and courage would be useless, and the worst of the unknown would become familiar.

On the Frontier does have its villains, and they are the stock villains of the Left: a fascist Leader, and the industrialists who support and expect to exploit him. But their villainy is more melodramatic than real. The Leader is a weak, hysterical neurotic, the Truly Weak Man of Auden's earlier psychologizing. 'You think I am strong?' he asks. 'No, I am weak, weak . . .'[18] And the industrialists, though they believe in their power, and think about it in essentially Marxist terms, are disproved by events. So Valerian, the principal industrialist, thinks:

> The world has never been governed by the People or by the merely Rich, and it never will be. It is governed by men like myself . . . Real political power is only made possible by electricity, double entry and high explosives.[19]

But in fact it is not economics or the will of capitalists that causes the war in the play: it is nationalistic feelings, xenophobia, and muddle. (Valerian, significantly, is shot by a worker, but for personal, not class reasons.) As in Spender's play, the force that moves and destroys men is no longer a political force; the centre of power is not in any class, but loose in the world, and everyone is a victim.

Because this is the case, *On the Frontier* is not focussed on individual characters, but is rather a contrapuntal structure of groups: the industrialists and their Leader, two ordinary families on opposite sides of the frontier, the People (workers, prisoners, soldiers, newspaper readers), and lovers—all helpless, all moved by events beyond their control. The momentum of the play is in the movement of the two countries into war, but no human character wills that movement. The effect is, as MacNeice put it in a review, 'a series of melodramatic cartoons . . . like a number of escaped posters and photographs blown by the wind in one's face'.[20] The image is an apt one, for the public action grows more and more chaotic as war approaches—as though war were simply another name for the end of all order. The final 'cartoon' is a scene in which five men read contrapuntally from five newspapers of different political positions, each with its own view of the chaos of Europe. They are mutually contradictory as to causes, but agreed as to consequences—a world war. It is the apocalypse, as reported in the press.

Like *Trial of a Judge*, this play takes as a theme correlative to the political one the love-destroying power of war. The two ordinary families are represented as occupying one room, divided into an Ostnian side and a Westland side. On the Ostnian side is a girl, Anna, and on the Westland a boy, Eric. Throughout the family scenes, while their elders express their hatred and prejudices, the two yearn toward each other, though they never meet; they speak, and even embrace, but this, one gathers, is not in this world of hate and fear, but somewhere else, in 'the good place'. ('The mystical love scenes of Eric and Anna made one long for a sack to put one's head in,' said MacNeice, who liked his sentiment and fancy kept separate.) And at the end of the play they both die, still yearning, still separated by war and the emotions that cause war.

The lovers have the final speeches of the play, and what they say sheds interesting light on the politics of *On the Frontier*. Eric, who has been a pacifist, dies on the barricades in an attempted revolution against the Leader; but his lines do not suggest that his cause was the right and only one:

> We cannot choose our world,
> Our time, our class. None are innocent, none.
> Causes of violence lie so deep in all our lives
> It touches every act.
> Certain it is for all we do
> We shall pay dearly. Blood
> Will mine for vengeance in our children's happiness,
> Distort our truth like an arthritis.
> Yet we must kill and suffer and know why.

> All errors are not equal. The hatred of our enemies
> Is the destructive self-love of the dying,
> Our hatred is the price of the world's freedom.[21]

The point, I take it, is that love's consummation must wait upon the consummation of hatred—that the enemies must be defeated before love can flourish; 'in the lucky guarded future,' says Eric, 'Others like us shall meet, the frontier gone, And find the real world happy.' But who exactly are the enemies? The fascists within, or the armies of the other side? And who, for that matter, are 'we'? Ostnians? Revolutionaries? Lovers? Politically speaking, the passage is remarkably obscure, considering its location in the play.

The final sixteen lines, spoken antiphonally by Eric and Anna (or to be precise by their spirits, since they are both dying in separate hospitals at the moment), are particularly striking in the way they anticipate Auden's later writing—poems, for example, like 'In Memory of W. B. Yeats' and 'Sept. 1, 1939'.

> ANNA. Europe lies in the dark
> City and flood and tree;
> Thousands have worked and work
> To master necessity.

> ERIC. To build the city where
> The will of love is done
> And brought to its full flower
> The dignity of man.

> ANNA. Pardon them their mistakes,
> The impatient and wavering will.
> They suffer for our sakes,
> Honour, honour them all.

> BOTH. Dry their imperfect dust,
> The wind blows it back and forth.
> They die to make man just
> And worthy of the earth.[22]

Not only the cadence, but the imagery of darkness, dust and earth, and the language of love and pardon belong to the poetry of Auden's later, post-political period. Here, at the end of a play about how war comes, these speeches deflect our attention from parties and causes, from Left versus Right and Choruses of Red Prisoners, to a theme beyond politics, the human effort to create the Just Place. As one contemporary critic remarked, these lines look 'uncommonly like a Christian hymn to a better world'.[23] In them, Auden wrote the first draft of his farewell to the 'thirties.

Like the two plays, Rex Warner's novel of 1938, *The Professor*, is about the failure and death of liberalism and the triumph of fascism. Warner was, like Spender, a committed communist, for a time a Party member, and like Spender he took the view in his book that liberalism was obsolete and that revolution was the only line of action left for the opponents of fascism. But his Professor, like Spender's Judge, is heroic and moving in his defeated liberalism—almost, it seems, against the author's will.

The novel takes place at a time of political crisis in an unnamed European country, in which fascists and communists are near to civil war, while the armies of a neighbouring fascist state wait on the borders for an invitation to invade. At this point the Professor, a classical scholar of international reputation, is offered the Chancellorship of the country; he is a man of known integrity and understanding, free of party attachments, and above all (like Spender's Judge) a man who believes in abstract justice and the rule of law. He accepts the position, and is swiftly and easily overthrown by the fascists; the foreign armies enter the country, and as he attempts to escape he is betrayed by his mistress, imprisoned, and shot in the back.

Much of this is highly dramatic, and Warner handles it with the rapid, terse intensity of a thriller. But the most dramatic passages in the book are not the moments of physical action, but the passionate monologues and debates, in which men holding different political positions argue them, and in so doing pass judgments on the Professor's liberalism. The force of these didactic passages is testimony to Warner's powers as a writer; but it is also a condition of the time that to argue for fascism could seem as violent an act as a blow struck in the street.

The debate begins at once, in the first scene, in which the Professor, lecturing to his students on Sophocles, digresses on the word 'Polis'—'an enclosure', he explains, a safety zone, or outpost against what to the Greeks (and in a very real sense their view was correct) was actually the barbarism of others who were outside this on the whole liberal organization.[24]

The Professor's son, a communist, interrupts him at this point. 'There is no enclosed space in Europe,' he says, the barbarians are inside as well as outside the defences, and so the 'Polis' no longer exists, and the man who goes on lecturing on it is helping to destroy civilization by preserving obsolete liberal ideals. He is answered by a fascist, who argues for discipline and the suppression of Reds and Jews. The Professor (like a good teacher) sums up: both speakers, he recognizes, have taken one assumption for granted—that the state no longer exists, but must be, in some way, either reconstituted or purged. 'If this were true,' he continues, 'it would be a terrible thing. It would mean that there would be no room within the framework of the laws for reason and persuasion to promote the growth towards that ideal state of affairs which we all seek.' But it *is* true, and that is the point of the novel; in a world in which fascism has power, none of the beliefs of liberalism can survive—order, law, and the power of reason are rendered obsolete by brute force.

In the episodes which follow, two dialogues are of particular importance. In one, the Professor meets an old school friend who has become a fascist officer, and listens while the fascist argues the morality of his cause. It is a strong, frightening speech; like Spender, Warner gives his fascist enough strength of argument, and enough rhetorical force, to make him threatening. The fascist's case rests on the assumption that the real human morality is based on instinct, 'the instinct to preserve and amplify one's own life'; 'we appeal,' he says, 'to the dark and vital and real forces in human nature which have so long been hypocritically oppressed by the teaching of men like you. We show our followers how to regain their self-confidence as individuals by hating their enemies. You offer them a whole world to love: we give them a tangible minority to hate.'[25] By arguing in this way, the fascist implicates the liberal Professor in the rise of fascism; liberalism, by preaching universal brotherhood and suppressing what is savage in men, has nourished the very forces of violence that it fears and deplores. (The whole speech echoes with the voice of that rejected hero of the generation, D. H. Lawrence.)

The second speaker is an elderly cobbler whom the Professor meets in his flight from the invading fascist armies. The cobbler lectures him on the damnation of the soul, arguing that pain, evil, poverty, and frustration are inevitable to the human condition, and that recognition of this common suffering is the necessary basis of brotherhood. 'We are brothers,' he says, 'not in the sense that we feel love, but because we know that we are the children of a common necessity. It is more a question of having felt hunger.'[26] Like the fascist, this religious fanatic holds the Professor and his liberal kind responsible for what has happened in the country; liberalism has taught men to see their lives as wretched, and to desire to escape from them:

> You urged us to be ambitious, to make good, to rise in the world, sometimes encouraging the most blatant and outrageous motives of greed and self-indulgence, sometimes pointing us towards the pleasures of the soul—culture, poetry, beauty of manners. Did you never observe that if we were to follow your advice we should have to fight and kill our brothers?'[27]

That is, the liberal tradition is a tradition of competition, and so eventually of exploitation and violence.

All of these speeches—by the communist son, by the fascist officer, by the religious fanatic—are indictments of the Professor's liberalism, and all make the same point, that he must take responsibility for the destruction of his country and of liberal civilization. The position that the novel proposes is absolutely clear: liberalism has created its own destroyers, and is guilty of its own death. Why then does one feel, reading the book, both affection and sympathy for the Professor, the character who represents liberalism? Is it simply because the sins of which he stands convicted—his belief in abstract justice, his faith in human goodness, his philosophical detachment—are the sins of a virtuous man? Not only that, I think, but also because, though the book may persuade us that the Professor's values are obsolete and actively destructive at this point in history, yet they remain moral. We feel that, and so, clearly, does Warner; the Professor dies a good, though defeated man, and his death is not history's execution of a criminally negligent governor, but a murder by fascists, a part of the darkness ahead.

The approaching darkness defines the imagined world that these three parables share: it is an apocalyptic world, in which the death of Europe is an immediate reality. Through the writings of the 'thirties one can see that apocalypse approaching, and the imaginable future shortening, until here, at the end of the decade, the future is almost non-existent, a year or two long, and literary works have a very curious perspective, like a landscape painting that is all foreground. The world they image is a world without history, for apocalypse is the end of history. Valerian, the industrialist in *On the Frontiers*, thinks about this:

> This is probably the last period in human history. The political régimes of the future may have many fancy names, but never again will the common man be allowed to rule his own life or judge for himself.[28]

And the Professor, a man accustomed to think in historical parallels, is no longer stirred by them:

> The actual process of life differed too remarkably from recorded history, and no imaginative insight could bridge the gulf between the living and the dead.[29]

Being without history, these parables are descriptive rather than prophetic. Fascism did not need to be predicted—it was already there—and beyond fascism there was no imaginable future. And so, though revolution is taken for granted as the only possible response to fascism, none of these books imagines a victorious one, or the new world after the war.

Insofar as these three books are political parables, they resemble the work done earlier in the 'thirties by the same authors. But if one compares *Trial of a Judge*, *On the Frontier*, and *The Professor* with earlier parables—with for example *Vienna*, *The Dog Beneath the Skin*, and *The Wild Goose Chase*—it is clear that a new element has entered the later work. Parable still seems the best term for this kind of non-realistic form, but these later examples are *tragic* parables. Tragedy, as I understand it, is the literary expression of men's sense of the forces in the world that are beyond human control, and especially of the forces of evil. Those forces in the late 'thirties seemed to have swept over Europe like some natural catastrophe, like the primal flood that is such a common image of the decade. In such a time, politics—men's efforts to govern rationally—becomes a tragic activity; and so political parables are tragic parables, ending in defeat and death.

Tragedy—if we mean by the term not a dramatic form but an acknowledgment of the power of evil—is a dominant mode of the late 'thirties; the human problem, as *The Times* leader-writer said, was how to live in an evil time, and that is a tragic question. Perhaps that is why Michael Roberts ended his 1938 study of T. E. Hulme with a personal essay, 'The Tragic Way', which has nothing to do with Hulme, but everything to do with Roberts' sense of his own time. 'In the tragic view,' Roberts wrote,

all doctrines of perfectibility are seen to be dangerous, whether in politics, philosophy or aesthetics. It is not merely that we are sometimes unlucky, and that we fail in our highest and most sustained endeavours: it is that this failure is intrinsic to our nature. As long as we are sensitive, thinking, moral creatures—as long as we are aiming, as we must aim, at perfection —we must find that any ultimate objective that we set ourselves is unattainable or unsatisfactory. That which is humanly good, or true, or beautiful, consists not in a final revelation and justification, but in particulars.[30]

This essay is an interesting one, historically speaking, because it is by the editor of *New Signatures* and *New Country*, and an early articulator of his generation's revolutionary enthusiasms. The change in his position over the intervening five years had been extreme, but it is no greater than the difference between 1933 and 1938. In the course of those five years, the revolutionary view had come to seem, for most writers, untenable, and the tragic view one that history and observation confirmed. So that I think one might say that Roberts was once more speaking for his generation, and articulating the sense of the world that the parables of his contemporaries also expressed.

One of Roberts' examples of the tragic view was Kafka's *The*

Trial, and in this, too, he was reflecting a generational taste. For Kafka was an important figure in the 'thirties sensibility. His works appeared in their first English translations through the decade—*The Castle* in 1930, *The Great Wall of China* in 1933, *The Trial* and *Metamorphosis* in 1937, *Amerika* in 1938—and they were accepted at once as significant for the time. What Kafka seemed to provide was a parabolic form for the perception of reality as nightmare that was increasingly the way the world looked. In Kafka's books, reality is fantastic and frightening, but is recorded as though it were ordinary and to be expected: authority is absolute and incomprehensible, and man is powerless, and only guilt and suffering are certain. One can see how, as young writers lived through the 'thirties, they came to see Kafka as the true realist of their reality.

It is impossible, of course, to prove that all the young writers of the 'thirties read Kafka, and one might reasonably argue that the necessity of nightmare was a conclusion that they all reached independently; but what is clear is that by the mid-'thirties Kafka-like effects were turning up in their writings, and that these effects increased in the later years of the decade. One could say, perhaps, that nightmare had become the parable-form of the time, and that what Kafka provided was a sophisticated example of how to turn nightmare into literature.

A principal example of this Kafka-like parable form is the 'thirties fiction of Edward Upward. Since his Mortmere days at Cambridge with Isherwood, Upward had published comparatively little, and by 1938 he was not so much a literary figure as a legend: Auden had learned from him, Isherwood deferred to him, Spender admired his 'strange sardonic power', and John Lehmann pursued him for *New Writing* and the Hogarth Press. He was, as a biographical note in an anthology of left-wing writing put it, 'the most interesting modern writer whose name does not show on the British Museum Catalogue'.[31] But not for what he had written.

What was interesting about Upward was the fantastic imagination that had invented Mortmere—an imagination that saw the ordinary world as hallucination, with everything clear, but nothing intelligible, like Kafka without the religious sense. That imagination was expressed in its purest state in 'The Railway Accident', written by Upward in 1928: 'a nightmare', said Isherwood, 'about the English'. In the years that followed, Isherwood escaped from that undergraduate nightmare world, and began to publish his first novels and stories; but Upward found escape more difficult. For him, the nightmare was real, and he spent the years of his early maturity in vain attempts to relate the vision of Mortmere to the reality of the world around him, 'to find the formula', as Isherwood put it, 'which would transform our private fancies and amusing freaks and bogies into valid symbols of the ills of society and the toils and aspirations of our daily lives.'[32]

The formula that he found was communism, and he was one of the first of his generation to join the Party. There he thought he found a way out of the pure subjectivity of fantasy: for Marxism affirmed the reality of the material world, independent of human thought. For Upward, Party membership seems to have been a mode of salvation in a desperate time, and he embraced it like a religion. 'I came to it,' he later said, 'not so much through consciousness of the political and economic situation as through despair.'[33] Like other emotional converts to a faith, he embraced the discipline of his new religion absolutely; he became the most doctrinaire of communist intellectuals, and he stayed in the Party long after the other writers of his generation had departed. But the conversion did not solve his problem: Marxism did not turn his fantasies into a symbolic system. Instead, the tension between his imagination and his political ideology shrivelled his natural gifts, and left him an arid, unimaginative, and unreadable realist. But in the 'thirties that had not yet happened, and Upward was thought of as potentially the English Kafka, the young writer who would make English Marxism imaginative.

When, in 1937, Upward contributed an essay titled 'Sketch for a Marxist Interpretation of Literature' to a volume of Marxist essays, he demonstrated his total commitment to the Party by taking a critical position of extreme rigidity: no book written at the present time, he wrote, could be good unless it was written from a Marxist or near-Marxist viewpoint, and no modern book could be true to life unless it recognized both the decadence of present-day society and the inevitability of revolution. By these

317

standards, all the great modern writers were failures: he specifically noted the shortcomings of Proust, Joyce, and Lawrence. No
modern book, apparently, was a success.

The most interesting and depressing point about Upward's
essay, though, is that it was an explicit repudiation of his own
gift; the kind of writing that he singled out for particular condemnation was the kind in which his odd, original imagination
most flourished. 'Literary allegories and fantasies,' he wrote,

> ... have survived the test of practical experience in former
> centuries when a more realistic view of the world could only
> have led to despair or to futile rebellion; and because their
> meaning was true in the past they may still have some value
> for us in the present. But a modern fantasy cannot tell the
> truth, cannot give a picture of life which will survive the test
> of experience; since fantasy implies in practice a retreat from
> the real world into the world of imagination, and though such
> a retreat may have been practicable and desirable in a more
> leisured and less profoundly disturbed age than our own, it is
> becoming increasingly impracticable to-day.[34]

This is a rejection, not only of the mode of most of his fiction
of the 'thirties, but of the most distinguished work of the best
writers of his generation. There was to be no more Mortmere,
and no more parables.

A note to this essay says of Upward that he 'is at present writing
a novel in which he hopes to deal more adequately and more
concretely with some of the problems he has raised in this essay.'[35]
The novel in question is *Journey to the Border*, apparently written
over several years, and with great difficulty, and published at
last through Lehmann's efforts in 1938. It does deal with one
basic problem raised in the essay—the problem of the relation
between the world of imagination and the material world—but
it does so in an odd way, not by demonstrating the correct
socialist-realist solution, but by rendering a negative example,
a fantastic, Mortmere-like inner life that becomes madness, and
is cured by a commitment to political action. It is a fantastic
confession, and an act of exorcism.

The situation of the novel is clearly drawn from Upward's own life. It concerns one day in the life of a young man who works as a tutor to an upper-middle-class family living in a country house (as Upward did for a time after leaving Cambridge). The young man despises the members of the family for their insensitive vulgarity, and himself for his dependence on them, but he is too weak and too neurotic to break away from the security that they offer. On the day of the action he is taken by his employer to a local race meeting; there he undergoes a series of visionary experiences that drive him to the border of madness, from which he is saved by a conversion to the revolutionary workers' movement.

Formally, the book is as far from socialist realism as a novel could be; it takes place entirely in the tutor's troubled mind, and there the perception of external reality is so shifting and ambiguous as to leave the reader certain of nothing except the tutor's deranged state. At the race-track ordinary objects change their appearance, sinister strangers appear and disappear, and the tutor engages in conversations that may or may not actually occur. One by one, characters appear who offer him the two things that his neurotic, withdrawn life lacks: contact with other people, and a mode of action. He talks with a girl who is a socialist, with a fascist, with a D. H. Lawrence/Homer Lane sort of psychologist, with a seductive woman. These are the stock allegorical tempters of the 'thirties myth; each represents a temptation to self-betrayal through the wrong kind of action—romantic socialism, fascism, the liberation of unreason, sexuality.

Other elements of the 'thirties myth also inhabit the tutor's mind. He is afraid of, and expects another war; he yearns for a 'genuine man of action', but feels threatened by fascism; he sees as inevitable the conflict of Left and Right, and identifies himself with the Left, though he does nothing about it. All of this makes the novel sound like a parable of the 'thirties situation—an ordinary young man psychologically disturbed by the fears and anxieties and the confusion of values of his time. The problems, if not the madness, are familiar themes, and one can see resemblances between this young man and other examples of the Truly Weak that have appeared in other books.

But the psychological state of the tutor is a problem: he is abnormal from the beginning, neurotically self-regarding, paranoid, solipsistic. He thinks, for example, early in the novel:

> All names were interchangeable. Any description, any explanation, was as futile as another. Think of all the moods, attitudes, opinions, theories, which the tutor had got through in a single morning. Which had been right? None. There was no such thing as being right. There were only mental and emotional exercises, some of them prettier than others . . . [36]

And he imagines solutions to his problems in terms of new fantasy-techniques—new ways of excluding reality—rather than in terms of action.

A change occurs in the tutor's state of mind in the final pages; he has reached the border of sanity, and there he carries on a dialogue with himself through which he is saved. The other self that he speaks with is the other Upward, the doctrinaire author of 'Sketch for a Marxist Interpretation of Literature', who instructs him in the true material nature of reality, and directs him to his cure:

> . . . let us suppose that you actually have been insane: you can be sure that, if your disease is curable, you could not find a better way of curing it than by joining the workers' movement. Because there is no other way of dealing *successfully* with the real external problems which confront you—and which, incidentally, confront the whole of humanity at the present time. [37]

This is Marxism understood as psychiatric treatment, and the whole passage reads like a conversation with a psychoanalyst. And, as sometimes happens in psychoanalysis, the patient is cured, but his imagination dies.

Is the novel really political, then? Can politics cause neurosis? And if so, can politics cure it? And can we take the tutor as representative of a general social problem of his time? Lehmann thought so; at least I assume that it was Lehmann who, having got the novel for the Hogarth Press, wrote the dust-jacket copy for it, and said:

> This book is an imaginative commentary on the predicament

of the more intelligent and honest members of the 'middle class' in England to-day.

But this is simply not true: the tutor is not such a generalized character. All madness is isolating, and the tutor's approach to madness, as we experience it through his consciousness, isolates him from the world around him. That world is capitalist society, and it shows signs of its own sickness, but the tutor's sickness is not to be explained simply as a manifestation of society's malfunctioning; his disorder is rooted in his own weakness, for which political commitment is a cure as neurotic as the disease.

Journey to the Border is much less a political parable than any of the three books previously discussed in this chapter, and though there are resemblances and a kind of parabolic kinship among them all, we will have to find a better way of describing this novel. We could say that it is a study of neurotic epistemology; or that it is a kind of confession, the convert exposing his past fantastic sins; or that it is a parable of modern madness, and of the neurotic function of political conversions. In any case, it must stand alone. The extended period of its composition makes Upward's novel less a parable of its particular date than of the whole 'thirties experience, and the evident subjective sources make it not so much a political statement as the veiled autobiography of a gifted man who traded his gift for the security of a cause, and wrote his only imaginative book to describe how and why he abandoned his imagination. In its realistic rendering of the fantastic the book does suggest the works of Kafka, and one can understand how Spender saw in Upward the promise of an English Kafka, but one can also see why Upward could not achieve that goal. For in the end he could not bear to inhabit a world of Kafka situations; he saw in fantasy a threat of madness, an abnormal state that he must break out of, and not, as he had hoped, a symbolic version of the madness of the world.

II

At the same time that Upward was completing his novel, other writers of his generation were turning to autobiography. It is difficult to explain why a generation should set out to assess and define itself at one time rather than another, but clearly the end of the 'thirties was such a time for the generation that I am concerned with. Perhaps they looked back because the view ahead was disheartening and obscure; perhaps they felt a need to understand the route by which they had reached this dark moment in history; perhaps they sought to define the past in order to repudiate it. Whatever the motive, young writers did begin to consider their own pasts then, and some of the best writing of these late 'thirties years is in this mode.

Autobiography belongs to the world of fact—it is a kind of documentary; and like documentary, it is also a self-conscious art form that may sometimes be read as parable. The writer of an autobiography is constructing a Myth of Himself, which by imposing shape and selection upon the past will explain his present existence. From this constructing process he will emerge as his own hero, or anti-hero, the agent or the victim of his destiny, and the events that he chooses to recall from his past will necessarily assume causal and symbolic roles in the making of the person that he has become. To the degree that he is conscious of his relation to history, his myth of self will also be a parable of his time; for writers of the late 'thirties, generation-conscious as they were, to write autobiography was also to write their generation's history.

Of the autobiographical-historical-parables of the time, the most interesting, as it is the most artful and self-conscious, is Christopher Isherwood's *Lions and Shadows*. The book appears to be a straightforward personal record: it is subtitled 'An Education in the Twenties', it carries a frontispiece captioned 'Myself, in 1921', and the first-person narrator is called Christopher Isherwood. But the author is careful to deny that the book is quite what it seems; it is not, he warns the reader in a note, an autobiography 'in the ordinary journalistic sense of the word . . .; it contains no "revelations"; it is never "indiscreet"; it is not even entirely "true".'[38] He has used a novelist's licence, he admits, in describing incidents and drawing characters, and he advises his reader to read the book as a novel.

If *Lions and Shadows* is neither quite fiction nor quite fact, then what is it? It is an account of the education of a novelist, Isherwood explains. It is therefore in the modern tradition of the portrait of the artist as a young man; and because it is self-consciously fictionalized, it must be not only a description of a novelist's education, but a demonstration of what he has learned. But it is also something more than one young Englishman's education. 'A young man,' Isherwood writes, 'living at a certain period in a certain European country, is subjected to a certain kind of environment, certain stimuli, certain influences'; all of these factors combine to make the book also a portrait of the artist's generation during its formative years—the first full-length portrait that a member of that generation had attempted.

The place to begin an examination of Isherwood's book is with his account of the factors that formed his generation. (Some of this I have quoted above, in Chapter One.) First, there is his sense of the psychological importance of the First World War for those who didn't fight in it:

> We young writers of the middle 'twenties were all suffering, more or less subconsciously, from a feeling of shame that we hadn't been old enough to take part in the European war.[39]

The war was a test that they had failed to take—a test of courage, maturity, sexual prowess, everything that makes a man a Man. And so they were uncertain of their manhood, and fearful of the Tests that would try them, which they nevertheless also desired. From this complex of fears and desires emerged the generation's typical protagonist, 'the neurotic hero, the Truly Weak Man'. The literary problem was how to render this sense of a generation's neurosis in a manner that was not itself neurotic.

The other characteristic of this generation, as Isherwood saw it, follows from its neurotic self-regard; it was totally unaware of economic and political realities in the public world outside. Isherwood mentions the General Strike, a Test which like most of his friends he failed by joining the wrong side, and he lists the figures in European politics—Hitler, Mussolini, Lenin, Trotsky—whom he and his friends had never heard of. The 'Education' of the subtitle comes to seem a heavily ironic term when one considers the life in the 'thirties for which these young men were being prepared.

The characters who inhabit this neurotic, ignorant world of Isherwood's 'twenties are his closest friends—Auden, Spender, and Upward among them—but transformed by the 'novelist's licence' into caricatures, grotesque figures in 'the vast freak museum of out neurotic generation'.[40] Auden is seen as a lunatic clergyman, Spender appears as a wild-looking giant howling a 'wild silly laugh', Upward is haunted, demonic, and lost. The plain, self-effacing prose in which Isherwood sets down their strange behaviour *sounds* rational and ordinary, but the behaviour is dream-like, extravagant, fantastic, and even the minor characters seem to belong more to the world of Mortmere than to ordinary reality: a typical paragraph begins, 'One morning the madman and I were standing together outside the pub . . .' The effect is to make the 'twenties seem not so much a period of history as an abnormal psychological state—but an abnormal state as observed by a normal and rational observer, with a scientific interest in the subject.

Of the examples that Isherwood offers of his generation's neurosis and ignorance, the most extreme case is Isherwood himself: the caricature who bears his name is the most neurotic, the most helpless and inept, the least comprehending of the book's characters. This caricature-Isherwood thinks of himself as 'Isherwood the Artist', and his romantic conception of the artist's role is subjected to a good deal of cold ridicule by Isherwood the actual writer of the book: Isherwood the Artist thinks of himself as 'an austere ascetic, cut off from the outside world, in voluntary exile, a recluse, a lonely, excluded, monastic figure', and he is last seen, like an adolescent Byron, 'still striking an attitude on his lonely rock'. This attitudinizing is treated throughout as a neurotic compensation for insecurity and artistic failure, and the efforts of the Artist to write novels are pitilessly exposed in the unkindest possible way—by quoting from his unsuccessful, unpublished works.

This method, by which autobiography becomes an anti-heroic Parable of the Self, is clearly a conscious, and apparently a necessary strategy. The Isherwood character in the book, the Truly Weak Man in the 'twenties, is in much the same situation that his friend Upward was—hating and despising his life, rejecting the values of his society and his class, living in an escapist world of self-dramatizing fantasy. But by assuming a detached attitude toward himself, Isherwood (the writer in the 'thirties who was writing the book) avoided the neurotic self-regard and self-loathing that had infected Upward's work; he turned his past self into an object for observation, and his present self into a coldly neutral instrument for observing. 'That the young man happens to be myself,' he says in his note to the reader in *Lions and Shadows*, 'is only of secondary importance: in making observations of this sort, everyone must be his own guinea-pig.' Escape from the neurosis of the 'twenties therefore becomes a matter of style; and *Lions and Shadows* is a demonstration of that style. If, as Isherwood says, it contains no revelations and is never indiscreet, that is because it is written in a manner that is too distanced and too impersonal for indiscretion. It records experience with the self-effacing neutrality of a camera—which becomes Isherwood's image of the artist's relation to his world.

Isherwood's book is a kind of companion piece to *Journey to the Border*, covering the years that brought Upward to his crisis and Isherwood to his release, and dealing with common problems. The *Daily Worker* shrewdly took note of the resemblance, and reviewed the two books together under the headline, ' "Heroes" Who Were Afraid'. 'Both books are remarkable,' the reviewer wrote, 'for their descriptions of an adolescent mind, dominated by fear, and out of touch with its environment.'[41] But by the end of *Lions and Shadows* Isherwood is on the way to making contact with reality; he too has made a journey to the border, but in his case the border is not the edge of insanity, but the edge of liberation. The book ends on 14 March 1929, in a train rolling through Germany. Isherwood the failed romantic writer, the inhibited neurotic, the Truly Weak Man, is leaving his past. Behind him lie England, Cambridge, Upward, his family and his fantasy life —his whole useless education in the 'twenties; ahead lies Berlin and the 'thirties, and another education for another time.

Lions and Shadows stops short of the 'thirties, and so avoids politics, Europe, fascism, the approach of war—all those urgent subjects of the next decade; the eight years' space between the last event and the writing of it stand as a temporal form of the distance between the writer and his former self. Cyril Connolly's *Enemies of Promise* is the opposite kind of autobiography, a book without distance. It goes back to a similar 'education in the 'twenties', but it relates that education to existence in the present time of composition, which is carefully dated at the end of the book as 'July 1937–Aug. 1938'. Those dates locate the book on several planes. In terms of European history they place it in the apprehensive period of the late 'thirties. 'This is the time of year,' the book begins, 'when wars break out . . .' and it ends, a year later, with Connolly 'meditating at this time of year when wars break out, when Europe trembles and dictators thunder'. In terms of literary history, 1937–8 is the date of what Connolly took to be a turning point in the Modern Movement, a point at which a change of style was to be predicted (and described at length). In personal terms, it was Connolly's thirty-fourth year, a date when he had been writing about books for ten years, but had not written a book that fulfilled the promise of his beginnings. His one ambition, he says in the first chapter, is 'to write a book that will hold good for ten years afterwards'. Perhaps this was the time. Perhaps if it was not done now, war would destroy the possibility. Existing as it does on these various planes, the book is various books: a guide book to the Modern Movement (a book which Connolly went on writing all his life, on a subject that he regarded as peculiarly his own); a theoretical study of modern prose style; an essay on the problems and pitfalls of the literary profession at the time; and a self-lacerating confession of his own failure.

The book begins, not with personal beginnings, as one might expect in an autobiography, but with the most abstract subject—style. Connolly's theory is that the Modern Movement (the capitals are his own) has oscillated between two extreme styles—the Mandarin (literary, artificial, decorated, best example Henry James), and the Vernacular or Colloquial (best example Hemingway), and that the time has come for a swing back to the Mandarin. He professes himself neutral in this matter, admiring both and merely recording their history, but the understanding of literary history in terms of style is itself a Mandarin trait, and Connolly's conclusion that 'the colloquial style of the last few years is doomed and dying' seems uttered with satisfaction. And when one notes that the book is dedicated to that arch-Mandarin,

Logan Pearsall Smith, one concludes that Connolly would have been a Mandarin, even in 1938, even with war coming, if he could. This whole section of his book, with its tables of important books by date and its reductions of modernism tó a problem in style, has an insulated, bookish quality that is rather unsettling: in 1937–8, in the midst of political crisis, Connolly had managed to write literary history in terms that are *only* literary, as though literature had no relation to the world at all.[42]

In the second part of the book, Connolly itemizes the 'enemies of promise', those obstacles and distractions in a literary man's life that threaten his career. Most of these are quite predictable: drink, journalism, success, sex, and domesticity would be on any writer's list. But politics is a rather surprising term to find here, in a book by a young writer in the late 'thirties. Connolly's attitude toward the subject is ambiguous; politics, he says,

> are more dangerous to young writers than journalism. They are dangerous because writers to-day feel that politics are necessary to them, but have not yet learnt how best to be political.[43]

But he sees the time as one which is suited to political writings, and he has a high opinion of the power of writing, at a time when many of his contemporaries had lost hope:

> To-day writers can still change history by their pleading, and one who is not political neglects the vital intellectual issues of his time, and disdains his material . . . He is not a victim of his time but a person who can alter it, though if he does not, he may well be victimised. He has to be political to realise himself, and he must go on being political to protect himself. To-day the forces of life and progress are ranging on one side, those of reaction and death on the other. We are having to choose between democracy and fascism, and fascism is the enemy of art. It is not a question of relative freedom, there are no artists in Fascist countries. We are not dealing with an Augustus who will discover his Horace and his Virgil, but with Attila, or Hulaku, destroyers of European culture, whose poets can contribute only

battle-cries and sentimental drinking songs. Capitalism in decline, as in our own country, is not much better as a patron than fascism. Stagnation, fear, violence and opportunism, the characteristics of capitalism preparing for the fray, are no background for a writer, and there is a seediness, an ebb of life, a philosophy of taking rather than giving, a bitterness and brutality about right-wing writers now which was absent in those of other days, in seventeenth-century Churchmen or eighteenth-century Tories. There is no longer a Prince Rupert, a Doctor Johnson, a Wellington, Disraeli, or Newman, on the reactionary side.[44]

I quote this passage at length because I find myself distrusting it, and the basis of my distrust is in the accumulative effect of the style: it seems to me an exercise in high rhetoric posing as conviction. Which side is Connolly really supporting here? Certainly not fascism, but if democracy includes present-day England, then not democracy either. What in fact he approves is the political writing of the past—politics in the context he is most comfortable in, the context of literary history. Because he is a literary man, he would like to believe that writing is powerful, and its influence crucial in the present crisis: 'unless writers do all they can it will be too late, war will break out, and the moment be past when the eloquence of the artist can influence the destiny of humanity.'[45] But the pages that follow are mostly prudential warnings to his fellow writers: politicians are low-brows, propaganda is inferior, political writing is honeycombed with clichés, the best work of the great writers was rarely their political writing; 'a writer who cannot assimilate with genius the harsh fare of contemporary politics,' Connolly concludes, 'had better keep out'.[46] The metaphor is a revealing one: in the end, politics is not an urgent human issue, but a matter of digestion, one more trouble for the aspiring writer, like his sex life and his bank balance, one more reason for failing to fulfil his promise.

For that is what this section is about—failure, and though the manner is one of Olympian generalization, the subject is really Connolly's own failure. By the end of the book, *promise* has become a term of bitter self-reproach, an accusation that he hears in the night and cannot answer: 'Promise is guilt—promise is the capacity for letting people down.' For the destruction of promise, one cause is as good as another—if it isn't sex it will be journalism, if it isn't drink it will be politics. But even if the destroyer is a public matter, like political commitment, Connolly sees it in its private consequences; his eye is turned always inward, away from the public world, toward that inward place where talent withers and turns sour.

That surely is why Connolly chose to begin his book with an essay on style, and to move through the problems of a writer's life to come at last to himself when young, the promising boy. First he shows his literary credentials, then his literary difficulties, and finally the golden promise that was not fulfilled. The environment of 'A Georgian Boyhood', the autobiographical third part of the book, is Eton, where Connolly spent the years just after the First World War. His attitude toward his school is deeply ambivalent; he condemns its 'culture of the lilies' for being 'rooted in the past, divorced from reality, and dependent on a foreign tongue'; it is sterile, and limited by good taste, it encourages aestheticism, it fosters adolescent vice, and it retards maturity. Deducing a system from his feelings on leaving Eton, he formulates what he calls the Theory of Permanent Adolescence:

> It is the theory that the experiences undergone by boys at the great public schools, their glories and disappointments, are so intense as to dominate their lives, and to arrest their development. From these it results that the greater part of the ruling class remains adolescent, school-minded, self-conscious, cowardly, sentimental, and in the last analysis, homosexual.[47]

But in his account of his life at Eton, these criticisms are swamped in a flood of nostalgia that makes this section seem, in comparison with earlier sections, uncontrolled and self-indulgent. Earlier, assessing the literary market, Connolly had remarked that there was room for 'planned autobiography (the only kind now worth writing)',[48] and he must have believed that he had written such a book. But if he did, he was wrong; or at least his plan was inadequate to bear the burden of his nostalgia.

In his discussion of the Vernacular, Connolly had chided Isherwood for his 'bland, anonymous' style; but it is Connolly's version of Mandarin prose that reveals the weakness of his book. His writing is constantly self-regarding and self-displaying, even when the ostensible subject is a general one: the style section is really about *his* style, the 'enemies of promise' are *his* enemies, and the autobiographical section, which he had intended to be an illustration of his solution to the problem of style, seems to express what Connlly says love meant for him then: 'a desire to lay my personality at someone's feet as a puppy deposits a slobbery ball'.[49] By then, in 1937–8 Isherwood had achieved a kind of eminence from which he could look back on his early follies with detachment; but Connolly was still caught in his past, still in love with Eton, still despising himself for not having written the book that would last ten years.

Enemies of Promise is an important bad book—bad because it is sentimentally self-regarding, but important because it nevertheless expresses realities of the generation and of the time (for after all, sentimentality may be a reality, too). As an account of the generation's early growth it is conventional, but just: the influence of the First World War, the mood of futility in the 'twenties, the distorting, retarding effect of public-school education are all treated intelligently and with the conviction that personal experience carries. And even at its worst, as in Connolly's gloomy, self-pitying vision of the future as the end of civilization (meaning *his* civilization) and the return of the Dark Ages, it is useful to the student of the time; for Connolly spoke for a privileged class, and his testimony reminds us that for many members of that class, however much they might talk socialism and visit Spain and face crises, the past retained a more vivid life than the present, casting the bright glow of its lost security and joy forward, and making the immediate moment shadowy and dim, not because it was a time of dictators and rumours of war, but because it was not childhood.

Enemies of Promise also reminds us, in passing, how generation-conscious the members of this generation were. Connolly brings forward all his literary contemporaries to testify or to offer cautionary examples: Auden, Isherwood, Day Lewis, MacNeice,

Orwell, Spender, Upward are there. They are present, I think, not simply to demonstrate Connolly's familiarity with the current literary scene, though that is surely a factor, but because he assumes that the problem he is dealing with—how to write a book that will last ten years—has a special meaning for his contemporaries in 1937–8, and that only their testimony can have current relevance and value.

One gets a similar sense of generation in Louis MacNeice's *Modern Poetry*, published in the same month as Connolly's book. MacNeice's intention, he explained in his preface, was to make 'a plea for *impure* poetry, that is, for poetry conditioned by the poet's life and the world around him';[50] but his book is in fact mainly a plea for the impure poetry of his contemporaries, the '*New Signatures* poets', and especially for the poetry of Auden and Spender. The assumption is that the conditioning elements in life and the world have been radically different for this generation, and the differences have compelled a 'change of attitude'. The new poets, MacNeice says, are different in two ways: they are 'emotionally partisan'—they take sides on modern issues, they affirm values, they are capable of tragic and heroic themes; and because of their partisanship they are willing to adapt forms to changing circumstances, and even to simplify reality in order to deal with it. All these are reasonable things to say about the young poets of the 'thirties, but only MacNeice said them all, and his book is the best account of his poetical generation to be written during the decade.

It is also in a way an autobiography. Like Orwell writing about poverty, and like Connolly writing about the literary life, Mac-Neice felt it necessary to base his general argument upon personal testimony. 'I intend,' he announced early in the book,

> ... to submit some literary autobiography, i.e. the history of my own reactions to and demands from poetry, in reading and writing it, over a number of years starting from early childhood. I think that this may throw a sidelight on the evolution of modern poetry in the same way that embryonic physiology throws a sidelight on the evolution of species or child-psychology throws a sidelight on adult activities.[51]

And so he devoted three chapters—roughly a third of the book—to 'My Case-book', an account of his literary evolution from childhood through school and university. What he records here is probably pretty much what other poetical youths of his time and class went through, from an early fondness for sentimental subjects and poetic diction, through a passion for Keats to the discovery of Eliot, on to the child-cult of the Sitwells and the blood-cult of Lawrence, and so out the other end into the mature world and the mature opinions that the book elsewhere expresses.

Like *Lions and Shadows* (and also like parts of *The Road to Wigan Pier* and *Enemies of Promise*), *Modern Poetry* is an 'education in the 'twenties', and an explanation of how the 'thirties generation evolved. MacNeice's account is less self-centred than the others, for though he was a sentimental man, he was also a reticent one, but it is nonetheless an important part of the record. His very sentimentalism is the source of one kind of value that the book has; for he was able to step back from himself and to describe the sentimental bases of his generation's attitudes. He stresses the generation's nostalgia, which was already in their childhoods a part of consciousness (to be post-war was to be nostalgic, almost by definition), and their bookish ignorance of life, and their essential elitism (which is simply class-sentimentality, after all). And he includes himself in the general judgment:

> I went down from Oxford and got married [he writes] while still holding firmly to these two tenets: (i) that what makes a poem a poem is its artificiality; (ii) that poetry is a pursuit for the few, that these few are the pick of humanity, and that when they speak they speak for themselves rather than for others.[52]

To recognize these late-'twenties attitudes is to recognize that in some ways the change in the 'thirties was primarily a rejection of sentimentality—or a shift from old sentimentalities to new ones.

MacNeice's version of his generation is based on a theory of personal psychology, as determined by personal factors (in his own case, for example, by the fact that his father was a clergyman, that his mother had died when he was young, that he had lived in the north of Ireland); he was impatient with theories that attributed individual character to general conditions. Nevertheless, his version is a generalization; he assumes that what was true of himself and of Auden and Spender was also true of other writers of their age, class, and background—and that includes *all* the writers of the 'thirties generation.

Of the poets of his generation, MacNeice was the most isolated, and the least political. He was never involved in movements, and he remained outside the political-literary cohorts of the period (he did not appear in either *New Signatures* or *New Country*). Living in the time that he did, he accepted left politics as necessary, but commitment went against his nature. There is an engagingly frank confession of his political feelings in his travel book, *I Crossed the Minch*, where he carries on a dialogue with his Guardian Angel, a severe, censorious spirit who doubts his political seriousness. MacNeice replies:

> My sympathies are Left. On paper and in the soul. But not in my heart or my guts. On paper—yes. I would vote Left any day, sign manifestoes, answer questionnaires. Ditto, my soul. My soul is all for moving towards the classless society. But unlike Plato, what my soul says does not seem to go. . . . With my heart and my guts I lament the passing of class.[53]

He was, he cheerfully admitted, a snob; but then, so was everyone else. 'All the people I know,' he wrote, 'have been conditioned by snobbery.'[54] The people he knew were mainly his own generation, and this is a generalization about the whole lot; the only difference was that MacNeice accepted his snobbery, and so found it easy to confess it. But his vestigial class feelings, and his political unease must have been shared by many of his contemporaries.

MacNeice published four books in 1938—*Modern Poetry, I Crossed the Minch*, a book on the London Zoo, and *The Earth Compels*, a volume of poems. All are to some degree autobiographical, and all are touched by the same strains—his nostalgia, his melancholy sense of the present, his apprehensiveness about the future. The world that he wanted was a world of ordinary pleasures, suited to the ordinary, sensuous man-in-the-street that he liked to imagine he himself was, and wished all poets would be.

I would have a poet able-bodied [he says in *Modern Poetry*], fond of talking, a reader of the newspapers, capable of pity and laughter, informed in economics, appreciative of women, involved in personal relationships, actively interested in politics, susceptible to physical impressions.[55]

But he did not expect to find that world in the near future; he expected a crisis that would silence the poetry and suspend the pleasures. Until that crisis came he would go on writing poetry, but the poetry that he wrote was autumnal and melancholy. Some of this quality was no doubt the tone of the professional lachrymose Irishman; but it was also the tone of the time, of living in the late 'thirties. That tone is movingly expressed in the last lines of 'On those Islands', MacNeice's farewell to the Hebrides which ends *I Crossed the Minch*:

> On those islands
> Where no train runs on rails and the tyrant time
> Has no clock-towers to signal people to doom
> With semaphore ultimatums tick by tick,
> There is still peace though not for me and not
> Perhaps for long—still peace on the bevel hills
> For those who still can live as their fathers lived
> On those islands.[56]

It is the familiar moral landscape of the 'thirties, in which islands symbolize escape into a simpler world than the real, present one (Iceland represented the same idea in *Letters from Iceland*). But there is no escape for the man who writes the poem, travelling back into his modern world, and no peace for him or for his world. The only possible posture was a melancholy waiting—at which, one must admit, MacNeice was very good.

III

The Munich Crisis of September 1938 was a symbolic event equal in its effect on literary consciousness to Hitler's rise to power in 1933, or the beginning of the Spanish Civil War in 1936. After Munich, writing in England had a different tone: the last calls to political commitment had been sounded, and had failed, and

334

there would be no heroic actions. The waiting for the end could begin in earnest.

This was more than a matter of literary sensibility—the tone of all English life changed during those late September days. While Chamberlain negotiated, England made preparations for war; trenches were dug in the London parks—in Kensington Gardens and Hyde Park, in St James's Park, and in Lincoln's Inn Fields—and passers-by paused to see how it was done, and then went home to dig their own air-raid shelters. Gas-masks were issued to civilians, and the evacuation of children began. Black-out precautions were issued, and air-raid wardens were recruited. The quality of life became essentially that of a nation at war.

A clear example of this change of tone is in the reception given to Day Lewis' new book of poems, *Overtures to Death*, when it appeared in October. Like the earlier collections of his short poems, this one shows the two conflicting sides of the poet's mind: his Georgian, nature-poet sensibility, and his political militancy. But it also contains a third kind of poetry—poems of passive waiting for disaster that one might call his 'post-political poems', such as 'Bombers', 'Newsreel', and the long title poem. The effect of the whole is more sombre, and more private, than the earlier Day Lewis had been; even the political poems seem less strident (the longest poem, 'The Nabara', a narrative account of a Spanish sea-battle, has the retrospective, historical quality that the narrative poems of Newbolt and Chesterton have).

John Lehmann reviewed the book in the *Daily Worker*, and, as one might expect, praised it. But his praise struck a new note. Day Lewis, he said, had withdrawn into himself, but he did not take this to be wrong:

When I say he has withdrawn into himself, I do not mean he has ceased to be interested in the immediate problems of society: far from it. The chief impression which the collection gives is of painful, rigorously honest self-examination, of bitter foreboding of impending disaster for the life around him, of struggles to decide questions of choice and action which experience has shown to be far harder and more complex than first enthusiasm counted.

335

But this mood seems to me the real 'iron' which Day Lewis had not yet achieved in 'From Feathers to Iron', and to create a poetry which is truly adequate for a thinking, civilised being face to face with the terrible future that the convulsions of capitalism are preparing for us.[57]

And he quoted, from 'February, 1936', and 'Bombers', passages which seemed to him 'the grim essence of thoughts and feelings which only came to most people in the "dream-house" for about three days at the end of September'. So the poems express the mood of Munich, and Munich confirms the poems.

Elizabeth Bowen also reviewed the book, and like Lehmann she read it as topical and necessary to the time. 'At any time,' she wrote,

> the appearance of a new collection of poems by Mr. Day Lewis is an event. But coming in this present unhappy autumn, *Overtures to Death* has an importance outside literary experience. Above the too many confused, urgent, uncertain voices we wait to hear the poet lift his note of authority. Stress, tension have tuned us up to listen: it is essential for us that what *is* essential should now be said. Where, under this constant threat to peace, do we stand—in our relation to the outside world, in our relation to ourselves? We hardly even know what questions to put to our own hearts. And at this moment when we must need vision, the everyday man's vision is cruelly blurred. Art keeps its immutable values, but if we are to draw strength from art (and we do need strength) we must have art that speaks in our own terms, that comprehends our entire experience. Mr. Day Lewis's poems seem most great now because of their double relevance—they have a poetic relevance to all time, and are at the same time relevant to our perplexing day.[58]

This sounds surprisingly like *The Times* leader-writer on 'Poets and the Crisis', though its example is a poet whom *The Times* would scarcely be expected to approve. The point is that in this mood, in this 'unhappy autumn', old and young, Right and Left were not essentially different in their notions of the poet's task: for both, art could only play a passive role—comforting, but not directing. No one could demand any longer that the writer 'make action urgent and its nature clear', for action no longer seemed possible. As the *TLS* said, Day Lewis' poems were 'dreadfully apposite at the moment; they are written under the stimulus and fear of death by air-raid'.[59] And what action should a poet urge against that destiny?

Another, different kind of expression of the end-of-the decade mood may be found in the autumn 1938, issue of *New Verse*. 'Commitments: A Double Number,' the cover reads, and inside are pieces by six *New Verse* regulars. 'A Note on this Number' explains that the contributors 'were asked to commit themselves on the relationship, more or less, between those who are not poets and those who are'.[60] What is striking about this note is the way it elaborately avoids mentioning politics; 'the aesthetic attitude is now decidedly out of place', the editor observes, but he takes pains not to say what is *in* place. The contributors were obviously puzzled, though most of them took their assignment to be one more profession of art's social role in a time of crisis.

The first piece in the issue is Auden's 'The Sportsmen: a Parable', an allegory of English poetic history in prose, in which the sportsmen shooting game birds represent poets writing their poems. The argument is essentially the economic view of literary history that Auden had already put into 'Letter to Lord Byron' and the introduction to the *Oxford Book of Light Verse*: poetry begins as an amateur activity, becomes professional, and loses its audience. News comes of another country where the inhabitants have cleared the land and made ducks plentiful, and where sportsmen are rewarded for their bags (i.e. the Soviet Union). Some sportsmen help to clear their own land, but the finest marksman of them all refuses. 'For many years now,' he explains,

> I have been spending all my waking hours in the study of eagles. I do not know if there are any others who share my passion; I do not suppose that there will ever be many who feel as I do about these rare and beautiful birds; but for me, it is my vocation and my life. So I must ask you to excuse me.[61]

The point could scarcely be more explicitly made: the commitment of the true artist is to his art.

Other contributors were less parabolic, and less categorical in their withdrawal from action, though all reflect to some degree a decline of political expectations. Kenneth Allott concluded his essay:

> I do not know much about society because I cannot do much to make or mar any society. I know a little more about poetry because I sometimes write it . . .[62]

And MacNeice wrote in the mood of *Modern Poetry*:

> The poet at the moment will tend to be moralist rather than aesthete. But his morality must be honest; he must not merely retail other people's dogma . . . It is quite possible therefore that at some period his duty as a poet may conflict with his duty as a man. In that case he can stop writing, but he must not degrade his poetry even in the service of a good cause . . .[63]

And even Spender, still at this time more politically-oriented than most of his fellow poets, contributed a disdainfully comical account of a meeting of the Writers' Association for Intellectual Liberty as an example of the kind of mindless bickering into which most meetings of left-wing writers degenerate.[64] The whole issue gives the effect of a defensive drawing-in by the poets, an abandoning of outposts so as to protect the central position, which is the artist's responsibility to his art. It is a considerable remove from the early, expansively political days of *New Verse*—though closer to what Grigson had intended, perhaps.

For the last word on the mood of this year of crises, what better voice than that of the generation's father-figure (or perhaps uncle-figure would be more precise), Forster? In December he reviewed Caudwell's *Studies in a Dying Culture* for the *New Statesman*, and took the occasion to make a personal assessment of communism, and to offer his personal counsel. Communism, he observed, was less sound than fascism, but that was because it was more human; 'it does care about ultimate happiness,' he thought, 'its final aims are thoroughly decent . . .' Yet he drew back from the Party, for moral reasons:

> As for their argument for revolution—the argument that we must do evil now so that good may come in the long run—

it seems to me to have nothing in it. Not because I am too nice to do evil, but because I don't believe the Communists know what leads to what. They say they know because they are becoming conscious of 'the causality of society'. I say they don't know, and my counsel for 1938–9 conduct is rather: Do good, and possibly good may come from it. Be soft even if you stand to get squashed. Beware of the long run. Seek understanding dispassionately, and not in accordance with a theory. Counsels of despair, no doubt. But there is nothing disgraceful in despair. In 1938–9 the more despair a man can take on board without sinking the more completely is he alive.[65]

So in the last year of the 'thirties despair was to be a sign of grace.

X

1939

I

If the decade of the 'thirties was like a tragic play, then Act Five is the year that began in September 1938, with the Munich agreement, and ended a year later—as tragedies must end—with the expected, necessary dying. That last year seems a strange period, as one looks back on it, a sort of war-year *before* the war, when the life of Europe had already become a war-time life, a period of waiting for the end, and of preliminary endings. The Spanish Civil War ended in March 1939, when Madrid surrendered; Czechoslovakia ended in the same month, when German troops occupied the country; Chamberlain's appeasement policy ended when Britain and France pledged their support to Poland (also in March); faith in the Soviet Union ended, for many left-thinking persons, when the Russo–German Pact was signed in August.

In the English literary world it was also a time of endings. Eliot's *Criterion* suspended publication in January 1939; the *London Mercury* published its last issue in April; *New Verse* stopped in May; *Twentieth-Century Verse* and *Fact* followed in June. They were a mixed collection of journals—from right-wing to left, from highbrow to middle, from contemporary poetry to documents—but all of them had played their role in the literary history of the decade, and literary life was diminished by their mass departure. It was as though the time itself recognized that a literary period—the years *entre deux guerres*—was over, and that henceforth the minds of men would be preoccupied with other things.

It was a time of endings, but of no beginnings, a time in which the great issues of the 'thirties, and the journals in which writers had argued those issues, were disappearing into the wings, and the stage emptied for the final scene. In such a time one might expect that the imaginations of writers would turn away from the immediate present, for the present would no longer seem a dramatic moral battlefield, but only a vacant space between the past and the future. They would turn instead backward, toward nostalgia, and forward, toward apocalypse. To do so would not be escapist, but merely preparative: if you examined the past honestly, as a displaced person might examine his belongings before he fled his home, you might find what was worth saving: and if you imagined the future fully and without flinching, you might be able to survive it. The 'thirties had been an unnerving decade, and some preparation was necessary for the worse that was coming; Orwell's George Bowling, in *Coming Up for Air*, explains his journey in search of the past by saying, 'I only wanted to get my nerve back before the bad times begin',[1] and that seems to have been a common need in 1939.

The major writings of this last year of the 'thirties constitute a Literature of Preparation, concerned more with assessment snd understanding than with action. In most ways they belong to the 'thirties: the forms that they use—the symbolic journey, the moral landscape, the documentary, the autobiography, the nightmare-parable—are the forms that developed through the decade, and the principal themes are the familiar ones—the relation of language to action, the interpenetration of public and private worlds, the failures of liberalism, the Truly Weak Man, the coming of war. What is different is the tone, which has become the tone of tragedy, taking for granted the suffering that must be endured, treating human history as the sum of things that are done to men, and accepting despair (as Forster had counselled) as the necessary cargo of a liberal mind in the bad times.

If war was the experience to be prepared for, then one way of preparing was obviously to seek war out, to journey beyond that frightening border and to return with the truth. Auden and Isherwood's *Journey to a War* is Literature of Preparation in this sense: it is *the* war-book of the period just before war became the Second World War. The authors were commissioned in the summer of 1937 to write a travel book, the itinerary to be left to their own discretion. That summer the Sino–Japanese War had been declared, and so they chose China. They made the journey in the first half of 1938, and wrote the book in the autumn (the foreword is dated 'December, 1938').

It is clear from the beginning that the book they put together is not a conventional travel book, or a conventional war book for that matter. Like *Letters from Iceland*, it is a discontinuous collection of parts in different forms: it begins with sonnets (Auden's) written on the ship en route to China, moves into a prose 'Travel-Diary' (Isherwood's) of the Chinese travels, then a group of photographs (Auden's), and ends with 'In Time of War', a sonnet sequence with a verse commentary (also Auden's). As a piece of reportage on a country at war this miscellany is limited and unsatisfactory; but it is hard to see how the two authors could have done much better. Neither spoke any Chinese, and they spent their time either with Europeans, or with English-speaking officials and interpreters, who were either comic ('Ha, ha, ha! Japan velly foolish') or entirely inscrutable. Though they travelled about, conscientiously looking for the war, they did not find it; their two trips to the 'front' were farcically unsuccessful, and they found no battles to describe.

Compared to war-reporting of the Spanish war (and of course the comparison would be made, and especially by critics of the Left), *Journey to a War* is superficial and uninformative. 'Many people will, I think, be annoyed by this book,' Randall Swingler wrote in the *Daily Worker*:

> There are only two good reasons for journeying to a country wracked with war: to find out what is really happening and to report it, or to participate. Here are one or two brilliant little pictures as of their first experience of a Japanese air-raid and an occasional good dramatic line of verse. But on the whole the authors are too preoccupied with their own psychological plight to be anything but helplessly lost in the struggle of modern China. [2]

That is clearly a judgment based on the experience of Spain; like a professional general, Swingler was prepared to fight the *last* war, not the next one. But Auden and Isherwood recognized that the war in China was different—that in its scale, its confusion, its huge destruction of cities and people, it was the war that was coming. And so the two young men travelled half-way round the world, not to report a war, and certainly not to participate in it, but to testify how they felt in the presence of war, and what meaning the experience had for them. They came to it as members of their generation, with the habits, the expectations, and the prejudices of their generation, and so the book is in a way about their own pasts; and they saw the war in China as the world war that would reach Europe soon, so the book is also about the future. But it is about the present, too and the present, to them in the late 'thirties, was a mélange of confused, uprooted, fragmentary experiences, as the book is.

Some reviewers—notably Evelyn Waugh—objected that the book was really two books, stuck together like the front and hind legs of a pantomime horse.[3] But the link between the two parts, the prose and the poetry, is in fact clear enough. There was a local, particular war being fought in China, which could only be experienced and described by travelling to it. This was Isherwood's function, to write the essentially documentary part of the book—a document both of the journey, with its confusions and disappointments, and of the two young men who made it. Isherwood was the best documentary writer of the 'thirties, and his Travel-Diary is a skilful example of the genre. Everything in it is rendered in terms of acutely observed detail: Auden dining with a general, a mayor giggling through an interview, peasants clinging to a train-roof, an old woman killed in an air-raid, a dog gnawing on a human arm, all are recorded with what seems photographic accuracy—photographic, that is, until one looks again and notices the images and metaphors that shape the feeling. Here, for example, is Isherwood's account of the first night air-raid that they experienced:

> The searchlights criss-crossed, plotting points, like dividers; and suddenly there they were, six of them, flying close together and high up. It was as if a microscope had brought dramatically into focus the bacilli of a fatal disease. They passed, bright, tiny, and deadly, infecting the night.[4]

The incident is dramatic, but it is also distanced by its imagery. The lights are geometric, mathematical, abstract; and the planes

343

are not the vehicles of a number of human beings, each engaged in a voluntary evil act, but *bacilli*, the neutral and natural carriers of sickness. War is impersonal as an infection—a disease that the whole world will contract, and suffer from, before the epidemic is over, an enormous, relentless destruction. Watching the raid, Isherwood thinks, 'It was as tremendous as Beethoven'.

This point of view is as meticulously maintained as it would be if the book were a modern, Jamesian novel. The observer is young, English, intelligent, and ignorant; even his superficialities are part of the characterization, part of the document. What he tells the reader is what such a character might have learned, in a few months in China, not speaking the language but looking with a camera eye: that war is sometimes hard to find, and always difficult to understand, that it is a mixture of tragedy and comedy, of great suffering and triviality, that it will not submit easily to the ordering pressure of art. But he tells us this entirely through the rendered first impressions of his two created characters.

Isherwood's document offers one war, or one version of it. The other is the universal war that all men were already involved in, the war between good and evil that is always being fought, more or less dramatically, in human hearts. That war was Auden's subject: his role in the book was to render the human meaning of what he had seen in the broadest, most general terms. He called that rendering 'In Time of War', and by leaving *war* unmodified, even by an article, he made his intention plain: his poem would be a parable of the nature and meaning of war, a theory and a morality rather than a history.

The twenty-seven sonnets in the sequence divide into three parts in a way that resembles the structure of Auden's 'Spain'. The first thirteen sonnets compose a parable-history of mankind, from the Creation and the exclusion from the Garden, through the phases of differentiation of social function, into actual history —the establishment and failure of the Church, the end of the Age of Faith, and the beginning of the Age of Economic Man. The similarity to the corresponding section of 'Spain' is considerable, but there are also important differences: Christian concepts appear, treated rather eccentrically, but without irony—the Garden, the Fall, the Incarnation are all there; and mankind, dealt with collectively in 'Spain' as the instrument of historical change, is here treated individually, as 'he', the human creature who has fallen into freedom, and must live by choice, necessarily. You couldn't call it a Christian poem, exactly, but you could say that its argument is consistent with Christian faith, and is not consistent with Marxism.

The key to the sequence is in the two sonnets that fall at the centre—the thirteenth and fourteenth. The thirteenth is a finale to the first movement, the parable of man's history to this moment. 'Certainly praise,' it begins,

>   let the song mount again and again
> For life as it blossoms out in a jar or a face,
> For the vegetable patience, the animal grace;
> Some people have been happy; there have been
>   great men.

But—the qualification comes:

> But hear the mourning's injured weeping, and know
>   why:
> Cities and men have fallen; the will of the Unjust
> Has never lost its power; still, all princes must
> Employ the Fairly-Noble unifying Lie.
>
> History opposes its grief to our buoyant song:
> The Good Place has not been; our star has warmed to
>   birth
> A race of promise that has never proved its worth;
>
> The quick new West is false; and prodigious, but wrong
> This passive flower-like people who for so long
> In the Eighteen Provinces have constructed the earth.[5]

There are two things to be said about this sonnet: first, that it is not an appeal to action, but to understanding and compassion; and second, that it says nothing specific about the war in China, or about any war. The moral condition of man that it describes underlies all aggressions of men against men, not any one in particular.

345

In the following sonnet the account of the present moment begins, with a significant line:

> Yes, we are going to suffer now . . .

Compare the refrain of 'Spain'—'Today the struggle'. The difference between struggle and suffering is the difference between the two poems, and between 1937 and 1939. When 'Spain' was written, the time was short, but there *was* time in which, it seemed, history might be changed by action. But 'In Time of War' makes no such proposition: *we*, all of us, are going to suffer *now*. Sonnet XIV uses images of a night raid, perhaps the same one that Isherwood described, but it uses them, not to describe an external enemy, but to draw an analogy between what the searchlights reveal and the evil that is in all men—the private hatred of which war is a metaphor and an enactment.

The six sonnets that follow are about Auden's experience of the war in China, but only in the sense that XIV is about an air-raid: that is, the war to which he had journeyed provided him with materials for a parable of the moral condition of man at this moment in his history. So the Japanese fliers in the raiding planes are examples of men who 'turn away from freedom'; the wounded Chinese are the human sufferings which we, the uninjured, cannot share; the dead soldier is any anonymous man who teaches us the Good by dying for it. And the war itself becomes parabolic, the acting out of the evil that has covered the earth:

> And maps can really point to places
> Where life is evil now:
> Nanking; Dachau.[6]

This is the present to which the history recorded in the earlier sonnets has brought us; we are going to suffer now, and in terms of suffering Nanking and Dachau are the same place.

Like 'Spain', 'In Time of War' turns in its final movement to questions of the moral values by which the future may be redeemed. The last seven sonnets address themselves to the examples of the defeated, the simple, 'all who seemed deserted'—all those, that is, whose lives deny the reigning values of war, violence, and power. The moral of those lives is not very complicated: man is free and fallible, 'Nothing is given: we must find our law', and the foundation of that law must be love. Our efforts will be imperfect, because men are imperfect; but we must go on trying. The sequence ends:

> We envy streams and houses that are sure:
> But we are articled to error; we
> Were never nude and calm like a great door,
>
> And never will be perfect like the fountains;
> We live in freedom by necessity,
> A mountain people dwelling among mountains.[7]

We are left with error, freedom, and imperfection. Nothing is said about action, or ephemeral pamphlets and necessary murders, and there are no imperatives, no tense warnings that time is short; compared to 'Spain', the ending is calm, resigned, even affirmative. What it affirms is the persistence of love, and the power of ordinary humanity to survive its leaders and destroyers.

The verse commentary that follows the sonnet sequence comments not so much on the sonnets as on the issue that the entire book treats—the moral meaning of war. The same points are made again, though in a somewhat more rhetorical, declamatory style: war is a necessary consequence of history; the enemy is an example of an eternal evil; good exists in ordinary persons: we are all involved in the general war, of which the struggle in China is only a local variant. It differs from the sonnets in one striking way, though—it ends with the voice of Man, *praying*:

> O teach me to outgrow my madness . . .
>
> Ruffle the perfect manners of the frozen heart,
> And once again compel it to be awkward and alive,
> To all it suffered once a weeping witness.
>
> Clear from the head the masses of impressive rubbish;
> Rally the lost and trembling forces of the will,
> Gather them up and let them loose upon the earth,
>
> Till they construct at last a human justice,
> The contribution of our star, within the shadow

> Of which uplifting, loving, and constraining power
> All other reasons may rejoice and operate.[8]

It is a religious response to the coming apocalypse, and in terms of man's life on this earth a tragic one: the 'general war' is eternal, suffering will not cease, evil continues its power; but human reason may yet rejoice. It sounds more like Yeats than like any of Auden's contemporaries.

'In Time of War' was criticized from the Left (the *Daily Worker*) and from the Right (Waugh), but other, more moderate critics received it with high praise, and a kind of relief, as though they were glad that at last the generation's first poet had said what was true but unspoken. Julian Symons called the sonnets Auden's best poems, and praised his tragic view of life; Spender agreed; Stonier in the *New Statesman* called the sonnets 'a remarkable achievement, a statement of faith comparable in dignity (such statements are rare to-day) with *In Memoriam*'. The comparison must have surprised Auden, who thought Tennyson the stupidest of English poets,[9] but it is a just one—the end of 'In Time of War' sounds a good deal like the end of *In Memoriam*.

The most acute and moving appreciation of 'In Time of War' came from Grigson. Grigson had read the sonnets, he said, after hearing Chamberlain's speech on the German occupation of Prague:

> ... it was a pure example of political mediocrity, at a time when even a Chamberlain might have *felt* human history, even if he had mixed his feelings with economic self-interest ... Then reading these sonnets, I did feel life instead of death.[10]

That is the right conjunction—the war in China, the death of Czechoslovakia, the imaginative failure of the leader of a democracy, and Auden's poem as a commentary on all of these, and an affirmation of humanity in spite of these defeats. Grigson grasped the general historical meaning of the sequence because he knew how Auden's mind worked, knew that he was thinking and feeling not about one particular war, but about human history. And he knew Auden's mind so well partly because Auden and *New Verse* had grown up together.

New Verse [he wrote] came into existence because of Auden. It has published more poems by Auden than by anyone else; and there are many people who might quote of Auden: '*To you I owe the first development of my imagination; to you I owe the withdrawing of my mind from the low brutal part of my nature, to the lofty, the pure and the perpetual.*' Auden is now clear, absolutely clear of foolish journalists, Cambridge detractors, and envious creepers and crawlers of party and Catholic reaction and the new crop of loony and eccentric small magazines in England and America. He is something good and creative in European life in a time of the very greatest evil.[11]

Grigson's praise of Auden has an elegiac tone that seems at first odd in a review of a poet still in his youthful prime. But the review was published in the last issue of *New Verse*, and Grigson was bidding farewell to his journal as well as to his greatest contributor, and to the decade in which they had functioned together. In 1939, the time of endings, *New Verse* had come to an end, and so had the English career of its star. In January, Auden and Isherwood had made another journey, out of England to self-imposed exile in America. To Grigson, who remained, it seemed that good and creative things were departing from European life, and leaving behind only the time's great evil.

Auden and Isherwood arrived in New York on 26 January 1939. That same day Barcelona fell, and with its fall the last hope of the Spanish Loyalists ended. Two days later there was another kind of ending—the death of Yeats. Auden must have begun at once to write his great elegy, 'In Memory of W. B. Yeats', in which he made these three endings merge into one vast human defeat: the old poet dead, the young poet in retreat from his lost causes, the city conquered seen as a single historical occasion, the end of the 'thirties.

The history of the composition of Auden's elegy is of some interest, as it relates to the history of the generation. Auden had a first draft of the poem written by the end of February, and published in the *New Republic* on 8 March. This version includes only two of the three parts of the poem—the first section, in which the death of the poet is compared to the death of a city, and the third, the moving, dirge-like address to poets in a time of defeat. It is a fine poem as it stands, but in the month that followed Auden added a new section, the central passage that begins 'You were silly like us: your gift survived it all', and it was this fuller version that appeared in England in April—appropriately enough, in the final issue of the *London Mercury*.

What had happened in that brief interval that led Auden to alter the poem, thrusting into the middle of it the section that so transforms it? The answer, I think, is that he had spent the time thinking about that obsessive theme of the 'thirties, the relation between poetry and action, and writing an essay on the subject— the essay that he entitled 'The Public vs. the Late Mr. William Butler Yeats'. The argument takes the form of a mock trial, with the Public Prosecutor speaking for the 'thirties idea of poetry-as-action (and sounding rather like Day Lewis), and the Counsel for the Defence taking the opposite position, and speaking in the voice of Auden. The defence gets the best lines, and the last speech, which ends: 'Just men will always recognize the author as a master.' The whole essay is a public gesture of a change of heart; Auden had abandoned the conviction that poetry could be an agent in history, and had accepted what he offers as Yeats' view— the vision of tragedy.

One speech in the trial has particular relevance to Auden's elegy. The Defence Counsel says:

> Art is a product of history, not a cause. Unlike some other products, technical inventions for example, it does not re-enter history as an effective agent, so that the question whether art should or should not be propaganda is unreal. The case for the prosecution rests on the fallacious belief that art ever makes anything happen, whereas the honest truth, gentlemen, is that, if not a poem had been written, not a picture painted, not a bar of music composed, the history of man would be materially unchanged.[12]

This is the argument of the added section of the poem. If it is true, then the left-wing poets of the decade were wrong, and their decade-long efforts to alter history were wasted. In this change of heart, by the generation's greatest poet, we might say that the 'thirties really ended. And only when Auden could say it in verse could he complete the decade's elegy. What he says in the added section of the poem is 'Poetry makes nothing happen', a statement that repeats the argument of the essay. But in the poem the line continues—'Poetry makes nothing happen: it survives/In the valley of its saying . . .' To his rejection of an old faith Auden has added a new, minimal affirmation; but it is a significant one, for in the bad times survival is a basic value, and poetry survives.

'In Memory of W. B. Yeats' is an historical poem, a point that Auden asserted by dating it, 'd. Jan. 1939'. Its subject is the relation between art and history (which is another way of putting the poetry-action theme, or the public-private one): what shall we do, those of us who are poets, as the dark night of Europe descends? Auden deals with this question specifically in the last section of the poem, where he brings together the makers of poetry and the world's disastrous happenings. It is the actual history of 1939 that presses in here:

> In the nightmare of the dark
> All the dogs of Europe bark,
> And the living nations wait,
> Each sequestered in its hate . . .

But poetry survives, to perform a role in this apocalyptic time that Yeats had understood, and that Auden expresses in very Yeatsian terms:

> Follow, poet, follow right
> To the bottom of the night,
> With your unconstraining voice
> Still persuade us to rejoice . . .

Rejoice is, of course, a Yeatsian word, and the theme, as it is stated here, is the theme of much of Yeats' tragic verse—that by rejoicing man creates something to rejoice about, that by affirming life in the face of the evidence man is testifying to human greatness. (It is a word that appears also in the last line of 'In Time of War', to make the same point.)

In one way this part of Auden's poem seems un-Yeatsian, though; Yeats tended to enter his public poems at the end, like a magus, to bless, forgive, and affirm. But Auden's appearance in the last section is confined to a single first-person-plural pronoun—

'Still persuade *us* to rejoice'. This is a characteristic Auden reticence, the self withheld from the poem, and identified only fleetingly, at a key moment. Here, the pronoun falls in the line with *rejoice*, so that the Yeatsian term encompasses the speaker and the class to which he belongs (but what is that class? poets? artists? or all feeling men confronting the apocalypse ahead?). But the pronoun does more than identify a speaker: it makes the last part of the poem a noble speech, the poet-as-poet addressing first the Earth, in which Yeats has been buried, and then 'poet', who is all the poets who must face the task of writing in a tragic time. It makes the ending of the poem an appeal and a testament.

In the course of that testament, Auden introduces an argument about language which has an important place in the poem, as it had in the critical debates of the decade. The argument had been a part of the Defence case in 'The Public vs. the Late Mr. William Butler Yeats', where it appeared in this form:

> But there is one field in which the poet is a man of action, the field of language, and it is precisely in this that the greatness of the deceased is most obviously shown. However false or undemocratic his ideas, his diction shows a continuous evolution towards what one might call the true democratic style. The social virtues of a real democracy are brotherhood and intelligence, and the parallel linguistic virtues are strength and clarity, virtues which appear even through successive volumes by the deceased.[13]

One can see why Auden wrote this: it is a rather desperate attempt to give political justification to his withdrawal from political action, and to justify aesthetic values by giving them political names. But in the poem he doesn't quite say that. What he does say is this:

> Time that is intolerant
> Of the brave and innocent,
> And indifferent in a week
> To a beautiful physique,
>
> Worships language and forgives
> Everyone by whom it lives;
> Pardons cowardice, conceit,
> Lays its honours at their feet.

> Time that with this strange excuse
> Pardoned Kipling and his views,
> And will pardon Paul Claudel,
> Pardons him for writing well.

The 'him' in the last line is Yeats: here are three reactionary poets, pardoned by Time. But why? The answer is Auden's answer to the central critical question of the 'thirties: what relation can there be between art and life, or art and history, in a time of political crisis? And it is all in that last line: 'Pardon him for writing well'. This does not mean, I take it, that art is a value in itself, but rather that to write well *in such a time* is to preserve the human imagination, and thus to defend a human value against the forces of inhumanity. It seems a confession of political powerlessness, and certainly it rejects the idea of poetry as a mode of action even more explicitly than 'In Time of War' did. It proposes instead poetry as a mode of survival, and this, too, is a political proposition of a kind. For, as Orwell observed, bad politics debases language, and misused language coarsens political thought. So that in a way Yeats and Kipling and Claudel were on the right side in spite of themselves.

Political poetry, Spender said, was that poetry which is 'concerned with the individual faced by an unprecedented crisis in the history of civilization . . .'14 Yeats was the modern master of that kind of poem, and Auden's elegy on his death is a great poem in the same tradition. Like other poems of this kind, it does not prescribe political ideas or actions; but it helps us to live in political history. Moving between private loss and public crisis, it brings the tragic past and the apocalyptic future together, and draws strength from that interaction; it is at once history and elegy, a work of art and a defence of art. Auden's poem makes nothing happen—what *could* be made to happen in that season of tragic endings?—but it does what is possible in art: it transforms calamity into celebration by an act of imagination, and so affirms the survival of art in a bad time. And if art survives, man survives too.

In the same month in which Auden's elegy appeared, Isherwood published a book that is also an elegy of a kind—*Goodbye to Berlin*. It is a book about the first years of the 'thirties that was

353

written in bits through the decade and published in the last year; so in a way it encompasses and expresses the whole period. Even in its form it seems expressive of the time: Isherwood had intended a vast novel of German life at the end of the Weimar years, to be called *The Lost*, but at the decade's end he had written only *Mr. Norris Changes Trains* and the 'short loosely-connected sequence of diaries and sketches'[15] that make up *Goodbye to Berlin*. He must have put these pieces together in the period between his return from China and his departure with Auden for America (the introductory note is dated September 1938); he was packing a book as a refugee might pack a suitcase, with all the bits of the past that he had managed to salvage. So the appearance of *Goodbye to Berlin* in 1939 records another kind of an ending—the ending of Isherwood's large ambition.

Like *Trial of a Judge*, Isherwood's book looks back to the years in Germany before the Nazis came to power. Those were the years when the young English writers—Isherwood, Auden, Spender, Lehmann—were in Berlin, but their returning to the period as a subject was more than an accident of personal experience; they sought there the history lesson that might explain how a civilized democracy with a liberal tradition could choose fascism. For a liberal, Germany's apparently voluntary reversion to authoritarianism must have seemed, as it still seems, the most terrible and threatening event of modern history, and the one that most demands an answer. The answer would have to be sought in the history of the Weimar period; or so it must have seemed to young liberals, looking back from the end of the 'thirties to the decade's beginnings.

Goodbye to Berlin is not, like Spender's play, about the failure of liberal leadership, but about the failure of feeling in an impoverished, demoralized, bankrupt city. There are no public figures in the book, and no great events: Hitler never appears, and the political struggles of the time are virtually ignored. There are only the Lost—the poor, the weak, the neurotic, the lonely and unloved, living their sad private lives. Together they compose the city in which fascism was possible.

It is the reality of that city that is Isherwood's essential subject. Like Eliot in *The Waste Land*, he made an image of his city out of

354

fragments of the lives of its inhabitants—a cabaret singer, a whore, a working-class hustler, a bartender, a Jewish merchant. The Berlin that their lives express is, like Eliot's London, a waste land of human isolation, of soiled love, of urban deadness and despair, and of inaction. It is a city in which no one acts, and no one feels, a frozen and lifeless place, like the bottom of Dante's hell. But it is also a city in history; it belongs to the 'thirties, as Eliot's city belongs to the 'twenties. And what makes it 'thirty-ish is that it can define its hell in political terms.

Though it is made of fragments, *Goodbye to Berlin* has a firm structure, which depends mainly on two factors. One is the symmetrical balancing of opposites—rich/poor, Jew/gentile, fascist/communist, German/alien, homosexual/heterosexual, all the polarities that separate and isolate human beings from one another. The opening diary section balances the closing one; 'Sally Bowles' is the opposite, in sexual terms, of 'On Ruegen Island'; the poverty in 'The Nowaks' contrasts with the wealth in 'The Landauers'. Among these separated groups there are no real contacts: human relationships falter and fail, love is sold, friendship is lost or betrayed. The book may in fact be *too* symmetrical, but it makes its point—that Berlin is a city without human connections.

The other structuring principle is the first-person narrator. He is called Christopher Isherwood, as though to encourage the reader to take the book as documentary, and the dispassionate objectivity with which he records his observations seems in the strict documentary style—seems indeed exactly the sort of writing that Storm Jameson wanted documentaries to be:

> As the photographer does, so must the writer keep himself out of the picture while working ceaselessly to present the *fact* from a striking (poignant, ironic, penetrating, significant) angle.[16]

But if you compare that statement with the narrator's remark on the first page of Isherwood's book, you see that in fact he would take the process one step farther:

> I am a camera with its shutter open, quite passive, recording, not thinking. Recording the man shaving at the window opposite and the woman in the kimono washing her hair. Some day, all this will have to be developed, carefully printed, fixed.[17]

This narrator is to be, not the photographer, whose consciousness selects and focusses, but the camera, the photographic mechanism itself. And thus the method becomes a metaphor. The vision of the camera eye is a symbol of isolation, and that is what the book is about.

On the surface, then, *Goodbye to Berlin* is documentary, but beneath that surface it is a personal testament; like Eliot, Isherwood recorded himself in recording his city. The first section, for example, 'A Berlin Diary (Autumn 1930)', begins like this:

> From my window, the deep solemn massive street. Cellar-shops where the lamps burn all day, under the shadow of top-heavy balconied façades, dirty plaster frontages embossed with scroll-work and heraldic devices. The whole district is like this: street leading into street of houses like shabby monumental safes crammed with the tarnished valuable and second-hand furniture of a bankrupt middle class.[18]

This is very much the camera eye at work, the city streets recorded in nouns, simply as *things*. But there is also an attitude and a judgment expressed—in the darkness and shabbiness, and in the final phrase; 'bankrupt middle class' is essentially a political judgment, but it suggests a further, more metaphorical meaning, a bankruptcy of values beyond the financial ones.

In the paragraph that follows, Isherwood establishes the camera metaphor quoted above. Then this passage ends the fragment:

> At eight o'clock in the evening the house-doors will be locked. The children are having supper. The shops are shut. The electric-sign is switched on over the night-bell of the little hotel on the corner, where you can hire a room by the hour. And soon the whistling will begin. Young men are calling their girls. Standing down there in the cold, they whistle up at the lighted windows of warm rooms where the beds are already turned down for the night. They want to be let in. Their signals echo down the deep hollow street, lascivious and private and sad. Because of the whistling, I do not care to stay here in the evenings. It reminds me that I am in a foreign city, alone, far from home. Sometimes I determine not to listen to it, pick up a book,

try to read. But soon a call is sure to sound, so piercing, so insistent, so despairingly human, that at last I have to get up and peep through the slats of the venetian blind to make quite sure that it is not—as I know very well it could not possibly be—for me.[19]

That is Isherwood's essential Berlin, a city of lonely people closed off from one another, of squalor, poverty, and despair, a city that is like the whistles of the young men—lascivious and private and sad. But it is also Isherwood's essential Isherwood, the lonely, passive voyeur who desires love, but knows that it could not possibly be for him. So that you might say that the representative Berliner in the book is the narrator, an isolated foreigner without real human contacts.

This is not a political fact, but it is a moral condition out of which political consequences may come. For among these passive, dispirited people there is one powerful source of energy—Nazism. In the stories, the Nazis are never in the foreground for long, but their hovering presence is always felt; fascism is as much a part of the tone of Berlin as the poverty and the perversions are. The camera eye records their behaviour dispassionately:

One night in October 1930, about a month after the Elections, there was a big row on the Leipzigerstrasse. Gangs of Nazi roughs turned out to demonstrate against the Jews. They manhandled sone dark-haired, large-nosed pedestrians, and smashed the windows of all the Jewish shops. The incident was not, in itself, very remarkable; there were no deaths, very little shooting, not more than a couple of dozen arrests. I remember it only because it was my first introduction to Berlin politics.[20]

Two points are made here: first, that Nazism is the source of such action as occurs in Berlin; and second, that the cold passivity of the camera eye is an inadequate response to their violence. Isherwood-the-author has drawn back from his camera-eye narrator, and is viewing his detachment with ironic disapproval.

The final section of the book is, like the first, a diary; it is dated 'Winter 1932-3', and covers the period during which Hitler became Chancellor and the Nazis became the rulers of Germany.

This diary is different from the earlier one, and the cause of the change is the same force that has changed Germany—the Nazis. This is most obvious in the closing pages, where Isherwood, having decided to leave the country, records his last impressions of Berlin:

> Today the sun is brilliantly shining; it is quite mild and warm. I go out for my last morning walk, without an overcoat or hat. The sun shines, and Hitler is master of this city. The sun shines, and dozens of my friends—my pupils at the Workers' School, the men and women I met at the I.A.H.—are in prison, possibly dead . . .
>
> I catch sight of my face in the mirror of a shop, and am horrified to see that I am smiling. You can't help smiling, in such beautiful weather. The trams are going up and down the Kleiststrasse, just as usual. They, and the people on the pavement, and the tea-cosy dome of the Nollendorfplatz station have an air of curious familiarity, of striking resemblance to something one remembers as normal and pleasant in the past—like a very good photograph.
>
> No. Even now I can't altogether believe that any of this has really happened. . . .[21]

The reference to a good photograph is there to remind us of the camera eye, and the narrator's initial assumption that he could record reality without engaging himself in it. But that is no longer possible in Berlin in 1933, when Hitler is master of the city; the reality is beyond replication, beyond belief. If the camera is the instrument of documentary, then one must conclude that in a world that contains fascism documentation is not enough. What the camera eye can document is the apparent city, smiling in the sun; but it cannot record possible death, or terror, or the reality of evil.

When *Goodbye to Berlin* appeared in 1939 it must have seemed almost an historical novel—a record of a time and a mood long past; 'the note of nostalgia', John Lehmann wrote, 'continually creeps in'.[22] *Nostalgia* seems at first glance an odd term to apply to the story of Berlin during the rise of the Nazis, but it is the correct term. For Isherwood's subject is a city that is dying of social sickness—of poverty, isolation, and despair—and is, at the end of the book, 'cold and cruel and dead'.[23] That dying city had engaged his imagination deeply—he never wrote so well about any other subject—and his book is a kind of elegy, a pained backward look at a city that had been a home of sorts for a shy, inverted young man, and to which he could not return, because it was dead.

That is to read the book as a private statement, which it is. But it is also a book about public issues; it is rather as though Isherwood had written the first act of a tragedy, but had written it very slowly, while the later acts were unfolding, and had published it only when Act Five was approaching its catastrophe. Perhaps it was only then, when the whole play had been acted out, that the first act could be seen as complete; like the dividing of Lear's kingdom, it took its meaning from its consequences.

Goodbye to Berlin is not a didactic book, but nevertheless it does contain a lesson in history. It tells us that poverty kills feelings, and isolates one man from another like freezing weather; that love and hate are political terms, and that hate feeds on human separateness; that violence is the energy of frozen hearts; that passivity and detachment are cold virtues. It is not a lesson that is taught abstractly; nobody makes political speeches in the book, and author and narrator are scrupulously reticent. Rather it is a lesson that is felt in the emotions, like a bad dream. 'Youth always demands its nightmares . . .' Isherwood wrote in 1939. 'Germany supplied them.'[24]

II

The withdrawal of Auden and Isherwood from the English literary scene is one sign of the breaking up of the 'thirties as a literary period. One may find other signs in the problems and pronouncements of those who stayed. Of these, Spender offers perhaps the best example, for throughout the 'thirties he had always seemed to represent an instance of his generation's general case. Spender was emotional, enthusiastic, naive, and quick to commit himself, but he was also intelligent and honest. He felt early in the decade the urgency of political circumstances, and he responded vigorously; but he also felt a deep and steady commitment to his vocation as a poet. Because he was naive, he believed, longer than most, that he could reconcile these two loyalties, not only to his own

satisfaction, but to the satisfaction of other poets and other Marxists, and so he was continually criticized, by literary men for being
too political, and by political men for being too literary.

Spender's 1939 began, characteristically, with yet another
attack on his good faith—this time in a letter to *New Verse* protest-
ing against his 'Left-Wing Orthodoxy' essay:

> It is a notable fact [wrote Yvonne Cloud]—giving rise to anger
> in some quarters and to jest in others—that whenever Mr.
> Spender finds himself in agreement with someone, it is—albeit
> reluctantly—with some near-Fascist spokesman; and whenever
> he finds himself obliged to criticize and condemn, it is—albeit
> regretfully—invariably some Left-wing work or writer.
>
> Since Mr. Spender feels, as he too obviously does, so uncom-
> fortable in the Left movement that he can only tolerate his false
> position at the price of doing incalculable petty damage to the
> cause he has espoused without even liking or understanding it,
> he would be well advised to limit his political pronouncements
> until he has ceased to confuse his personal with the class
> struggle.[25]

This is a fair account of Spender's troubles as a public figure. He
had always found orthodoxy difficult, and he had always tended
to take great issues personally, as though every public event were
a potential lyric poem. And yet one side of his nature desired the
sure solutions of orthodoxy—hence the personal struggle that got
confused with the class struggle.

There are evidences of this struggle in virtually everything that
Spender wrote in this last year of peace. For example, in the late
autumn of 1938 he twice reviewed a memorial volume of John
Cornford's writings, and expressed one side of his struggle in one
review and the other side in the other. In *Now and Then* he wrote:

> This book inspires me and fills me with shame. It is a collection
> of accounts of a disinterested life led with honesty, single-
> mindedness and great intelligence, in the cause of Socialism . . .
> He may seem to have abandoned the poet's problems, for what
> was to him the central problem, that of defeating fascism by the
> directest possible means. But the challenge he leaves poets, in

face of which it is impossible not to feel inadequate and ashamed, is to live his view of life through our poetry as seriously as he lived and died for freedom.

At about the same time he wrote in the *New Statesman*:

One may feel, as I do, that the pattern of this young hero is over-simplified; his vision of life is impatient and violent, it leaves too many questions unanswered, he burns out too quickly, rushing headlong to his death; but nevertheless it is a pattern which in other lives may take on a greater richness without losing Cornford's power and determination.[26]

In the first quotation, Spender was feeling the complex man's envy of the life and death of simple commitment; but in the second he was thinking as a poet, of the consequences for poetry of such a commitment. Even in his most militant political days Spender had not managed to still that second voice for long; in the last months of the decade it grew stronger, as the hopes of the Left grew weaker, and spoke with a sombre authority.

One name for that authority is the tragic sense. Spender had come to feel, as others had, that the good causes had suffered too many defeats, that it was now too late for any opposition except the disastrous opposition of war. That feeling is very clear in the introduction that he wrote for *Poems for Spain*, an anthology of poems of the Spanish Civil War that was published in March 1939. That was the month in which the Loyalists surrendered at Madrid, and though Spender's essay was written earlier, it is in the mood of that ending.

At Guernica, at Irun, wherever the Republic has sustained defeat, its cause represents pure tragedy, because these defeats are the real and entire destruction of a life and a principle by the death-bearing force that opposes them. In the rest of Europe one sees principles confused, betrayed, compromised: but in Spain the idea clothed in flesh and blood is continually being destroyed, and therefore as continually and as surely reborn in the mind of a world which remains a spectator.[27]

As so often in Spender's writing, this is a public statement about a political issue that is also a private confession of feeling. What

Spender is recording here is the end of the Spanish struggle as an issue in history: it had been a cause that action might win; now, being tragic, it can only be a meaning to be understood.

In the face of such defeats, Spender drew back from political commitment, as Auden had done, to a defensive position from which poetry, at least, might be defended. *The New Realism*, a pamphlet published in May 1939, is his definition of that position. The point of view of the pamphlet is ostensibly socialist and revolutionary, but the principal arguments are not ones that Spender's Marxist acquaintances would have found agreeable, for they amount to a theory of disengagement from the world of action. 'The duty of the artist,' Spender writes in his opening paragraph, 'is to remain true to standards which he can discover only within himself.'[28] In his art he will seek to analyze modern life, and if he is a true realist, and an artist, that analysis will be revolutionary, because it will reveal the sickness of society. But the artist himself may be a reactionary (Spender takes admiring note of Rilke, Yeats, Eliot, and Lawrence). 'What is important is the analysis, and not the *means* of achieving the change, which is not the primary concern of art.'[29]

The analysis need not, then, be socialist. It *cannot* be proletarian, for there are no proletarian writers, and will be none until there is a working-class audience and a working-class tradition. In the meantime, bourgeois writers will have to go on analyzing what they know—that is, their own bourgeois world. On this point Spender attacks Caudwell, who had written in *Illusion and Reality* that the writer's only hope was to join the communist movement and identify himself with the interests of the working class. Spender rejects this notion entirely, and in so doing rejects the entire left-wing political commitment of his generation, including his own; the passage reads like a farewell to the hopes and illusions of the mid-decade, the years when action seemed possible:

Writers who have attempted to throw off their bourgeois environment to enter a revolutionary one, have only succeeded in uprooting themselves, in getting killed, or in ceasing to be writers and becoming politicians. Ashamed of the environment to which they are accustomed, they have not been able to acquire a convincing knowledge of any other. This is particularly true of those who have not been able to take the final plunge, but have merely immersed themselves in every kind of committee meeting and agitation. They have sacrificed a life of which they did after all know something, and entered a whirlwind where nothing is tangible.[30]

Caudwell appears again a few pages later, as the antagonist in another, related argument. In *Studies in a Dying Culture* he had called writers like Shaw and Wells pathetic because, though they were disillusioned with bourgeois culture, they were unable to wish for something better. Spender responds with a defence of such divided men:

> The fundamental weakness of Caudwell's position is in assuming that the writer who is in a divided position is not in a position to portray historic truth. Surely, the fact that he derides, the 'illusionment' that makes these writers 'pathetic', is precisely that thing in their historic situation which makes them interesting and valuable. The divisions between their interests is a fact, and one of the most significant facts in the history of our time.[31]

The point is the one that Spender had already made: that the artist's function is not to change the world, but to analyze and understand it. But in personal terms it means that the artist accepts his inability to alter reality, and makes that inability his subject. It is, therefore, another aspect of that view of life which starts from the sense of human limitation—that is, the *tragic* view.

This separation of art from action is, like so many of Spender's utterances, a personal as well as a theoretical statement: it is a renunciation of his militant years, a confession of the failure of such effort. But it is also, more positively, a renewed commitment to art, not as an instrument of political change, but as a human value. This confessional note is especially clear in the final paragraph of the essay, in which Spender pleads for a new kind of criticism which would judge writers by the truth of their analysis rather than by their stated opinions.

It would follow from such a critical approach that we judged writers by the amount of life felt in their works, rather than by

363

their political actions and opinions. In practical affairs this would mean that instead of appearing on political platforms and writing about aspects of life of which they know nothing, writers would write about the kind of life they knew best, learning as much about it as possible and saying what they believe to be true of it, without airing too much their opinions. Far too many writers and artists have been driven away from the centre of their real interest towards some outer rim of half creating, half agitation. A great deal is said about saving culture, but the really important thing is to have a culture to save.[32]

Spender called this position 'The New Realism', but it was not new for him; it was rather a return to the position that he had taken in 'Poetry and Revolution' in 1933. And so this later essay seems a judgment, at the decade's end, of all the activist effort of the intervening years; poetically speaking, it had all been a mistake, a wasteful diversion of energies from the creative centre of his life to the political rim.

That image of centre and perimeter appears also in *The Still Centre*, the book of poems that Spender published in the same month in which *The New Realism* appeared. It was Spender's first collection since *Poems* in 1934, and he put into it all the work that he wished to preserve from the intervening five years; it therefore amounts to a record of Spender's ideas and concerns through those years, and is a parallel in poetry to the account of his career that he gives in *The New Realism*. The book is divided into four parts, which are roughly chronological: Part One contains the earliest poems, continuous in manner with *Poems*—emotional, high-pitched, full of unspecified feeling; Parts Two and Three are the occasional poems of the political years, including poems concerned with the Spanish War. Coming after these poems, the fourth part makes a dramatic contrast, a contrast which Spender was at pains to emphasize in his manifesto-like Foreword:

I think that there is a certain pressure of external events on poets today, making them tend to write about what is outside their own limited experience. The violence of the times we are living in, the necessity of sweeping and general and immediate action, tend to dwarf the experience of the individual, and to make his immediate environment and occupations perhaps something that he is even ashamed of. For this reason, in my most recent poems, I have deliberately turned back to a kind of writing which is more personal, and I have included within my subjects weakness and fantasy and illusion.[33]

He had chosen, as a conscious alternative to the earlier, more public, committed poetry, to write the kind of poetry that he had defended against Caudwell—the poetry of the divided man.

The first poem of this final section, 'Darkness and Light', is about this choice; it begins:

> To break out of the chaos of my darkness
> Into a lucid day is all my will;

but continues in the second stanza:

> Yet, equally, to avoid that lucid day
> And to preserve my darkness, is all my will.

Day and darkness, the objective world and the self, are also imaged as the centre and circumference of a circle—the antithetical impulses toward and away from subjectivism, which are equally part of human identity. The resolution of the poem is an acceptance of both in the whole circle of the self:

> The world, my body, binds the dark and light
> Together, reconciles and separates
> In lucid day the chaos of my darkness.[34]

The relation of this poem to Spender's expressed intention is obviously very close; it is a programmatic poem, a demonstration of his turn back to the personal.

'Darkness and Light', and the poems that follow it, are most interesting for what they exclude: there are no suffering poor here, no exiles, no heroes, and no politics. Spender takes his body as the world, and self as the whole subject. There are poems of childhood and of lost love, and introspective self-examinations, and even a poem entitled 'The Human Situation' is entirely concerned with subjective experience. Only in the last poem in the book does Spender return to the other, public world. It is an elegy for a Spanish poet, and is inevitably set in the context of the Civil War;

but even that world becomes an inner landscape, a parable of the sense of personal loss.

> Oh let the violent time
> Cut eyes into my limbs
> As the sky is pierced with stars that look upon
> The map of pain,
> For only when the terrible river
> Of grief and indignation
> Has poured through all my brain
> Can I make from lamentation
> A world of happiness,
> And another constellation,
> With your voice that still rejoices
> In the centre of its night,
> As, buried in this night,
> The stars burn with their brilliant light.[35]

The similarity between this poem and Auden's elegy on Yeats is unavoidable. It is not a matter of influence or imitation, but of a common occasion and a shared mood: a dead poet, a lost cause, a violent time, and a felt need to rejoice (the word occurs at the end of both poems) in spite of the darkness. They are poems of their time, *for* their time.

Together *The New Realism* and *The Still Centre* announced the end of Spender's uneasy alliance with communism, and the communist reaction was, as one might expect, unfavourable. Alick West reviewed the two books together in the *Daily Worker*, and had no good word for either. West took the argument of *The New Realism* to be a way of letting the writer out of political commitment:

> He need not try to make himself single-hearted for the new world. Instead, he can persuade himself that his vacillations have historical importance, that the most significant dialectical contradiction is his own mind.

Moving on to the poems, he wrote:

> There is more than a hint of this in Spender's new collection of

poems, 'The Still Centre'. The 'still centre' is a secret retreat where Spender watches Spender's conflicts. Spender is not interested in solving his conflict, but in having one. For he can then feel that his special task is to stand aside and watch it.[36]

This is all perfectly true: Spender had reached the point of believing that poetry makes nothing happen, and to do so was to be confronted with the problem of finding a new subject matter. He had ceased to believe in the 'new world', or that he could make himself single-hearted by any possible effort. And so he turned back, as he said, to the personal; if the conflicts that he had felt in the troubled 'thirties could not be solved by action, then the best thing for a poet was to make those conflicts his subject, to re-enter the self and the personal past.

III

If nostalgia and apocalyptic apprehension, the sad look back and the depressed look ahead, were the dominant characteristics of end-of-the-'thirties writing, then the most representative books of that time are MacNeice's *Autumn Journal* and Orwell's *Coming Up for Air*. MacNeice and Orwell seem at first an oddly matched pair— the melancholy, rather elegant Irish poet and the scruffy English chronicler of the down and out—but they shared certain qualities that are important to the whole history of the decade. Both were by nature isolated men, who withheld themselves from the group movements of their time; both were pushed to the political Left by the necessities of the time, but were anti-Marxist by nature; both valued and celebrated the ordinary pleasures of existence; both viewed the future with a prophetic gloominess. Neither man fits the stock notion of the 'thirties writer as a *New Country* parlour-communist; but both are as important, as artists and as representative sensibilities, as any of the *New Country* gang. And both spoke with special significance to the mood of the decade's end.

Autumn Journal is, most simply, what its title says it is: a personal record of the period from August through December 1938. Those were the months when Chamberlain found 'peace in our time' at Munich, while London prepared to be bombed and the Loyalists at Barcelona fought their last defence, and those events all enter the poem. But even in times of crisis the private life goes on, and MacNeice's achievement in his poem was to interweave the constituent part of his life, and to show how those parts acted upon each other: how the past affected his responses to the present, and how the present forced him to judge the past; how the public world invaded private life, and how private losses coloured his attitude toward public crises. It is a poignant last example of that insistent 'thirties theme, the interpenetration of public and private worlds.

The poem takes its primary structure from the chronology of public events, the sequence of:

> Conferences, adjournments, ultimatums,
> Flights in the air, castles in the air,
> The autopsy of treaties, dynamite under the bridges,
> The end of *laissez faire*.[37]

These are the events of that autumn that will get into the history books. But there is also another chronology, less causal and less consequential—the sequence of private occasions and private feelings of a man living an ordinary lonely life. In less critical times one might expect that these two chronologies would exist separately—what have politicians to do with a man's loneliness?—but in the autumn of 1938 they intermingle, seem to become analogies of each other. MacNeice is very good on this relationship; he was always a poet of private living, but in this poem he counterpoints private and public circumstances in a way that creates the mood of crisis as it must have been felt by men like himself.

For example, a principal theme of the poem is his lingering love for his first wife, who had left him and had married another man. Some passages of *Autumn Journal* are love poems to that lost love, and they are intimate and moving; but the mood is the mood of England in that critical autumn, the private loss is an analogue of public loss, and the poet's helpless misery is an appropriate response to the public situation as well as to the private one.

The relation works in the opposite way, too—public events echo private feelings. In September, MacNeice hears preparations for war going on outside his flat near Regents Park:

> Hitler yells on the wireless
>   The night is damp and still
> And I hear dull blows on wood outside my window;
>   They are cutting down the trees on Primrose Hill.
> The wood is white like the roast flesh of chicken,
>   Each tree falling like a closing fan;
> No more looking at the view from seats beneath the
>   branches,
>   Everything is going to plan . . .[38]

This is a public action, for a public reason (an anti-aircraft emplacement was being built); but it is felt as a private loss, a part of the plan that is the loss of everything valued. So public and private interweave, and have one theme—loss: the loss of a by-election, the loss of a dog, the loss of Czechoslovakia, the loss of love, all together composing the mood of the autumn of 1938.

In a time of crisis, men feel an impulse to review their pasts, and a good deal of *Autumn Journal* is retrospective autobiography. I have called such backward glances nostalgic, and they are very much that in MacNeice's case; his habitual sentimental melancholy was especially suited to nostalgia. But the autobiographical passages are more than that: they are also judgments of the past imposed by the disastrous present. So, for example, he remembers the early days of his marriage:

>   But Life was comfortable, life was fine
>   With two in a bed and patchwork cushions
>   And checks and tassels on the washing-line,
>   A gramophone, a cat, and the smell of jasmine.
>   The steaks were tender, the films were fun,
>   The walls were striped like a Russian ballet,
>   There were lots of things undone
>   But nobody cared, for the days were early.
>   Nobody niggled, nobody cared,
>   The soul was deaf to the mounting debit,
>   The soul was unprepared
>   But the firelight danced on the ply-wood ceiling.[39]

There is tender feeling here for those careless days; but still, *careless* is a judgment. Not a very precise one, to be sure—what *was* it that

was left undone? But somehow that life of careless love in the careless early 'thirties is made to share responsibility for the way things
are at the end of the decade, for the general loss.

As with marriage, so with the other elements that composed
MacNeice's past: Ireland, his public school, Oxford, a classical
education. Each is treated with nostalgic affection, but also with
the ironic knowledge that it is irrelevant to the present crisis.
Ireland is 'a faggot of useless memories', school is a place where
boys were taught to expect everything and deplore nothing,
Oxford is recollections of Greek composition and idealist philosophy. All were fun in their day, but their day is past:

> Good-bye now, Plato and Hegel,
>   The shop is closing down;
> They don't want any philosopher-kings in England,
>   There ain't no universals in this man's town.[40]

That is really the time, not MacNeice, speaking; clearly if the
time allowed, he would have been content to go on as he was, a
charming Irish classicist with upper-class tastes and a gift for
making melancholy poems. But the time determined its exclu-
sions, and the poet acknowledged them; they were all part of the
loss.

Nostalgia is one element in the response of writers to the mood
of the decade's end; the other I have called the sense of apocalypse
—the conviction of approaching terror that everyone seemed to
share. MacNeice felt it, too, and invoked it in his poem, as a
nightmare vision of the dead, as 'the coming/Of the unknown
Uebermensch', and 'the beast/That prowls at every door and
barks in every headline'. There was no way of avoiding that prowl-
ing beast—like everyone else, MacNeice took the war against
fascism as already determined; the only question was how to
confront it.

Perhaps it was because of that question that MacNeice travelled
to Barcelona in December 1938, and made the record of his journey there, and his night thoughts of New Year's Eve in that
beleaguered city, the substance of the closing sections of his poem.
The presence of the Spanish War gives the poem an oddly ana-
chronistic quality, for by the time it was published Barcelona had

fallen, and the war was over; *Autumn Journal* must be the last poem
written in which the struggle in Spain functioned as a symbolic
event. But on that New Year's Eve Barcelona was still a flicker of
light in the widening darkness, the Loyalists were still heroes. And
so MacNeice lay in the dark, while the bombers droned overhead,
and made a harsh assessment of himself in the context of the war
that was being fought around him, and the war that waited to be
fought:

> I have loved defeat and sloth,
>   The tawdry halo of the idle martyr;
> I have thrown away the roots of will and conscience,
>   Now I must look for both,
> Not any longer act among the cushions
>   The Dying Gaul;
> Soon or late the delights of self-pity must pall
>   And the fun of cursing the wicked
> World into which we were born . . .[41]

It is an indictment that seems more than personal, that spreads
out from the poet to involve his class and his generation, and the
postures of the 'thirties. On the last night of 1938, MacNeice was
acknowledging the end of a time.

The poem ends, not with a call to action, but with an invoca-
tion of love and life that is like a blessing, or a prayer:

> The New Year comes with bombs, it is too late
>   To dose the dead with honourable intentions:
> If you have honour to spare, employ it on the living;
>   The dead are dead as 1938.
> Sleep to the noise of running water
>   To-morrow to be crossed, however deep;
> This is no river of the dead or Lethe,
>   To-night we sleep
> On the banks of Rubicon—the die is cast;
>   There will be time to audit
> The accounts later, there will be sunlight later
>   And the equation will come out at last.[42]

Like other works of the time, this is Literature of Preparation: the die is cast, and there seems a kind of relief in that knowledge. What is coming will be terrible, but less terrible, perhaps, than waiting for the end.

Autumn Journal is a passive poem, a record of a private life carried on the flood of history. It has no personal momentum, no important decisions are made; the most positive thing that Mac-Neice does is to work in an Oxford by-election (which his candidate loses). Nor does it propose any positive values, any programme for confronting the future; England has come to the end of *laissez faire*, but MacNeice has no alternatives to offer, beyond a vague solidarity of resistance against the common enemy. I don't wish to suggest that the poem *should* have these elements in it in order to be excellent, but simply that the state of mind that Mac-Neice recorded in his journal did not include them, and that MacNeice, who was honest about his feelings even when they were self-pitying and sentimental, would not falsify what he had felt. In an introductory note to the book, he acknowledged inconsistencies and over-statements, but refused to alter them; he was not, he said,

> attempting to offer what so many people now demand from poets—a final verdict or a balanced judgement. It is the nature of this poem to be neither final nor balanced. I have certain beliefs which, I hope, emerge in the course of it but which I have refused to abstract from their context. For this reason I shall probably be called a trimmer by some and a sentimental extremist by others. But poetry in my opinion must be honest before anything else and I refuse to be 'objective' or clear-cut at the cost of honesty. [43]

He was not, so far as I am aware, called either a trimmer or an extremist; he was called *bourgeois*. The poem, said Julian Symons, might be called 'The Bourgeois's Progress', and Roy Fuller wrote that MacNeice was 'a *type* of the bourgeoisie at the end of its epoch'. [44] Such remarks were meant to be pejorative, but they had in fact a certain objective validity. MacNeice, like every other important writer of his generation, was a member of the educated middle class, and like other members of his generation he was concerned to understand and to record what had happened to himself and to his class that had brought them to this crisis. Fuller was perhaps premature in assuming that it was the epoch of the bourgeoisie that was ending, but certainly a kind of life was coming to its close, and MacNeice knew that it was. But he was not writing a poem about the bourgeoisie, he was writing a personal journal, and the critics of the Left were insensitive in not seeing that the subject of the poem was a life in a time of crisis, and not a generalization about politics and class.

Autumn Journal is the best personal expression of the end-of-the-'thirties mood. Only one other book that I know gives that mood with equal intensity—George Orwell's last pre-war novel, *Coming Up for Air*. Orwell shared in the feelings of nostalgia and apprehension that mark the writing of the period; what makes his book exceptional is the intensity of his visions of the lost past and the apocalyptic future. His protagonist, George Bowling, is a petit-bourgeois visionary, and the novel is a visionary novel, though it is disguised as flat colloquial realism, like an Old Testament prophet in a cloth cap.

The prophetic role is one that Orwell had played before, both in his fiction and in his private letters. The Orwell-character in *Keep the Aspidistra Flying* (1936) imagines civilization dying, 'the whole western world going up in a roar of high explosives',[45] and Orwell was just as gloomy to his friends: 'Everyone with any imagination can foresee that Fascism . . . will be imposed on us as soon as the war starts', he wrote to Geoffrey Gorer in September 1937, and in the following spring he remarked to Cyril Connolly that 'we might as well pack our bags for the concentration camp'.[46] The interesting thing about these private observations is that they treat fascism not as an external enemy, or as an opposing and appalling philosophy, but simply as a destiny, a terrible fate that is going to strike *our* side as well as *theirs*. *Coming Up for Air* is a novel inspired by such thoughts.

In the novel George Bowling, a 'five to ten quid a week' insurance inspector, escapes from his suburban family and revisits his childhood home town, to get his nerve back 'before the bad times begin'. The date is June 1938, and to Bowling, who is the most ordinary of ordinary men, it is clear that a war is near, and so he tries to come up for air, once, while there is still time, to go home, to go fishing, to recover his lost life. Bowling's return to Lower Binfield gives Orwell an opportunity to recover, in vision, the nostalgic world of the past, and to set it against the world that is coming:

> ... in a manner of speaking [Bowling says] I *am* sentimental about my childhood—not my own particular childhood, but the civilisation which I grew up in and which is now, I suppose, just about at its last kick. And fishing is somehow typical of that civilisation. As soon as you think of fishing you think of things that don't belong to the modern world. The very idea of sitting all day under a willow tree beside a quiet pool—and being able to find a quiet pool to sit beside—belongs to the time before the war, before the radio, before aeroplanes, before Hitler. There's a kind of peacefulness even in the names of English coarse fish. Roach, rudd, dace, bleak, barbel, bream, gudgeon, pike, chub, carp, tench. They're solid kind of names. The people who made them up hadn't heard of machine-guns, they didn't live in terror of the sack or spend their time eating aspirins, going to the pictures and wondering how to keep out of the concentration camp.[47]

There are two worlds here: one is the stable, changeless world that existed before the Great War; the other is the present and everything that is coming—Orwell assumes a continuity between the world of the radio and the movies and the world of the concentration camp. The quality that gave that earlier life value has already been lost in 1938. 'What was it,' Bowling asks himself, 'that people had in those days?'

> A feeling of security, even when they weren't secure. More exactly, it was a feeling of continuity. All of them knew they'd got to die, and I suppose a few of them knew they were going to go bankrupt, but what they didn't know was that the order of things could change.[48]

What Bowling is seeking, when he returns to Lower Binfield, is the sacred world of childhood, where that feeling of continuity still exists; in his memory it is a secret pool full of giant carp, which he had found as a child but had never fished. If he could catch those fish, he could somehow catch the past. But he returns to find the pond drained to make a rubbish-dump for a suburban development; where the great fish swam there are only tin cans.

Bowling goes back, not simply because he yearns for the security of the past, but because he hates the present and fears the future. He takes it for granted that a war is coming, and that everyone else thinks so, too. He has visions of what that war will be like, which are vivid and violent and terrible; but what is most striking about them is that they are home-front visions, of an England that is bomb-torn and starved, but has grown used to war:

> I looked forward a few years. I saw this street as it'll be in five years' time, say, or three years' time (1941 they say it's booked for), after the fighting's started.
>
> No, not all smashed to pieces. Only a little altered, kind of chipped and dirty-looking, the shop windows almost empty and so dusty that you can't see into them. Down a side street there's an enormous bomb-crater and a block of buildings burnt out so that it looks like a hollow tooth . . .
>
> I can hear the air-raid syrens blowing and the loud-speakers bellowing that our glorious troops have taken a hundred thousand prisoners. I see a top floor back in Birmingham and a child of five howling and howling for a bit of bread. And suddenly the mother can't stand it any longer, and she yells at it, 'Shut your trap, you little bastard!' and then she ups the child's frock and smacks its bottom hard, because there isn't any bread and isn't going to be any bread. I see it all. I see the posters and the food-queues, and the castor oil and the rubber truncheons and the machine-guns squirting out of bedroom windows.[49]

The suffering will not only be at the hands of the enemy, then; the castor oil and the truncheons will be the instruments by which Englishmen torture Englishmen, and so fascism will become an *English* way of governing, when the war comes.

Bowling's vision of war is the nightmare vision of *1984*, and *Coming Up* is like a first draft of the later book. The greatest similarity, and the most exceptional aspect of Bowling's sense of apocalypse, is that he fears the world after the war more than he fears the war. Through the novel he broods on what that world will be like:

. . . it isn't the war that matters, it's the after-war. The world we're going down into, the kind of hate-world, slogan-world. The coloured shirts, the barbed wire, the rubber truncheons. The secret cells where the electric light burns night and day, and the detectives watching you while you sleep. And the processions and the posters with enormous faces, and the crowds of a million people all cheering for the Leader till they deafen themselves into thinking that they really worship him, and all the time, underneath, they hate him so that they want to puke. It's all going to happen.[50]

And that last sentence becomes a refrain: *It's all going to happen.* Indeed it does begin to happen, ironically, while he is in Lower Binfield; a bombing plane flies over the town, a bomb is accidentally dropped, a greengrocer's shop is destroyed and three people are killed. The bomb also blows up Bowling's dream, and he goes home to his nagging wife.

Bowling's venture has been a failure; the town is changed, the pool is drained, nothing of the past remains. But Orwell does not treat his journey as foolish, as simply a middle-aged man's attempt to escape reality. The date makes it more than that. For in 1938 a journey in search of the past was a kind of affirmation, an occasion for celebrating what was good in that past, and Bowling's journey has been a preparation, an attempt, at least, to come up for air before the bad times begin.

Contemporary critics of Orwell's novel seem to have been peculiarly blind to what it was about. Anthony West in the *New Statesman* took it to be 'skilful propaganda against cruelty and ugliness', and the *TLS*'s reviewer called it a 'cautionary tale'. But it is neither of these—it does not set out to warn, nor to persuade, but to *prophesy*. There is, in the end, nothing to be done except what Bowling does, which is to live his old life, and to wait.

Prophecy is the most pessimistic of modes, because it assumes that the future is already fixed, inherent in the present. And it seems appropriate that Orwell's prophetic novel should have appeared when it did, at the fag-end of the 'thirties, in the summer of 1939. What he prophesied did not, of course, come to pass, or at least not all of it, though the bombed city that he visualized was pretty much what London became. But the fact that he did prophesy as he did is a significant fact about the mood of the time, when the apocalypse was there, round the corner or across the Channel, and there seemed nothing to be done.

XI

1939-40

On 1 September 1939 German armies entered Poland, and that
was that: England and France declared war on the 3rd, and the
decade of the 'thirties was over. Immediate responses to the end
they had all been waiting for varied among writers according to
temperament and private circumstances, but they shared certain
death-bed moods—shock, depression, a sense of having been
abandoned by history, a loss of motivation and direction. Spender,
on the first day of the war, found himself unable to write at all,
and began a journal because he could do nothing else. The first
entry begins:

> *September 3rd*
> I am going to keep a journal because I cannot accept the fact
> that I feel so shattered that I cannot write at all . . . I feel as if
> I could not write again. Words seem to break in my mind like
> sticks when I put them down on paper. I cannot see how to
> spell some of them. Sentences are covered with leaves, and I
> really cannot see the line of the branch that carries the green
> meaning.[1]

Spender's sense of shock was partly public and partly personal: the
end of the peace and the end of his marriage had come at the same
time. His journal mixes these two kinds of defeat into one com-
pound record of the end of hopes: his wife is gone, he is alone and
unhappy, and in London the streets are empty and there are
black-outs at night; public and private details follow one another
on a single page, as though they were metaphors of each other, or
of one common loss: 'There was an air raid warning last night.
A— seems so far away now, I imagine her in her red dressing
gown and she looks pale and dazed.[2]

In the days that followed, Spender thought about fascism, and
the war, and the reasons for fighting; and he also thought about

personal things—about love and sex, about personal relationships, and poetry, and art. But mostly he thought about the past, and particularly about the years in the early 'thirties when he had lived among Germans. Those were the days of *Freundschaft*, of sexual freedom and peace. They were gone—Nazism and the war had destroyed that world—and perhaps Spender could think about them because they *were* gone; perhaps the past was a tolerable subject simply because it was past. 'During these first days of the war,' Spender wrote,

I have tended to live in the past, partly because the present is so painful, partly because it is so fragmentary and undecided. We live in a kind of vacuum now in which the events on which we are waiting have not yet caught up on us . . .[3]

But even in the midst of recollection, the present intrudes: Hitler rants on the wireless, the feeling of loneliness and lost love becomes intense. An entry written at the end of September sums up the mood:

When I drew the blinds I felt the Autumn chill in my bones, and because of the decision I have taken which is simply a recognition of existing facts, I had a sense of the desolation of the world.[4]

The desolation of the world was something that other writers felt, too. MacNeice, travelling in Ireland when the war began, felt it. He had just begun work on a book on Yeats' poetry, and in the first chapter of that book he recalls his feelings at the time:

I had only written a little of this book when Germany invaded Poland. On that day I was in Galway. As soon as I heard on the wireless of the outbreak of war, Galway became unreal. And Yeats and his poetry became unreal also.

This was not merely because Galway and Yeats belong in a sense to a past order of things. The unreality which now overtook them was also overtaking in my mind modern London, modernist art, and Left Wing politics. If the war made nonsense of Yeats's poetry and of all works that are called 'escapist', it also made nonsense of the poetry that professes to be 'realist'. My friends had been writing for years about guns and frontiers and factories, about the 'facts' of psychology, politics, science, economics, but the fact of war made their writing seem as remote as the pleasure dome in Xanadu.[5]

Unlike Spender, MacNeice was able to respond to desolation by writing poems, but the mood of his poems of those days is much like the mood of Spender's journal. During August and September he wrote a sequence that he called 'The Coming of War'. It is about his journey around Ireland; but it is also, like Spender's journal, about two kinds of loss—the end of a love affair, and the beginning of the war. In the sequence the place and the public and private themes interpenetrate: the Irish scene, war, and lost love become simply three kinds of endings.

One of the poems begins, 'Running away from the War', and that was what MacNeice was doing when he went to Ireland, but he could not have gone with any expectation of success, for to run was simply to arrive and find that the war had got there first. So, in a poem titled 'Cushendun', he comes to a remote, old-fashioned, comfortable village (it is in the extreme north-east corner of Northern Ireland), and finds there

> Forgetfulness: brass lamps and copper jugs
> And home-made bread and the smell of turf or flax
> And the air a glove and the water lathering easy
>   And convolvulus in the hedge.
>
> Only in the dark green room beside the fire
> With the curtains drawn against the winds and waves
> There is a little box with a well-bred voice:
>   What a place to talk of War.[6]

But one did talk of war there; it was, as he said, the only reality.

'The Coming of War' is a very personal sequence, full of the Irish melancholy that was MacNeice's most distinctive poetic quality, but it is also expressive of the time in which it was written. One finds in the poems, for example, that only the past has a sharp, defined existence: Irish history and personal history adhere to particular things, but present and future are only feelings, anxious and acute, yet unattached to any substantial reality. The war itself is a feeling, a doom that is lapping at the door;

but it is not a subject to be treated specifically, as possible history or as a cause. It is only an abrupt and final ending, like a fifth-act curtain or a slammed door, beyond which there is nothing imaginable except death.

Neither Spender nor MacNeice responded to the war by becoming a 'War Poet', nor did any of their contemporaries. Their failure to do so was a disappointment to the press, which understood how poets were supposed to react when a war began. *The Times Literary Supplement*, for example, in a leader published in December 1939, exhorted 'the Poets of 1940' to do their duty; 'it is for the poets to sound the trumpet call,' the *TLS* declared; '. . . the monstrous threat to belief and freedom which we are fighting should urge new psalmists to fresh songs of deliverance.'[7] But the trumpet did not sound, and the psalmists did not appear.

This failure to deliver poetically was no doubt partly a consequence of the way in which the war had begun. The fall and winter of 1939 were the time of the 'phoney war', when England and Germany were officially at war, but were not doing any fighting. British troops were in France, but engaged no enemy there, and in London there were air-raid alerts, but no air-raids. The first British casualty did not occur until December (when an English soldier assigned to the defence of the Maginot Line was killed), and serious fighting did not begin until the German armies marched into the Netherlands and Belgium in May 1940. In the meantime, the end that had been predicted with such grim certainty through the 'thirties had come, and nothing had happened. It must have been an odd and unsettling experience, to wake up on the day after the Apocalypse and find that the world was going on much the same as before.

But there was another, more fundamental reason for the lack of war-writing by members of the 'thirties generation. Spender explained it in an essay that is a reply to the *TLS* leader:

At the beginning of the last war Rupert Brooke and others were 'trumpets singing to battle'. Why did not Rupert Brooke step forward 'young and goldenhaired' this time? No doubt, in part, precisely because one had done so last time. There is another reason: the poetry of the war of democracy versus fascism had already been written by English, French, Spanish, German and Italian émigré poets during the past five years, and particularly during the Spanish war.[8]

For the 'thirties generation, the battle had already been fought and lost; the final curtain had fallen on the tragedy of the decade, and what followed was not essentially a part of the drama.[9] For the writers *as writers*, the appropriate response to the end of the 'thirties was silence, or a retrospective brooding over what had happened. Some of them would fight in the war, or support it in various other ways, but they would not write much about it; it was not really their war, and when it overtook their lives it came not as a cause, but as a consequence of a cause that had already been lost.

It was that lost cause that remained in the generation's imaginations. The end of the 'thirties had been a long death-bed vigil, and now that the waiting was over, the deceased became a subject for discussion, to be analyzed, simplified, generalized about, and judged. In the first year of the war the decade that had just ended was more prominent in the writings of the 'thirties generation than the war that was present. And so the 'thirties passed out of immediate reality into myth, while the war that had been an apocalyptic myth waited to become reality.

The creation of the Myth of the Thirties begins with Auden. Perhaps his location, in New York, removed from the immediate experience of air-raid alerts and uniforms and rumours, gave him the detachment to look back on the decade that was behind him; but more than that, Auden was his generation's generalizer, its diagram-maker, its historian. It seems appropriate that he should have written the generation's first 'war poem', a poem set in a bar in Fifty-second Street, and concerned not with the war itself, but with its moral causes in history.

'September 1, 1939' begins with the death of the 'thirties:

> I sit in one of the dives
> On Fifty-second Street
> Uncertain and afraid
> As the clever hopes expire
> Of a low dishonest decade . . .[10]

Clever is a pejorative term here, by which all the hopes of the decade—pacifism, the Peace Ballot, the Popular Front, the Loyalist cause—are dismissed; they were clever hopes, invented by clever people, but reality was always elsewhere and uglier, and they deserved to expire. The decade in which such hopes existed Auden calls *low* and *dishonest*. These seem at first odd terms to apply to a period of history—how can a *decade* be dishonest? The rest of the poem is an explanation of what Auden means, of why these terms are in fact appropriate ones.

Auden takes the war to be a consequence, not of the wickedness of Hitler, or even of politicians in general, but of human evil. His lines:

> Those to whom evil is done
> Do evil in return

have an immediate historical reference—the initial evil was the Treaty of Versailles, of which the Second World War was an inevitable consequence—and also a longer-range meaning—'the whole offence/From Luther until now', protestantism and its correlative capitalism begot imperialism, and imperialism brought war. But Auden's inversion of the Golden Rule has another, more fundamental meaning: it is a generalization about human nature, a proposition about the role of Original Sin in history; and a generation that denied that role, and built its hopes on human goodness, was a dishonest one.

The eighth stanza of the poem, the one that Auden came to dislike and which he eventually cut from the text, contains another important judgment of the decade. 'All I have is a voice,' Auden says, 'to undo the folded lie.' The lie must refer back to the decade's intellectual and moral dishonesty, and so the poem is a corrective, almost a penitent gesture, made by a member of the 'thirties generation as the decade ended. The lie to be refuted is

> The romantic lie in the brain
> Of the sensual Man-in-the-street,
> The lie of Authority
> Whose buildings grope the sky:
> There is no such thing as the State

And no one exists alone;
Hunger allows no choice
To the citizen or the police,
We must love one another or die.

It is an odd, startling passage for a poet of the political 'thirties to
write: Authority is a liar (out go the Party, leaders, rulers, and
governors); there is no such thing as the State (out goes politics
altogether, along with patriotism, frontiers, and national identity);
neither citizen nor police has a choice (and so these antagonists
become brothers, and out go the class struggle and the human
enemy). What is left is a proposition about brotherly love (which
Auden later came to see contained its own lie—we must die
anyway).

Auden's poem is a re-assessment of human nature and human
history that the occasion compelled; and because the 'thirties was
a time of such strong imperatives and beliefs, his re-assessment is
necessarily a judgment of the decade, and the beginning of the
emergent Myth. Auden compresses the whole history of the decade
into one historical unit, to all of which he applies his two dismissive adjectives—*low, dishonest*. The war that has come is a
deserved punishment for moral errors inherent in political ideas;
mankind is more evil than the clever hopers had thought. Such a
judgment could not have been made while the hopes survived,
and Auden's poem is the decade's first epitaph.

At about the same time that Auden was writing his poem,
Malcolm Muggeridge, a journalist turned Army private, was saying his own mordant farewell to the 'thirties in the first full-length
study of the decade. Like Auden, he assumed that the period had
ended when war was declared, and his book, entitled simply *The
Thirties*, was begun in the autumn of 1939 and completed before
the last month of the decade had actually passed. Muggeridge
had a sharp eye for the ironic fact and the ridiculous figure, and
his book is crammed with details—so much so that some reviewers
complained that it was all trees and no wood. But in fact there was
a simple principle of selection operating. Muggeridge looked over
the history of the decade for whatever could be debunked, satirized, or caricatured, for anything that would demonstrate the

folly and the failure of the ten years that had just passed. He found, when he looked, that this category was all-inclusive, and so his book is one unrelenting condemnation—sometimes wittily ironic, sometimes savagely contemptuous, sometimes a bit hysterical-sounding, but never approving or admiring.

Muggeridge's book contributed two elements to the emerging Myth of the Thirties. First, he assumed that the entire decade should be regarded as an unmitigated failure (like Auden, he regarded the whole period as subject to a single judgment). And secondly, he assumed that the appropriate attitude toward that failure was not sympathy, compassion, or regret, but contempt— an attitude not unlike that felt by the post-war generation of the 'twenties for the Old Men.

The tone of the book is captured precisely in the final paragraph, which describes the way the decade died:

> In so confused a state of mind, the Thirties drew to an end— looking for freedom that it might be defended, looking for a war that it might be fought; Shape of Things to Come, coming, come. Soldiers were ready; aeroplanes flew through the sky, dropped leaflets which might have been bombs; threats were uttered—like Lear's 'I will do such things—what they are yet I know not, but they shall be the terrors of the earth'; back to London drifted some of those who had fled, opened cinemas which had been closed, recovered their self-confident voices which had momentarily become plaintive, when no sirens sounded bravely demanding cessation of bureaucratic control, bravely railing against regulations imposed. After all, though there was a war, still there might be no war; after all, still it was only on other countries that bombs fell—Poland, Finland, Holland perhaps; after all, the Nazi régime might collapse, Hitler die, or, under the stress of a blockade, sue for peace. Fighting a war which might not have to be fought, defending what no more existed to defend, following campaigns which did not take place, mourning for the living and looking for strength to the dead, strangely, sadly and rather foolishly, the Thirties drew to a close.[11]

Here all values and all dignity are denied to the English people, who are treated as no more than the sum of the follies of their time; and their time is nothing but follies. The very way in which the decade ended is taken as a confirmation of its foolish life, as though the phoney war was an inevitable and proper consequence of a phoney peace.

Orwell reviewed Muggeridge's book in the spring of 1940, and endorsed its message. Muggeridge could find no line of action, Orwell wrote, except 'an indiscriminate walloping of all human activities whatever. But,' he continued,

> as a social historian this does not altogether invalidate him, because the age we live in invites something of the kind. It is an age in which every *positive* attitude has turned out a failure. Creeds, parties, programmes of every description have simply flopped, one after another. The only 'ism' that has justified itself is pessimism. Therefore at this moment good books can be written from the angle of Thersites, though probably not very many.[12]

Among the possible good books Orwell no doubt meant to include his own *Inside the Whale*, which had just been published, for it contains, in the title essay, Orwell's principal contribution to the Thirties Myth, from the angle of Thersites. One might regard Orwell's book as a literary supplement to Muggeridge's, for the literature of the decade had been pretty much ignored in *The Thirties*—perhaps because Muggeridge could not find sufficient folly in it. But Orwell could, and did.

The primary subject of 'Inside the Whale' is the writings of Henry Miller, but Orwell takes the occasion to sketch a literary history of the two decades between the wars as a context for Miller's extreme non-political, non-moral passivity. He dwells particularly on the *New Signatures* poets, whom he treats as a homogeneous group—public-school-university-Bloomsbury—with a common political bent toward communism. The set piece of this account is Orwell's attack on Auden, as an example of the 'soft-boiled emancipated middle class who were too young to have effective memories of the Great War'.

> To people of that kind such things as purges, secret police, summary executions, imprisonment without trial, etc., etc., are

too remote to be terrifying. They can swallow totalitarianism *because* they have no experience of anything except liberalism.

Orwell then quotes two stanzas from the end of 'Spain', beginning 'Tomorrow for the young the poets exploding like bombs', and ending with 'the flat ephemeral pamphlet and the boring meeting'. This is the passage in which the line 'the conscious acceptance of guilt in the necessary murder' occurs, and Orwell has sport with it:

> The second stanza is intended as a sort of thumbnail sketch of a day in the life of a 'good party man'. In the morning a couple of political murders, a ten-minutes' interlude to stifle 'bourgeois' remorse, and then a hurried luncheon and a busy afternoon and evening chalking walls and distributing leaflets. All very edifying. But notice the phrase 'necessary murder'. It could only be written by a person to whom murder is at most a *word* . . . Mr. Auden's brand of amoralism is only possible if you are the kind of person who is always somewhere else when the trigger is pulled.[13]

'On the whole,' Orwell concludes, 'the literary history of the 'thirties seems to justify the opinion that a writer does well to keep out of politics.'[14] This is an odd conclusion to get from the author of *The Road to Wigan Pier* and *Homage to Catalonia*, but it became a commonplace of the Thirties Myth: for a decade, so the Myth goes, young writers were seduced into political actions that they didn't understand, and both politics and literature suffered.

The most important point about 'Inside the Whale' is that it helped to fix the relation between politics and literature in the Thirties Myth. But it also added further authority to the established cast of characters in the Myth. The *New Signatures* poets had been considered central figures in the literary history of the decade from 1932 on, but Orwell was the first of the later myth-makers to adopt this view. His essay offers a handy list of who was *in*:

> The leading figures in this group are Auden, Spender, Day-Lewis, MacNeice, and there is a long string of writers of more or less the same tendency, Isherwood, John Lehmann, Arthur

Calder-Marshall, Edward Upward, Alec Brown, Philip Henderson, and many others.[15]

The only surprising names here are the last two. Alec Brown was a Marxist who had written *The Fate of the Middle Classes* (reviewed unfavourably by Orwell in the *Adelphi*), and a novel, *Daughters of Albion* (described by Orwell as 'a huge wad of mediocre stuff'); Henderson was a Marxist literary critic, author of *The Novel Today* (which Orwell had called 'badly written and thoroughly dull' in a review in the *New English Weekly*). The two are inserted here for an obvious reason—to increase the communist content of the list, and to do so with two obviously inferior writers.

Another significant contribution to the Myth is Gascoyne's 'Farewell Chorus', which is dated New Year 1940—the first day of the new decade. In the poem Gascoyne imagines the 'thirties as a railway station, from which 'the long black pullman' of history is departing, leaving behind those people who are not fit for the journey—the weak, the 'too indelicately tender', the indifferent, all those in retreat from life. The decade that they are left behind in is described in terms that are a summary of negative judgments that form the Myth: it is a place of delusive peace and false hope, of self-deception, complacency, and ineffectual indignation. Ahead, in the new decade of the 'forties, violence waits— planes hum, guns roar, fire rages—but it is nevertheless a future that Gascoyne describes in positive terms:

> So silent is the ray
> Of naked radiance that lights our actual scene,
> Leading the gaze into those nameless and unknown
> Extremes of our existence where fear's armour falls away
> And lamentation and defeat and pain
> Are all transfigured by acceptance; where men see
> The tragic splendour of their final destiny.[16]

By the end, 'Farewell Chorus' has become a war-poem.

Much of Gascoyne's poem is put together out of second-hand 'thirties properties: the train as an emblem of energy, the catalogue of life-denying persons, the frontier, the Apocalypse ahead are all familiar to a reader of the early work of Auden, Spender, and Day Lewis. What is different is Gascoyne's assumption that since war had come in spite of the efforts of men of good will, those efforts must have been delusive and self-deceptive. This is an alternative version of Auden's 'dishonest decade', and it becomes another part of the Myth. The very conception of the poem as a train-side farewell—as though one could leave the unsuccessful past behind on the platform and steam unencumbered into the future—is a part of the Myth, too. The decade came to be considered as a collective mistake, which could be rejected and replaced by reality, just as the reality of war had replaced the false hopes of peace.

Day Lewis had spent the first year of the war like an old soldier retired from the battle, living in a Devon village and translating Virgil's *Georgics*. Both the retirement and the translation were political acts; he had physically withdrawn from his commitment to the Communist Party, and from politics in general, and he had underlined that change by choosing to work on Virgil's country poems, thus acknowledging that his true poetic place had always been in the tradition of natural, pastoral poetry, a tradition that seemed to him profoundly English. The foreword that he wrote for his translation, dated 'June 1940', makes this point very clearly; it is both a celebration of and a commitment to the tradition:

> The fascination of the Georgics [he writes] for many generations of Englishmen is not difficult to explain. A century of urban civilization has not yet materially modified the instinct of a people once devoted to agriculture and stock-breeding, to the chase, to landscape gardening, to a practical love of Nature . . . In our love of domestic animals, in the millions of suburban and cottage gardens, we may see the depth and tenacity of our roots in earth today.[17]

Politics is not mentioned at all (though the vision of English rural life is essentially a Tory vision); the war enters only as an event which might lead in the end to a decentralization of industry, and thus a new 'rural-urban civilization'. By the end of the first paragraph it is clear that Day Lewis had come home.

As a preface to his translation Day Lewis wrote a set of 'Dedicatory Stanzas' addressed to Stephen Spender—the last example of that network of cross-dedications and cross-references among members of the generation that MacNeice called the 'myth of themselves'. It is an appropriate dedication, for the verses that follow are a valedictory assessment of the generation and its decade, seen from a point beyond the end, from a new decade and a new war. Two passages in particular offer a theory of the generation's behaviour that is at once a self-justification and a version of the Myth. In the second stanza Day Lewis writes:

> Where are the war poets? the fools inquire
> We were the prophets of a changeable morning
> Who hoped for much but saw the clouds forewarning:
> We were at war, while they still played with fire
> And rigged the market for the ruin of man:
> Spain was a death to us, Munich a mourning.
> No wonder then if, like the pelican,
> We have turned inward for our iron ration,
> Tapping the vein and sole reserve of passion,
> Drawing from poetry's capital what we can.[18]

This is essentially a recapitulation of what Spender had said about the absence of war poets—that *their* war had already been fought and lost. This being the case, the right action for poets is that which will help them to survive; the failure of the political hopes of the 'thirties justifies the poet in turning inward, away from politics, toward poetry itself (which becomes not simply a medium for the expression of ideas, but a value).

Toward the end of the poem Day Lewis compares his own time with Virgil's:

> Different from his own age and myths, our toil
> The same. Our exile and extravagances,
> Revolt, retreat, fine faiths, disordered fancies
> Are but the poet's search for a right soil
> Where words may settle, marry, and conceive an
> Imagined truth, for a regimen that enhances
> Their natural grace.[19]

Here is a catalogue of terms for the desperate gestures of the 'thirties—exile, extravagances, revolt, retreat, fine faiths, disordered fancies—implying a displacement of poets from their proper places, and a common error, a departure from reality. The goal of all these turbulent gestures is not seen as a political end (there is nothing here about justice, or peace, or brotherhood) but simply as a 'right soil' in which poetry might flourish. So they were all really behaving as poets all along—it was only the soil of poetry that had shifted.

The most surprising thing about the 'Dedicatory Stanzas' is the tone in which Day Lewis deals with the present. If the poem was written at the same time as the foreword—and it must have been —then while the poet wrote France was falling before the German armoured columns, and the British were desperately withdrawing from Dunkirk. Day Lewis wrote about this moment in history like this:

> Meanwhile, what touches the heart of all, engrosses.
> Through the flushed springtime and the fading year
> I lived on country matters. Now June was here
> Again, and brought the smell of flowering grasses
> To me and death to many overseas:
> They lie in the flowering sunshine, flesh once dear
> To some, now parchment for the heart's release.[20]

One is tempted to be ironic about this passage, to say that the *TLS* need not have worried, that Rupert Brooke had risen from the dead. But this attitude toward death in battle, though it seems naive after Wilfred Owen, is in keeping with Day Lewis' commitment to an apolitical pastoral tradition. This is the way men have died in verse before; it is not an original stanza, or even a very good version of the old words, but it is another expression of Day Lewis' return to the subjects, the language, and the customary emotions in which he felt secure. And the very fact of the difference between this kind of poetical dying and the things that Spender and Cornford had said about the Spanish dead is another way of saying that for Day Lewis the 'thirties were over.

By the spring of 1940 the Thirties Myth had become pretty well defined in its principal premises. One further contribution of that time is important because it came from a distinguished member of an older literary generation, and because it gained a certain amount of attention. In May of 1940 Virginia Woolf travelled to Brighton to address the Workers' Educational Association. Her subject was the relation between class and creativity. All English writers since Chaucer, she said, have been middle-class and educated; the writer 'sits upon a tower raised above the rest of us; a tower built first on his parents' station, then on his parents' gold'. (The 'rest of us' here is of course disingenuous; Mrs Woolf was in the same elevated position.) But in the time between the First World War and the Second the tower had begun to lean, and Mrs Woolf was persuaded that the current war would topple it: 'the world after the war will be a world without classes or towers'.[21]

Her lecture, which she entitled 'The Leaning Tower', is a diagnosis and an obituary of the 'thirties generation, the last generation to be elevated above 'the rest of us' by their class and their education, and the only generation compelled to write while their superior position was crumbling. Everything that was true of the generation, everything that was wrong with its members and their writing, Mrs Woolf thought stemmed from this fundamental insecurity: they were class-conscious, self-pitying, angry; they became political-minded; they sought out scapegoats on whom to cast the blame; they attacked bourgeois society; they preached; they wrote a 'bastard language'. In all this, Mrs Woolf argued, they were compelled by their unique position in history:

> Trapped by their education, pinned down by their capital they remained on top of their leaning tower, and their state of mind as we see it reflected in their poems and plays and novels are full of discord and bitterness, full of confusion and compromise.[22]

No other generation, she thought, had been exposed to such pressures. 'It may be,' she observed, 'that none has had such an appallingly difficult task. Who can wonder if they have been incapable of giving us great poems, great plays, great novels?'[23] That sentence was her spadeful of earth on the coffin of the 'thirties generation; they had written nothing great, because they were incapable of greatness, and their incapacity was an historical necessity (one had not expected such strict historical determinism to come out of Bloomsbury).

It should not surprise anyone that Mrs Woolf was severe in her obituary notice of the generation; she had not liked their work when she first commented on it in 'A Letter to a Young Poet' in 1932, and their writing since then had pleased her no better. She had wanted beauty and fine language, and they had given her politics and polemics, and so in 1940 she was prepared to dismiss the entire generation as casualties of history.[24]

What is most important about Mrs Woolf's judgments is that they became—indeed had already become—orthodox elements in the Thirties Myth. If we put her remarks with those of the other writers discussed above, we will have a set of assumptions about the 'thirties and the younger writers of that decade that remain the commonplace of literary history. That set will include the following propositions:

The 'thirties may be treated critically as a single historical entity with a fixed and definable character;

It was a period marked by intellectual error, false hopes, delusion, and dishonesty;

The fact that it ended in war may therefore be considered as a deserved destiny, a just punishment for moral failure;[25]

Its writers were all of necessity politically motivated;

Their efforts to make literature a mode of action failed, and their writing shared in that failure.[26]

These are all arguable propositions, but none is entirely true; they are the constituents of a myth by which a complex, confused, often contradictory time has been simplified in order that it might be comprehended. There is no way of reducing the period (or any historical period for that matter) to order except by such simplifications, and of course all history is myth-making in this sense. But some myths come closer to reality than others, incorporate more of the disorderly facts into their orders; and all historical myths must be re-examined from time to time, and a new effort made to make them stretch farther, to assimilate more, and to approach more nearly to the complexity of truth.

'What a decade!' Orwell wrote in 1940:

A riot of appalling folly that suddenly becomes a nightmare, a scenic railway ending in a torture-chamber. It starts off in the

393

hangover of the 'enlightened' post-war age, with Ramsay MacDonald soft-soaping into the microphone and the League of Nations flapping vague wings in the background, and it ends up with twenty thousand bombing planes darkening the sky and Himmler's masked executioner whacking women's heads off on a block borrowed from the Nuremberg museum. In between are the politics of the umbrella and the hand-grenade. The National Government coming in to 'save the pound', MacDonald fading out like the Cheshire Cat, Baldwin winning an election on the disarmament ticket in order to rearm (and then failing to rearm), the June purge, the Russian purges, the glutinous humbug of the abdication, the ideological mix-up of the Spanish war, Communists waving Union Jacks, Conservative MPs cheering the news that British ships have been bombed, the Pope blessing Franco, Anglican dignitaries beaming at the wrecked churches of Barcelona, Chamberlain stepping out of his Munich aeroplane with a misquotation from Shakespeare, Lord Rothermere acclaiming Hitler as 'a great gentleman', the London air-raid syrens blowing a false alarm as the first bombs drop on Warsaw.[27]

What a decade indeed; reported in this headlong chronicle of follies it is depressing piece of history, the sooner closed the better. But Orwell's account is itself a part of the Myth, and one could compose a different summary that would alter the picture; it might simply contain the titles of novels and poems and plays, of books of travel and criticism and reportage—poems by Auden and Spender and MacNeice and Empson, novels by Isherwood and Greene and Warner, *The Road to Wigan Pier*, *Homage to Catalonia*, *Journey to a War*, *Some Versions of Pastoral*, *Illusion and Reality*. On the basis of that summary, one would exclaim 'What a decade!' in a different tone of voice. Both summaries would be true—or rather, both would be a *part* of reality; putting them together, we will come as close, perhaps, as we can come to the true literary history of the 'thirties.

APPENDICES,
NOTES AND
INDEX

APPENDIX A

from *Oxford Poetry 1927* (Oxford: Basil Blackwell, 1927)

PREFACE

Did it serve no other purpose, this volume should at least offer a rebutment of the tendency, shared by many serious-minded and a few single-minded persons, contemptuously to credit Oxford with 'the undergraduate mind'. We confess ourselves able neither to comprehend such an abstraction nor to surmise what increment may result from the fitting of any intellectual caption to so many diverse heads. Our minds are sparse enough, in all conscience: they must not also be held obnoxious to the charge of uniformity.

On the other hand, the chaos of values which is the substance of our environment is not consistent with a standardization of thought, though, on the political analogy, it may have to be superseded by one. All genuine poetry is in a sense the formation of private spheres out of a public chaos: and therefore we would remind those who annually criticize us for lack of homogeneity, first, that on the whole it is environment which conditions values, not values which form environment; second, that we must hold partly responsible for our mental *sauve-qui-peut*, that acedia and unabashed glorification of the subjective so prominent in the world since the Reformation.

> Im Winkel König Fahrenheit
> hat still sein Mus gegessen
> —'Ach Gott, sie war doch schön, die Zeit,
> die man nach mir gemessen![1]

A tripartite problem remains, and may be stated thus:

(a) The psychological conflict between self as subject and self as object, which is patent in the self-consciousness and emotional stultification resultant from the attempt to synchronise within the individual mind the synthesis and the analysis of experience. Such appears to be the prime development of this century, our experiment in the 'emergent evolution of mind'. Emotion is no longer necessarily to be analysed by 'recollection in tranquillity': it is to be prehended emotionally and intellectually at once. And this is of most importance to the poet; for it is his mind that must bear the brunt of the conflict and may be the first to realize the new harmony which would imply the success of this synchronization.

(b) The ethical conflict; a struggle to reconcile the notion of Pure Art, 'an art completely isolated from everything but its own laws of operation and the

[1]Christian Morgenstern. 'Galgenlieder.'

397

object to be created as such',[2] with those exigencies which its conditions of existence as a product of a human mind and culture must involve, where the one cannot be ignored nor the other enslaved.

(c) The logical conflict, between the denotatory and the connotatory sense of words, which is the root-divergence of classic and romantic; between, that is to say, an asceticism tending to kill language by stripping words of all association and a hedonism tending to kill language by dissipating their sense under a multiplicity of associations.

In what degree this problem is realized and met in these pages, the individual reader must decide. Those who believe that there is anything valuable in our youth as such we have neither the patience to consider nor the power to condone: our youth should be a period of spiritual discipline, not a self-justifying dogma. As for the intelligent reader, we can only remind him, where he experiences distaste, that no universalized system—political, religious or metaphysical—has been bequeathed to us; where pleasure, that it is but an infinitesimal progression towards a new synthesis—one more of those efforts as yet so conspicuous in their paucity.

[2]Jacques Maritain, 'Poetry and Religion'; New Criterion, V, 1.

W.H.A.
C.D.-L.

---

from the theatre programme, GROUP THEATRE SEASON:
Sweeney Agonistes and *The Dance of Death*. Westminster
Theatre, Oct. 1, 1935.

I WANT THE THEATRE TO BE . . .

By W. H. Auden

Drama began as the act of a whole community. Ideally there would be no spectators. In practice every member of the audience should feel like an understudy.

Drama is essentially an art of the body. The basis of acting is acrobatics, dancing, and all forms of physical skill. The music hall, the Christmas pantomime, and the country house charade are the most living drama of to-day.

The development of the film has deprived drama of any excuse for being documentary. It is not in its nature to provide an ignorant and passive spectator with exciting news.

The subject of drama on the other hand, is the commonly known, the universally familiar stories of the society or generation in which it is written. The audience, like the child listening to the fairy tale, ought to know what is going to happen next.

Similarly the drama is not suited to the analysis of character, which is the province of the novel. Dramatic characters are simplified, easily recognisable and over life-size.

Dramatic speech should have the same confessed, significant, and undocumentary character, as dramatic movement.

Drama in fact deals with the general and universal, not with the particular and local, but it is probable that drama can only deal, at any rate directly, with the relations of human beings with each other, not with the relation of man to the rest of nature.

NOTES

PREFACE

1. Poem XXX ('August for the people and their favourite islands'), *Look Stranger!* (London: Faber & Faber, 1936), pp. 65–6.
2. 'Psychology and Art To-day', in Geoffrey Grigson, ed., *The Arts To-day* (London: John Lane The Bodley Head, 1935), p. 20.
3. 'Introduction', *The Poet's Tongue*, An Anthology chosen by W. H. Auden and John Garrett (London: G. Bell & Sons Ltd, 1935), p. ix.

CHAPTER
[I]

1. See for example Cyril Connolly, *Enemies of Promise*; Graham Greene, *A Sort of Life*; Christopher Isherwood, *Kathleen and Frank*; C. Day Lewis, *The Buried Day*; Louis MacNeice, *The Strings Are False*; Stephen Spender, *World Within World*; Evelyn Waugh, *A Little Learning*; and the essays by Elizabeth Bowen, William Plomer, and Anthony Powell in Graham Greene, ed., *The Old School*.
2. Quoted in Peter Stansky and William Abrahams, *The Unknown Orwell* (London: Constable, 1973), p. 61.
3. Powell, 'The Wat'ry Glade', in Greene, ed., *The Old School* (London: Cape, 1934), pp. 160–1.
4. Orwell, *The Road to Wigan Pier* (London: Gollancz, 1937), pp. 170–1.
5. Cockburn, *In Time of Trouble* (London: Rupert Hart-Davis, 1956), p. 65.
6. Waugh, *A Little Learning* (London: Chapman & Hall, 1964), p. 170.
7. Isherwood, *Lions and Shadows* (London: Hogarth, 1938), pp. 74–5. Orwell, 'My Country Right or Left', in *Collected Essays, Journalism and Letters*, vol. 1 (London: Secker & Warburg, 1968), pp. 537–8.
8. Toynbee, *Friends Apart* (London: MacGibbon & Kee, 1954), p. 91.
9. For example in Auden's 'The Malverns', poem XVII of *Look, Stranger!* (London: Faber & Faber, 1936), p. 46: ' "The poetry is in the pity," Wilfred said . . .'; also Spender, *The Destructive Element* (London: Cape, 1935), p. 135, and Day Lewis, *A Hope for Poetry* (Oxford: Blackwell, 1934), p. 15.
10. Roberts, *Critique of Poetry* (London: Cape, 1934), p. 153.
11. Lehmann, *The Whispering Gallery* (London: Longmans Green, 1955), p. 139.
12. Waugh, *Brideshead Revisited* (London: Chapman & Hall, 1945), pp. 30–1.

13. Quennell, *The Sign of the Fish* (London: Collins, 1960), p. 37.
14. Coghill, 'Sweeney Agonistes', in Richard March and Tambimuttu, eds., *T. S. Eliot A Symposium* (London: Editions Poetry London, 1948), p. 82.
15. Quoted in Valerie Eliot, ed., *The Waste Land: Facsimile and Transcript of the Original Drafts* (London: Faber & Faber, 1971), p. [1].
16. Isherwood, *Lions and Shadows*, p. 121.
17. Richards, *Science and Poetry* (London: Kegal Paul, Trench, Trubner & Co., 1926), pp. 64–5.
18. Eliot, 'Ulysses, Order, and Myth', *The Dial*, 75 (Nov. 1923), 483.
19. Auden and Plumb, 'Preface', *Oxford Poetry 1926* (Oxford: Basil Blackwell, 1926), p. v.
20. *Oxford Outlook*, 8 (Dec. 1926), 308–9.
21. Auden and Day-Lewis, 'Preface', *Oxford Poetry 1927* (Oxford: Basil Blackwell, 1927), p. v.
22. *Oxford Poetry 1927*, p. vii.
23. Hugh Gordon Porteus, 'W. H. Auden', *Twentieth Century*, 4 (Feb. 1933), 15.
24. Eliot, 'Last Words', *Criterion*, 18 (Jan. 1939), 271.
25. Isherwood, *Lions and Shadows*, p. 177, and MacNeice, *The Strings Are False* (London: Faber & Faber, 1965), p. 101. See also M. P. Ashley and C. T. Saunders, *Red Oxford: A History of the Growth of Socialism in the University of Oxford* (Oxford: Oxford University Labour Club, 1933).
26. Isherwood, *Lions and Shadows*, p. 73. Auden remembered his generation at Oxford in very similar terms: 'We were far too insular and preoccupied with ourselves to know or care what was going on across the Channel. Revolution in Russia, inflation in Germany and Austria, Fascism in Italy, whatever fears or hopes they may have aroused in our elders, went unnoticed by us. Before 1930 I never opened a newspaper.' 'As It Seemed to Us', *The New Yorker*, 41 (3 Apr. 1965), 180.
27. Isherwood, foreword to 'The Railway Accident', in Upward, *The Railway Accident and Other Stories* (London: Heinemann, 1969), p. 1.
28. Isherwood, foreword, p. 2.

CHAPTER

[II]

1. Roberts, Preface to *New Country* (London: Hogarth, 1933), p. 9.
2. Spender, *Poems* (London: Faber & Faber, 1933), p. 31.
3. Quoted by Hugh Sykes, 'The League of Nations', *Experiment*, 5 (Feb. 1930), 9.
4. Brophy, Introduction to *The Soldier's War. A Prose Anthology* (London: Dent, 1929), p. ix.
5. Introduction to *The War 1914–1918*. A Booklist compiled by Edmund Blunden, Cyril Falls, H. M. Tomlinson and R. Wright (London: The Reader, n.d.), p. 2.

6. *The Soldier's War*, pp. x–xi.

7. Herbert Read, 'The Pity of War', *Adelphi*, 1 (Oct. 1930), 69. Note that the title is taken from Owen's preface.

8. F. Le Gros Clark, 'Footnote to "Journey's End"', *Purpose*, 2 (Jan.–Mar. 1930), 36.

9. Waugh, *Decline and Fall* (London: Chapman & Hall, 1928), p. 84.

10. For other examples of the two wars in the early writings of the younger generation, see Spender's 'Written Whilst Walking Down the Rhine', in *Twenty Poems* (Oxford: Blackwell, [1930]), pp. 15–16, and John Lehmann, 'Talk on the River', in *A Garden Revisited* (London: Hogarth, 1931), pp. 20–1.

11. Blunden, 'An Institution and a Moral', *Oxford Outlook*, 11 (Nov. 1931) 191–2.

12. *Criterion*, 9 (Apr. 1930), 569.

13. Day Lewis, *Transitional Poem* (London: Hogarth, 1929), p. 69.

14. Roberts, preface to *New Signatures* (London: Hogarth, 1932), p. 15.

15. Philip Henderson, *The Poet and Society* (London: Secker & Warburg, 1939), p. 220.

16. MacNeice, 'Poetry', in Grigson, ed., *The Arts To-day* (London: John Lane The Bodley Head, 1935), p. 56. One should note also the way members of the generation invented extravagant roles for themselves: Auden, for example, as an undergraduate, in his room with the curtains drawn, wearing an eye-shade and interrogating young poets, and Upward with his Dürers, inventing Mortmere.

17. Eliot called Auden's play 'a brilliant piece of work', and claimed Auden as 'about the best poet that I have discovered in several years'. Letter to E. McKnight Kauffer, quoted in B. C. Bloomfield and Edward Mendelson, *W. H. Auden: A Bibliography* (Charlottesville, University Press of Virginia, 1972), p. 3.

18. Isherwood, 'Some Notes on Auden's Early Poetry', *New Verse*, 26–7 (Nov. 1937), 5–6.

19. *Poems* (London: Faber & Faber, 1930), pp. 8–9.

20. *Poems*, p. 17.

21. *Poems*, p. 34.

22. Empson, 'A Note on W. H. Auden's "Paid on Both Sides"', *Experiment*, 7 (Spring 1931), 61.

23. *Poems*, p. 51.

24. Waugh, *Vile Bodies* (London: Chapman & Hall, 1930), pp. 132–3.

25. *Vile Bodies*, p. 143.

26. *Vile Bodies*, p. 223.

27. *Vile Bodies*, p. 65.

28. *Vile Bodies*, pp. 136–7.

29. *Vile Bodies*, pp. 144–5.

30. *Vile Bodies*, pp. 247–8.

31. Huxley, *Ends and Means* (London: Chatto & Windus, 1937), p. 274.

[III]

1. Stephen Spender, *World Within World* (London: Hamish Hamilton, 1951), p. 137.

2. See A. J. P. Taylor, *England 1914–1939* (Oxford: Oxford University Press, 1965), p. 298, and Noreen Branson and Margot Heinemann, *Britain in the Nineteen Thirties* (London: Weidenfeld & Nicolson, 1971), Ch. 2, for two accounts of 1931 as a 'watershed'.

3. Noël Coward, *Cavalcade* (London: Heinemann, 1932), p. 138.

4. Spender, *Poems* (London: Faber & Faber, 1933), p. 25.

5. 'Obituary: John Cornford', *Cambridge Review*, 58 (5 Feb. 1937), 228. The correspondent was Professor Ernest Barker.

6. Day Lewis, *From Feathers to Iron* (London: Hogarth, 1932), p. 31.

7. Roberts, 'First and Second Impressions', *Poetry Review*, 23 (Jan.–Feb. 1932), 66.

8. Leonard Woolf, *Downhill All the Way* (London: Hogarth, 1967), p. 174; Peter Stansky and William Abrahams, *Journey to the Frontier* (London: Constable, 1966), p. 77.

9. Lehmann, *The Whispering Gallery* (London: Longmans, 1955), p. 178.

10. Quoted in Stansky and Abrahams, *Journey to the Frontier*, p. 76.

11. Roberts, Preface to *New Signatures* (London: Hogarth, 1932), pp. 12–13.

12. Preface to *New Signatures*, pp. 18–19.

13. Spender, *World Within World*, p. 249.

14. Unsigned review of *From Feathers to Iron* and *New Signatures*, in *Twentieth Century*, 3 (Apr. 1932), 30. Lehmann also recalled 'the sense of menacing war, implicit or explicit in so many of the contributions', *Whispering Gallery*, p. 182.

15. Priestley, *Evening Standard*, 12 May 1932, 7; Murry, *Adelphi*, 4 (June 1932), 643; Barker, *Adelphi*, 4 (June 1932), 642; Leavis, *Listener*, 7 (13 Apr. 1932), 540.

16. 'The Promethean Society. A Survey', *Twentieth Century*, 1 (Mar. 1931), 23.

17. *Twentieth Century*, 4 (Sept. 1932), 1–2.

18. *Daily Express*, 27 July 1932, 3.

19. Woolf, *Letter to a Young Poet* (London: Hogarth, 1932), p. 26.

20. Quennell, *Letter to Mrs. Virginia Woolf* (London: Hogarth, 1932), pp. 15–17.

21. Hayward, *Criterion*, 12 (Oct. 1932), 131.

22. Auden, 'Private Pleasure', *Scrutiny*, 1 (Sept. 1932), 193.

23. 'Autumn Books Supplement', *New Statesman*, 4 (15 Oct. 1932), x.

24. Auden, *The Orators* (London: Faber & Faber, 1932), p. 34.

25. Auden, Preface to *Collected Poetry* (New York: Random House, 1945), p. [vii].

26. Philip Henderson, *The Poet and Society* (London: Secker & Warburg, 1939), p. 205.

27. Auden, Foreword to 3rd edition of *The Orators* (London: Faber & Faber, 1966), p. 7.

28. Foreword to 3rd edition, p. 7. Auden got the first Lawrence title wrong: it is *Fantasia of the Unconscious*.

29. *Adelphi*, 4 (June 1932), 643.

30. 'The Poet and Revolution', *Adelphi*, 4 (Sept. 1932), 863.

31. Auden, 'Writing, or The Pattern Between People', in Naomi Mitchison, ed., *An Outline for Boys & Girls and Their Parents* (London: Gollancz, 1932), p. 868.

CHAPTER

[IV]

1. Quoted in F. R. Leavis' review, 'This Poetical Renascence', *Scrutiny*, 2 (June 1933), 70.

2. Read, *Adelphi*, 5 (Feb. 1933), 379.

3. *Times Literary Supplement*, 6 July 1933, 463.

4. 'Editorial', *New Oxford Outlook*, 1 (May 1933), 3.

5. *Cambridge Left*, 1 (Summer, 1933), 10.

6. L. J. Romsey, 'On Some Pacifist Solutions', *Outpost*, 1 (June 1932), 75.

7. Day Lewis, 'Letter to a Young Revolutionary', *New Country* (London: Hogarth, 1933), p. 36.

8. *New Country*, pp. 41–2.

9. For another text making the same point, see Michael Roberts, 'A Knack to Know a Knave', *Twentieth Century*, 4 (Jan. 1933), 8–10:

How shall I choose a leader? Not by his wealth, nor his command of votes, nor any accidental attributes, but as I would choose a wife, by simple recognition.

You do know. That is the first thing, the datum: let theorizing follow. If you are intelligent and honest it isn't likely that you will choose a rogue or a fool, but take your quivering chance. Give service where service is due; you will at least attain integrity . . .

Democracy denies the authority of one man over another which, in private life, we all accept.

10. *New Country*, p. 226. The poem is no. 32 in *The Magnetic Mountain*.

11. *New Country*, p. 69.

12. Spender, 'Upward, Kafka and van der Post', *The Destructive Element* (London: Cape, 1935), p. 238. The phrase in single quotes is from Richards' passage on *The Waste Land* in *Science and Poetry*.

13. *New Country*, p. 189.

14. *New Country*, p. 19.

15. *New Country*, pp. 13, 11, 14, 15, 11.

16. *New Country*, pp. 253, 229.

17. Poem no. XI in *Reconstruction* (Oxford: Shakespeare Head Press, 1933), p. 19.

18. *New Country*, pp. 231–2.

19. *New Country*, pp. 193–4, 225, 233.

20. Dobree, 'New Life in English Poetry', *Listener*, 9 (14 June 1933), 958; Leavis, ' "This Poetical Renascence",' *Scrutiny*, 2 (June 1933), 74.

21. G. E. G., 'Why', *New Verse*, no. 1 (Jan. 1933), 1–2.

22. 'Politics: and a Request', *New Verse*, no. 2 (Mar. 1933), 1.

23. Grigson, 'Faith or Feeling?', *New Verse*, no. 2 (Mar. 1933), 15.

24. Madge, 'Poetry and Politics', *New Verse*, no. 3 (May 1933), 1. For a communist's critique of the Spender–Madge argument, see John Cornford, 'Left?', in *Cambridge Left*, 1 (winter 1933–4), 25–9; reprinted in Pat Sloan, ed., *John Cornford: A Memoir* (London: Cape, 1938), pp. 125–33.

25. Dilys Powell, *Descent from Parnassus* (London: Cresset Press, 1934), p. 203.

26. *The Magnetic Mountain* (London: Hogarth, 1933), pp. 30–1.

27. *Magnetic Mountain*, p. 11.

28. *Magnetic Mountain*, p. 44.

29. MacNeice, 'Poetry', in *The Arts To-day*, ed. Geoffrey Grigson (London: John Lane The Bodley Head, 1935), pp. 56–7.

30. *Magnetic Mountain*, p. 50.

31. *Magnetic Mountain*, pp. 50, 43.

32. *Magnetic Mountain*, p. 47.

33. 'The Witnesses', *Listener*, 10 (12 July 1933), Poetry Supplement, iii.

34. 'A Happy New Year', *New Country*, p. 205. This part of the poem was later reprinted as poem no. 10 of *Look, Stranger!* (London: Faber & Faber, 1936).

35. The manuscript of the lecture, which was delivered in 1937, is in the possession of Janet Adam Smith (Mrs John Carleton). It was never published.

36. Nicolson, *Diaries and Letters 1930–1939* (London: Collins, 1966), p. 153. The poem was never published in its entirety; it is in the Auden manuscript notebook in the Swarthmore College Auden Collection.

37. Auden borrowed a good deal from Lawrence's commentary on the Witnesses of *Revelation*, and the passage in Lawrence provides an excellent gloss on Auden's poem, as for example:

> They testify before the god of earth or fecundity all the time. And all the time, they put a limit on man. They say to him, in every earthly or physical activity: thus far and no further.—They limit every action, every 'earth' action, to its own scope, and counterbalance it with an opposite action. They are the gods of gates, but they are also gods of limits: each forever jealous of the other, keeping the other in bounds. They make life possible; but they make life limited.   *Apocalypse*
> (London: Martin Secker, 1932), pp. 148–9.

Dilys Powell first noted Auden's sources for the poem, in *Descent from Parnassus*, p. 183.

38. Eugen Bleuler, *Textbook of Psychiatry* (London: George Allen & Unwin, n.d. [1924]), p. 531. Auden cites the same passage from Wagner, as quoted in William MacDougall, *An Outline of Abnormal Psychology* (London: Methuen, 1926), p. 338.

39. Isherwood, *Lions and Shadows*, p. 207.

40. Auden, *The Dance of Death* (London: Faber & Faber, 1933), p. 7.

41. *Dance of Death*, p. 38.

42. Bell, 'Politics in Cambridge', *New Statesman*, 6 (9 Dec. 1933), 731.

43. See David Caute, *The Fellow-Travellers* (London: Weidenfeld & Nicolson, 1973), p. 134.

44. The only specific reference I have come across is Herbert Read's poem, 'The Brown Book of the Hitler Terror', in *New Verse*, no. 6 (Dec. 1933), 2.

CHAPTER

[V]

1. Lehmann, *The Noise of History* (London: Hogarth, 1934), p. 44.

2. Spender, 'Politics and Literature in 1933', *The Bookman*, 85 (Dec. 1933), 147.

3. The Very Rev. H. R. L. Sheppard, in *Fascists at Olympia, A Record of Eye-Witnesses and Victims*, compiled by 'Vindicator' (London: Gollancz, 1934), p. 11.

4. Auden, 'Summer Night', *The Listener*, 11 (7 Mar. 1934), 421. Auden described the same occasion in prose in his introduction to Anne Fremantle, *The Protestant Mystics* (1964); in this version the experience is offered as an example of 'The Vision of Agape', and emphasis is placed on the feelings among the participants, not on the world outside.

5. Greene quotes the note in *A Sort of Life* (London: Bodley Head, 1971), p. 210.

6. See A. W. Kinglake, *The Invasion of the Crimea*, 8 vols. (Edinburgh and London: Blackwood, 1863–87), vol. 5, pp. 476–7.

7. Greene, *It's a Battlefield* (London: Heinemann, 1934), p. 174.

8. *It's a Battlefield*, p. 237.

9. *It's a Battlefield*, pp. 224–5.

10. *Times Literary Supplement* (8 Feb. 1934), 90; D. A. Willis, 'New Life for the Novel', *Viewpoint*, 1 (Apr.–June 1934), 14.

11. *It's a Battlefield*, pp. 175–6.

12. Introduction to *It's a Battlefield*, Collected Edition (London: Heinemann/Bodley Head, 1970), p. ix. Greene explains why he had to restore to the text the episode of the trunk murderer's arrest, which had been removed from an earlier edition: 'Without the mad murderer of the Salvation Army the battlefield of the title lacked the sense of violence and confusion. The metaphor became a political and not an ironic one . . .'

13. Michael Roberts, in *The Criterion*, 14 (Apr. 1935), 499. For other 'thirties writing on the Vienna Uprising see Naomi Mitchison, *Naomi Mitchison's Vienna Diary* (London: Gollancz, 1934); Charles Madge, 'Loss', in *The Year's Poetry 1934*, ed. Roberts, Gould, Lehmann (London: John Lane The Bodley Head, 1934), p. 127; Julian Bell, 'Vienna', *The Year's Poetry 1935*, pp. 117–18; John Lehmann, *Down River* (London: Cresset Press, 1939), and 'Arthur Pumphrey' [Alan Pryce-Jones], *Pink Danube* (London: Martin Secker, 1939).

14. Lehmann, *The Noise of History*.

15. 'A Little Distance Off', *The Noise of History*, p. 12.

16. 'The Door Flies Open', *The Noise of History*, p. 29.

17. 'Five to Twelve', *The Noise of History*, p. 55.

18. Grigson, 'The Year's Poetry', *Bookman*, 87 (Dec. 1934), 151; A.L.M., 'A Poet Writes of Real Things', *Daily Worker* (24 Oct. 1934), 4.

19. Spender, *Vienna* (London: Faber & Faber, 1934), p. 25.

20. *Vienna*, p. 42.

21. *Vienna*, pp. 42–3.

22. *Times Literary Supplement*, 13 Dec. 1934, 890.

23. Spender, *World Within World* (London: Hamish Hamilton, 1951), p. 191.

24. *World Within World*, p. 192.

25. Muir, 'Society and the Poet', *London Mercury*, 31 (Feb. 1935), 382.

26. See, as an example of how conscious this process was, the passage from Montagu Slater, 'A Story Everybody Knows', *Left Review*, 1 (Mar. 1935), 227, quoted below, p. 187.

27. Michael Roberts, 'The Return of the Hero', *London Mercury*, 31 (Nov. 1934), 72.

28. Dilys Powell, *Descent from Parnassus* (London: Cresset, 1934), xvi–xvii.

29. Day Lewis, 'The Road These Times Must Take', *Left Review*, 1 (Nov. 1934), 35.

30. Auden, 'Prologue', *New Country*, p. 194; revised for *Look, Stranger!* (London: Faber & Faber, 1936), p. 12.

31. *Viewpoint*, 1 (Apr.–June 1934), 1.

32. Zhdanov, in *Problems of Soviet Literature*. Reports and Speeches at the First Soviet Writers' Congress. By A. Zhdanov, Maxim Gorky, N. Bukharin, K. Radek, A. Stetsky (London: Martin Lawrence Ltd, n.d. [1935]), p. 21.

33. An unidentified writer, quoted in Charles Madge, 'Writers under two flags', a review of *Problems of Soviet Literature*, in *Left Review*, 2 (Feb. 1936), 228.

34. Gilbert Armitage, 'The New Wyndham Lewis', *New Verse*, no. 7 (Feb. 1934), 14.

35. Spender, 'A New Defence of Poetry', *Now and Then*, no. 47 (Spring, 1934), 25.

36. 'Answers to an Enquiry', *New Verse*, no. 11 (Oct. 1934), 2.

37. 'Answers to an Enquiry', 7 and 15.

38. 'Answers to an Enquiry', 12.

39. Day Lewis, *A Hope for Poetry* (Oxford: Blackwell, 1934), p. 1.

40. *A Hope for Poetry*, p. 76. This is the source of Roberts' remarks on heroes in 'The Return of the Hero', which is a review of Day Lewis' book.

41. For other 1934 versions of these common views of the generation see Michael Roberts, *Critique of Poetry* (London: Cape, 1934), p. 238 ff., and John Strachey, 'The Education of a Communist', *Left Review*, 1 (Dec. 1934), 63–9.

42. *A Hope for Poetry*, p. 47.

43. *A Hope for Poetry*, pp. 55–6.

44. *A Hope for Poetry*, pp. 37–8.
45. Grigson, 'The Year's Poetry', *Bookman*, 87 (Dec. 1934), 151.

CHAPTER

[VI]

1. C. Day Lewis, 'Controversy', *Left Review*, 1 (Jan. 1935), 128; Michael Roberts, 'Poetry and Propaganda', *London Mercury*, 31 (Jan. 1935), 231; Stephen Spender, 'Writers and Manifestos', *Left Review*, 1 (Feb. 1935), 145.
2. Spender, *The Destructive Element* (London: Cape, 1935), p. 13.
3. *Destructive Element*, pp. 14–15.
4. *Destructive Element*, pp. 14, 190–1.
5. Richards acknowledged his relation to the 'thirties generation in the second edition of *Science and Poetry* (1935) by adding a new set of epigraphs including three from Auden's poems and one from Empson. This edition also added to the *Waste Land* footnote:

    The original footnote [Richards wrote] seems to have puzzled Mr. Eliot and some other readers. Well it might! In saying, though, that he 'had effected a complete severance between his poetry and all beliefs' I was referring not to the poet's own history, but to the technical detachment of the poetry. And the way in which he then seemed to me to have 'realised what might otherwise have remained a speculative possibility' was by finding a new order through the contemplation and exhibition of disorder. (pp. 70–1).

    This endorses even more strongly the notion of a formal solution to the modern problem; it offers, one might say (with the terminology of the present study in mind) an authority for the writing of parables in a critical time.
6. *Destructive Element*, pp. 222–3.
7. *Destructive Element*, p. 224.
8. *Destructive Element*, pp. 67, 182.
9. *Destructive Element*, p. 254.
10. Naturally enough, he was severely attacked by his more orthodox communist colleagues. For example, John Lehmann wrote: 'Further evidence that he is still fairly deeply confused about Communism and the poet's relation to revolutionary politics, is provided by his book of criticism published in 1935, *The Destructive Element*. There is an immense amount of valuable material in this book, in scattered comments and sudden imaginative flashes of criticism, and its main theme . . . is really illuminating. It is when he gets down to those writers who are his contemporaries that his judgment seems to stray, and his general theoretical remarks on war, and propaganda, and Marxism can often only be considered an insult to his own intelligence.' Lehmann, 'Some Revolutionary Trends in English Poetry: 1930–1935', *International Literature*, no. 4 (Apr. 1936), 80.
11. Montagu Slater, 'The Turning Point', *Left Review*, 2 (Oct. 1935), 19, 20.

12. 'Introduction', *The Poet's Tongue*, An Anthology chosen by W. H. Auden and John Garrett (London: G. Bell & Sons Ltd, 1935), pp. ix–x. The anthology was published in two forms, a two-volume text edition and a one-volume trade edition; the front matter is essentially the same in both.

13. *Poet's Tongue*, p. ix.

14. Auden, 'Psychology and Art To-day', in *The Arts To-day*, ed. Geoffrey Grigson (London: John Lane The Bodley Head, 1935), p. 18.

15. 'Psychology and Art To-day', pp. 18–19.

16. 'Psychology and Art To-day', p. 19.

17. 'Psychology and Art To-day', p. 20.

18. A. Desmond Hawkins, *Criterion*, 15 (Jan. 1936), 302. It is worth noting that of the eight essays in the volume Auden's was the one that received the most critical attention, and that in his essay it was the passage on parable-art that was the most quoted; it was as though critics had been waiting for Auden to name the concept, so that they could use it. See for example Grigson in *New Verse*, no. 15 (June 1935), 17; and the *Times Literary Supplement*, 26 Sept. 1935, 592.

19. Empson, *Some Versions of Pastoral* (London: Chatto & Windus, 1935), p. 3.

20. *Some Versions*, pp. 3, 15, 23.

21. *Some Versions*, p. 11.

22. *Some Versions*, p. 21.

23. *Times Literary Supplement*, 7 Dec. 1935, 838.

24. J. Brian Harvey, 'Proletarian or Pastoral?' *Left Review*, 2 (Feb. 1936), 231.

25. Day Lewis, *Revolution in Writing* (London: Hogarth, 1935), p. 16.

26. *Revolution in Writing*, p. 17.

27. Day Lewis quotes this passage at the end of his second essay, 'Writers and Morals', *Revolution in Writing*, p. 31.

28. Lehmann, *Whispering Gallery*, p. 225.

29. Spender, *World Within World*, p. 126.

30. Isherwood, 'Prologue: Gerald and Mr. Norris', in Gerald Hamilton, *Mr. Norris and I* (London: Allan Wingate, 1956), p. 10.

31. The link between liberation, revolution, and homosexuality was evident to many writers of the time. Laura Riding, for example, writing in response to the *New Verse* questionnaire, asked: 'How do you explain the connexion between homosexuality and communism—suggested by their happy union in so many unhappy contemporary poets?' *New Verse*, no. 11 (Oct. 1934), 5. And both MacNeice and Day Lewis made the connection in essays. Day Lewis, defining 'our talented, average, vaguely revolutionary young writer,' wrote:

He is generally free from those sexual conflicts with which orthodox Christian morality tormented his forebears for centuries. At the same time, the War-environment in which he grew up, combined possibly with a radical weakening of morale in the class from which he springs, tends to drive him to homosexualism for refuge from responsibilities.

Revolution and Writing, pp. 29–30.

And MacNeice observed that the comradeship of extreme political movements led to an idealization of homosexuality (see above, pp. 121–2).

32. Isherwood, *Mr. Norris Changes Trains* (London: Hogarth, 1935), p. 130.

33. Quoted in *The Whispering Gallery*, p. 225.

34. *Mr. Norris Changes Trains*, pp. 76–7.

35. *Mr. Norris Changes Trains*, p. 232.

36. *Times Literary Supplement*, 14 Mar. 1935, 161; William Plomer, 'Fiction', *Spectator*, 154 (1 Mar. 1935), 346.

37. The play is described in Mardi Valgemae, 'Auden's Collaboration with Isherwood on *The Dog Beneath the Skin*', *Huntington Library Quarterly*, 31 (Aug. 1968), 373–83. The play has never been published.

38. The manuscript is in the library of Exeter College, Oxford.

39. Valgemae, 'Auden's Collaboration', 378.

40. Spender, 'The Poetic Drama of W. H. Auden and Christopher Isherwood', *New Writing*, n.s. 1 (autumn 1938), 105.

41. Montagu Slater, 'The Turning Point', *Left Review*, 2 (Oct. 1935), 20–2; A. L. M., 'Shocked Satirists', *Daily Worker*, 3 July 1935, 4.

42. E. D. Randall, 'Speaking Personally', *Action*, no. 1 (21 Feb. 1936), 10.

43. *Times*, 31 Jan. 1936, 12.

44. J. M., *Janus*, 1 (May 1936), 30.

45. Auden and Isherwood, *The Dog Beneath the Skin* (London: Faber & Faber, 1935), p. 11.

46. *The Dog Beneath the Skin*, p. 43.

47. Poem no. 30 in *Look, Stranger!* (London: Faber & Faber, 1936), pp. 65–6. The poem was first published as 'To a writer on his Birthday', in *New Verse*, no. 17 (Oct./Nov. 1935), 7–9.

48. Slater, 'A Story Everybody Knows', *Left Review*, 1 (Mar. 1935), 227.

49. Quoted in Phyllis Bentley, 'Literature and Society', *Left Review*, 1 (Sept. 1935), 488.

50. Maxim Gorky, 'Soviet Literature', in *Problems of Soviet Literature*, p. 44.

51. C. St John Sprigg, *Great Flights* (London: Thomas Nelson & Sons, 1935), p. 1.

52. *Great Flights*, p. 3.

53. Fox, 'Lawrence the 20th Century Hero', *Left Review*, 1 (July 1935), 391. For another Communist version of Lawrence, see Caudwell, 'T. E. Lawrence: A Study in Heroism', in *Studies in a Dying Culture* (London: John Lane, 1938).

54. City of Oxford High School for Boys, *Proceedings at the Unveiling of the Memorial to Lawrence of Arabia* (Oxford: J. Thornton & Sons, 1937), pp. 10–11.

55. 'T. E. Lawrence. By his Friends', *Listener*, 17 (9 June 1937), 1160. [An unsigned review by Isherwood.]

56. Auden, 'T. E. Lawrence', *Now and Then*, no. 47 (spring, 1934), 30.

1. 'Buy this Book', an unsigned review of Frederic Prokosch's *The Assassins*, *New Verse*, no. 22 (Aug./Sept. 1936), 16.

2. Julian Bell, 'Introduction', *We Did Not Fight* (London: Cobden-Sanderson, 1935), pp. xviii–xix.

3. Bell, 'War and Peace: A Letter to E. M. Forster', in Quentin Bell, ed., *Julian Bell: Essays, Poems and Letters* (London: Hogarth, 1938), pp. 373, 380.

4. Bell, 'On Roger Fry—a Letter to A', in *Essays, Poems and Letters*, p. 294. The letter is datelined, Wu Han University, Hupeh, China, Jan. 4, 1936'. Bell was a teacher there, and it was during this absence from England that he wrote the three long letters that define his own position and his sense of his generation One, 'On Roger Fry', was apparently intended for publication in the Hogarth Press series of letters to which Lehmann, Forster, and Virginia Woolf had already contributed, but it was not published, and appeared for the first time in the posthumous collection edited by Bell's brother, Quentin.

5. Lehmann, 'Some Revolutionary Trends in English Poetry: 1930–1935' *International Literature*, no. 4 (Apr. 1936), 71, 72; G. W. Stonier, 'Auden, Then and Now', *New Statesman*, 12 (14 Nov. 1936), 778; Spender, 'Fable and Reportage', *Left Review*, 2 (Nov. 1936), 779.

6. The poems quoted are David Gascoyne's 'Five Poems', *New Verse*, no. 15 (June 1935), 6, and A. J. M. Smith's 'The Face', *New Verse*, no. 22 (Sept. 1936), 7. The critic of Grigson is D. Mirsky, in 'About Stephen Spender and C. Day Lewis', in *International Literature*, no. 10 (Oct. 1936), 86.

7. 'Manifesto', *New Writing I*, ed. John Lehmann (London: John Lane The Bodley Head, 1936), [v]; R. W. Fletcher, '*New Writing* is Good Writing', *Daily Worker*, 14 Oct. 1936, 7; Frank Chapman, *Criterion*, 16 (Oct. 1936), 163.

8. Lehmann, *The Whispering Gallery*, p. 232.

9. Day Lewis, *Noah and the Waters* (London: Hogarth Press, 1936), pp. [7], [9].

10. *Noah and the Waters*, pp. 46–7.

11. *Noah and the Waters*, p. 50.

12. Unsigned review (but certainly by Grigson), 'Two Whiffs of Lewisite', *New Verse*, no. 21 (June–July 1936), 17–18.

13. *Daily Worker*, 22 Apr. 1936, 7.

14. Day Lewis, *The Buried Day* (London: Chatto & Windus, 1960), p. 222.

15. Edwin Muir, 'The Flood', *Spectator*, 156 (13 Mar. 1936), 482, 484.

16. *Julian Bell. Essays, Poems and Letters*, p. 322.

17. Roberts, 'Stammering Prophets', *Listener*, 15 (11 Mar. 1936), 'Early Book Supplement', p. xii.

18. Day Lewis, *A Hope for Poetry*, Reprint with a Postscript (Oxford: Basil Blackwell, 1936), pp. 80, 83, 98.

19. Roberts, 'Introduction', *Faber Book of Modern Verse* (London: Faber & Faber, 1936), p. 3.

20. Mirsky, 'About Stephen Spender and C. Day Lewis', 83.

21. Spender, 'Fable and Reportage', 782.

22. Gollancz, 'The Left Book Club', *Left Book Club News*, no. 1 (May 1936), 2.

23. Strachey, '1936 Has Been a Great "Left" Year', *Daily Worker*, 2 Dec. 1936, supplement, p. i.

24. See for example the review of John Lewis' *The Left Book Club* in the *Times Literary Supplement*, 18 Sept. 1970, 1016, and the subsequent correspondence.

25. Harold J. Laski, 'Editorial: The Labour Party and the Left Book Club', *Left News*, no. 16 (Aug. 1937), 456.

26. Grierson, 'Propaganda', *Sight and Sound*, 2 (winter 1933–4), 119.

27. Grierson, 'The Story of Documentary Film', *Fortnightly Review*, 152 (Aug. 1939), 122.

28. Rotha, *Documentary Film* (London: Faber & Faber, 1936), p. 15.

29. Grierson, Preface to *Documentary Film*, pp. 7, 13. For Left criticism of Grierson's position, see Arthur Calder-Marshall, *The Changing Scene* (London: Chapman & Hall, 1937), pp. 36–40.

30. GPO Film Library, *Notes and Synopses 1938*, p. 24.

31. Stonier, 'An Exceptional Story', *New Statesman*, 12 (12 Dec. 1936), 998; Frank Chapman, *Criterion*, 16 (Oct. 1936), 163.

32. Brophy, 'New Fiction. The Need for More Imagination', *Daily Telegraph*, 20 Oct., 1936, 10.

33. Roberts, 'Notes on English Poets', *Poetry*, 39 (Feb. 1932), 278; Porteus, 'W. H. Auden', *Twentieth Century* (Promethean Society), 4 (Feb. 1933), 15.

34. 'Notes on Contributors', *Contemporary Poetry and Prose*, no. 1 (May 1936), 15.

35. *New Statesman*, n.s. 10 (14 Dec. 1935), 946.

36. Mortimer, 'The Art of Displeasing', *Listener*, 15 (17 June 1936), 1150–2; 'A Worker's Notebook', *Daily Worker*, 12 June 1936, 4; 'Exhibition—or Exhibitionism?', *Action*, 2 July 1936, 11.

37. Read, 'Introduction', catalogue of the *International Surrealist Exhibition* (London: New Burlington Galleries, 1936), p. 13.

38. See Peter Quennell, 'Surrealism and Revolution', *New Statesman*, 6 (26 Aug. 1933), 237–8; and C.M. [Charles Madge], 'The Meaning of Surrealism', *New Verse*, no. 10 (Aug. 1934), 13–15.

39. Gascoyne, *A Short Survey of Surrealism* (London: Cobden-Sanderson, 1935), p. xii.

40. 'Speech by Herbert Read at the Conway Hall', *International Surrealist Bulletin*, no. 4 (Sept. 1936), 9.

41. [Lord] Hastings, 'The Surrealists', *Left Review*, 2 (Jan. 1936), 186.

42. Roger Roughton, 'Barber's bust with loaf on head', *Daily Worker*, 8 Apr. 1936, 7; J. K., 'Explodes an Illusion', *Daily Worker*, 30 Dec. 1936, 7.

43. [Roughton], 'Surrealism and Communism', *Contemporary Poetry and Prose*, nos. 4–5 (Aug.–Sept. 1936), 74.

44. 'Surrealism and Communism', 75.

45. [Roughton], 'Fascism Murders Art', *Contemporary Poetry and Prose*, no. 6 (Oct. 1936), 106.

46. [Roughton], 'Announcements: Policy', *Contemporary Poetry and Prose*, no. 8 (Dec. 1936), 143.

47. Hugh Sykes Davies, 'Extracts from the Lecture: Biology and Surrealism', *International Surrealist Bulletin*, no. 4 (Sept. 1936), 13.

48. Roughton, 'Lady Windermere's Fan Dance', *Contemporary Poetry and Prose*, no. 6 (Oct. 1936), 117.

49. Quennell, 'Surrealism and Revolution', *New Statesman*, 6 (26 Aug. 1933), 238.

50. Derek Kahn, 'They See Where the Menace Lies', *Daily Worker*, 14 Oct. 1936, 7.

51. Roger Hinks, 'Art Chronicle: Surrealism', *Criterion*, 16 (Oct. 1936), 72.

52. Greene, *Journey Without Maps* (London: Heinemann, 1936), p. 107.

53. *Journey Without Maps*, p. 102.

54. *Journey Without Maps*, p. 262.

55. Guy Hunter, ' "The Waste Land" in Liberia', *London Mercury*, 34 (June 1936), 178.

56. Orwell, *Keep the Aspidistra Flying* (London: Gollancz, 1936), p. 30.

57. Introduction to *A Gun for Sale*, Collected Edition (London: Heinemann/The Bodley Head, 1973), p. vi.

58. Greene, *A Gun for Sale* (London: Heinemann, 1936), pp. 57, 256.

59. Rosamund Lehmann, 'New Novels', *New Statesman*, 12 (1 Aug. 1936), 164.

60. Forster, 'Chormopuloda', *Listener*, 16, Early Autumn Book Supplement (14 Oct. 1936), vii.

61. *The Ascent of F6* (London: Faber & Faber, 1936), pp. 49–50.

62. 'The Ascent of F6', *Group Theatre Paper*, no. 6 (Dec. 1936), 5.

63. A. R. Humphreys, 'The Ascent of F6', *Cambridge Review*, 58 (30 Apr. 1937), 355.

64. Spender, 'Fable and Reportage', 781; Day Lewis, 'Paging Mankind', *Poetry*, 49 (Jan. 1937), 227. Day Lewis shared the common inability to quote Lord Acton correctly, and made the famous passage more categorical than it in fact is. What Acton wrote was this: 'Power tends to corrupt, and absolute power corrupts absolutely. Great men are almost always bad men.'

65. For example John Beevers, 'Topical Morality', *New Statesman*, 12 (10 Oct. 1936), 531.

CHAPTER

[VIII]

1. Connolly, 'To-day the Struggle', New Statesman, 13 (5 June 1937), 928.

2. In *Mithraic Emblems* (London: Boriswood, 1936).

3. *The Whispering Gallery*, p. 279.

4. When the *Left Review* asked 148 writers to take sides on the war in the autumn of 1937, 127 supported the Loyalists, 16 were neutral, and only 5 sided with Franco. One should note, of course, that a poll conducted by a left-wing journal and signed by twelve leading left intellectuals would

scarcely be objective. Even the way in which the question was put was highly polemical:

The Question
To the Writers and Poets of England, Scotland,
Ireland and Wales

It is clear to many of us throughout the whole world
that now, as certainly never before, we are determined or compelled to take sides. The equivocal
attitude, the Ivory Tower, the paradoxical, the ironic
detachment, will no longer do.

We have seen murder and destruction by Fascism in
Italy, in Germany—the organisation there of social
injustice and cultural death—and how revived, imperial
Rome, abetted by international treachery, has conquered her place in the Abyssinian sun. The dark
millions in the colonies are unavenged.

To-day, the struggle is in Spain. To-morrow
it may be in other countries—our own.
But there are some who, despite the martyrdom of
Durango and Guernica, the enduring agony of Madrid,
of Bilbao, and Germany's shelling of Almeria, are
still in doubt, or who aver that it is possible that
Fascism may be what it proclaims it is:
'the saviour of civilisation'.

This is the question we are asking you:
Are you for, or against, the legal Government
and the People of Republican Spain?
Are you for, or against, Franco and Fascism?
For it is impossible any longer to take no side.

Writers and Poets, we wish to print your answers. We
wish the world to know what you, writers and poets,
who are amongst the most sensitive instruments of a
nation, feel.

The signatories were Louis Aragon, Auden, José Bergamin, Jean Richard Bloch, Nancy Cunard, Brian Howard, Heinrich Mann, Ivor Montagu, Pablo Neruda, Ramon Sender, Spender, and Tristan Tzara.

5. The first English casualty, whose death preceded all the others by several months, was a woman. Felicia Browne was a sculptor and a communist who was in Spain on a sketching trip when the war broke out; she refused to be evacuated, joined a militia unit, and was killed in an attack on a munitions train on 29 August 1936. A pamphlet of her drawings was published in

414

London in October, with an anonymous appreciation of her life and work that drew the following conclusion:

There was a tremendously strong thread of consistency running through her life and this came to some objective expression in her Party work. But the tragedy lies in the fact that she was unable to realise her use to Communism as an artist . . . There was a split between her imagination and her practice which, with better fortune, might have been healed by realisation of her practical revolutionary use. ('Felicia Browne: An Appreciation', in *Twenty Drawings by Felicia Browne*, London, n.d. [1936], p. 2.)

A similar epitaph might have been written for Cornford and Caudwell, and indeed for most Left-leaning artists; 'use to Communism *as an artist*' was the problem.

6. Orwell, 'Eye-Witness in Barcelona', *Controversy*, 1 (Aug. 1937), 85–8; John Sommerfield, 'To Madrid', *New Writing*, 3 (spring 1937), 43–8; Auden, 'Impressions of Valencia', *New Statesman*, 13 (30 Jan. 1937), 159; Spender, 'Miscellany: Heroes in Spain', *New Statesman*, 13 (1 May 1937), 714–15.
7. Cornford, 'A Letter from Aragon', *Left Review*, 2 (Nov. 1936), 771.
8. Cornford, 'A Letter from Aragon', *Left Review*, 2 (Nov. 1936), 771.
9. Cornford, 'Full Moon at Tierz: Before the Storming of Huesca', *Left Review*, 3 (Mar. 1937), 69–70.
10. Spender, 'Miscellany: Heroes in Spain', 715.
11. Spender, 'Poetry', *Fact*, no. 4 (July 1937), 26.
12. Spender, 'Regum Ultima Ratio', *New Statesman*, 13 (15 May 1937), 811. The title was changed to its present form, 'Ultima Ratio Regum', when the poem was included in *The Still Centre* (1939).
13. It is perhaps this aspect of Spender's relation to the war in Spain that led Hugh Kingsmill and Malcolm Muggeridge to satirize his war poems in their *1938: A Pre-view of Next Year's News* (London: Eyre & Spottiswoode, 1937). The book is a series of imaginary news items for the year ahead. The item for 20 June reads:

Mr. Stephen Spender and Spain

At a literary luncheon in the Holborn Restaurant yesterday, the guest of honour, Mr. Stephen Spender, gave readings from poems written while on active service in Spain. Proposing a vote of thanks, Miss Maude Royden said that whatever their political views might be, they must all surely recognise in the poems they had just listened to the most poignant expression, since Rupert Brooke, of youth going gallantly into battle. Certain lines of those they had just heard would, she knew, for ever linger in her memory:

> If I die in Spain
> I do not die in Spain
> I die in the future
> And shall live again
> When the future has overtaken the past.

14. *Daily Worker*, 12 Jan. 1937, 3.

15. Auden, in *Modern Canterbury Pilgrims*, ed. the Dean of New York (London: Mowbray, 1956), p. 41.

16. Auden, Introduction to *The Poet's Tongue*, p. ix.

17. Auden, *Spain* (London: Faber & Faber, 1937), p. 10. Auden cut much of this passage from later versions of the poem.

18. Goodman, 'Perspectives for Poetry', *Daily Worker*, 2 June 1937, 7.

19. Rickword, 'Auden and Politics', *New Verse*, nos. 26–7 (Nov. 1937), 22.

20. Dyment, 'Poetry', *Time and Tide*, 18 (12 June 1937), 794.

21. *New Verse*, no. 25 (May 1937), 22.

22. For example Storm Jameson, 'Documents', in *Fact*, no. 4 (July 1937), 9–10: The type of socialist here is a revolutionary . . . and here, if he is a novelist, the writer is not likely to be able to create a revolutionary hero under the eyes of the living Dimitroff . . . Note that in Ralph Bates's very fine novels his heroes are least convincing when they are behaving as revolutionaries. In quarrelling, in gathering olives, in enduring, they appear as whole men. Compare the hero of Malraux's last book with the figure of Dimitroff; he is a shadow.

23. Ralph Fox, *The Novel and the People* (London: Lawrence & Wishart, 1937), p. 130.

24. Auden, in *New Verse*, no. 25 (May 1937), 22.

25. *Listener*, 18 (29 Sept. 1937), 691.

26. For other examples of the Left's rejection of Richards, see Alick West, *Crisis and Criticism* (London: Lawrence & Wishart, 1937), Ch. VI; and Edward Upward, 'A Marxist Interpretation of Literature', in Day Lewis, ed., *The Mind in Chains* (London: Frederick Muller Ltd, 1937), pp. 44–5.

27. Caudwell, *Illusion and Reality* (London: Macmillan, 1937), p. 295.

28. *Illusion and Reality*, pp. 171–2.

29. *Illusion and Reality*, p. 306.

30. *Illusion and Reality*, p. 319.

31. Compare MacNeice's remark to Auden: 'I think you have shown great sense in not writing "proletarian" stuff . . . You realise that one must write about what one knows. One may not hold the bourgeois creed, but if one knows only bourgeois one must write about them.' 'Letter to W. H. Auden', *New Verse*, nos. 26–7 (Nov. 1937), 12.

32. Spender, 'Oxford to Communism', *New Verse*, 26–7 (Nov. 1937), 10.

33. Spender, *Forward from Liberalism* (London: Gollancz, 1937), p. 169.

34. *Forward from Liberalism*, p. 196.

35. Laski, *Left News*, no. 9 (Jan. 1937), 205.

36. Strachey, 'Topic of the Month: Democracy and Freedom', *Left News*, no. 11 (Mar. 1937), 273, 275; J. R. Campbell, 'Forward from Liberalism—but Whither?', *Daily Worker*, 1 Feb. 1937, 4; Randall Swingler, 'Spender's Approach to Communism', *Left Review*, 3 (Mar. 1937), 112; Pollitt, 'Liberalism and Communism', *Labour Monthly*, 19 (Mar. 1937), 188.

37. *Daily Worker*, 19 Feb. 1937, 4.

38. *Authors Take Sides on the Spanish War* (London: Left Review, n.d.).

39. Day Lewis, 'Regency Houses', *London Mercury*, 36 (May 1937), 5.

40. Empson, 'Just a Smack at Auden', *Contemporary Poetry and Prose*, no. 10 (autumn 1937), 24.

41. Roberts, 'Aspects of English Poetry: 1932–1937', *Poetry*, 49 (Jan. 1937), 213–14.

42. Roberts, *The Modern Mind* (London: Faber & Faber, 1937), p. 5.

43. George Every, *Criterion*, 17 (Oct. 1937), 133.

44. Russell, 'The Fairly Modern Mind', *New Statesman*, 13 (26 June 1937), 1048.

45. 'Is the Army a Concentration Camp?', *Truth*, 121 (2 June 1937), 861.

46. Spender, 'Poetry', *Fact*, no. 4 (July 1937), 21.

47. Storm Jameson, 'Documents', *Fact*, no. 4, 13.

48. 'Documents', 11, 15.

49. 'Documents', 12. Two years later, when Miss Jameson reprinted her essay, she was a good deal less positive about it. She changed the title to 'New Documents', and wrote in a preparatory note: 'This essay was written for *Fact*, for an issue called "Writing in Revolt". It was a singularly inapt title— foolish, too: writers may revolt, though surely not in a vacuum, but writing? Neither the theory nor the examples offered could have been labelled revolutionary in any proper sense of that bundle-word. This essay is as mild, orthodox and one-sided as the annual conference of the Conservative Party, and much more so than any Mothers' Meeting.' Storm Jameson, *Civil Journey* (London: Cassell, 1939), p. 261.

50. Jameson, 'Socialists Born and Made', *Fact*, no. 2 (May 1937), 87.

51. 'Documents', 15–16.

52. 'Documents', 15.

53. For example Seán O'Faoláin, 'The Proletarian Novel', *London Mercury*, 35 (Apr. 1937), 584:
Those of us who are dissatisfied with the heritage of Naturalism, with its inherent pessimism, its destructivism, its distaste for what it handles, its bitterness, its aimless objectivity, its accurate descriptions of insignificant detail, have but few alternatives, and, in each case, if we think honestly about the thing at all, we are brought up sooner or later against the real reasons for our dissatisfaction—the philosophical values, or lack of values, inherent in these alternatives. The crude materialism of the Communist is at least understandable, and in that lies a great deal of its seductive power. We cannot afford merely to state, in opposition, a merely artistic credo.

54. Orwell, *The Road to Wigan Pier* (London: Gollancz, 1937), p. 5.

55. *Road to Wigan Pier*, p. 17.

56. *Road to Wigan Pier*, pp. 34–5.

57. For a contemporary account of mining by a real miner, see B. L. Coombes, 'The Flame', *New Writing*, 3 (spring 1937), 131–4.

58. *Road to Wigan Pier*, pp. 148–9.

59. *Road to Wigan Pier*, p. 159.

417

60. Laski, *Left News*, no. 11 (Mar. 1937), 275; Pollitt, 'Mr. Orwell Will Have to Try Again', *Daily Worker*, 17 Mar. 1937, 7.

61. Charles Madge and Tom Harrisson, *Mass-Observation* (London: Frederick Muller Ltd, 1937), p. 10.

62. *New Statesman*, 12 (12 Dec. 1936), 974.

63. *New Statesman*, 13 (2 Jan. 1937), 12.

64. Humphrey Jennings was a maker of documentary films who was also a poet and painter. He was a member of the English Committee of the International Surrealist Exhibition in 1936, and exhibited six of his own works in the show. Like Madge, he seems to have seen Mass-Observation as a kind of collective surrealism.

65. *New Statesman*, 13 (30 Jan. 1937), 155.

66. See for example Geoffrey Gorer, 'Notes on the Way', *Time and Tide*, 18 (24 July 1937), 1003–5, and subsequent correspondence with Harrisson; also T. H. Marshall, 'Is Mass-Observation Moonshine?', *The Highway*, 30 (Dec. 1937), 48–50.

67. Observers' expressed motives are quoted in Madge and Harrisson, eds., *First Year's Work by Mass-Observation* (London: Lindsay Drummond, 1938), pp. 65–79.

68. *Mass-Observation*, pp. 47–8.

69. Harrisson, 'Mass-Observation and the W.E.A.', *The Highway*, 30 (Dec. 1937), 47.

70. C.M. and H.J., 'They Speak for Themselves: Mass-Observation and Social Narrative', *Life and Letters*, 17 (autumn 1937), 37.

71. C.M., 'Poetic Description and Mass-Observation', *New Verse*, no. 24 (Feb.– Mar. 1937), 3.

72. Humphrey Jennings, Charles Madge, and others, *May the Twelfth* (London: Faber & Faber, 1937), p. 335.

73. *May the Twelfth*, p. 414.

74. 'Oxford Collective Poem', *New Verse*, no. 25 (May 1937), 18–19.

75. Auden and MacNeice, *Letters from Iceland* (London: Faber & Faber, 1937), pp. 25, 26.

76. *Letters from Iceland*, p. 30.

77. *Letters from Iceland*, p. 93.

78. *Letters from Iceland*, pp. 236, 258.

79. Prokosch, *New Verse*, nos. 26–7 (Nov. 1937), 24.

80. *Letters from Iceland*, p. 212.

81. *Letters from Iceland*, p. 261.

82. See above, pp. 100–102.

83. See, for example, *The Protection of the Public from Aerial Attack* (London: Gollancz, 1937), and *Air Raid Protection: the Facts*, published as issue no. 13 of *Fact* (1938).

84. For example, 'Radio News-reel', *Listener*, 18 (21 July 1937), 136–7, included photographs of a family, with gas-masks ready, in a model gasproof shelter in Plymouth, air-raid wardens in masks on bicycles, anti-aircraft gunners in

masks, and 'gasmasked men of the Portsmouth City Engineers Demolition and Rescue Squad at work on a bombed house, removing casualties . . .'

85. MacNeice, *Out of the Picture* (London: Faber & Faber, 1937), p. 113.
86. *Out of the Picture*, p. 125.
87. 'In Defence of Vulgarity', *Listener*, 18 (29 Dec. 1937), 1408.
88. *Out of the Picture*, p. 120.
89. Montagu Slater, 'They Try to Be Honest', *Daily Worker*, 25 Aug. 1937, 7.

CHAPTER
[IX]

1. 'Poets and the Crisis', *The Times*, 26 Sept. 1938, 13.
2. 'Topical Note', *New Verse*, nos. 31–2 (autumn 1938), 9.
3. Prokosch, 'Ode', *New Verse*, no. 29 (Mar. 1938), 5, 8.
4. G.E.G., 'New Poems by MacNeice and Prokosch', *New Verse*, no. 30 (summer 1938), 18.
5. Spencer, 'Waiting', *New Verse*, no. 29 (Mar. 1938), 12.
6. 'New Poems by MacNeice and Prokosch', 18.
7. Orwell, *Collected Essays, Journalism and Letters*, vol. I, p. 311.
8. MacNeice, *Modern Poetry: A Personal Essay* (Oxford: Oxford University Press, 1938), p. 205.
9. The speech was published in *Abinger Harvest* in 1936 as 'Liberty in England'.
10. Forster, 'Credo', *London Mercury*, 38 (Sept. 1938), 398.
11. Toynbee, 'Too Good for This World', *Town Crier*, 9 Dec. 1938, 2.
12. Rees, 'Politics on the London Stage', *New Writing*, n.s. 2 (spring 1939), p. 109.
13. Spender, *Trial of a Judge* (London: Faber & Faber, 1938), pp. 109–10.
14. *Trial of a Judge*, pp. 49–50.
15. *Trial of a Judge*, p. 91.
16. Rees, 'Politics on the London Stage', p. 110.
17. Auden and Isherwood, *On the Frontier* (London: Faber & Faber, 1938), p. 91.
18. *On the Frontier*, p. 81.
19. *On the Frontier*, p. 25.
20. MacNeice, 'The Theatre', *Spectator*, 161 (18 Nov. 1938), 858.
21. *On the Frontier*, pp. 120–1.
22. *On the Frontier*, pp. 122–3.
23. F. McEachran, 'Topical Drama', *Adelphi*, 15 (Jan. 1939), 202.
24. Warner, *The Professor* (London: John Lane The Bodley Head, 1944), p. 20. (I quote from the more readily available uniform edition; the novel was first published in 1938 by Boriswood.)
25. *The Professor*, pp. 113, 118.
26. *The Professor*, p. 217.
27. *The Professor*, pp. 217–18.
28. *On the Frontier*, p. 26.

29. *The Professor*, p. 202.

30. Roberts, *T. E. Hulme* (London: Faber & Faber, 1938), pp. 251–2.

31. E. Allen Osborne, ed., *In Letters of Red* (London: Michael Joseph, 1938), p. 248.

32. *Lions and Shadows*, p. 274.

33. 'A Conversation with Edward Upward', *The Review*, nos. 11–12 (1964), 67.

34. Upward, 'Sketch for a Marxist Interpretation of Literature', in C. Day Lewis, ed., *The Mind in Chains* (London: Frederick Muller Ltd, 1937), p. 48.

35. *The Mind in Chains*, p. 40.

36. Upward, *Journey to the Border* (London: Hogarth Press, 1938), p. 42.

37. *Journey to the Border*, p. 215.

38. 'To the Reader', *Lions and Shadows*, p. [7].

39. *Lions and Shadows*, p. 74.

40. *Lions and Shadows*, p. 217.

41. Ralph Wright, ' "Heroes" Who Were Afraid', *Daily Worker*, 30 Mar. 1938, 7.

42. Compare the sketches of literary history that Auden was writing at the time—for example in 'Letter to Lord Byron' and in his Introduction to the *Oxford Book of Light Verse* (1938)—which stress social and economic factors.

43. *Enemies of Promise* (London: Routledge, 1938), p. 127.

44. *Enemies of Promise*, pp. 129–30.

45. *Enemies of Promise*, p. 130.

46. *Enemies of Promise*, p. 138.

47. *Enemies of Promise*, p. 325.

48. *Enemies of Promise*, p. 176.

49. *Enemies of Promise*, p. 246.

50. MacNeice, 'Preface', *Modern Poetry*; the page is unnumbered.

51. *Modern Poetry*, p. 34.

52. *Modern Poetry*, pp. 73–4.

53. MacNeice, *I Crossed the Minch* (London: Longmans, Green, 1938), pp. 125, 127.

54. *I Crossed the Minch*, p. 130.

55. *Modern Poetry*, p. 198.

56. *I Crossed the Minch*, p. 248.

57. Lehmann, 'The Advance of C. Day Lewis', *Daily Worker*, 19 Oct. 1938, 7.

58. Elizabeth Bowen, 'Overtures to Death', *Now and Then*, no. 61 (winter 1938), 32–3.

59. 'A Poet of Warfare', *Times Literary Supplement*, 8 Oct. 1938, 637.

60. *New Verse*, nos. 31–2 (autumn 1938), 2.

61. *New Verse*, nos. 31–2, 3.

62. *New Verse*, nos. 31–2, 7.

63. *New Verse*, nos. 31–2, 7.

64. The Association responded in the following issue of *New Verse*. See below, p. 360.

65. Forster, 'The Long Run', *New Statesman*, 16 (10 Dec. 1938), 971–2.

CHAPTER

[X]

1. Orwell, *Coming Up for Air* (London: Gollancz, 1939), p. 206.
2. Swingler, 'Two Intellectuals in China', *Daily Worker*, 29 Mar. 1939, 7.
3. Waugh, 'Mr. Isherwood and Friend', *Spectator*, 162 (24 Mar. 1939), 496.
4. Auden and Isherwood, *Journey to a War* (London: Faber & Faber, 1939), p. 71.
5. *Journey to a War*, p. 271.
6. *Journey to a War*, p. 274.
7. *Journey to a War*, p. 285.
8. *Journey to a War*, pp. 300–1.
9. He said so in his introduction to *A Selection from the Poems of Alfred, Lord Tennyson* (Garden City, N.Y.: Doubleday, Doran & Co., 1944), p. x.
10. G.E.G., 'Twenty-seven Sonnets', *New Verse*, n.s. I, 2 (May 1939), 48.
11. 'Twenty-seven Sonnets', 49.
12. Auden, 'The Public vs. the Late Mr. William Butler Yeats', *Partisan Review*, 6 (spring 1939), 51.
13. 'The Public vs. the Late Mr. William Butler Yeats', p. 51.
14. Spender, 'Poetry', *Fact*, no. 4 (July 1937), 21. The passage is quoted at greater length above, p. 270.
15. Introductory note to *Goodbye to Berlin* (London: Hogarth, 1939), p. 7.
16. Jameson, 'Documents', *Fact*, no. 4, 15.
17. *Goodbye to Berlin*, p. 13.
18. *Goodbye to Berlin*, p. 13.
19. *Goodbye to Berlin*, p. 14.
20. *Goodbye to Berlin*, p. 219.
21. *Goodbye to Berlin*, pp. 316–17.
22. Lehmann, *New Writing in England* (New York: Critics Group Press, 1939), p. 31.
23. *Goodbye to Berlin*, p. 288.
24. Isherwood, 'German Literature in England', *New Republic*, 98 (5 Apr. 1939), 254.
25. Yvonne Cloud, 'Criticizing the Left', *New Verse*, n.s. I (Jan. 1939), 25–30.
26. Spender, 'A Communist in Action', *Now and Then*, no. 61 (winter 1938), 26; Spender, 'The Will to Live', *New Statesman*, 16 (12 Nov. 1938), 772.
27. Stephen Spender and John Lehmann, eds., *Poems for Spain* (London: Hogarth, 1939), p. 9.
28. Spender, *The New Realism. A Discussion* (London: Hogarth, 1939), p. 5. The essay was originally delivered as a lecture to the Association of Writers for Intellectual Liberty.
29. *The New Realism*, p. 12.
30. *The New Realism*, p. 19.
31. *The New Realism*, p. 21.

32. *The New Realism*, pp. 23–4. Spender returned to the subject in July 1939, in a review of Philip Henderson's *The Poet in Society*:

The mistake lies in supposing that it matters whether poets return to tradition or build up private fantasies or rush out into the world and sit bravely on committees or 'interpret the crisis that is taking place in the mind of man', or join a Church, or anything else that can provide a rallying cry. All this is like advice about people's love affairs: to the neighbours, it is a matter of social relations; to the people concerned, it is a matter of experience. Poetry is also a matter of experience. To be a poet one must have the courage of one's own experiences, to be a critic one must be able to test the integrity of felt and expressed experiences. Therefore, it is better to judge poets by their poetry than by their expressed opinions.

'Poetry and Politics', *Spectator*, 163 (26 July 1939), 156.

33. Spender, *The Still Centre* (London: Faber & Faber, 1939), pp. 10–11.

34. *The Still Centre*, pp. 77–8.

35. *The Still Centre*, p. 107.

36. Alick West, *The Daily Worker*, 10 May 1939, 7.

37. MacNeice, *Autumn Journal* (London: Faber & Faber, 1939), p. 30.

38. *Autumn Journal*, pp. 30–1.

39. *Autumn Journal*, pp. 33–4.

40. *Autumn Journal*, p. 53.

41. *Autumn Journal*, pp. 91–2.

42. *Autumn Journal*, p. 96.

43. *Autumn Journal*, pp. 7–8.

44. Symons, *Life and Letters Today*, 21 (June 1939), 152; Roy Fuller, 'Two Alive, One Dead', *New English Weekly*, 15 (29 June 1939), 176.

45. Orwell, *Keep the Aspidistra Flying*, p. 30.

46. Orwell, *Collected Essays, Journalism and Letters*, vol. I, pp. 284, 309.

47. Orwell, *Coming Up for Air*, pp. 92–3.

48. *Coming Up for Air*, p. 131.

49. *Coming Up for Air*, pp. 35–6.

50. *Coming Up for Air*, p. 184.

CHAPTER

[XI]

1. Spender, 'September Journal', *Horizon*, 1 (Feb. 1940), 102.

2. 'September Journal', 111.

3. 'September Journal', *Horizon*, 1 (Mar. 1940), 214.

4. 'September Journal', 222.

5. MacNeice, *The Poetry of W. B. Yeats* (London: Oxford University Press, 1940), pp. 1–2.

6. MacNeice, 'The Coming of War', *The Last Ditch* (Dublin: Cuala Press, 1940), p. 6.

7. *Times Literary Supplement*, 'To the Poets of 1940', 30 Dec. 1939, 755.

8. Spender, 'The Creative Imagination in the World Today', *Folios of New Writing*, autumn 1940 (London: Hogarth Press, 1940), p. 145.

9. Cyril Connolly made the same point in the opening editorial statement of *Horizon*, the journal that he began in January 1940: 'So far this is a war without the two great emotions which made the Spanish conflict real to so many of us. It is a war which awakens neither Pity nor Hope . . .', 'Comment', *Horizon*, 1 (Jan. 1940), 5.

10. Auden, 'September: 1939', *New Republic*, 100 (18 Oct. 1939), 297.

11. Muggeridge, *The Thirties* (London: Hamish Hamilton, 1940), p. 318.

12. Orwell, 'The Limit to Pessimism', *New English Weekly*, 17 (25 Apr. 1940), 5.

13. Orwell, *Inside the Whale* (London: Gollancz, 1940), pp. 168–70.

14. *Inside the Whale*, p. 172.

15. *Inside the Whale*, p. 161.

16. Gascoyne, 'Farewell Chorus', *Poems 1937–1942* (London: Editions Poetry, London, 1943), p. 54.

17. Day Lewis, 'Foreword', *The Georgics of Virgil* (London: Cape, 1940), p. 7.

18. 'Dedicatory Stanzas', *The Georgics of Virgil*, p. 9. See also Day Lewis, 'Where Are the War Poets?', in *Word Over All* (London: Cape, 1943), p. 30.

19. 'Dedicatory Stanzas', pp. 10–11.

20. 'Dedicatory Stanzas', p. 10.

21. Woolf, 'The Leaning Tower', *Folios of New Writing*, autumn 1940 (London: Hogarth, 1940), p. 30.

22. 'The Leaning Tower', p. 23.

23. 'The Leaning Tower', p. 27.

24. She was answered in a later issue of *Folios of New Writing* by four 'thirties writers: Upward, B. L. Coombes, MacNeice, and Lehmann. None of them makes a strong rebutting case, and all seem rather weary and sad, like the self-justifying survivors of some great catastrophe. 'We may not have done all we could in the Thirties', MacNeice wrote, 'but we did do something', and he left it at that. See *Folios of New Writing*, spring 1941 (London: Hogarth, 1941), pp. 24–46.

25. Consider, as an example, the remark of Graham Greene: 'Violence comes to us more easily because it was so long expected—not only by the political sense but by the moral sense. The world we lived in could not have ended any other way.' 'Notes on the Way', *Time and Tide*, 21 (19 Oct. 1940), 9. The essay was later included in his *Collected Essays* under the title 'At Home'.

26. For example Cyril Connolly: 'The flight of Auden and Isherwood to a land richer in incident and opportunity is also a symptom of the failure of social realism as an aesthetic doctrine . . .', 'Comment', *Horizon*, 1 (Feb. 1940), 70.

27. Orwell, 'The Limit to Pessimism', 5.

INDEX

424